Language and Equilibrium

Language and Equilibrium

Prashant Parikh

The MIT Press
Cambridge, Massachusetts
London, England

For information about special quantity discounts, please e-mail special_sales@mitpress.mit.edu

This book was set in Times New Roman and Syntax on 3B2 by Asco Typesetters, Hong Kong.
Printed and bound in the United States of America.

Library of Congress Cataloging-in-Publication Data

Parikh, Prashant.
Language and equilibrium / Prashant Parikh.
p. cm.
Includes bibliographical references and index.
ISBN 978-0-262-01345-1 (hardcover : alk. paper)
1. Pragmatics. 2. Grammar, Comparative and general—Syntax. 3. Game—theoretical semantics. 4. Semantics (Philosophy) I. Title.
P99.4.P72P365 2010
401'.43—dc22 2009015862

10 9 8 7 6 5 4 3 2 1

For Avani and Neal

riverrun, past Eve and Adam's, from swerve of shore to bend of bay, brings us by a commodius vicus of recirculation back to Howth Castle and Environs.
—James Joyce, opening of *Finnegans Wake*

A way a lone a last a loved a long the
—James Joyce, closing of *Finnegans Wake*

We shall not cease from exploration
And the end of all our exploring
Will be to arrive where we started
And know the place for the first time.
—T. S. Eliot, *Little Gidding*

Contents

List of Figures

Acknowledgments

Professionally, my deepest debt is to Kenneth Arrow, Aravind Joshi, and Robert Stalnaker. Their support over two decades in a myriad ways has been invaluable. David Israel and Terry Langendoen have also been generous well-wishers and I have consulted them often.

The mathematician Ray Hoobler read key portions of the text and asked many penetrating questions about the heart of the mathematical framework. The economist Ennio Stacchetti offered insightful comments on the game-theoretic models in the book. The mathematician Hans Mathews pinpointed a gap or two in the new version of situation theory I was developing. My debt to all three scholars is immense. Any infelicities that still remain are very much my own.

Robin Clark suggested the link with Saussure and translated relevant passages from the French. He also helped articulate the comparison with Montague grammar and parts of chapter 3. More broadly, he was present through the writing of the book, and the many conversations we had, especially about definite descriptions, pushed me to clarify various formulations and arguments. We have co-authored papers within this framework and I have greatly enjoyed our joint work.

Two anonymous referees each read through the manuscript twice and provided many constructive comments. Their remarks improved the book considerably.

I am grateful to Kent Bach, Noam Chomsky, Herb Clark, Sol Feferman, Joe Halpern, Larry Moss, David Mumford, Venkat Rao, R. K. Shyamsundar, Brian Skyrms, and Terry Winograd, all of whom read parts of the text or supported this work in other ways.

Personally, my deepest debt is to my parents, Jagdish and Shaila, my wife, Avani, and my son, Neal. Neal is a young mathematician and computer scientist in his own right and made many creative suggestions in our numerous conversations about language and meaning. The book would not have seen the light of day without Avani.

1 Introduction

I learned very early the difference between knowing the name of something and knowing something.
—Richard Feynman, *The Making of a Scientist*

In this book, I present a new account of meaning for natural language.

The account has three levels. Most concretely, it offers a tool to derive and compute the meanings of all possible utterances, at least in principle. More generally, it provides a method to produce variant theories of meaning and to address the many problems and puzzles that beset its study. Most abstractly, it advances a way to think about meaning and language through the lens of a broad and powerful idea and image.

At the first level the account is a theory, at the second a framework, and at the third a paradigm.

The paradigm embodies the leading idea and image of *equilibrium*—or balance among multiple interacting forces. The framework draws primarily upon game theory and situation theory. These are the best tools available at present to implement the idea of equilibrium in our context of language and meaning. The theory uses the constraints that arise from game theory and situation theory to capture the meanings of utterances. This renders their derivation a more or less straightforward computational task.

The resulting account is called *equilibrium semantics*.

1.1 Brief Background

Although the study of meaning goes back to classical times in multiple cultures,[1] there have been two broad traditions in the philosophy of

1. See, for example, Deutsch and Bontekoe (1997) and Raja (1977).

language that have addressed meaning in the twentieth century. One is the ideal language tradition and the other is the ordinary language tradition.[2] Frege, Russell, Whitehead, and the early Wittgenstein were among the first contributors to the former, and the later Wittgenstein, Austin, Grice, and Strawson were among the first contributors to the latter. In the second half of the twentieth century, both traditions have borrowed a great deal from each other and have partly even merged, albeit uneasily.

From all the details of both traditions, it is possible to extract two central ideas, one from each tradition. The first tradition has contributed the idea of *reference*, of language's being *about* the world (or about extralinguistic entities in particular); the second tradition has contributed the idea of *use* or *communicative activity* in a broad sense. The first tradition tried to understand reference or the aboutness of language; the second tradition tried to understand use or the communicative function of language. Both ideas, incidentally, are nicely captured in the happy phrase *the flow of information*, a composite idea that underlies and undergirds the account of meaning in this book.

Ideal language philosophy originated in the study of mathematics and the logic of mathematical statements, which led to its emphasis on the idea of reference. In the main, it did not see mathematics as a *situated activity*, partly on account of its abstract and formal nature. This led to its ignoring the dimension of use and to its focus on formal logic and especially on translating natural language utterances into logical languages.[3] In fact, in the early days, the often inconvenient facts of use were treated as a kind of defect that would be removed by *idealizing* language. While this tradition has yielded many insights of continuing relevance including, crucially, its use of mathematical methods—expressed perhaps most of all in what is called formal semantics after Montague (1974b)—its attempt to extend its ideas from mathematical languages to natural languages has led to many difficulties as elaborated in section 1.4.[4]

2. See the collection of essays in Rorty (1988).

3. Perhaps the classic example of this is Russell (1905, 1919). To be fair to these philosophers, their interest in semantics was secondary to their interest in the philosophical problems they were attempting to solve. Semantics was a means to a philosophical end.

4. Indeed, there are problems with its account of the semantics of mathematical activity as well such as the problem discussed in section 7.3.

The practitioners of ordinary language philosophy, reacting to this artificial and ersatz[5] view of natural language, started from the vision that natural language was an inherently situated activity and that the use of language in communication should be at the heart of its study. Unfortunately, they also appeared to believe in the main that this attribute of natural language made formal methods relatively inapplicable. This tradition too has afforded many insights into the nature of linguistic meaning, although its lack of a mathematical approach has often made its arguments imprecise and vague.

The awkward state of affairs that exists at present can be best seen in there being the two distinct disciplines of semantics and pragmatics, each concerned with meaning, one primarily with its referential aspect and largely formal and conventional, the other primarily with its use-related or communicative aspect and largely informal and contextual.[6] While both disciplines have drawn upon each other and have developed a great deal since their originating ideas were established, in the mainstream view, semantic meaning is still generally identified with a sentence's conventionally given and formally represented truth-conditions, and pragmatic meaning is generally identified with some combination of contextually inferred and informally represented Gricean implicature and Austinian illocutionary force.[7] These two types of meaning typically coexist and may coincide or diverge in ways best exemplified perhaps in Grice (1975, 1989) and Kripke (1977).

Kaplan (1969), building on Montague's index semantics and Lewis's (1972) contextual coordinates, introduced context into semantics proper via his two-dimensional notion of *character* but this was intended for just a limited set of expressions, primarily tense and pronouns. Stalnaker (1970, 1978, 1998, 1999b), noting the ubiquity of context-sensitive

5. This word is used to indicate that the notion of an "ideal" language was an *inferior substitute* for natural language and is not meant pejoratively.

6. In the literature, there are many different ways of drawing the distinction between semantics and pragmatics. Two of the most important are: between the formal representation of meaning and the communicative aspect of meaning, and between literal meaning seen as conventional and rule-based and implicature and illocutionary force seen as contextual and inferential. These two different distinctions can be and are often merged. A third related distinction is that between the truth conditions of an utterance and the felicity conditions of an utterance.

7. The origins of the idea of force go back to Frege, so the neat picture presented above should be seen as a vast schematic oversimplification for expository purposes.

expressions in language, generalized the concept of a context from an index to a *context set*—an entire "body of information"—for literal meaning, which is essentially the underlying idea of context that is prevalent today, including roughly the one used in this book, except that Stalnaker's notion is couched in the framework of possible worlds. The question of exactly how context obtruded into the sphere of semantics, whether conventionally or inferentially, or a combination of both, was largely unaddressed.

Barwise and Perry (1983) tried to reorganize these insights in a radical rather than moderate way by extending model-theoretic or referential methods to accommodate Austin's focus on use by inventing the key idea of a *situation*, something Austin had used informally[8] and something that captures Stalnaker's idea of a body of information directly rather than circuitously via possible worlds.[9] Among other advances, this led to a blurring of the boundaries between the two traditions and between semantics and pragmatics, although not in any very precise way. One problem was that situation semantics, as their account was called, involved an overly abstract and impoverished notion of use, as did the earlier efforts

8. See, for example, Austin (1979a).

9. To quote from Stalnaker (1999b):

> My central assumption was that a context should be represented by a body of information that is presumed to be available to the participants in the speech situation. A *context set* is defined as the set of possible situations that are compatible with this information—with what the participants in the conversation take to be the common shared background. The contextual factors relevant to interpreting John's utterance of "I love Mary" will then be, not simply the index, but the fact that the relevant body of information includes the information that John is speaking and that the utterance is taking place on June 14, 1998.

Stalnaker's (1998) context set plays a dual role: it provides both the initial body of information within which an utterance takes place as well as the final body of information that results from the utterance. So there is a single entity (a set of possible worlds) that changes through a discourse. An utterance situation and the resulting described situation, in Barwise and Perry's sense, are more general than this, as they need not be fully shared by the participants in the discourse (a point I discuss in detail in section 3.3.4 on common knowledge and section 5.7 on the indeterminacy of contexts) and the relation between them is different. As I see it, the described situation resulting from an utterance then affects the succeeding utterance situation in an ongoing discourse. I say more about this in section 2.6 and section 7.2.

Situation theory also transcends situation semantics and has been applied to areas other than language.

by Montague, Lewis, Kaplan, and Stalnaker[10]: they had no *theory* of use, just some notational "stand-ins" for broad aspects of use.[11] Nevertheless, I have found Barwise's development of a theory of information—called situation theory—as well as a few aspects of their attempt to combine the two traditions to be of great value in developing my own approach to language and meaning. Part of the reason for this is the conviction that if things are done correctly there ought to be just one unified theory of meaning rather than two uneasily juxtaposed accounts. This Hegelian *aufhebung* of the two traditions and the two disciplines is what will be attempted in *Language and Equilibrium*.[12]

The erosion of the barrier separating semantics from pragmatics has been underway from other quarters as well. Recanati (2004b, 2004c) as well as the Relevance Theorists (see Sperber and Wilson 1986a, 1986b, 2004; and Carston 2004 among others) have also been chipping away at this distinction (most strikingly with examples of so-called *free enrichment*[13]) and offering a more imbricated picture of meaning. The view that many linguistic phenomena that were previously seen as belonging to semantics in fact belong to pragmatics has come to be called *radical pragmatics* though, of course, in my view, these are all part of a *radical semantics* that I have chosen to call equilibrium semantics.

10. It is notable that Stalnaker (1996, 2006) has himself turned to game theory more recently.

11. Like "speaker connections," for those familiar with their account.

12. Despite the dynamic turn of Kamp (1981), Heim (1982), and Gronendijk and Stokhof (1991), most of these developments remain squarely within the tradition of Montague-inspired formal semantics where the focus is on finding appropriate meaning representations rather than on *deriving* intended and optimal meanings through use. Discourse representation theory, file change semantics, and dynamic logic are concerned more with the *results* of the communicative process than with communication itself, with the *what* rather than with the *how*. They address what Austin (1979b) called the perlocutionary act and effects of communication, not the locutionary and illocutionary acts and the securing of uptake and understanding. As such, they do not appear to question the *syntax-semantics-pragmatics* trichotomy and pipeline view of meaning bequeathed by Morris (1938) and Grice (1989) despite their undoubted technical accomplishments.

13. For example, when an utterance of a sentence such as "*Casablanca* is playing" is being interpreted, it has to be *enriched* or *completed* with a partial content such as *in New York this evening*. This enrichment is part of the literal content of the utterance. See Parikh (2006b) and section 4.4.1 for a detailed game-theoretic analysis of this phenomenon.

Typically, following Charles Morris's (1938) original trichotomy *syntax–semantics–pragmatics*, semantics is identified with what comes from the linguistic representation or with the conventional meaning of the representation and pragmatics is identified with the contributions of the ambient circumstances. Linguists especially use the term *underspecification* to describe this—semantics first underspecifies content that is later filled in by pragmatics. It is better to identify semantics with the problem of inferring the entire content,[14] regardless of what contributes to this content, the linguistic representation or the context. Indeed, it has often been assumed in the past that conventions suffice for getting at content so there is an ambiguity in the original identification of semantics with convention since it was implicit that convention would yield content. This perhaps explains the origin of the term *literal* content. That is, it is not clear whether the commitment should be to the literal, purportedly conventional source of content or to content per se. The mainstream view[15] of semantics has identified with the former, but I am urging the latter, especially since even literal content is ineluctably contextual.

A major advantage of the identification of semantics with the determination of content rather than with convention is that it allows a uniform view of all representations and symbols, whether they are linguistic, or belong to other modes such as the visual or gestural, or whether they are mental representations. The uniform view is that content of any kind is a function of two variables, the representation φ and its embedding ambience u. That is, the content can be written as $C(\varphi, u)$, where φ stands for any representation, whether it is linguistic, visual, gestural, or mental. Indeed, φ can stand for any *sign* as well, including tree rings, footprints, or black clouds.

Secondly, this view of a single discipline for meaning prevents an artificial division into two subfields—semantics and pragmatics—of all the factors that should jointly contribute a unified theory of content. The former view takes the representations themselves as primary and more or less exclusive (the first variable in $C(\varphi, u)$) and as the starting point for scientific inquiry, the latter view takes the flow of information and commu-

14. "Meaning" and "content" are used interchangeably in most places in this book. When "meaning" is used differently, as it will be later in certain contexts, it will be pointed out explicitly.

15. Even Austin (1979c) assumed that demonstrative *conventions* correlated utterances (statements) with historic situations. Perhaps Grice (1989) is ultimately responsible for the mainstream view.

nication and thought as primary (*C* itself) and as the starting point for scientific inquiry. If the field of language and meaning is seen as falling within the larger domain of information flow with human behavior as one central component of it, then we ought to be more inclined to the second view. Language then becomes just a *part* of all that makes meaning possible. As Dretske (1981) writes, "In the beginning there was information. The word came later." An exclusive focus on language takes hold of the wrong end of the stick and makes grammar primary, and meaning secondary and an afterthought. This leads to a parallel exclusion of context by focusing on "semantic meaning" (meaning derived almost entirely from the linguistic representation) as primary and "pragmatic meaning" (meaning arising from contextual factors) as secondary. Restoring the centrality of information and its flow enables a balanced view of the sources of meaning as such. And, as will be seen later in this chapter as well as throughout the book, the subject matter, including even syntax,[16] is best viewed not as a linear "stick" but as a *circle* instead.

Third, Austin (1975, 1979b) offered a critique of the semantics–pragmatics distinction that appears to have been largely ignored. His dialectical argument started by making a persuasive case that the meaning of at least some utterances is not a matter of truth conditions alone. While assertions require truth conditions, performative utterances require felicity conditions. Semantics would then be concerned with truth conditions and pragmatics with felicity conditions. But this argument places us on a slippery slope. Austin argued that truth conditions are themselves just part of the felicity conditions for uttering a sentence. This suggests that semantics is really a part of pragmatics or, to put the thesis in its most radical form, that there is no principled distinction between semantics and pragmatics. If illocutionary force is taken as an aspect of the content of an utterance, then once again this leads to a unified view of semantics and pragmatics.

Of course, to be convincing, the viewpoint being advanced requires a homogeneous framework that actually enables a uniform derivation of the full content of an utterance. I show it is possible to create such a framework from first principles.[17]

16. See section 7.1.1.

17. As will be seen later, content will be divided into locutionary and illocutionary content, but because context will play an essential role in the derivation of both types of content, this distinction is quite different from that between semantics and pragmatics.

An added advantage to offering a comprehensive and detailed *mathematical* framework for meaning is that many arguments offered today for or against a theory of particular phenomena remain inconclusive because their proponents often presuppose different views of semantics and pragmatics and also give *nonuniform* accounts for different classes of phenomena. For example, in the fascinating arguments over the last century for or against Russell's (1905) theory of definite descriptions, different theorists often assume different and incompatible positions on the notion of meaning itself and then advance a very particular theory of definite descriptions that may be at odds with theories of other, even adjacent, phenomena.[18] Such arguments may be seen as offering a perspective at *two* levels simultaneously, both an implicit argument for an idea of meaning and an explicit one for a particular theory. In contrast, this book provides a *uniform* approach to the derivation of the full contents of more or less all utterances, couched within an explicit and unified framework for meaning that synthesizes semantics and pragmatics. This does not obviate the need for particular theories but it makes these accounts reasonably uniform across phenomena.

Besides combining the central ideas of reference and use stemming from ideal language and ordinary language philosophy, I also depart from both traditions in fundamental ways. I see content as *indeterminate* in a number of specific ways, a facet of meaning that has not been seriously addressed before. Finally, of course, I introduce the idea of *equilibrium* to explain its many aspects, both traditional and new, in a manner that unifies them and provides a single idea and image of the system of language and meaning.

Thus, in a simplified and abstract way, it would be accurate to say that equilibrium semantics, the account of meaning presented here, combines four distinct ideas in a single unified framework: *reference*, *use*, *indeterminacy*, and *equilibrium*.

1.2 The Origins of Symbols

Observational cosmology suggests that the universe is roughly fourteen billion years old. By contrast, it appears that a little over sixty thousand years ago the human race broke into a *symbolic* consciousness, a new kind of consciousness that allowed it for the first time to use objects and events

18. See, for example, the papers in Reimer and Bezuidenhout (2004). Not all views—even in the collection cited—are so fragmented of course.

to *represent* other objects and events. The experience of death or the experience of play may have been among the first events that triggered this fateful break with our "prehuman" past. Until then, presumably, man[19] was submerged in a kind of *presymbolic* awareness that allowed him just "direct" perception and "direct" actions and interactions in the world, not unlike the condition of other animals. See Terrence Deacon (1997) for one account of what is involved in man's achievement of a symbolic consciousness.[20]

It is difficult for us to imagine this presymbolic state because this new cognitive ability must have suddenly transformed the universe into a miraculously different place, one with myriad individuals, properties, and relations. Of course, these entities had been there all along, and had been perceived, reasoned about, and acted upon in direct and unmediated ways, but their richer existence as we know it today required the ability to *name* them, to form discrete mental and public symbols corresponding to them, to pluck them out of the relatively undifferentiated store of the world. Overnight, the world must have become a repository of *information*, a novel ontological space in place of the old continuum. It seems reasonable to surmise that it was this fresh and unfamiliar power to represent the world to ourselves and communicate it to others, especially through language, that made us human.[21]

19. This word and its cognates are used in their gender-neutral sense.

20. See also the book by Ian Tattersall (2002). I quote two paragraphs:

> If the modern human brain, with all its potential capacities, had been born along with modern human skull structure at some time around 150 to 100 kyr ago, it could have persisted for a substantial amount of time as exaptation, even as the neural mass continued to perform in the old ways. We have much less evidence than we would like that directly bears on the origin and spread of *Homo sapiens*. However, we do know that our species originated in this general time frame, probably in Africa. And we know as well that it quite rapidly spread Old World-wide from its center of origin, wherever that was.
>
> Further, if at some point, say around 70 to 60 kyr ago, a cultural innovation occurred in one human population or another that activated a potential for symbolic cognitive processes that had resided in the human brain all along, we can readily explain the rapid spread of symbolic behaviors by a simple mechanism of cultural diffusion.

21. The presymbolic Neanderthals were able to build beautiful stone tools, and, as far as we know, communicate like many other mammals, but they do not appear to have possessed language as we know it (see Tattersall, 2002). The dramatic experience of Helen Keller in modern times may also throw some light on this transformation, although in her case she clearly had private representational capabilities—what she discovered was public symbolic communication.

In this book, I take as my starting point this informational space of individuals, properties, relations, and other entities, and study how we use language to talk about the world and do things in the world.

I now describe in broad terms my conception of meaning and language and how they fit into the larger scheme of things.

1.3 Information and Meaning

The breakthrough transformation described above allowed *reality*, that is, the world, to be construed as a space of entities. This space is what we call *information*. It contains individuals, properties, and relations; it also contains entities involving individuals *having* properties and *standing in* relations as well as collections of such states of affairs.

Intuitively and epistemologically, it is perhaps such collections that people first learn to discriminate and identify, chunks and slices of reality called *situations*. It is from situations, from these parts of the world that agents may observe or find themselves in, that they isolate individuals standing in relations.

An ancestor who had emerged into a symbolic awareness of the world may have noticed footprints in the snow or may have found himself fashioning a tool: both are situations the ancestor encountered and identified. Equally, modern man may read a report on a company or find himself in a restaurant: again, both circumstances are situations in our special sense of the term.

Beyond these rudimentary individuations, the ancestor may have realized that such footprints *meant* that a bear had passed by recently or that the hardness of the piece of stone he was using to fashion a tool *meant* that he could use it to chip away at various rocks. Similarly, the modern man in question may also have drawn the conclusion that the company report *meant* that its stock price was about to rise or that his being in a restaurant *meant* that he could order some food. Such observations point to another type of basic entity in our informational space: links between situations that allow one situation to carry information about another. This kind of link, called a *constraint*, is the essence of *meaning*. Put metaphorically, meaning is *the flow of information*.[22]

22. As I wrote above, "meaning" also refers to content or, in other words, to *information* itself. Thus, it can stand for both the *flow* of information from one situation to another and for the *information* that flows. It is useful to have this dual sense for our central concept.

Smoke means fire, black clouds mean rain, footprints in the snow mean that a bear has passed by there recently. The natural presymbolic order that exists prior to man is full of constraints that enable one part of the world to be systematically linked to another and to carry information about another.[23]

Of course, if there is no one around to observe these natural regularities, they remain undiscovered and unexploited. But it was an essential part of man's survival that he was able to register these constraints and choose his actions on their basis. Many such causal constraints were instinctively recognized by presymbolic man and even other animals and lower forms, but it was the ability to mentally represent and manipulate such systematic links and communicate them to others that enabled *Homo sapiens* to succeed so spectacularly.

Thus, the informational universe contains not just individuals standing in relations and situations but also constraints. My theory of this space is called *situation theory*, first invented by Barwise (1989b), who was influenced by Dretske's (1981) account of information flow, and who in turn was inspired by the classic theory of information transmission developed by Shannon (1949). The version of situation theory presented in this book is very much my own, though it draws a great deal from Barwise and Perry (1983) and Barwise (1989b).

Another way to describe the causal links that are part of the natural order is to say that smoke is a *sign* of fire, black clouds a sign of rain, and footprints a sign of a bear's presence. The term "sign" will be used to refer to constraints that do not involve human agency in a basic way. Once man broke into a symbolic consciousness, a new type of entity arose that I will call a *symbol.* Symbols are *artificial* constructs that involve human intention and agency in a basic way and that are at least partly social. Our modern man's company report is a collection of symbols. Symbols are organized in systematic ways and such structures are called *symbol systems*. The system of traffic lights is one example of a symbol system, but the major symbol systems are those of language. Once again, see Terrence Deacon (1997) for one account of the distinction.

The object of a theory of meaning should be symbols and symbol systems and how they are used by agents to bring about a flow of

23. All these constraints are causal and causality is therefore the basic cement of the universe. If causality implies regular succession of causally related events, then this statement would need to be modified to take account of the nondeterministic implications of quantum mechanics. See chapter 1 of Dretske (1981) for an illuminating discussion of the connection between causality and information.

information. For an entity to be a symbol, it must *stand for*, *be about*, *refer to*, or *represent* some other entity in the world and this relation must owe its existence ultimately to human intention and agency. Both signs and symbols involve "aboutness," but the requirement of human intention and agency is what distinguishes symbols from signs. The relation of a symbol to its referent is the relation of *reference* or *representation*.[24] This relation can be expressed as a constraint between two situations and thus enables one situation to carry information about another, the hallmark of meaning. A red light *means* you have to stop and a green light *means* you can go. The universe of symbols and symbol systems is very wide because it includes not only verbal languages, but also images, gestures, and other symbol systems. Peirce (1867–1913/1991) and Saussure (1916/1972) were perhaps the first figures to build explicit semiotic theories of this generality, but this kind of attempt has since fragmented into the separate study of each symbol system with little underlying unity.[25]

While the relation of reference or representation may be said to be the central aspect of meaning, it is also in some ways its most obvious attribute.[26] A less obvious aspect, indeed one that still eludes many, is the equally central relation of use. This is the aspect connected with the requirement of human intention and agency. It would perhaps not be an exaggeration to say that the subtlety of the relation of use is what makes semantics (or what many call pragmatics today) difficult. This is not to diminish the great strides that made referential semantics possible, but once the basic ideas of Tarskian model theory were in place, the rest has

24. Usually, the term "reference" is reserved for the relation between a symbol and an individual and "representation" is used more widely. I will use "reference" more or less interchangeably with "representation."

25. Interestingly, some semblance of unity prevails in the so-called Continental tradition in the work of figures such as Jakobson, Barthes, Derrida, and Eco because they all draw upon Saussure. See, for example, Colapietro (1993). While my book is entirely in the analytic tradition, readers more inclined to Continental semiology may also find it of interest as problems of common concern to both traditions are addressed. An explicit connection with the Continental tradition and Derrida is made in section 5.7.

26. Some philosophers deny this referentiality altogether while some others—like most Continental thinkers—assert that the relation of meaning is one between a symbol and a mental entity. I will simply take reference as the starting point of our study. This is not to deny that language has mental significance of course.

been a matter of working out details, however innovative they may be. A similar revolution has yet to occur in the domain of use, although part of the difficulty is that its subtlety makes many philosophers and linguists deny its importance and sometimes even its existence. The main reason for this skepticism is that there is as yet no systematic theory and mathematical apparatus to model use; this is a lacuna I hope to fill in this book in a compelling way.

In addition to the two central aspects of reference and use, a third equally fundamental attribute of natural language and many other symbol systems is the indeterminacy of meaning. Except for the relatively copious literature on vagueness, this property has also remained largely unexplored in its other dimensions. It is primarily this attribute of meaning that has allowed writers such as Derrida (1988) to make some amazingly outlandish claims about language and meaning. But if approached systematically and mathematically, this vital but amorphous attribute becomes easier to grasp and allows one to understand some rather commonsensical facts about language that have been ignored by many. It also makes clear why, along with the relation of use, this property of meaning is responsible for many of the difficulties faced by computational linguists.

Finally, the fourth entirely new feature of natural language that appears to have gone almost completely unnoticed is that of equilibrium. While Lewis (1969) was a precursor, Parikh (1987b, 2001) may have been the first to bring this aspect *squarely* into the realm of meaning. The *generative* idea in philosophy, linguistics, and artificial intelligence, the idea of starting with a stock of simple objects and combining them according to formal rules to derive more complex objects, was enormously fruitful, but perhaps too much has been attempted with this single idea. What semantics (and language more widely) needs in addition is the equally powerful idea of equilibrium. Essentially, equilibrium allows one to consider the *interactions* of objects at multiple levels, something that generativity precludes. Earlier, I considered *Language and Interaction* for the title of this book. There was a deliberate ambiguity in this title: "interaction" was meant to refer not only to the interactions between agents involved in the flow of information, but also to the interactions among various entities at multiple levels in the system of language and meaning.

Equilibrium semantics rests on the four fundamental ideas of reference, use, indeterminacy, and equilibrium because these features *inhere* in meaning; they are not imposed on it by the framework. The account I construct is like any other empirical theory in the sciences; in addition, a science of meaning is a *social* science.[27]

Situated games of partial information play a central role in capturing all four of these ideas in a unified mathematical framework.

1.4 Language

The focus in this book is on language although the methods developed will also be applicable to other symbol systems. Language is possibly our most sophisticated symbol system and is certainly the most intricately structured. Meaning is also almost completely social: the relation between a word and its referent is in the main not fixed by a "natural" relation such as resemblance. The relation is, in a specific sense, *arbitrary*. "Table" could have meant "chair" and vice versa if English had evolved differently.[28]

I now discuss the four key ideas introduced above in some more detail.

1.4.1 Reference

The concept of reference came to be better appreciated and more precisely understood in modern times. Since this happened via the work of logicians such as Frege, Russell, and Tarski working with formal languages, and since these methods were then extended to natural languages, it seems best to start with a long quote from one of the more elegant modern texts on formal semantics by L. T. F. Gamut (1991a, 1991b).

> The semantics of standard logic can be seen as a referential theory of meaning (and thus as a correspondence theory of meaning). When defining a model for predicate logic, the first thing we do is choose some set of entities[29] as our domain. The set is independent of the expressions which collectively form a predicate-logical language. We then specify a relation between the predicate-logical language in question and the domain. By means of an interpretation function, the constant symbols are assigned individual domain elements, and the predicate symbols are assigned sets of domain elements (or sets of ordered se-

27. It is a social science for two reasons: because both speaker and addressee are integrally involved in communication and meaning and because the entire society plays a part in contributing to meaning. The first point is discussed throughout the book, the second briefly in section 1.5 and section 7.1.2.

28. This arbitrariness of conventional meanings is dealt with partially in section 7.1.2.

29. Here "entity" stands for "individual" in our sense. For us, "entity" is used to refer to any object in the ontology introduced in section 1.3.

quences of *n* domain elements in the case of *n*-ary predicate letters) as their references. With this as a basis, we are in a position to define the reference relative to this model of all sentences in our language (that is, their truth-values), in the so-called truth definition.

The semantics of predicate logic is indifferent to the kinds of things we choose to put in the domains of our models. And whatever the domain may be, the theory of meaning is always a referential one: the meanings of the symbols are always their references.

One important characteristic of the semantic interpretation process, a characteristic which also happens to be shared by the nonstandard systems we shall meet up with, is that a strict parallelism is maintained between the syntactic constructions and their semantic interpretations. The truth definition mirrors the syntactic definition of the formulas of the language in question. There is a methodological consideration underlying this practice, one which can be traced back to Frege. This German logician and mathematician gave the first satisfactory analysis of sentences with relational predicates and multiple quantification in 1879, in his *Begriffsschrift*. Now the fundamental insight behind his solution to these age-old problems is that every sentence, no matter how complex, is the result of a systematic syntactic construction process which builds it up step by step, and in which every step can receive a semantic interpretation. This is the well-known *principle of semantic compositionality*.

This extract explains clearly how reference is conceptualized and set up for formal languages. The framework of formal semantics for natural language has largely taken over this conceptualization and added to it more complex entities to handle the more complex devices of natural language. Montague Grammar and its derivatives such as Discourse Representation Theory[30] represent in some sense the pinnacle of this approach to meaning.

But some aspects of the underlying conceptualization that formal semantics shares with the semantics of predicate logic are problematic for natural language for the following reasons:

- Restriction of the domain to individuals
- Holism of truth values
- Reference as assignment
- Compositionality
- Extensionality and intensionality

As we have already seen in section 1.3, and will see in greater detail in the next chapter, there are a plurality of entities in the informational space. It is this significantly richer space that will be seen to be required for the semantics of natural language because natural language is much

30. See Kamp and Reyle (1993).

richer than (first-order) formal languages. Individuals and sets of (sequences of) individuals may be adequate for predicate logic but they are far too impoverished to handle the complexities of natural language. Some of these inadequacies have been addressed in formal semantics by bringing in properties and relations as entities in their own right (as opposed to modeling them as sets), but what is needed is a thoroughgoing revision of the ontology. This is provided by situation theory, both in its original form and especially in the version presented here.

The second assumption of the holism of truth values is a particular instance of the previous assumption. Instead of supplying appropriate structured entities to play the role of the contents of utterances, formal semantics and philosophy have continued to deal with truth values as their (referential) "meanings." Barwise and Perry (1975, 1983) have criticized this holism in very thorough ways and there is little point in repeating this criticism here. Unfortunately, situation theory and situation semantics have fallen out of favor[31] and so their solution to the problems posed by this holism have been largely ignored.

Third, reference has been treated simply as *assignment*, a move that is perfectly legitimate for formal languages, but leaves much to be desired for natural languages. This is one reason for the split in the study of meaning: formal semanticists have contented themselves with simply addressing the problem of representing meanings and have left the messy facts of use that lie at the core of reference to pragmatics and the philosophy of language. Unfortunately, by and large, these latter disciplines have simply replaced assignment by *convention*, that is, (literal) contents

31. Partee (2005) identifies two reasons why this may have happened: Barwise avoided the notion of possible situations and Barwise and Perry never gave a satisfactory account of quantified noun phrases such as "every student." While this may be true from the viewpoint of the Montague grammar community, I believe the reason for their falling out of favor is more fundamental, one that plagues even the formal semanticists: as I said above in section 1.1, they had no *theory* of use, and so failed to deliver the breakthrough of incorporating Austin into model theory bruited by situation semantics. They could not develop such a theory partly because of fundamental gaps in situation theory, something I rectify in chapter 2, and partly because they had no access to the ideas of game theory. This led to an inability to carry the entire program forward, not just to a lack of solutions to the particular problems posed by possibility and quantifiers. I address noun phrases in chapter 6 and I have no objection to possible situations when required as long as they do not lead to a modal realism. Indeed, they arise in a natural way in the situation-theoretic construction of games described in chapter 3 and sections A.2 and A.4 of Appendix A.

are generally taken as conventionally given. What is required is both an adequate ontology *and* an account of reference in its full complexity that meshes with these representations. I attempt to do this via a combination of game theory and situation theory that allows one to actually construct a formal definition of reference.[32]

The fourth shared assumption is Frege's venerable *principle of compositionality.*[33] Again, this is perfectly valid for formal languages because it is always assumed that such languages are perfectly precise and unambiguous. But natural languages are notoriously ambiguous and vague and then Fregean compositionality breaks down. This is because the meaning of one word (and phrase) in an utterance of a sentence can affect and be affected by the meanings of the other words (and phrases) in the sentence.[34] When no ambiguity or vagueness are present, these interdependencies and interactions of meaning are otiose and superfluous. But when they are present, as they almost always are in natural language, the simple generative idea of Fregean compositionality falls short. As I said earlier, generativity prohibits the *interactions* of various objects. Equilibrium semantics offers a generalization of the *Fregean principle of compositionality*, called the *fixed point principle* or *fixed point compositionality*, that is able to accommodate these pervasive attributes of natural language; when they are absent, the *fixed point principle* reduces to the special case of Fregean compositionality.

Finally, Frege's (1980) classic paper appeared to make it clear that reference could not be *direct*, that there had to be some intervening layer such as that of his "sense." These issues have been hotly contested after Kripke's (1972/1980) dramatic work on direct reference for a subclass of words. I will side with Frege and offer a picture of word meaning that is a generalization and refinement of the traditional observation that the ordinary word "meaning" is ambiguous and needs to be split into two parts

32. I do not actually give this definition of reference in the book because it is messier than similar definitions. It follows the general line of definitions discussed in chapter 6 of Parikh (2001) with appropriate modifications to accommodate the more general framework for meaning presented here. It is analogous to Definition 2 in section 5.10 of this book.

33. Frege himself may or may not have put forward this principle, but it is widely known as such and I will stick to this appellation.

34. In an utterance of "The waiter is rude," all four words are ambiguous as will be seen in chapter 6, and their intended meanings affect and reinforce one another. Indeed, it will be seen in section 7.1.1 that meaning and grammar are also interdependent.

that have variously been called connotation and denotation, sense and reference, and intension and extension. I call these two tiers conventional meaning and referential meaning.[35] In this book, I do not offer any argument for this position, as it would mean a long detour and require addressing a large literature including, most prominently, Kripke (1972/1980) himself. I hope to do this on another occasion but some inkling of my views may be gleaned from chapter 6 on noun phrases where I briefly address proper names and where I offer detailed counterarguments to Kripke's (1977) critique of Donnellan (1966) based on my theory of definite descriptions. In any case, I hope the theory will be immune to the kinds of criticisms Kripke (1972/1980) and Putnam (1975) (among many others) have made. A somewhat surprising consequence of my account is that while every word in a natural language has at least one conventional meaning, phrases and sentences have no conventional meanings; on the other hand, when used in an utterance, words, phrases, and sentences all receive referential meanings or contents. Each word in an utterance of a sentence such as "The waiter is rude" has at least one conventional meaning, but the various phrases and the entire sentence have no conventional meaning. On the other hand, all words, phrases, and sentences acquire contents when uttered. This again is a failure of compositionality at the level of sense or intension or conventional meaning.

Despite these departures from the many assumptions shared by the standard semantics of formal and natural languages, equilibrium semantics does share its foundational assumption that language requires a referential theory of meaning. Indeed, my account requires that every word, phrase, and sentence in an utterance have a reference, even apparently syncategorematic words such as THE and OR.

1.4.2 Use

There are at least two reasons why the concept of use is subtle and has resisted analysis. One is that it involves a number of other concepts that are often poorly understood. The other is that it is difficult to develop a mathematical apparatus that can accommodate all these concepts and that does justice to interactions between agents. With formal languages, it is possible to abstract from use and pretend we are dealing just with inert symbols rather than with their use. With natural languages, this

35. When the context is clear, I will use just the term "meaning" instead of the longer "referential meaning." This sense of "meaning" is identical with that of "content."

becomes impossible as we will see below. Those who have tried to ignore the relation of use as central to semantics have had to resort to many awkward contortions such as positing all kinds of entities at multiple layers of sentential representation, whose connection with empirical reality becomes increasingly tenuous and ad hoc, reminiscent of the epicycles of pre-Copernican astronomy.[36]

Minimally, the following concepts are intimately related to, if not included in, the concept of use:

- Belief, desire, intention, and agency
- Sentence and utterance
- The situatedness of language
- The efficiency of language
- Ambiguity
- Communication and information flow

36. A single example should suffice: Recanati (2004b) cogently confutes the "representationalist" analysis of an utterance of "It is raining." I quote:

> John Perry (1986) and many others after him have argued as follows. Even though nothing in the sentence "It is raining" stands for a place, nevertheless it does not express a complete proposition unless a place is contextually provided. The verb "to rain," Perry says, denotes a dyadic relation—a relation between times and places. In a given place, it doesn't just rain or not, it rains at some times while not raining at others; similarly, at a given time, it rains in some places while not raining in others. To evaluate a statement of rain as true or false, Perry says, we need both a time and a place. Since the statement "It is raining" explicitly gives us only the two-place relation (supplied by the verb) and the temporal argument (indexically supplied by the present tense), the relevant locational argument must be contextually supplied for the utterance to express a complete proposition. If Perry is right, the contextual provision of the place concerned by the rain is an instance of saturation like the assignment of a contextual value to the present tense: both the place and the time are constituents of what is said, even though, unlike the time, the place remains unarticulated in surface syntax.
>
> But is Perry right? If really the contextual provision of a place was mandatory, hence an instance of saturation, *every* token of "It is raining" would be unevaluable unless a place were contextually specified. Yet I have no difficulty imagining a counterexample, that is, a context in which "It is raining" is evaluable even though no particular place is contextually singled out.

Then Recanati (2004b, 9–10) goes on to provide an irrefutable counterexample and thereby argue against the representationalist view. I should add that the main thrust of Perry's (1986) paper is antirepresentationalist, so even his failing to avoid this tendency is especially revealing of the pervasiveness of the mainstream view that can ultimately be traced back to logicism.

It is astonishing that mainstream linguistics in the twenty-first century has no theoretically grounded conception of agency.[37] Whatever our innate endowment may be, language (its dimension of meaning in particular) is surely a social institution and as such supervenes on use and human agency. Ever since Grice, the philosophy of language has had recourse to the concept of rational agency, but it has remained informal. The only framework today that has an apparatus with a mathematically formulated and philosophically sound conception of agency is that of game and decision theory. This conception has undergone exciting changes since the work of Tversky and Kahneman (Kahneman, Slovic, and Tversky 1982) and is still evolving. In this sense, my earlier work (Parikh 1987b, 1992, 2000, 2001; Fehling and Parikh 1991) and others' subsequent contributions (e.g., the volume edited by Benz et al. 2006 and the volume edited by Pietarinen 2007) to the now burgeoning field of game-theoretic semantics and pragmatics have been the only approaches that involve the concept of agency in a full-blooded way. Belief, desire, and intention are integral to action and it is the singular virtue of decision and game theory that they offer a way to integrate these component factors that result in action. Any systematic approach to questions of use must draw upon a theory of action and especially interaction that includes its constituents of belief, desire, and intention. Indeed, we will see in the paragraphs that follow that all the other elements of use listed above can be addressed adequately only because we have recourse to game theory and situation theory.

Perhaps equally astonishing is the insistence of many philosophers and linguists on dealing with sentences rather than utterances despite the contributions of ordinary language philosophy. A sign or symbol seldom carries information by itself. It is only when we take account of the circumstances in which the sign or symbol occurs that we can infer a referential meaning.[38] Likewise, a sentence by itself does not have a meaning. It is only an utterance, an act involving the production of a sentence (or other symbol) in some situation, that carries information. While words and sentences appear to mean things in the abstract, only a moment's reflection is required to see that a name such as HARVEY or common noun

37. Even Optimality Theory does not, just as it does not have many of the other concepts listed above. See Blutner and Zeevat (2004).

38. This observation is in fact a little subtler for images and similar symbols than for words.

such as BANK can only carry their conventional meanings[39] when abstracted from their circumstances of use. Without an embedding utterance, a name cannot possibly refer (which one of countless Harveys is being referred to?) nor can a noun, verb, preposition, or article.[40] Identifying utterances with sentences may be permissible only for formal languages. The *circumstances* of utterance simply cannot be ignored in the case of natural language. Put differently, a sentence and its component parts cannot ever connect with reality, cannot ever be about anything without being ensconced in an utterance. I suspect the reason for the reluctance to deal squarely with utterances is that, as hinted above, there simply appears to be no mathematical or otherwise solid apparatus to deal with the messiness and unruliness of *contexts*. Sentences are well-behaved, rule-governed objects and so we feel more comfortable with them and have ways of manipulating them. I hope that equilibrium semantics, with its use of game theory and situation theory, will dispel these doubts.

I have already referred to the situatedness of language when talking about contexts and circumstances, just alternative words for what will technically be called the *utterance situation*. Indeed, agents are always in situations of one sort of another, and not just our utterances, but all our actions as well as their constituents—beliefs, desires, and intentions—are situated. In the case of utterances, as with all actions, this situatedness implies that meaning is a result of both the sentence uttered and the utterance situation. In fact, as already mentioned earlier, we will write $C(\varphi, u) = C_u(\varphi)$ for the content of a sentence φ uttered in situation u. The context makes many contributions to the meaning of an utterance in general unlike the case of formal languages where one can effectively write $C_u(\varphi) \equiv C(\varphi)$ for all situations u. This situatedness occurs more widely than just with natural language. When someone waves his hand to extend a greeting, there is a situation in which he performs the action and thereby conveys a greeting. In a different situation, the same action could have meant a goodbye.

Intimately related to this situatedness is the efficiency of language. The fact that the same sentence can be used to convey different contents in different circumstances is precisely what makes language efficient. Partly,

39. That is, the suitably indexicalized properties and relations corresponding to what one might find in a dictionary for a common noun as explained in section 7.1.2; the case of names is a little different and is dealt with in sections 3.2 and 6.3.

40. In the extended sense of reference I am using.

efficiency is purely linguistic, that is, it resides in the lexical ambiguity of words and structural ambiguity of sentences, thereby allowing one word or one sentence to carry multiple semantic values via linguistic mechanisms, but by and large it is contextual. Context is central to efficiency as it provides the ambient information that gets *added* to the purely linguistic information a sentence provides to produce meaning. In these two ways, efficiency is an entirely observable and empirical fact about language and meaning. However, when we begin to build theories of language and meaning, then another dimension of efficiency enters the picture. *Agency* is central to contexts and agency itself is *more or less* efficient because it is more or less *rational*. While few agents (including human beings) are always perfectly rational in ways sometimes required by game and decision theory, they are not entirely irrational either. In any case, whatever our variable degree of rationality, it is arguable that it lies at the center of the efficiency of language, not only in its contextual aspect, but even in its purely linguistic aspect. Indeed, it is at the center of all human institutions, let alone just the institutions of language and meaning. (That is why game and decision theory have such wide applicability.) Until it is known better and more empirically how we make choices, one aspect of efficiency then is that it provides a way of *idealizing* language and meaning via the idea of rationality, just as earlier the predicate calculus had provided a way to regiment the messiness of natural language. However, this time it is not language itself that is being idealized but its use. Moreover, because game and decision theory are increasingly open to all kinds of *behavioral* modes of choice, not just perfectly rational ones, the degree of idealization involved can be "tuned" for greater or lesser realism in our theory-building. These two dimensions of efficiency, one purely empirical (involving both language and context), the other more or less theoretical (involving agency), are both what make semantics difficult and what make language an extraordinarily rich symbol system.

I have alluded to ambiguity in language a few times in the foregoing. I see ambiguity in an extended sense as an essential part of language. Generally, linguists and philosophers think of ambiguity as being either lexical or structural; I use the term very widely to cover any and all cases where more than one possible interpretation of an utterance may exist. This includes not just lexical and structural ambiguity, but all those cases that result from the efficiency of language. It turns out, as shown especially in Parikh (2001, 2006b) and Clark and Parikh (2007), that more or less the same game-theoretic models can be applied to disambiguating all multiple possible interpretations. It is because of this uniformity of application that I feel that "ambiguity" should be broadened to encompass all these varied cases.[41] In section 7.1.1, the notion of ambiguity will be generalized even further.

The essence of use lies in communication and information flow between agents. Grice (1957, 1969) was the first person to introduce and explore the related concept of nonnatural meaning. Strawson (1964) and Schiffer (1972) refined Grice's attempts at definition. Parikh (2001) expanded this exploration into an infinite lattice of concepts of communication and information flow as well as related infinite lattices of concepts associated with speaker meaning and addressee interpretation, and gave rigorous game-theoretic definitions of these concepts. We will see in section 5.10 that these game-theoretic definitions need to be generalized to account fully for the indeterminacy of meaning.

The six interlocking notions above are all integral parts of the concept of use. It is the complexity of these constituent notions that makes it difficult to incorporate the concept of use into semantics in a smooth way and this is why it has been consigned to the "dustbin of pragmatics." It is fortunate that the situated game theory I will present is ideally suited to tackle each of these component notions in a thorough way that allows a seamless unification of semantics and pragmatics.

To summarize, by and large, meaning involves utterances as actions and is situated. Different situations with the same signs or symbols typically carry different information. In one situation, smoke may mean fire, in another, a cigarette smoker. Or, as remarked above, a hand wave may mean hello or goodbye. To paraphrase Wittgenstein (1953/1968), an utterance of "This chair is brown" could mean a variety of things in different circumstances. This situatedness of meaning goes hand-in-hand with the efficiency of language whose flip side is a pervasive ambiguity in signs and symbols, particularly those of language. All of these together make communication and the flow of information between agents possible.

1.4.3 Indeterminacy

A consequence of the fact that meaning depends on use is that it may be indeterminate in a number of ways.[42] Three of these are:

41. This extended applicability of my games of partial information has sometimes been misunderstood as applying only to the narrower, traditional concept of ambiguity.

42. An extended discussion of this feature of meaning can be found in Parikh (2001, 2006b).

1. Content is not always fully intended.
2. Content is not always deterministically given.
3. Content is not always the same for speaker and addressee.

Overwhelmingly in the literature of the last century, both in linguistics and in the philosophy of language, the negations of these statements have been the shared beliefs. Even Wittgenstein, Austin, and Grice, three philosophers who were very sensitive to aspects of the use of language, and their many followers, appear to have made these assumptions.

At least part of the meaning of an utterance is explicitly intended by speakers because they are engaged in purposive activity. Indeed, there are corresponding intentions on the side of the hearer as well.[43] But intentions are themselves *situated* so that speakers do not need to explicitly intend everything. For example, did Dostoevsky explicitly intend the entire literal and implicated content of *Crime and Punishment*? It is perhaps even physically impossible to do so because, even minimally, there would be so much implicit information being conveyed. The way to think about content is to allow for some of it not to be explicitly intended and to inquire if the speaker might assent to the unintended part of the content. This will be shown in detail once our game-theoretic models are in place. However, since in practice we are seldom in a position to ask such questions of speakers and addressees about their utterances and interpretations, we have to reconcile ourselves to saying that content is partly indeterminate in this sense, since it may have partly not been explicitly intended and we cannot know whether it has been correctly inferred. Of course, since intentions are invisible, it is not possible to be sure even about the intended parts of the content. Perhaps Grice (1989), who introduced intention-based derivations of content, expected too much to be resolved by intentions.

Grice was also probably the first philosopher to allow that content may be partly indeterminate in a direct sense, but he restricted this indeterminacy just to implicature, assuming that literal content was always determinately given in communication. It is natural to extend this type of indeterminacy to all aspects of meaning. The principal insight here is that linguistic communication and information flow can be *probabilistic*, something that does not seem to have been noted before at this general level.[44]

43. See Strawson (1964) and Parikh (2001).

44. Except in Parikh (2001, 2006a, 2006b). More recently, probabilistic approaches to particular phenomena such as conditionals have appeared in Kaufmann (2005). See Cohen (2003) as well. Probabilistic methods have, of course, been common in computational linguistics.

Probabilistic communication is important in the determination of both literal content and implicature as well as illocutionary force. Once we take note of this fact, we begin to see it everywhere, even in the simplest information flows. This makes the need for probabilistic approaches to interpretation such as that used in game and decision theory even more apparent. That is, all aspects of content may be probabilistic and indeterminate, and an addressee may not infer just propositions from an utterance, but also the probabilities with which they are being conveyed.

Finally, in practically all the relevant literature, it has been assumed that communication and information flow consist in just an identity between a proposition conveyed and a proposition grasped. Closer examination of this assumption shows that this is the simplest case, and in a sense that will become clear later, it is an ideal case that is seldom realized in practice. Essentially, contents will usually be different for different participants in a communicative interaction. This fact introduces yet another aspect of indeterminacy into meaning.

Other sources of indeterminacy, some of a more technical kind, will be introduced in chapter 5.

1.4.4 Equilibrium

Our final and central unifying idea and image is that of equilibrium. This idea has a long history: it goes back to Newton's mechanics, and then, especially via Adam Smith in the eighteenth century and the mathematician Cournot in the nineteenth, finds its way into economics and later into game theory in the twentieth. Today, the idea of equilibrium occurs in practically every natural and social science. Indeed, it is arguable that Saussure (1916/1972) had an inkling of this notion in his idea of phonology (and semiology, generally) as a *system of differences.* While I initially saw equilibrium in language and meaning via the application of game theory, it is possible to abstract from the game theory and see equilibrium as an inherent and empirical part of this system.

Equilibrium simply means balance among multiple interacting elements. In each context where the idea of equilibrium is applicable, we have to determine what these elements are and what the nature of their interactions is. Once we have these, all that remains is to describe the conditions under which these multiple interactions "balance." In some contexts, the only observable states of a system are those in equilibrium; in other contexts, disequilibrium may also be observable. Equilibrium may also be dynamic and evolve over time.

For language, equilibrium enters essentially through the element of *choice*: the speaker must choose his utterance and the addressee must choose her interpretation and these choices must be in *balance*. As we will see, the speaker and addressee participate in multiple games at multiple levels in a single utterance—at the level of words, phrases, and the sentence itself—and so there are multiple equilibria that occur in communication. Not only does each equilibrium involve a balance among the choices and strategies available to the speaker and addressee in each game, but the multiple equilibria are themselves in balance: an equilibrium of equilibria!

Saussure (1916/1972) viewed language as a system of opposing elements that underlay a process of choice. "What idea or phonological material there is in a sign matters less than what there is around it in the other signs."[45] Saussure's position seems to be that a sign has significance not simply because of the association between sound and meaning but because this association is embedded in a larger system of sound-meaning associations.[46] The significance of this notion becomes apparent in the context of making a linguistic choice; it is worth quoting Saussure (1916/1972) at length:

> Our memory holds in reserve all kinds of more or less complex phrases, regardless of their type or length so that, when we employ them, associated groupings can be called upon to fix our choice. When someone says *marchons!* ("Let's walk!"), he thinks unconsciously of a divers group of associations in the midst of which the phrase *marchons!* finds itself. On the one hand, it is part of the series *marche!* ("Walk!" [familiar]) *marchez!* ("Walk!" [formal, plural]), and it is the opposition of *marchons!* with these forms that determines the choice; on the other hand, *marchons!* evokes the series *montons!* ("let's go up/get aboard!") *mangeons!* ("let's eat!") among which it is chosen by the same process. For each series, we know what must be varied to obtain the correct contrast with the desired unit. If we change the idea to be expressed, then other oppositions will be needed to make the correct value appear; we say, for example *marchez!* or perhaps *montons!*...
>
> This principle applies to phrases and to sentences of all kinds, even the most complex. At the point where we say the sentence «que *vous* dit-il?» ("What does he say to you?"), we vary an element in a latent form, for example: «que *te* dit-il?» ("What does he say to you [familiar]?")—«que *nous* dit-il?» ("What does he say to us?"), etc., and it is in this way that our choice is fixed upon the pronoun *vous*. So in this operation, which consists in mentally eliminating anything that

45. "*Ce qu'il y a d'idée ou de matière phonique dans un signe importe moins que ce qu'il y a autour de lui dans les autres signes.*" (Chapter VI, section 4) Note that all translations in this section are by Robin Clark.

46. Thus, changing one part of a system should ramify throughout the system, causing all the other associations to change as well.

does not lead to the desired differentiation at the desired point, associative groupings and phrasal patterns are both in play.[47]

Accordingly, Saussure's insight is that a language is defined by a system of choices that can bear meaning, and the fact of choosing one sign instead of another is, in itself, a critical act that is an inherent part of the linguistic system. The content of this insight has been far from clear, however, and most theoretical linguistics has shied away from using an action such as choice as part of its theoretical machinery in favor of the study of linguistic representations, a static object that seems more amenable to formal investigation.

Philosophers influenced by the ordinary language tradition, on the other hand, have always had recourse to the idea of an *utterance* and therefore of an *action* and even implicitly of an *interaction*. While Grice (1989) may have been the first to introduce the idea of interaction into the philosophy of language, it remained relatively implicit in his analysis of speaker meaning. Strawson (1964) was perhaps the first to explicitly consider the interaction between a speaker and addressee by noting that there were reciprocal intentions and actions on the addressee's side in communication, but his insight has been ignored in subsequent work by philosophers and linguists. By and large, the addressee remains a ghost in mainstream semantics, at most a passive recipient of the speaker's actions.

47. "*Notre mémoire tient en réserve tous les types de syntagmes plus ou moins complexes, de quelque espèce ou étendue qu'ils puissent être, et au moment de les employer, nous faisons intervenir les groupes associatifs pour fixer notre choix. Quand quelqu'un dit* marchons!, *il pense inconsciemment à divers groupes d'associations à l'intersection desquels se trouve le syntagme* marchons! *Celui-ci figure d'une part dans la s'erie* marche! marchez!, *et c'est l'opposition de* marchons! *avec ces formes qui détermine le choix; d'autre part,* marchons! *évoque la série* montons! mangeons! *etc., au sein de laquelle il est choisi par le même procédé; dans chaque série on sait ce qu'il faut faire varier pour obtenis la différenciation propre à l'unité cherchée. Qu'on change l'idée à exprimer, et d'autres oppositions seront nécessaires pour faire apparaître une autre valeur; on dira par exemple* marchez!, *ou bien* montons!...

"*Ce principe s'applique au syntagmes et aux phrases de tous les types, mêmes les plus complexes. Au moment où nous pronon cons la phrase: «que* vous *dit-il?»*, *nous faisons varier un élément dans un type syntagmatique latent, par exemple «que* te *dit-il?»—«que* nous *dit-il?»*, *etc., et c'est par là que notre choix se fixe sur le pronom* vous. *Ainsi dans cette opération, qui consiste à éliminer mentalement tout ce qui n'amène pas la différenciation voulue sur le point voulu, les groupements associatifs et les types syntagmatiques sont tous deux en jeu.*" (Chapter VI, section 2)

Further, except for the singular work of David Lewis (1969), neither linguists nor philosophers have quite conceived of utterances and interactions within a system of choices. Unfortunately, Lewis thought of game theory as mere "scaffolding" that was ultimately dispensable.[48] More importantly, he conceived of speaker meaning as entirely conventional because his primary aim was to analyze the concept of convention and he believed Grice's concept of nonnatural or speaker meaning fell within his concept of convention. The particular types of game models he considered, based on the work of Schelling (1960), were also fairly basic and lacked the complexity required for modeling communication that was ambiguous and contextual and costly. (The first work to develop appropriate game models was Parikh 1987b.)[49]

Thus, Saussure considered choice but not interaction between speakers and addressees, and philosophers with the exception of Lewis considered action and interaction but not choice. Both these elements of choice in the context of strategic interaction need to be brought together in a way that results in an equilibrium, a composite idea that neither component idea by itself suggests. To the best of my knowledge, the only mathematical framework that does this *adequately* is game theory, particularly situated games of partial information, the kinds of games invented in Parikh (1987b) and developed throughout this book. The kind of system that emerges from taking choice and strategic interaction as fundamental

48. To quote from Lewis's (1969) introduction:

> My theory of convention had its source in the theory of games of pure coordination—a neglected branch of the general theory of games of von Neumann and Morgenstern, very different in method and content from their successful and better known theory of games of pure conflict. Coordination games have been studied by Thomas C. Schelling and it is he who supplied me with the makings of an answer to Quine and White.
>
> Yet, in the end, the theory of games is scaffolding. I can restate my analysis of convention without it. The result is a theory along the lines of Hume's, in his discussion of the origin of justice and property.

49. The key insight required was the modeling of communication by representing the relevant interactions and choices via games in so-called *extensive* form as initially developed by Kuhn (1953) and as elaborated by Kreps and Wilson (1982) for games of incomplete information. The extensive form enabled making explicit certain crucial information involving ambiguity, something that is obscured in the so-called *strategic* form representations Lewis used. These ideas are introduced in chapter 3 and in Appendix A. Lewis also never considered the costs of communication.

properties of linguistic and communication systems is rather different from what has emerged in the past.

To take just one important example, the approach taken here is very different from the approach that Montague (1974b) took in "The Proper Treatment of Quantification in Ordinary English." There, Montague gave a method of translating an interesting fragment of English into the language of Intensional Logic (IL). Since the interpretation of IL relative to a model is a straightforward affair, English could then be interpreted indirectly by piggybacking on IL. Montague's accomplishment is an impressive one, standing as the culmination of the "logicist" approach that has its origins in the work of Frege and Russell. This type of approach, which remains the dominant paradigm in (linguistic) semantics, maps surface linguistic forms into an abstract logical representation, Logical Form. Logical Form is a syntactic level of representation that shares many properties with an artificial logical language such as First Order Logic. This abstract language can then be interpreted relative to a model.

However, unlike an artificial language—such as standard First Order Logic or a computer programming language, both of which can be interpreted directly—Logical Form necessarily contains elements that can only be interpreted relative to a context. Thus, Logical Form requires a pragmatic component that will fill in details from the context and yield the content of the utterance. Thus, these theories give the linguist (and philosopher) *two* degrees of freedom: first, there is the unseen level of Logical Form, which can be quite remote from observable sentences;[50] second, the fact that one then maps Logical Forms to contents means that Logical Form can be remote from intended contents as well. While this situation is not, in itself, a fatal one, these two degrees of freedom with an unobservable and relatively remote Logical Form in the center do mean that theories of this sort will be relatively unconstrained by empirical factors. Any evidence contradicting such a theory could, in principle, be fixed by ad hoc adjustments to the intermediate layer of Logical Form. It seems therefore that conceptually simpler theories responsive to the empirical facts of language use might be preferred.[51]

50. Notice that surface syntax is already quite remote from what we can observe directly since it involves abstract objects such as constituents and grammatical categories. Logical Form adds another level of unobservable structure.

51. It appears that the neuroscientific evidence also indicates that choices are actively considered in the brains of interlocutors during communication (see Glimcher, 2004, and more recent books on neuroeconomics); interactions

The approach developed here shares some properties with the analysis found in Montague's (1974a) "English as a Formal Language." There, he tried to interpret a fragment of English directly relative to a model. However, the objects he chose to translate were sentences and their parts, not utterances. My approach is similar though I connect *utterances* directly to model-theoretic structures, that is, to situation theory, and give a method for computing the interpretation of complex expressions and their parts in a non-Fregean way via the *fixed point principle*. As will be shown, because my objects of analysis are utterances and not sentences, and because utterances involve both choice and strategic interaction, game theory plays a fundamental role in this computation.

I am thus advancing an empirical hypothesis about choice, strategic interaction, and equilibrium, and the nature of linguistic meaning and communication as well as developing a set of mathematical tools for linguistic and philosophical exploration. A consequence of the analysis will be that there is no principled distinction between semantics and pragmatics. There are currently many views about the relationship between semantics and pragmatics, but they all appear to share the view that certain things are inherently semantic—for example, conventional meanings—and other things are inherently pragmatic—for example, the role of context. This starting point originated perhaps in Grice's (1975) pioneering work on implicature, but it has now become almost an a priori commitment for researchers.

My suggestion is that it is worthwhile to start afresh from first principles and see what kind of framework emerges before we draw a line between the two subfields, if any such line needs to be drawn. In the end, it is the techniques and analyses of natural language meaning that are interesting, not some putatively inherent distinction between subfields. Game theory and equilibrium semantics allow us to look at "the problem of meaning" in a new way.

To return to the main theme of equilibrium, the details of this idea in the framework will become clear as we develop it. It incorporates the other three principal features we have discussed: reference, use, and indeterminacy. Below I describe a global view of the idea.

Language and its use may be viewed as a system of constraints in the specific sense of "constraint" introduced earlier. I will not bother to con-

---

among agents are of course obviously observable. So the elements underlying equilibrium—choice and strategic interaction—appear to have empirical validation.

vert a relationship that obtains into a formal constraint in this sense, but when this word is used, my intention is that the relationship can be so expressed. In other words, equilibrium semantics will itself be expressible as a system of constraints within situation theory.

My concern in this book will be with the following four sets of constraints:

1. Syntactic constraint (**S**)
2. Conventional constraint (**C**)
3. Informational constraint (**I**)
4. Flow constraint (**F**)

Equilibrium semantics may be described compactly via its system of constraints **SCIF**. When speech is considered, a fifth set of phonological constraints **P** would have to be added. This last constraint will be addressed very briefly in chapters 5, 6, and 7.

S contains some account of the syntax of the language being considered. I will not adopt any particular approach to grammar, but will use this constraint informally as it is not my chief concern. Syntax interacts with and is influenced by meaning, that is, the other three constraints in **SCIF**, but we will simply take it as given, except in chapter 7. **S** plays a critical role in the derivation of content. As an aside, we observe that it is primarily with respect to this constraint that different symbol systems differ: language is the symbol system with the most elaborate and determinate syntax.

C is a set of conventional constraints that maps every word into one or more properties or relations. This map is called the *conventional map* and can be largely extracted from a dictionary,[52] except for a relatively small class of syncategorematic words such as determiners and conjunctions. The conventionality of the meanings implies that they are independent of context.[53] Again, to a lesser degree, different symbol systems differ with respect to this constraint as well: some symbol systems such as language are more or less fully conventional whereas others such as images may be partly naturalistic. The exact role and place of conventional meanings in communication will be examined from chapter 3 onward.

52. With appropriate modifications to take account of the kinds of criticisms Kripke (1972/1980) and Putnam (1975) have made. See section 7.1.2.

53. This independence is actually partial in a sense that is made precise in section 7.1.2.

I maps the properties and relations obtained from the conventional map into certain special situation-theoretic objects introduced in the next chapter. Which particular objects they get mapped into is in part determined by **S** and in part by our informational space or ontology relative to a context or utterance situation u. This map is called the *informational map*. The general form of this constraint is by and large the same for all symbol systems, but as **S** influences its behavior, its details vary from system to system.

Finally, **F** is in some sense the main constraint, the one that embodies much of the framework of equilibrium semantics. Essentially, a system of situated games provides a model of the utterance situation u, so that together with the sentence and its phrase structure, we can infer its meaning. Again, this constraint works in the same way for different symbol systems at a general level, but differs in particulars.

At this stage, this very brief description of **SCIF** will necessarily be rather abstract. The rest of the book will spell it out.[54]

The general idea of equilibrium in equilibrium semantics is that all four sets of constraints are in equilibrium—within each constraint and across constraints, both in the context of the system of meaning and grammar and in the context of utterances. In this book, we explore the central part of this ideal conception.

1.5 The Scope of Game Theory in Language

As explained in Parikh (2007), there are broadly two levels at which game theory can address the problems posed by language, a situational level and a structural level. At the situational level, the interest is in solving the problem of content in situated communication. At the structural level, the interest is in solving the problem of how the various structures—conventional meaning, semantical rules, linguistic variation—emerge to enable communication. Of course, both these levels coexist and codetermine each other, as discussed in section 7.1.2, but this book will try to offer a more or less complete account at the situational level since this is the central problem of semantics in philosophy and linguistics. I hope to address the structural level and also relate the two levels elsewhere. In analogy with the field of economics where the main division is between microeconomics and macroeconomics, these two levels could well be called *microsemantics* and *macrosemantics* since the first deals with com-

54. See Parikh and Clark (2006, 2007) for a short introduction to this framework.

munication between and among individuals and the second deals with attributes of language that emerge in entire populations.

As I have argued in this chapter, a new framework that reorganizes and reconceptualizes semantics and pragmatics is badly required. The mainstream consensus has reached an impasse. The account of equilibrium semantics does *three* things: it provides a new theory, a new framework, and a new paradigm for language and meaning. It would therefore be a fatal mistake to view the game-theoretic and related apparatus developed in *Language and Equilibrium* as simply grafting a piece of mathematical machinery onto a mainstream, largely Grice-inspired framework in order to formalize relatively informal areas of the field such as implicature or lexical disambiguation. It is a great deal more than this: I am seeking a radical reframing of the problem of meaning and, indeed, am promising a whole new way to think about it.

In contrast, much other recent game-theoretic work primarily in the field of linguistics, especially by Arthur Merin, Robert van Rooij, Gerhard Jäger, Anton Benz, and others,[55] while notable in its own right, has generally taken the mainstream view of semantics and pragmatics as *given* and so works primarily within what has come to be called *formal pragmatics* as there is relatively little that can be done within the sphere of literal meaning if it is assumed to be given by conventional rules. As a result, much though perhaps not all such work has focused on the formalization of *received* pragmatic factors (like the Gricean maxims and various types of implicature) involved in communication rather than attempting something more fundamental to transform our very view of meaning and, in particular, the relation between semantics and pragmatics. In all of this work, the idea of equilibrium is simply a computational technique to solve games rather than a pervasive empirical fact about language. For such work, game theory is, in a sense, *everything*. Without it, there would be nothing to say. Reading such work, a philosopher or linguist could be reasonably secure that not much will need to change in his or her broad picture of language. But, of course, this is a serious problem because many (e.g., those favoring a more radical

55. See Merin (1999) and Benz et al. (2006) for instance. The title of the latter collection of papers—*Game Theory and Pragmatics*—indicates that their contributions are viewed as belonging only to pragmatics and, indeed, this is what they have been in the main. The corresponding semantics is left primarily to researchers in formal semantics and the combination of the two to a Gricean view of the whole.

pragmatics) feel that this foundational mainstream view of language is breaking down.

For my account, on the other hand, game theory (and situation theory) are merely the best currently available tools to forge this new way of thinking about language and meaning that I have called equilibrium semantics. My primary interest is not in the apparatus but in the reframing and transformation it makes possible. Indeed, I have added significantly to the tools where they fell short of the task.

As such, I urge the reader to be open to this omnipresent but largely unnoticed idea and image of equilibrium in language.

1.6 A Note to the Reader

Meaning is central to life. It is what makes us human. As such, this book is intended for a wide readership in the cognitive sciences: philosophers influenced by either Anglo-American or Continental or non-Western thought, linguists, artificial intelligence researchers, computer scientists, neuroscientists, psychologists, economists and other social scientists interested in language and communication, and even formally inclined theorists in the arts, especially literary and visual.

Readers will bring their own projects and philosophical commitments to the book and I want to alert them to one overriding principle as a guide to their reading: while the material is presented largely as a tightly knit and almost seamless framework, it has in fact many separable and interacting parts and levels that can be discerned. I have selected these constituents because I believe they are the components best suited to the ends I had in mind, but people with different goals or with different tastes may make different choices for these individual elements. A reader may accept my view of a foundational issue without being persuaded by some particular analysis or vice versa. I naturally hope that readers will find the entire structure credible and appealing, but some may pick and choose from the offerings and build their own wholes. I want readers to keep such variant architectonic possibilities in mind as they read the book.

It is also useful to briefly go over what is background and what is new. There are three principal elements that form the context for this book.

Foremost is the rich backdrop of the last century of semantics itself. I have tried to identify some weaknesses in mainstream approaches to meaning and to relate my proposals to this setting in chapter 1. Some more discussion is presented later, especially in chapter 5 where I consider the issue of indeterminacy and the Gricean challenge of defining meaning and communication, and in chapter 6 where I address especially Kripke's arguments for a Russellian view of definite descriptions. I hope to attempt a more detailed comparative analysis with other semantic accounts in the future.

The second has to do with the perspective of situation theory, the required parts of which I have recounted in chapters 1 and 2 for the uninitiated reader. I hope this background will also help those who are familiar with its history to break free of some of the prejudices that have surrounded its decline. As I have argued, especially in chapter 2, it proved inadequate because some key pieces were missing, and I have tried to supply these items in what follows. Among these are a new perspective on infons (and therefore on partiality and fine-grainedness, two of situation theory's important strengths) and a new operation of unification.

The last is the context of game theory which has now been around for almost a century.[56] I have presented its basic ideas from scratch in chapter 3 but from my own perspective of *situated* choice. It is difficult to separate the background from this viewpoint but the experienced reader will have no trouble differentiating between the two. For newcomers, I have provided references to standard texts in the field.

Classical game theory is also concerned largely with single games (or with repetitions of a single game). A key innovation is the idea of interactions between and among games. This has led to many new elements, not least the product operation on games, conceiving the initial probability distributions as strategic variables, and interdependent games with a double fixed point solution—all introduced in chapter 4—but, again, it is not easy to produce a complete list of additions and alterations. Appendix A also contains an elaboration of my perspective on situated games and their solution that exploits an analogy made possible by the universality result of chapter 4.

I have followed a certain convention throughout the book: unless displayed, linguistic expressions are almost always mentioned in double quotes or small capitalization, and meanings or contents are italicized. The use of different alphabets or styles for the many symbols also follows a pattern that is harder to describe but should become familiar as the reader progresses through the book.

56. Zermelo (1913) was probably the first person to publish a theorem in the theory of games.

2 Information, Meaning, and Language

In the same way, the world is not the sum of all the things that are in it. It is the infinitely complex network of connections among them. As in the meanings of words, things take on meaning only in relationship to each other.
—Paul Auster, *The Invention of Solitude*

Reality consists of situations linked by constraints. A situation with smoke in it usually involves a situation with fire in it and this constraint is expressed by saying that smoke *means* fire. Linguistic constraints are similar and allow the utterance "There is a fire" to carry the information that there is a situation with a fire in it.

The central type of circumstance considered throughout this book is a situation with two persons Alan and Barbara, $\mathcal{A}$ and $\mathcal{B}$, engaged in some activity, with $\mathcal{A}$ uttering a natural language sentence φ in order to convey some information to $\mathcal{B}$. Since the utterances will involve a miscellany of sentences, the situations described will also be varied.

Alan and Barbara may be contemplating one of two actions, either to go to a concert or to dinner and a movie. In such a context, they may discuss their plans in order to arrive at a decision. Part of this conversation may be an utterance by $\mathcal{A}$ suggesting they go to dinner and a movie. This kind of setting will be described more precisely in chapter 3 once some of the terminology and mathematical tools to model this situation are developed in this chapter.

2.1 The Informational Space

There are a number of entities in the circumstances identified above. To start with, there is a *situation*, a limited part of the world, containing two persons seated in the living room of a New York apartment talking about what they might do one evening.

In the situation, it is possible to single out various *individuals* such as the two protagonists $\mathcal{A}$ and $\mathcal{B}$, a living room with furniture in it, restaurants in New York they may visit, movies they may watch, and so on.

Simultaneously with the individuation[1] of these discrete objects like persons, rooms, and restaurants, it may be noticed that these individuals have various *properties* and stand in various *relations* to one another. Alan is male and likes Japanese food; Barbara is female and prefers French food. It may or may not be raining outside. $\mathcal{A}$ may want to go to a movie that evening while $\mathcal{B}$ may prefer a concert. Individuals relate to one another in various ways. When we abstract across instances of these, we get properties and relations.[2] Relations are basic in that they are not words, sets of n-tuples, ideas, or concepts. They are the glue that holds things together.

When we abstract across both the glue and the items glued together, that is, across both relations and individuals, we get *infons*. Thus, infons are individuals having properties and standing in relations. People sometimes find infons mysterious. It may not be clear if they are objective things "out there" or are subjective things in our heads. An analogy might be helpful.

If there is a wooden chair in a room, a human agent can see the woodenness of the chair and *detach*, as it were, this property of being made of wood from the chair as an entity in its own right. Is the property then "out there" or is it something that exists only in the agent's mind? The chair's woodenness is certainly something "out there," what has been called the *glue*, though it requires an agent with appropriate capacities to notice it and isolate it. It is possible to think of the property as being "out there" and the agent having a mental concept or representation corresponding to it that is more or less accurate.[3] Infons are similar: the chair's *being* wooden is an infon and is equally something out there but, again, an agent is required to notice and represent it more or less faithfully.

1. Agents do not always need to *individuate* various objects and situations. They may sometimes merely *discriminate* them "behaviorally," as Devlin (1991) has pointed out.

2. Since properties can be thought of as relations applying to a single individual, just one of the terms "properties" or "relations" will sometimes be used as shorthand for the more cumbersome "properties and relations."

3. This simple picture of properties and relations raises many difficult metaphysical questions, partly in connection with their identity conditions and vagueness, that are sidestepped here.

Alternative names for infons are *states of affairs*, *items of information*, and, when true of some existing situation, *facts*.[4]

Situations are essentially collections of infons and may be factual or not, possible or not.

There are three levels of *partiality* in these entities. First, situations themselves are limited parts of the world and agents usually encounter the parts rather than the whole world, itself the maximal situation. Second, it should be evident that many situations will be only partially specifiable. It may be impossible to *exhaust* many real situations, itemizing all their infons. Third, agents may often have only partial access to infons. This third level of partiality (together with an operation on these partial infons) is the key new element of the situation theory presented here. Thus, the information that agents individuate or discriminate and then represent is often partial in multiple ways. All three types of partiality are the joint result of the interaction between finite agents and their environments.

Epistemically, agents observe situations first, identify some of the infons those situations contain next, and extract as uniformities some of the infons' constituent relations and individuals last. When these entities are described more formally below, it is convenient to do it in the reverse order, starting with individuals, properties, and relations, going on to infons, and then defining situations.

A more complex entity mentioned in chapter 1 is a *constraint*, a link between two situations that captures the essence of meaning. Mathematically, constraints can be represented simply as (higher-order) infons with a special relation *involves* or $\Rightarrow$ and at least two arguments for the two linked situations. Much of the system of language and meaning can be expressed as a set of interacting constraints.

The information available to an agent in a situation is always relative to one or more constraints. If A sees a situation outside with black clouds and is aware of the constraint that black clouds mean rain, then he can infer the existence of a second situation with rain. The meaning of an utterance is the information that is available to an agent who has access to the relevant constraints involved in communication. This meaning is usually just a part of the total information available to an agent with respect to the situation of utterance.

I now introduce two more kinds of entity.

4. Infons are never true or false by themselves, they may only be so relative to some situation.

Properties are accessed in two different ways, *ascriptively* or *objectually*. That is, sometimes properties are regarded as the kind of entity that is *attached* to other objects, as descriptive of objects. When Alan is said to like Japanese food and Barbara, French food, these two properties are being treated ascriptively. But properties are also handled as individual objects themselves, especially when ascribing other properties to an objectually viewed property. For example, the furniture in the agents' room being brown involves ascribing the property of being brown to the furniture; but, saying that brown is a color involves ascribing another property, that of being a color, to this objectually treated property. A *type* or *kind* of object is an abstract object obtained by objectifying or *reifying* a property. Types are intimately connected with properties. For every property there is a plurality of corresponding types, one for each situation relative to which the property is being considered. Often, the relevant situation for a type is just the world.[5]

The *extension* of a property in some situation is the collection of objects with that property in that situation. If all and only the tables and chairs in the room are brown, then this collection of furniture is the extension of the property of being brown in this situation. Given the intimate connection between a property and corresponding types, types have extensions as well. The extension of a type of object will be just the extension of the corresponding property in the relevant situation. Thus, both types and extensions are situated objects, being defined only relative to situations.

In the mathematical theory of these entities, other more complex entities are considered in the sections to follow. Since one sense of "information" refers to this universe of entities, it should now be clear how information arises in a natural way via man's cognitive apparatus and activity in an environment. Its generality should also clarify how all of reality may be viewed *informationally*. The collection of all such entities is called the ontological or informational space $\mathcal{O}$. As Quine (1960) has famously observed, ontologies are not unique. There are other ways of construing information but $\mathcal{O}$ is an optimal one. As far as human beings are concerned, $\mathcal{O}$ *is* reality and contains all the objects that language can be about. If there were an interest in other agents—such as birds and

5. The situation for the type formed from the property of being brown could have been smaller—just the room they are in, for example—but nothing in the utterance may indicate the need to restrict it to this smaller situation. Usually, statements involving types are of a general nature and so the situation relative to which they are formed is the whole world.

bees—then different and simpler spaces for these simpler agents would be needed. Much of the complexity of $\mathcal{O}$ arises from language and other symbol systems that are unique to human beings.

The mathematical theory of this space $\mathcal{O}$, called situation theory, was first developed by Barwise (1989b). Other more recent accounts are by Devlin (1991) and Seligman and Moss (1997). While situation theory is at one level an extension of model theory, it also comes with the underlying philosophy of information and meaning articulated above. The version of it in this book contains a number of departures from its earlier formulations. Only the parts of situation theory needed here are considered. The treatment is also largely informal.

2.2 Situation Theory

Situation theory has two key features. The first is that much information is available and representable only partially. An agent in an environment seldom has full information about the situation he is in, or is perceiving or contemplating. He has to act with only partial information in hand.

The second feature is the attempt to make as fine-grained distinctions in the ontology as required for language and meaning. Properties and relations are distinct from sets or extensions, and types are distinct from properties. One way to think of this fine-grainedness is that situation theory is a little like the dual of category theory, which attempts to capture the most abstract aspects of algebraic systems.[6]

The world $\mathcal{W}$, itself a situation, consists of smaller parts that are situations, collections of individuals standing in relations. The latter form the basis for more abstract objects called parameters, types, and extensions. The collection of all these entities is denoted by $\mathcal{O}$.

At the simplest level, $\mathcal{O}$ contains various individuals, properties, and relations. Individuals such as chairs, restaurants, and persons are typically denoted by a_i or b_j, properties such as being brown or being male by P_i or Q_j, and relations such as preferring French food to Japanese food by R_i. A property or relation may have an indexical component. The property of being brown may be "a color like x" where x is some "brown" object in the agent's experience.

6. The interested reader may want to refer to Lawvere and Schanuel (1997) and Mac Lane (1971).

Infons are represented informally by tuples such as $\langle\langle R; a_1; \ldots; a_n; 1\rangle\rangle$ or $\langle\langle R; a_1; \ldots; a_n; 0\rangle\rangle$, with the polarity of 1 indicating that the relation R holds of the n objects and the polarity of 0 indicating that it does not. When a positive polarity is clear from the context, it can be dropped to simplify the notation. Often, relations will have special location arguments, one for space and the other for time.[7] We may have $\langle\langle R^{prefers}; a_1; a_2; l; t; 1\rangle\rangle$ where $R^{prefers}$ stands for the relation of preference, a_1 for the French restaurant Cafe Boulud, a_2 for the Japanese restaurant Nobu, l for New York, and t for this evening. This infon captures the informational item that Cafe Boulud is preferred to Nobu this evening in New York. Letters such as σ, τ, and υ (i.e., the Greek letter upsilon) are used to denote such infons.

Abstractly considered, each infon has a set of argument places or roles that can be filled by appropriate and compatible objects. Infons can be thought of in two ways: as individuals standing in relations or as functions that map these argument places into compatible objects. That is, they can be conceived either as the values of certain functions or as functions just as a sequence of numbers may be given by listing the numbers or by a function from the natural numbers.[8] This ambiguity is deliberately left intact, as it is convenient. Thus, it is possible to write the infon above as $\langle\langle R^{prefers}; (1, a_1); (2, a_2); l; t; 1\rangle\rangle$ where the prefixes 1 and 2 indicate which item is preferred to which. The relation itself is given the special index 0 and the location and time -1 and -2, respectively. When there is no doubt about which argument occupies which role, I will leave these indices out to avoid clutter.

In a given situation, it may be known only that Cafe Boulud is preferred, without knowing what it is preferred to. Or an agent may not know which evening the temporal argument refers to, and so on. This is because there is usually just partial information, not only about the world and not only about a situation, but also about an infon. Both of the following are valid but partial ways of rendering the same item of information: $\langle\langle R^{prefers}; a_1; l; t; 1\rangle\rangle$ or $\langle\langle R^{prefers}; a_1; a_2; 1\rangle\rangle$. Every possible combination of arguments is admissible, including the empty infon. Indeed, the tuple $\langle\langle R^{prefers}; a_1; a_2; l; t; 1\rangle\rangle$ mentioned earlier is itself partial: it omits the agent whose preference it is. Therefore, a more complete expression of this infon might be $\langle\langle R^{prefers}; a_1; a_2; a_3; l; t; 1\rangle\rangle$ where a_3 denotes the agent

7. In the subatomic realm, in the context of something like string theory, more than four dimensions would need to be considered.

8. I thank Hans Matthews for this analogy.

$\mathcal{B}$. This partiality of infons allows their representation to stretch from the empty infon to more and more arguments until the infon is *saturated.*

The main relation and other objects that make up an infon are called its *constituents*. The arity of an infon or of its main relation is the number of argument roles needed to saturate the infon minus the number 3.[9] Properties are just unary relations.

As I said above, the argument roles have to be filled in by *compatible* objects. It is possible to have an infon with $\mathcal{A}$ eating an apple, but one cannot have an infon with an apple eating $\mathcal{A}$. This relation of compatibility among the constituents of an infon is taken as primitive and externally given.

To handle expressions such as "the large room" or "ate with a fork," *conditioned* or modified individuals and relations are used. The general form for such modified individuals and relations is $(a \mid \sigma)$ and $(R \mid \sigma)$. These can be read "the room such that it is large" and "ate such that the eating was with a fork." Determiners and tense will also be expressed via such conditioning devices. The other objects in $\mathcal{O}$ can also be conditioned in exactly the same way.

So far, I have considered individuals, properties, relations, and infons. Situations, the next type of entity in $\mathcal{O}$, are just collections of infons and are denoted by letters such as *s*, *t*, and *u*. Situations have always been implicit in model-theoretic semantics, since they are parts of reality that correspond to the model-theoretic structures used to specify truth conditions. In situation theory they are, like everything else in it, "first class citizens." As Barwise (1989e) has noted, "the move of admitting situations as first class citizens in semantics is analogous to the admission of sets as first class citizens in mathematics." Many situations, like the situation this evening in the apartment where $\mathcal{B}$ prefers Cafe Boulud to Nobu, are just

9. It is often not obvious what the arity of an infon or relation is. Think of a relation like "sells": it would seem to need a seller, a buyer, an object sold, a price, and a time and location. This would suggest that its arity is $7 - 3 = 4$. But it may need many other arguments depending on the complexity of the object sold—information about all kinds of restrictions on the use of the object, possible warranties, and so on. Even the price may not be a single number but a whole "scheme." The list of possible conditions can be quite long and, more importantly, would be different for different objects. In practice, we would just take the union of all the possible argument roles for the domain in question to obtain the arity of the relation. The number 3 is subtracted from the number of roles to discount the three roles for the relation and its time and space locations.

partially specifiable, and the relation between a situation s and an infon σ that holds in it is written $s \models \sigma$ or $\sigma \in s$, and is described by saying s supports σ or σ holds in s.[10]

The information expressed by the relation $\models$ is special and is called a *proposition*. Thus, if $\sigma = \langle\langle R^{prefers}; a_1; a_2; a_3; l; t\rangle\rangle$, s is the situation in the apartment, and $s \models \sigma$, then this latter information is a proposition and is denoted by letters such as p_i and q_j. Only propositions are true or false; infons by themselves do not admit of truth values. The proposition $s \models \sigma$ is true because in the situation s Barbara prefers Cafe Boulud to Nobu. Utterances typically convey multiple propositions, although these are usually just multiple infons relative to some common described situation. A proposition $s \models \sigma$ can also be expressed as the infon $\langle\langle \models; s; \sigma\rangle\rangle$ whose relation is $\models$ and whose first and second arguments are s and σ.

Parameters are indeterminates or variable-like placeholders for any of the entities above. We write $\dot{a}$, $\dot{R}$, $\dot{\sigma}$, and $\dot{s}$ for parameters involving individuals, relations, infons, and situations, respectively. The letters x, y, and z are also used to denote parameters. The precise difference between variables and parameters is that a variable is an object in a logical language while a parameter is an object in a mathematical model. Thus, parameters *model* variables.[11] With parameters go *anchors*, functions that anchor a parameter to an object of an appropriate type. An anchored infon would be written $\sigma[f]$ where f is the anchor with domain the set of parameters in σ and range a contextually given set of appropriate objects. Likewise, when one or more parameters in an infon σ supported by a situation s are anchored via f, we write $s[f]$.

Types, mentioned above, are either basic or are formed by abstraction. Basic types include *IND, REL^n, INF, SIT, PROP, PAR*, and *TYP*, where the symbols stand for individual types, relation types, infon types, situation types, proposition types, parameter types, and type types, respectively. Given an object x of type T, we write $x : T$. For example, an individual type is written **a** and a situation type is written **s**.

Types formed by abstraction, like the type of object that is, say, a restaurant, are intuitively what is obtained when some individual or property is considered objectually or generically. Types are always relative to some situation and so are written $[x \mid s \models \langle\langle \ldots; x; \ldots\rangle\rangle]$ (or, more simply,

10. There are distinctions to be made, as between real and abstract situations, but I omit this fuller consideration here.

11. See Gawron and Peters (1990) for further elaboration.

$[x \mid s \models \sigma(x)])$ where s is the relevant *grounding* situation. The grounding situation may be the whole world W. In an appropriate utterance of "The room is a part of the house," both definite descriptions could be used generically rather than referentially to pick out the corresponding types rather than particular individuals, as will be seen in chapter 6.

Extensions, as explained above, are just the sets corresponding to properties or relations *relative* to some situation and do not need any elaboration. Perhaps the most common type of extension is $\{x \mid s \models \langle\langle P; x \rangle\rangle\}$, which is the set of objects satisfying the property P in situation s.

It is convenient to define $e(P, s)$ to be the individual $a = (x \mid s \models \langle\langle P; x \rangle\rangle)$ when the condition $s \models \langle\langle P; x \rangle\rangle$ yields just one object and the set $\{x \mid s \models \langle\langle P; x \rangle\rangle\}$ otherwise. Equivalently, $e(P, s) = a \in \{x \mid s \models \langle\langle P; x \rangle\rangle\}$ when $\mathrm{card}(\{x \mid s \models \langle\langle P; x \rangle\rangle\}) = 1$, where "card" is the cardinality of the relevant set, and $e(P, s) = \{x \mid s \models \langle\langle P; x \rangle\rangle\}$ otherwise. This entity $e(P, s)$, which can be either an individual or a set depending on whether a single object has P in s or not, will occur frequently in our study of noun phrases. Clearly, when *no* object has P in s, $e(P, s)$ will just be the empty set ϕ.

I set out this definition formally as it will be required often:

$$e(P, s) = \begin{cases} a & \text{if there is exactly one object } a \\ & \text{having } P \text{ in } s \\ \{x \mid s \models \langle\langle P; x \rangle\rangle\} & \text{otherwise} \end{cases} \tag{2.1}$$

When one situation s (or situation type $\mathbf{s}$) involves another s' (or $\mathbf{s}'$), there is a constraint between them, written $s \Rightarrow s'$ (or $\mathbf{s} \Rightarrow \mathbf{s}'$). Constraints are objects in their own right and can be nomic, conventional, or of other types. They can be represented as infons like $\langle\langle \Rightarrow; s; s' \rangle\rangle$. They provide the mechanism through which agents perceive, infer, and act in the world. It will be shown later that equilibrium semantics can be compactly expressed through four sets of constraints.

Finally, an object can be formed by a process akin to lambda abstraction, writing $\hat{x}(y \mid \sigma(x, y))$ or similar variants, where the parameters can refer to any appropriate object. The difference between this process, called *hat abstraction*, and lambda abstraction is similar to the difference between parameters and variables. That is, hat abstraction is a model of lambda abstraction.

This more or less completes the entire range of objects required for natural language. The subset of infons is now explored more fully as these are the primary objects needed in equilibrium semantics.

2.3 The Space of Infons

In the ontology $\mathcal{O}$, there are individuals, relations, infons, situations, and other objects. The sets of individuals and relations in $\mathcal{O}$ are denoted by **IND** and **REL**, respectively. **REL** is the union of $\mathbf{REL}_n$, the set of n-ary relations for each $n \in \mathbb{N}$. For the present purposes, these sets are taken to be finite. Thus, our interest is in a small part of reality called the *environment* $\mathcal{E}$, a finite subset of $\mathcal{O}$. The set of spatial locations is denoted by **LOC** and the set of temporal locations by **TIM**. These two sets are subsets of $\mathcal{P}(\mathbf{IND})$, the power set of **IND**.[12]

The set of infons and their associated parts $\mathcal{I}$ will be built up informally in stages, first with basic unconditioned infons, then compound unconditioned infons, and then conditioned infons. Finally, even this last set will be expanded to include higher-order infons. Just for completeness, **SIT** is defined to be the set of situations under consideration and **PROP** to be the set of propositions.

We start with individuals $a_i \in \mathbf{IND}$ and n-ary relations $R_i \in \mathbf{REL}$ for any $n \in \mathbb{N}$. Let $\mathbf{n} = \{-2, -1, 0, 1, 2, \ldots, n\}$ where $n \in \mathbb{N}$. Intuitively, this set stands for the set of argument places of an n-ary infon. An n-ary infon has $n + 3$ argument places. A partial function from **n** to the ontology is now defined in a way that allows us to construct infons. One key restriction on this function is the primitive relation of *compatibility*. The objects assigned to the argument places provided by **n** have to be compatible with each other. As I said above, while one can have $\mathcal{A}$ eating an apple, one cannot have an apple eating $\mathcal{A}$. There is no general way to characterize this relation of compatibility, so I take it as primitive and given.

A partial function $\mathbf{A_n}$ from **n** to $\mathbf{TIM} \cup \mathbf{LOC} \cup \mathbf{REL} \cup \mathbf{IND} \cup \mathcal{P}(\mathbf{IND})$ is an *assignment* for an n-ary infon if and only if

1. If $\mathbf{A_n}(-2)$ is defined, then it is in **TIM**.
2. If $\mathbf{A_n}(-1)$ is defined, then it is in **LOC**.
3. If $\mathbf{A_n}(0)$ is defined, then it is in $\mathbf{REL}_n$.
4. For $1 \leq i \leq n$, if $\mathbf{A_n}(i)$ is defined, then it is in $\mathbf{IND} \cup \mathcal{P}(\mathbf{IND})$.
5. The values $\mathbf{A_n}(i)$ for all $i \in \mathbf{n}$ have to be compatible with each other.

12. This allows us to deal with spatial and temporal regions and points in a natural way.

An assignment is therefore a specification of a function that maps the members of **n** to times, locations, relations, and individuals or sets of individuals in a way that does not lead to any incompatibility among the objects. This definition is similar to Barwise's (1989e) except that I have associated the argument places with the entire infon instead of with relations. In the fourth clause, the value of the function $\mathbf{A_n}(i)$ for $1 \leq i \leq n$ is either an individual or a *set* of individuals. This makes it possible to consider the entity $e(P, s)$ described in the previous section as the value of $\mathbf{A_n}(i)$ for $1 \leq i \leq n$. This entity may be either an individual or a set of individuals based on whether $\{x \mid s \models \langle\langle P; x \rangle\rangle\}$ is a singleton or not. The utility of this will be clear when noun phrases are considered in chapters 3, 4, and 6.

Intuitively, the collection of assignments will form the basis for our initial infons. Let $\mathcal{I}$ contain the set of tuples $\langle\langle \mathbf{A_n}; i \rangle\rangle$ for all assignments $\mathbf{A_n}$ for each n where i, the polarity, is either 1 or 0. These tuples are called *basic unconditioned infons* and are denoted by symbols such as σ and τ. When the assignment is not total, the infons are said to be unsaturated or partial. Note that only compatible tuples are admitted into $\mathcal{I}$.

Example 1 An assignment for a binary infon may be $\mathbf{A_2}(-2) = t$, $\mathbf{A_2}(0) = R$, $\mathbf{A_2}(1) = a$, and $\mathbf{A_2}(2) = b$. A corresponding infon with positive polarity would be $\langle\langle \mathbf{A_2}; 1 \rangle\rangle = \langle\langle (0, R); (1, a); (2, b); (-2, t); 1 \rangle\rangle$. If the relation R is the relation of eating and a picks out Alan and b picks out an apple and t is this evening, then the infon may also be written $\langle\langle (0, R^{eating}); (1, \text{Alan}); (2, \text{apple}); (-2, \text{this evening}); 1 \rangle\rangle$[13] and it expresses the information that Alan is eating an apple this evening. The time t can be a single time or an interval. No location has been specified, so the function is partial. Note that its arguments are compatible with one another. This is a basic unconditioned infon and is unsaturated.

As mentioned above, the notation can be simplified to make it convenient to write expressions for infons. Instead of a set of ordered pairs, which is what assignments $\mathbf{A_n}$ are, it is possible to write just the values of the function when the context makes it clear what their first coordinates are. So instead of an infon $\langle\langle (0, R); (1, a); (2, b); (-1, l); (-2, t); i \rangle\rangle$ where the location and time arguments are written at the end just before the polarity i, we would write simply $\langle\langle R; a; b; l; t; i \rangle\rangle$ with the understanding that

13. I will usually not put such context-dependent items directly into the argument roles of an infon. I have done this here to convey the intuitive idea more clearly.

0 is mapped into R, 1 into a, 2 into b, -1 into l, and -2 into t. That is, the elements in the tuple are written in a certain order even though the actual argument places are not ordered. These elements are called the constituents of the infon. When it is necessary to refer to a constituent abstractly without specifying whether it is an individual or a relation, parameters x, y, z will be used.[14] When the polarity is 1, it will often be omitted. Thus, a saturated n-ary infon can now be written as a tuple of elements $\langle\langle R; a_1; \ldots; a_n; l; t; i \rangle\rangle$. Unsaturated infons look the same except that some constituents are dropped. Sometimes, when a binary relation is involved, infix notation will be used.

Some assumptions that apply to the set of infons are now listed. I have followed Barwise (1989e) in this, although there are some differences.

Assumption 1 If $\sigma = \langle\langle \mathbf{A_n}; i \rangle\rangle$ and $\sigma' = \langle\langle \mathbf{A'_n}; i' \rangle\rangle$, then $\sigma = \sigma'$ if and only if $\mathbf{A_n} = \mathbf{A'_n}$ and $i = i'$.

The intuitive idea is that two infons are identical if and only if each constituent in one is identical to the corresponding constituent in the other and the polarities are identical.

Example 2 $\langle\langle R; a; b; i \rangle\rangle = \langle\langle R'; a'; b'; i' \rangle\rangle$ if and only if $R = R'$, $a = a'$, $b = b'$, and $i = i'$.

2.3.1 A Lattice of Infons

Once we have this initial set of infons, it is natural to think of ways in which they may be related. Recall that a partial order over $\mathcal{I}$ is a binary relation $\Rightarrow_\ell$ over $\mathcal{I}$ that is reflexive, antisymmetric, and transitive; that is, for all σ, τ, and υ in $\mathcal{I}$, we have:

- Reflexivity: $\sigma \Rightarrow_\ell \sigma$
- Antisymmetry: If $\sigma \Rightarrow_\ell \tau$ and $\tau \Rightarrow_\ell \sigma$ then $\sigma = \tau$
- Transitivity: If $\sigma \Rightarrow_\ell \tau$ and $\tau \Rightarrow_\ell \upsilon$ then $\sigma \Rightarrow_\ell \upsilon$

A partial order $\Rightarrow_\ell$ on $\mathcal{I}$ that intuitively captures the relation "is at least as informative as" or "is at least as strong as" is now assumed.

Assumption 2 $\Rightarrow_\ell$ is a partial order on $\mathcal{I}$.

Certain infons are naturally more informative or stronger than others.

Example 3 $\langle\langle P^{crimson}; a \rangle\rangle \Rightarrow_\ell \langle\langle P^{red}; a \rangle\rangle$ where a is some physical object because anything crimson is also always red. So the first infon is more in-

14. Of course, these letters can stand for any object in the ontology, leaving it to the context to make clear what type of object is being referred to.

formative than the second. Likewise, $\langle\langle P^{spinster}; a\rangle\rangle \Rightarrow_\ell \langle\langle P^{female}; a\rangle\rangle$ where a now stands for a person. Note that the polarities in all these infons are positive and so have been dropped for convenience.

It is also true that $\langle\langle R; a; b\rangle\rangle \Rightarrow_\ell \langle\langle R; a\rangle\rangle$. If R is the relation of eating, then if a is eating b, a must be eating. Likewise, $\langle\langle R; a; 0\rangle\rangle \Rightarrow_\ell \langle\langle R; a; b;\ 0\rangle\rangle$ because if a is not eating, then a is not eating b. In each case, the infon on the left is more informative than the infon on the right. The values of eating, a, and b must be compatible with each other. This more specific kind of informativeness is encoded below.

Assumption 3 Suppose $\mathbf{A_n}$ is a sub-assignment of $\mathbf{A}'_\mathbf{n}$. For $i = 0, 1$, let $\sigma_i = \langle\langle \mathbf{A_n}; i\rangle\rangle$ and $\sigma'_i = \langle\langle \mathbf{A}'_\mathbf{n}; i\rangle\rangle$. Then $\sigma'_1 \Rightarrow_\ell \sigma_1$ and $\sigma_0 \Rightarrow_\ell \sigma'_0$.

Intuitively, it is clear that if we have two items of information, say that a is red and b is blue, then it is possible to combine these states of affairs in two obvious ways, by conjoining them or by disjoining them. With this in mind, the partially ordered set $(\mathcal{I}, \Rightarrow_\ell)$ is further assumed to be a lattice.

A lattice is a partially ordered set in which every pair of elements has a unique supremum (the elements' least upper bound called their join)[15] and a unique infimum (their greatest lower bound called their meet).[16] Let $\vee$ and $\wedge$ be the induced join and meet operations.[17] The natural language words OR and AND are related to these two operations but are different from them because the behavior of the natural language words is more complex.[18] In any case, we now have the operations of conjoining and disjoining infons.

A lattice is complete if all of its subsets (whether finite or infinite) have both a join and a meet. Intuitively, there does not appear any reason to restrict $\vee$ and $\wedge$ to finite subsets so we also assume the lattice is complete.

15. The supremum or least upper bound of a pair of elements, if it exists, is the least element of $\mathcal{I}$ that is greater than or equal to each element of the pair.

16. The infimum or greatest lower bound of a pair of elements, if it exists, is the greatest element of $\mathcal{I}$ that is less than or equal to each element of the pair.

17. If $\tau = \sup\{\sigma, \sigma'\}$, then $\tau = \sigma \vee \sigma'$. Likewise, if $\tau' = \inf\{\sigma, \sigma'\}$, then $\tau' = \sigma \wedge \sigma'$.

18. I believe it is desirable to give up Grice's blanket injunction against multiple senses (or what I call conventional meanings) for words such as AND and OR but I cannot defend this view here. Since I take them to be lexically ambiguous (e.g., AND also carries the conventional meanings *and then* and *and so*), they are different from $\vee$ and $\wedge$.

Finally, since $\mathcal{I}$ now has the two binary operations $\vee$ and $\wedge$, we assume each distributes over the other.[19] This can also be checked against the intuitive behavior of informational items, although non-distributive lattices famously turn up in quantum mechanics.[20] I now record this assumption below.

Assumption 4 $\mathcal{I}$ is a complete distributive lattice under $\Rightarrow_\ell$.

The supremum of the whole lattice is denoted by **1** and the infimum is denoted by **0**. The former is sometimes expressed as $\langle\!\langle\ \rangle\!\rangle$ to emphasize that it also corresponds to the "empty" infon or to "no information." Intuitively, **1** will hold in any situation because every situation supports "no information" vacuously. **0** is the contradictory infon. Intuitively, it will not hold in any situation because no (coherent) situation can support contradictory information. It plays an important role in the framework as the interpretation of *meaningless* utterances or utterances involving incompatible constituents such as "Colorless green ideas sleep furiously" or "The apple is eating Alan." It is also equivalent to the conjunction of two identical infons of opposite polarity, expressing information such as *a* is red and *a* is not red.

Basic infons can also be quantified over with $\exists$ and $\forall$ in the usual way except that these quantifiers are not interpreted as part of a logical language but as part of the world. Likewise, as was said earlier, we can adopt λ notation keeping in mind that it is an informational rather than a linguistic device. It was called *hat* notation to emphasize this difference.

With these operations, $\mathcal{I}$ is expanded to include *compound infons*. These are infons that combine basic infons via $\vee$ and $\wedge$ and quantify and abstract over them.[21]

2.3.2 Conditioned Infons

Conditioned infons are now introduced informally. To capture something like THE TALL BLOND MAN WITH ONE BLACK SHOE, which is basically about

19. That is, it is assumed that $\sigma \wedge (\tau \vee \tau') = (\sigma \wedge \tau) \vee (\sigma \wedge \tau')$ and $\sigma \vee (\tau \wedge \tau') = (\sigma \vee \tau) \wedge (\sigma \vee \tau')$.

20. See chapter 21 of Barwise and Seligman (1997).

21. For a basic infon σ with polarity i, its complement $\neg\sigma$ would just be the infon with the opposite polarity. If complements (or pseudo-complements) are defined generally, the lattice can be converted into a commutative ring with identity in the usual way, defining $\sigma + \sigma' = (\sigma \wedge \neg\sigma') \vee (\neg\sigma \wedge \sigma')$ (i.e., the symmetric difference) and $\sigma * \sigma' = \sigma \wedge \sigma'$. The multiplicative identity would be **1**.

a man with various attributes, it is necessary to introduce conditions or conditioning infons. Simply put, the more general conditioned form of $\langle\langle R; a_1; \ldots; a_n; l; t; i \rangle\rangle$ is just $\langle\langle R \mid C_0; a_1 \mid C_1; \ldots; a_n \mid C_n; l \mid C_{-1}; t \mid C_{-2}; i \rangle\rangle$ where the C_i are themselves infons. Often, these infons C_i will just be unconditioned but compound infons, though there is nothing to rule out the possibility of nested conditions. The noun phrase above would be rendered roughly as $\langle\langle a_1 \mid \langle\langle P^{tall} \rangle\rangle \wedge \langle\langle P^{blond} \rangle\rangle \wedge \langle\langle R^{with}; a_1' \mid \langle\langle P^{one} \rangle\rangle \wedge \langle\langle P^{black} \rangle\rangle\rangle\rangle; i \rangle\rangle$ where a_1 and a_1' stand for the man and shoe respectively.[22] Notice that there are two levels of conditioning. The positive polarity on the conditions has been omitted to avoid clutter.

Conditioned infons are ubiquitous in modeling tense and aspect. To render the present continuous in an utterance of "Harvey is playing," the auxiliary verb IS would correspond to the infon $t \mid (t \parallel t_u) \wedge t, t_u \in [t_0, t_\infty]$ where $\parallel$ means "overlaps with" and where t_u is the time of utterance. Infix notation was used to make the infon easier to read.

Unconditioned infons can now be seen as just a special case of conditioned infons where the conditioning infon on each constituent is **1** (or, in other words, $\langle\langle\ \rangle\rangle$). When an item in an infon is conditioned by $\mathbf{1} = \langle\langle\ \rangle\rangle$, that is, by "no information," the **1** will just be omitted.

It may happen that a condition on a constituent of an infon is contradictory. An infon $\langle\langle a \mid C \rangle\rangle$ where $C = \mathbf{0}$ would just be $\langle\langle a \mid \mathbf{0} \rangle\rangle = \mathbf{0}$. That is, the overall infon is itself contradictory when it is conditioned by a contradictory infon. This also makes intuitive sense because a contradictory condition can never be realized and so makes the overall infon contradictory as well.

An interesting example arises when the entity $e(P, s)$ is used for a. Recall from Equation 2.1 that $e(P, s)$ is the individual $a = (x \mid s \models \langle\langle P; x \rangle\rangle)$ when the condition $s \models \langle\langle P; x \rangle\rangle$ yields just one object and the set $\{x \mid s \models \langle\langle P; x \rangle\rangle\}$ otherwise. When *no* object has P in s, $e(P, s) = \{x \mid s \models \langle\langle P; x \rangle\rangle\} = \phi$, the empty set.

Now consider $\langle\langle e(P, s) \mid C \rangle\rangle$ where $C = \langle\langle =; \mathrm{card}(\{x \mid s \models \langle\langle P; x \rangle\rangle\}); 1 \rangle\rangle$ with "card" standing for the cardinality of the set in question. With infix

22. This is a rough and incomplete rendering because dealing with determiners such as THE and ONE takes some more machinery that is developed later. Here I have used the individual a_1 to represent THE MAN, though this phrase would also need to be built up from its constituent parts. The phrase ONE SHOE is composite in a similar way. In particular, $\langle\langle P^{one} \rangle\rangle$ is an incomplete rendering of the conditioning infon, but I leave it here as a suggestive indication. There is also the issue of predicates such as TALL that will not be addressed here. The fully worked out content of this description will be given in chapter 6.

notation, $C = (\text{card}(\{x \mid s \models \langle\!\langle P; x \rangle\!\rangle\}) = 1)$ and $\langle\!\langle e(P,s) \mid C \rangle\!\rangle = \langle\!\langle e(P,s) \mid \text{card}(\{x \mid s \models \langle\!\langle P; x \rangle\!\rangle\}) = 1 \rangle\!\rangle$.

There are three possible cases. One is when exactly one object a has P in s. Then $e(P,s)$ is just that individual a. We can replace C with $\mathbf{1}$ because $\langle\!\langle e(P,s) \mid C \rangle\!\rangle = \langle\!\langle a \mid \text{card}(\{x \mid s \models \langle\!\langle P; x \rangle\!\rangle\}) = 1 \rangle\!\rangle = \langle\!\langle a \mid (1 = 1) \rangle\!\rangle = \langle\!\langle a \mid \mathbf{1} \rangle\!\rangle$ since $(1 = 1)$ is always true. Therefore, $\langle\!\langle e(P,s) \mid C \rangle\!\rangle = \langle\!\langle a \mid \mathbf{1} \rangle\!\rangle = \langle\!\langle a \rangle\!\rangle$.

What if there are either no objects satisfying P in s or there is more than one object satisfying P in s? In such situations, $e(P,s)$ is defined to be the *set* $\{x \mid s \models \langle\!\langle P; x \rangle\!\rangle\}$ and will be either the empty set ϕ or a set with at least two members. But C requires that this very set be a singleton and so is contradictory. That is, C reduces to something like $0 = 1$ or $2 = 1$ and so $C = \mathbf{0}$. This implies $\langle\!\langle e(P,s) \mid C \rangle\!\rangle = \langle\!\langle e(P,s) \mid \mathbf{0} \rangle\!\rangle = \mathbf{0}$.

I display these cases below for greater clarity:

$$\langle\!\langle e(P,s) \mid C \rangle\!\rangle = \langle\!\langle e(P,s) \mid (\text{card}(\{x \mid s \models \langle\!\langle P; x \rangle\!\rangle\}) = 1) \rangle\!\rangle$$
$$= \begin{cases} \langle\!\langle e(P,s) \mid (1 = 1) \rangle\!\rangle & \text{if exactly one object } a \text{ has } P \text{ in } s \\ \langle\!\langle e(P,s) \mid (0 = 1) \rangle\!\rangle & \text{if no object has } P \text{ in } s \\ \langle\!\langle e(P,s) \mid (n = 1) \rangle\!\rangle & \text{if } n \geq 2 \text{ objects have } P \text{ in } s \end{cases}$$

This simplifies to:

$$\langle\!\langle e(P,s) \mid C \rangle\!\rangle = \begin{cases} \langle\!\langle e(P,s) \mid (1 = 1) \rangle\!\rangle = \langle\!\langle a \mid \mathbf{1} \rangle\!\rangle = \langle\!\langle a \rangle\!\rangle \\ \langle\!\langle e(P,s) \mid (0 = 1) \rangle\!\rangle = \langle\!\langle \phi \mid \mathbf{0} \rangle\!\rangle = \mathbf{0} \\ \langle\!\langle e(P,s) \mid (n = 1) \rangle\!\rangle = \langle\!\langle \{a_1, \ldots, a_n\} \mid \mathbf{0} \rangle\!\rangle = \mathbf{0} \end{cases} \tag{2.2}$$

To make these possibilities more concrete, think of P as the property of being tall and situations s with either one tall person or none or more than one. In the first case, $\langle\!\langle e(P,s) \mid C \rangle\!\rangle$ will contain the one tall person, and in the others it will be $\mathbf{0}$. This kind of occurrence of contradictory infons will be very useful in chapters 3, 4, and 6 where names and definite descriptions and other noun phrases are considered.

These assumptions may be summarized thus:

Assumption 5 $\langle\!\langle x \mid \mathbf{0} \rangle\!\rangle = \mathbf{0}$ and $\langle\!\langle x \mid \mathbf{1} \rangle\!\rangle = \langle\!\langle x \rangle\!\rangle$ where x is any entity in $\mathcal{O}$.

It is also natural to assume that:

Assumption 6 $\langle\!\langle \mathbf{0} \rangle\!\rangle = \mathbf{0}$ and $\langle\!\langle \mathbf{1} \rangle\!\rangle = \mathbf{1}$.

Assumptions 1 through 4 above can be extended to conditioned infons in the obvious way. Essentially, an enlarged lattice $\mathcal{I}$ (with multiple sublattices with the same $\mathbf{1}$ and $\mathbf{0}$) is the result. In what follows, assignments will be used as before, but keep in mind that the elements of $\mathbf{n}$ are now mapped not just into relations or sets of individuals, but conditioned versions of these.[23]

2.3.3 A New Operation

Barwise (1989e) had fleetingly mentioned a distinct third operation $\odot_s : \mathcal{I}^2 \to \mathcal{I}$ that captures the unification or merging of infons. His definition is now expanded to take account of more cases. It is also stipulated that infons can be combined in these ways only relative to some situation s in which they hold. Since this operation on infons is central to equilibrium semantics and since its recursive definition involves many cases, it is developed step by step with examples.

Case 1: Incompatible Merging If two assignments $\mathbf{A_n}$ and $\mathbf{A_n'}$ involve incompatible objects, then the basic infons $\sigma = \langle\langle \mathbf{A_n}; i \rangle\rangle$ and $\sigma' = \langle\langle \mathbf{A_n'}; i \rangle\rangle$ are incompatible, and in this case $\sigma \odot_s \sigma' = \mathbf{0}$.

This case ensures that merges resulting in incompatible tuples will not occur.

Example 4: Incompatible Merging If there are two infons $\langle\langle R \rangle\rangle$ and $\langle\langle (1, b) \rangle\rangle$ where the individual b is incompatible as the first argument of the relation R, then their merge results in $\mathbf{0}$. If R is the relation of eating and requires an agent as its first argument and if b is an apple instead, then their merge would be incompatible as one cannot have an apple eating something. In such a situation, instead of the merge resulting in the intuitively expected $\langle\langle R, b \rangle\rangle$, we get the contradictory infon $\mathbf{0}$ instead.

The next two cases apply to situations where the objects in the tuples being merged are compatible.

Case 2: Ordinary Merging If two assignments $\mathbf{A_n}$ and $\mathbf{A_n'}$ are compatible as functions,[24] and their objects are also compatible with one another, we say the basic infons $\sigma = \langle\langle \mathbf{A_n}; i \rangle\rangle$ and $\sigma' = \langle\langle \mathbf{A_n'}; i \rangle\rangle$ are compatible, and in this case $\sigma \odot_s \sigma' = \langle\langle \mathbf{A_n} \cup \mathbf{A_n'}; i \rangle\rangle$.

Example 5: Ordinary Merging If there are two binary infons $\langle\langle R; (1, a) \rangle\rangle$ and $\langle\langle R; (2, b) \rangle\rangle$ then their assignments are compatible and if the

23. Expressing this formally leads to a tangle of symbols because one has to consider multiple and nested assignments, so just the same top-level symbols are used, but with this extended meaning.

24. That is, their values agree on all common elements in their domains. This compatibility of functions is different from but related to the compatibility of objects in an assignment.

objects in their tuples are also compatible, we can merge them to get $\langle\langle R;(1,a)\rangle\rangle \odot_s \langle\langle R;(2,b)\rangle\rangle = \langle\langle R;a;b\rangle\rangle$. Here R could be the relation of eating, a may stand for the agent $\mathcal{A}$ doing the eating and b may stand for an apple, the object being eaten. In this case, the first infon $\langle\langle R;(1,a)\rangle\rangle$ encodes the information that $\mathcal{A}$ is eating and the second infon $\langle\langle R;(2,b)\rangle\rangle$ that an apple is being eaten. Since these assignments are compatible as functions and since the tuples are also compatible with respect to their objects, their merge $\langle\langle R;a;b\rangle\rangle$ represents the combined information that $\mathcal{A}$ is eating an apple. The polarities of the two infons have to be the same, either 1 or 0. It is the situation s that licenses the infons being merged in this way rather than in one of the other ways described below. If there had been two infons $\langle\langle(1,b')\rangle\rangle$ and $\langle\langle R;(2,b)\rangle\rangle$ where b' is also an apple, then while the assignments are compatible as functions, they are not compatible as tuples since one cannot have one apple eating another. This implies that Case 1 applies and their merge is contradictory. It is also possible to merge two infons $\langle\langle(1,a)\rangle\rangle \odot_s \langle\langle(0,R)\rangle\rangle = \langle\langle(0,R);(1,a)\rangle\rangle$ if there are no incompatibilities.

The next case involves hat notation.

Case 3: Hat Merging $\langle\langle\hat{y}\langle\langle y;x;i\rangle\rangle;j\rangle\rangle \odot_s \langle\langle z;j\rangle\rangle = \langle\langle z;x;i\rangle\rangle$.

Example 6: Hat Merging For example, $\langle\langle\hat{R}\langle\langle\dot{R};a;i\rangle\rangle;i'\rangle\rangle \odot_s \langle\langle P;i'\rangle\rangle = \langle\langle P;a;i\rangle\rangle$. In chapter 6, it will be seen that the determiner THE has the approximate referential meaning $\langle\langle\hat{P}(e(\dot{P},r))\rangle\rangle$.[25] When this is merged with the referential meaning $\langle\langle P^{waiter}\rangle\rangle$ for a noun such as WAITER, we get $\langle\langle\hat{P}(e(\dot{P},r))\rangle\rangle \odot_s \langle\langle P^{waiter}\rangle\rangle = \langle\langle e(P^{waiter},r)\rangle\rangle$, exactly what would be expected from a process akin to λ-conversion. Conjunctions are not addressed in the book but they are treated similarly.

The cases above were appropriate for the "internal" fusing of infons where the constituents of each infon enter into the same tuple when they are compatible. With ordinary merging, we obtained a composite infon containing the relevant constituents within a single tuple. With hat merging, we replaced a parametric property or relation in one infon by inserting a property or relation from another infon into the first infon. Now we look at cases where such internal blending is not possible but where we still need to be able to put infons together.

25. The full accurate meaning can only be given later as it requires defining another special infon *Unique*. For now, I use this approximation just to illustrate Hat Merging. r stands for the (resource) situation, a term described in section 2.6.

Case 4: Miscellaneous Cases These come into play when the other cases do not apply.

Case 4a: Meet Merging If both polarities are 1 then $\sigma \odot_s \sigma' = \sigma \wedge \sigma'$.

Intuitively, this occurs when there are two infons with positive polarity that are being combined "externally." The relevant operation is $\wedge$ here because when the polarity is 1, the combined infon should intuitively be stronger (relative to $\Rightarrow_\ell$) than the infons being merged.

Example 7: Meet Merging For instance, $\langle\!\langle R; a\rangle\!\rangle \odot_s \langle\!\langle R'; a'\rangle\!\rangle = \langle\!\langle R; a\rangle\!\rangle \wedge \langle\!\langle R'; a'\rangle\!\rangle$. More concretely, if R is the relation of eating and R' is the relation of drinking, and a and a' are agents, the infons cannot be unified internally, and since their polarities are positive, their merge reduces just to meet. Informally considered, we have the stronger information that a is eating "*and*" a' is drinking. This stronger information is most naturally represented by the meet.

Case 4b: Join Merging If both polarities are 0 then $\sigma \odot_s \sigma' = \sigma \vee \sigma'$.

This case is or should be treated as the dual of case 4a. Here, since the polarities are negative, we should intuitively expect the product infon to be weaker than the multiplicands.

Example 8: Join Merging Dually, $\langle\!\langle R; a; 0\rangle\!\rangle \odot_s \langle\!\langle R'; a'; 0\rangle\!\rangle = \langle\!\langle R; a; 0\rangle\!\rangle \vee \langle\!\langle R'; a'; 0\rangle\!\rangle$. Again, if R, R', a, and a' are as above, the informal result is the weaker information that a is not eating "*or*" a' is not drinking. An alternative construal of this case could have been that neither is a eating nor is a' drinking, but the duality of the case with meet merging would then be lost.

Case 4c: Contradictory Merging If both polarities are different[26] then $\sigma \odot_s \sigma' = \mathbf{0}$.

Example 9: Contradictory Merging $\langle\!\langle R; a; 1\rangle\!\rangle \odot_s \langle\!\langle R'; a'; 0\rangle\!\rangle = \mathbf{0}$. While it is possible to combine two infons with opposing polarities with meet or join, the result with the merge operation is just the contradictory infon.

Case 4d: Identity Merging $\sigma \odot_s \mathbf{1} = \mathbf{1} \odot_s \sigma = \sigma$.

This case preserves the intuitive meaning of **1** as "no information." Keep in mind that all these subcases of Case 4 apply only when no other case does.

We now come to a recursive case.

26. The polarity of a basic infon is always 1 or 0 but the polarity of a compound infon may be 1, 0, or undefined.

Case 5: Conditional Merging $\langle\!\langle x \mid \sigma; i \rangle\!\rangle \odot_s \sigma' = \langle\!\langle x \mid \sigma \odot_s \sigma'; i \rangle\!\rangle$.

Example 10: Conditional Merging $\langle\!\langle a; i \rangle\!\rangle \odot_s \langle\!\langle R \rangle\!\rangle = \langle\!\langle a \mid \langle\!\langle R \rangle\!\rangle; i \rangle\!\rangle$. Here R may be a property such as being tall and a may be the agent $\mathcal{A}$. Since a is not conditioned by any infon explicitly, it is in effect conditioned by **1**, so, in more detail, this case is as follows: $\langle\!\langle a \mid \mathbf{1}; i \rangle\!\rangle \odot_s \langle\!\langle R \rangle\!\rangle = \langle\!\langle a \mid \mathbf{1} \odot_s \langle\!\langle R \rangle\!\rangle; i \rangle\!\rangle = \langle\!\langle a \mid \langle\!\langle R \rangle\!\rangle; i \rangle\!\rangle$. This is the case that gets activated when the infons corresponding to a noun phrase such as THE TALL MAN are combined.

These component cases are now collected together for convenience. The situated binary operation $\odot_s : \mathcal{I}^2 \to \mathcal{I}$ involves five cases:

1. **Incompatible Merging** If two assignments $\mathbf{A_n}$ and $\mathbf{A'_n}$ involve incompatible objects, then the basic infons $\sigma = \langle\!\langle \mathbf{A_n}; i \rangle\!\rangle$ and $\sigma' = \langle\!\langle \mathbf{A'_n}; i \rangle\!\rangle$ are incompatible, and in this case $\sigma \odot_s \sigma' = \mathbf{0}$.
2. **Ordinary Merging** If two assignments $\mathbf{A_n}$ and $\mathbf{A'_n}$ are compatible as functions, we say the basic infons $\sigma = \langle\!\langle \mathbf{A_n}; i \rangle\!\rangle$ and $\sigma' = \langle\!\langle \mathbf{A'_n}; i \rangle\!\rangle$ are compatible, and in this case $\sigma \odot_s \sigma' = \langle\!\langle \mathbf{A_n} \cup \mathbf{A'_n}; i \rangle\!\rangle$.
3. **Hat Merging** $\langle\!\langle \hat{y} \langle\!\langle \dot{y}; x; i \rangle\!\rangle; j \rangle\!\rangle \odot_s \langle\!\langle y; j \rangle\!\rangle = \langle\!\langle y; x; i \rangle\!\rangle$.
4. **Miscellaneous Cases** Otherwise:

a. **Meet Merging** If both polarities are 1 then $\sigma \odot_s \sigma' = \sigma \wedge \sigma'$.
b. **Join Merging** If both polarities are 0 then $\sigma \odot_s \sigma' = \sigma \vee \sigma'$.
c. **Contradictory Merging** If both polarities are different then $\sigma \odot_s \sigma' = \mathbf{0}$.
d. **Identity Merging** $\sigma \odot_s \mathbf{1} = \mathbf{1} \odot_s \sigma = \sigma$.

5. **Conditional Merging** $\langle\!\langle x \mid \sigma; i \rangle\!\rangle \odot_s \sigma' = \langle\!\langle x \mid \sigma \odot_s \sigma'; i \rangle\!\rangle$.

Incompatible merging results in **0**. When this case does not apply, merging involves squishing infons together when possible (ordinary merging, hat merging, and conditional merging); if this is not possible, it reduces to meet or join or **0** depending on their polarity. As defined, the operation may be ambiguous between ordinary merging and conditional merging. It is the situation s in which the operation is carried out that will determine which case is indicated. In conditional merging, $\odot_s$ is just pushed recursively into one level lower than the top level. When it reaches the base level where the operation has to be actually performed, one of the other cases will apply. When an infon is expressed simply as $\langle\!\langle (1, a); i \rangle\!\rangle$ where $a \in \mathbf{IND}$, it may be necessary to check what its arity is before merging it with another infon. In applications, it will usually just be assumed in certain contexts that the arity is appropriate for unification.

This is not the most intuitive of operations to define and the unification of infons poses some real difficulties. My own construal is tentative at best and refinements and possibly more cases may well be required. Putting our thinking about the lattice of infons and the merge operation together results in the following facts.

Fact 1 $\odot_s$ is associative and has $\mathbf{1}$ as an identity.[27]

Fact 1 can be shown in detail by going through each case. When an algebraic system has an associative operation, it is called a semigroup. A semigroup with an identity is called a monoid. Thus, our system of infons $(\mathcal{I}, \odot_s)$ is a monoid. It turns out, as will be shown partly in section 2.8 and fully in chapter 4, that the monoidal structure of this algebraic system plays a crucial role in making possible a tightly knit framework for meaning with the powerful result of the universality of games of partial information in semantics. It is essentially the associativity of $\odot_s$ and other operations ($\circ$ and $\otimes$) that will be introduced later that is required.

Fact 2 $\mathbf{0}$ is a zero for the monoid $(\mathcal{I}, \odot_s)$, that is, for all σ in $\mathcal{I}$, $\sigma \odot_s \mathbf{0} = \mathbf{0} \odot_s \sigma = \mathbf{0}$.

Fact 2 follows directly from contradictory merging because the polarities of the multiplicands are either different or both are undefined.

I now mention a fact that connects the lattice with the monoid.

Fact 3 If the polarity of two infons σ and σ' is 1 then $\sigma \odot_s \sigma' \Rightarrow_\ell \sigma \wedge \sigma'$ and if it is 0 then $\sigma \vee \sigma' \Rightarrow_\ell \sigma \odot_s \sigma'$.

Fact 3 relates both to the internal (Cases 1, 2, 3, 5) and the external (Case 4) ways of merging infons. Intuitively, $\sigma \odot_s \sigma' \Rightarrow_\ell \sigma$ and $\sigma \odot_s \sigma' \Rightarrow_\ell \sigma'$ when all polarities are positive because the merged infon has more information than its individual operands. Since $\sigma \wedge \sigma'$ is the infimum (or the *greatest* lower bound) of σ and σ', we have $\sigma \odot_s \sigma' \Rightarrow_\ell \sigma \wedge \sigma'$ when the polarities are 1. Dually, for the other case when the polarities are 0.

When the context is clear, it is possible to write simply $\sigma\tau$ instead of $\sigma \odot_s \tau$ for the product of two infons.

27. Any binary operation $\bullet$ over some set S is said to be associative if $x \bullet (y \bullet z) = (x \bullet y) \bullet z$ for all triples x, y, and z in S. Associativity is extremely important to have as it is usually not possible to do much with an algebraic system (i.e., $(S, \bullet)$) without it. An element 1 in S is an identity for $(S, \bullet)$ if $x \bullet 1 = 1 \bullet x = x$ for all x in S. An element 0 in S is a zero for $(S, \bullet)$ if $x \bullet 0 = 0 \bullet x = 0$ for all x in S.

2.3.4 Extending $\mathcal{I}$

First, basic unconditioned infons were introduced. Then compound infons and later conditioned infons were added. Now $\mathcal{I}$ is extended further by allowing the constituents of infons to be other objects that are not individuals. There is nothing preventing situations, types, infons, and other objects, if they are appropriate and compatible, from filling in the argument roles of infons. These objects are treated as individuals. For example, a proposition $s \models \sigma$ can also be expressed as an infon $\langle\langle \models; s; \sigma \rangle\rangle$ and a constraint $s \Rightarrow s'$ can be written $\langle\langle \Rightarrow; s; s' \rangle\rangle$.

This extension makes $\mathcal{I}$ significantly more complex even though the structure uncovered in the foregoing can be extended to this larger set. A formal definition of $\mathcal{I}$ would require a simultaneous recursive definition for multiple sets. Such forms will just be used when required without much ado.

2.3.5 Situations and Infons

Assumption 7 For all situations s and all infons σ and τ:

1. $s \not\models \mathbf{0}$ and $s \models \mathbf{1}$.
2. If $s \models \sigma$ and $\sigma \Rightarrow_\ell \tau$ then $s \models \tau$.
3. $s \models \sigma \wedge \tau$ if and only if $s \models \sigma$ and $s \models \tau$.
4. $s \models \sigma \vee \tau$ if and only if $s \models \sigma$ or $s \models \tau$.

The first assumption above will be used in chapters 3, 4, and 6. All it says is that no situation can support the contradictory infon and, dually, that all situations support the empty infon. This makes intuitive sense as we want our situations to be coherent. The rest of the assumptions do not really get used in this book but they are useful to record. They are relevant when the propositional contents of utterances are considered.

2.3.6 Infons and Shannon's Information Theory

As mentioned in chapter 1, Shannon's[28] quantitative theory of information inspired Dretske's account of the flow of information, which in turn influenced Barwise's development of situation theory. So far, nothing has been said about how the two theories of information, one qualitative and the other quantitative, are connected. A small beginning is made here.

28. Though the name of Shannon is usually cited in accounts of this theory of information transmission, there were several others who also contributed to its development: Boltzmann, Gibbs, Nyquist, Hartley, Szilard, and Weiner among other physicists and electrical engineers. See http://en.wikipedia.org/wiki/Timeline_of_information_theory for a timeline of quantitative information theory.

Just as an infon may be true or false only relative to a situation, likewise the amount or quantity of information in an infon is also determined only with respect to an embedding situation. Unlike engineering applications of information theory, the interest here is not in the average amounts of information a source may generate or a channel may transmit, but in the amount of information contained in a particular content (i.e., infon) relative to a situation. Thus, our interest is in the *surprisal* of an infon with respect to a situation rather than in the *entropy* of the situation that "generates" the infon.

If we assume that an infon σ or its complement may be realized in situation s with probabilities $p(\sigma \mid s) = \pi$ and $p(\neg\sigma \mid s) = 1 - \pi$, then the surprisal of σ with respect to s is given by $S(\sigma \mid s) = \log_2(1/p(\sigma \mid s)) = -\log_2 \pi$ and the surprisal of $\neg\sigma$ with respect to s is given by $S(\neg\sigma \mid s) = \log_2(1/p(\neg\sigma \mid s)) = -\log_2(1 - \pi)$.

Any situation s taken in isolation may be viewed as a generator of information. In the situation with $\mathcal{A}$ and $\mathcal{B}$, assume their furniture may a priori have been any of eight equally likely colors. Then the fact σ that it is brown is a reduction in uncertainty that has a surprisal of $S(\sigma \mid s) = \log_2(1/p(\sigma \mid s)) = \log_2 8 = 3$ bits.

If $s \models \sigma$ to start with and there is no reduction of uncertainty involved then of course $S(\sigma \mid s) = 0$. A more likely infon will have a lower surprisal and vice versa. In particular, $S(\mathbf{1} \mid s) = 0$ and $S(\mathbf{0} \mid s) = \infty$ for all s. Since a more informative infon is less likely than a less informative one, the following implication holds.

Fact 4 If $\sigma \Rightarrow_\ell \tau$ then for all s $S(\sigma \mid s) \geq S(\tau \mid s)$.

Often, objective probabilities are not available and then surprisal may have to be interpreted subjectively based on subjective probabilities. That is, an agent may have to rely on his subjective construal of the surprisal of a state of affairs.

It turns out that the surprisal or amount of information in an infon relative to a situation is *not* the key factor in communication. What matters is the *value* of this information, as spelled out in Parikh (2001, 2006b) and in chapter 3. In many situations, agents do prefer more information to less, in which case the value of more information will also be greater. But agents always convey and interpret information relative to the goals of the conversation, as Grice (1975) pointed out in his maxims, and as implied by the notion of the *value* of information, and this frequently implies that speakers convey less than they know about a topic. If someone asks where a person lives, for example, the appropriate response may be the country, city, area, or street depending on the context. Such optimal withholding of information is ubiquitous.

Incidentally, I mention in passing that this discussion also links up with the notion of possibility as the surprisal of an infon with respect to a situation involves countenancing the different possible ways a situation might be.

2.3.7 Questions and Commands

The infons considered so far may be used to describe possible states of affairs that hold in some situation and that may serve as the contents of statements made by speakers to addressees. To capture the content of questions or commands, slight modifications of these infons are introduced.

If $\mathcal{A}$ asks $\mathcal{B}$ "Where is Nobu?" then the infon representing this question would be expressed as $?\langle\langle R; a_1; x; 1\rangle\rangle$, where R stands for some appropriate relation involving location, a_1 refers to Nobu, and x is a parameter that together with the "?" indicates that the argument corresponding to Nobu's location is missing. The polarity is 1 because such questions carry a "positive" presupposition.[29] Note that the location of the utterance is different from the location of Nobu referred to in the question. For a question like "Is Nobu downtown?" we would write $?\langle\langle R; a_1; a_2; x\rangle\rangle$ where a_2 stands for "downtown" and where the polarity is now the missing information.

Commands are even simpler and we write just $!\sigma$ to indicate the imperative mood.

This completes the description of the space of infons. It should be easier now to appreciate how these information packets or "quanta" are constituted and how they combine with each other and relate to the other enti-

29. I have yet to consider how best to formulate the notion of presupposition within equilibrium semantics (e.g., whether presuppositions can be fully assimilated to conditions as described in section 2.3.2) and so I do not elaborate on it here or elsewhere in the book. Construing presuppositions as conditions is both "semantic" and "pragmatic" though it does not involve truth-value gaps and does not involve speakers exclusively but the use of an expression by a speaker. One advantage of this view is that it permits any *part* of an utterance—like a definite description—to carry a presupposition. This is similar to implicatures and enrichments being carried by subsentential clauses. See section 4.4.1 and 4.4.2 and also footnote 26 in section 4.4.4. See also section 6.1.1 for a discussion of presupposition in the context of definite descriptions.

ties in $\mathcal{O}$. There is certainly a great deal more structure to be uncovered in this space but how relevant it would be for semantics is unclear.

2.4 Ontological Maps

It is possible to define partial maps that transform the entities in $\mathcal{E}$ into other entities in $\mathcal{E}$.

A property P in $\mathcal{E}$ can be transformed into a number of different entities in $\mathcal{E}$. To start with, P can be mapped into an individual $(a \mid s \models \langle\langle P; a \rangle\rangle)$ that has P relative to some situation s in $\mathcal{E}$. Instead of mapping the property into an individual, it turns out to be more useful to consider the infon containing the relevant individual as it is infons (rather than individuals themselves) that are the contents of uttered expressions. Thus, the map actually defined is $ind(P, s) = \langle\langle (a \mid s \models \langle\langle P; a \rangle\rangle) \rangle\rangle$; this is called *instantiation*. In our setting, the property of being male would be instantiated by $\langle\langle \mathcal{A} \rangle\rangle$. Alternatively, P can be mapped into its extension $ext(P, s) = \langle\langle \{x \mid s \models \langle\langle P; x \rangle\rangle\} \rangle\rangle$ relative to s; this is *extensionalization*. The property of being brown would have as its extension the collection of furniture in the room. These two transforms go together intuitively as they will enable us to get at the referential uses of noun phrases.

It is also possible to transform P into its corresponding type $typ(P, s) = \langle\langle [x \mid s \models \langle\langle P; x \rangle\rangle] \rangle\rangle$ and name this *reification*. $\mathcal{A}$ and $\mathcal{B}$ might, in their discussion about what to do in the evening, discuss the narrative as a form in movies. This would be an instance of reification. Next, there is just the *identity* map $id(P, s) = \langle\langle P \rangle\rangle$, taking P essentially into itself. Finally, P can be mapped into an indeterminate object, that is, a parameter $par(P, s) = \langle\langle (\dot{a} \mid s \models \langle\langle P; \dot{a} \rangle\rangle) \rangle\rangle$ that satisfies P. If $\mathcal{A}$ and $\mathcal{B}$ were to go to a restaurant that evening and ask for the waiter, they would be referring not to a particular person but indeterminately (or attributively) to a waiter, whoever he or she might be.[30] Such maps are called *parametrizations*. These three transforms pertain to other uses of noun phrases and also to other types of phrases.

There are thus five maps that transform properties into infons containing corresponding entities—instantiation, extensionalization, reification, identity, and parametrization. These are all the operations required; there are, of course, all sorts of other operations (e.g., taking an individual into

30. This and other uses of definite descriptions will be examined in detail in chapter 6.

a property it has, or an infon into its constituent property). I display these five maps for convenience:

$ind(P, s) = \langle\langle (a \mid s \models \langle\langle P; a \rangle\rangle) \rangle\rangle$ instantiation

$ext(P, s) = \langle\langle \{a \mid s \models \langle\langle P; a \rangle\rangle\} \rangle\rangle$ extensionalization

$typ(P, s) = \langle\langle [a \mid s \models \langle\langle P; a \rangle\rangle] \rangle\rangle$ reification

$id(P, s) = \langle\langle P \rangle\rangle$ identity

$par(P, s) = \langle\langle (\dot{a} \mid s \models \langle\langle P; \dot{a} \rangle\rangle) \rangle\rangle$ parametrization

It is possible, in principle, to study both the underlying space and the space of transformations on $\mathcal{E}$ (or $\mathcal{O}$), just as we may study an Euclidean space and its group of, say, rotations about an axis. Situation theory can be conceived of as a theory of the underlying space of ontological entities. However, we can also consider spaces of transformations on the underlying space. It is interesting that, unlike the case of Euclidean and many other spaces, the ontological space is not available to us in any obvious way. Our primary routes to discovering the objects that populate this space are linguistic and epistemic situations, and also some intuitive ideas about how we might transform an entity to generate another entity. In an important sense, both the underlying ontological space and its associated space of transformations have to be discovered more or less simultaneously. This is reflected partly by the need to define one collection of entities in terms of another, for example, properties in terms of infons, or types in terms of properties. But these two spaces can also be viewed abstractly, as independent but related mathematical structures.[31]

2.5 Agents

The informational space and its corresponding theory presupposes the existence of agents who are required for the processes of individuation and discrimination that generate the objects in $\mathcal{O}$ and $\mathcal{I}$. Agents such as $\mathcal{A}$ and $\mathcal{B}$ are always in some situation. Agents can be persons but, more generally, they can be any entity capable of perception and action. Birds and bees are also agents and so are certain sorts of artificial devices we call robots. $\mathcal{A}$ and $\mathcal{B}$ and other agents are typically finite and have limited capacities. They try to do the best they can given these constraints and so are seldom

31. The space of transforms of concern here is essentially a small subset of $T_{\mathcal{E}} = \{f_s : \mathcal{E} \rightarrow \mathcal{E}\}$, where the functions in $T_{\mathcal{E}}$ are partial maps. Since there are many environments, there will be many corresponding spaces.

perfectly rational in the sense made precise in game and decision theory. Our interest here will be in agents that have the ability to use language to a greater or lesser degree and that are able to reason in more or less complex ways. Indeed, the focus will almost exclusively be on people, although the reader should keep a broader notion of agency in mind.

Our agents perceive facts in the world, form beliefs about the world, interact with each other, and choose to perform certain actions in the world. Not much will be said about their perceptual capabilities or about their belief formation, but these capacities will be assumed in discussing how they interact and choose actions—in particular, how they choose utterances and interpretations of these utterances. Their ability to interact and choose essentially allows them to engage in playing situated games or solving situated decision problems. Since these agents represent such choice situations and reason about them, it will be necessary to make some assumptions about how they make choices. Situated games and decision problems and how agents reason about them are introduced in the next chapter.

2.6 Language and its Situations

We start with a natural language that is taken as given. I assume that a grammar for this language is also available and that it generates all the parses for all the words, phrases, and sentences in the language.

Given the language, we collect its words in the finite set $\mathcal{V}$, standing for its vocabulary. A string on $\mathcal{V}$ of length n is then a function from $\{1, 2, 3, \ldots, n\}$ to $\mathcal{V}$. The unique string of length 0, the empty string, is denoted by e. The concatenation $\cdot$ of two strings is defined in the usual way and $v \cdot w$ is written vw. $\mathcal{V}^*$ is the set of all strings on $\mathcal{V}$ and is called the free monoid on $\mathcal{V}$. We add the special zero element 0 to $\mathcal{V}^*$ which can be thought of as an illegitimate or contradictory string.

Consider now the following proper subset $\mathcal{L}$ of $\mathcal{V}^* \cup \{0\}$. It is formed by defining the following special modification of concatenation: $v \circ w = v \cdot w = vw$ when vw has at least one parse and $v \circ w = 0$ otherwise. Then $\mathcal{L}$ is the set formed by freely generating all strings from $\mathcal{V}$ by this special concatenation operation and also includes the empty string e and the zero element 0. It is just the set of all words, phrases, and sentences in the language together with the empty and zero elements.[32] The operation $\circ$, also

32. I will simply ignore the question of how to handle the concatenation of two sentences. Something is said about this in section 7.2 on discourse.

called concatenation (or grammatical concatenation), is associative and has the empty string e as an identity which makes $(\mathcal{L}, \circ)$ a monoid just like the monoid $(\mathcal{I}, \odot_s)$ identified in section 2.3.3. It has the zero element 0 just as $(\mathcal{I}, \odot_s)$ had the zero element $\mathbf{0}$. That is, $v \circ 0 = 0 \circ v = 0$ for all strings v. As mentioned earlier, it is the associativity of $\circ$ and other operations ($\odot_s$ and $\otimes$, the latter of which will be introduced in chapter 4) that is important for equilibrium semantics.

A sentence φ is made up of individual words and may be represented as $\varphi_1 \circ \varphi_2 \circ \cdots \circ \varphi_n$ for some natural number n. When no ambiguities arise, this is written $\varphi_1\varphi_2 \ldots \varphi_n$. Sentences are usually denoted by letters such as φ, ψ, μ, v, and ω. As I mentioned in section 1.4.2, my view is that a sentence by itself is completely inert and has no *referential* content. It is only an utterance (i.e., an action of an appropriate kind) involving a sentence that results in some (referential) meaning being generated. Words do have *conventional* contents that are independent of context and utterance but, once again, as mentioned in section 1.4.1, sentences do not. Why is it then that when a sentence such as JOHN SAW THE PRETTY GIRL WITH A TELESCOPE is considered abstractly apart from any context, it appears that it can be partially interpreted? This happens because the reader implicitly supplies an abstract utterance situation that is partially filled out, leaving a number of constituents as parameters. I will show this in greater detail in the next section.

A single utterance is a complex event and is thus associated with a number of situations and other entities. Typically, $\mathcal{A}$ and $\mathcal{B}$ will be in some *utterance* situation u that is part of a larger *discourse* (or *dialogue*) situation d in which the two interlocutors are engaged in a conversation interspersed with other actions.[33] In the example, $\mathcal{A}$ and $\mathcal{B}$ are considering whether to go to a restaurant and movie or to go to a symphony and one of them may say something pertaining to this setting. This description of an utterance situation is intended to be very broad and cover a wide range of interactions. The situation u contains various ambient facts and a parameter $\dot{\varphi}$ for the sentence to be uttered. This parameter is a constituent of an infon $\langle\!\langle hu; \mathcal{A}; \dot{\varphi} \rangle\!\rangle$ where hu is the special relation of having uttered something.[34] We have $u \models \langle\!\langle hu; \mathcal{A}; \dot{\varphi} \rangle\!\rangle$. The parameter $\dot{\varphi}$ is an-

33. The latter is called a *discourse* situation rather than, say, an "interaction" situation because the interest is in the linguistic aspect of the interaction. However, the nonlinguistic actions that take place in d obviously contribute to the meaning of the discourse and dialogue.

34. See section A.2 in Appendix A. Of course, there would also be arguments for a spatiotemporal location for the utterance.

chored via an anchor f to the sentence φ uttered in u, that is, $f(\dot{\varphi}) = \varphi$. More generally, we would have $f(\dot{\varphi}) = \alpha$, where α is any expression uttered in u, not necessarily a whole sentence. When it is required that we make the anchor f explicit, we write $u[f]$ rather than just u, as mentioned in section 2.2. I will usually leave the anchor implicit with the understanding that $\dot{\varphi}$ is tied to the expression α being considered. The situation d contains parameters for all the sentences uttered up to and including $\dot{\varphi}$ and a larger set of nonlinguistic facts; it is a dynamic situation that unfolds over time. These parameters are then anchored via an anchoring function to the particular sentence(s) being interpreted. The sentence φ itself is not inserted into u (or d) for technical reasons: this allows consideration of alternative sentences being uttered in the same utterance situation. u can itself be decomposed into *lexical* subsituations $u_1, u_2, \ldots,$ u_n, each u_i containing an utterance of its corresponding word φ_i together with other ambient information. l_u and t_u are the location and time of the utterance. They will usually play a role in restricting the contents of verb tenses and also in delimiting the contents of words such as HERE and NOW.

As d evolves, it generates a description of some situation, called the *described* situation c.[35] Each utterance in d typically adds multiple infons to c. If d is made up of a sequence of utterances each taking place in utterance situations $u, u', \ldots,$ then, just as u contributes to constructing c, c in turn contributes to modifying u to establish the next utterance situation u', which generates c', and so on. Both u's contribution to c and c's contribution to u' are *partial* as there may be other things going on in the ambient situation that also need to be taken into account when interpreting the sequence of utterances. As mentioned in footnote 8 in section 1.1, this contrasts with Stalnaker's (1998) view in which a single entity called the context set plays both roles and in which the only changes allowed are those issuing from the utterance itself. The added generality and finer grain one gets by keeping the utterance situation and described situation apart are useful in different ways. One is that the described situation is used in identifying the proposition expressed by an utterance and this role cannot be played by the utterance situation as it has many extraneous facts such as the speaker's uttering the sentence that are not part of what is described.[36] Another is that the utterance situation and described

35. c is a mnemonic for content.

36. This is also the problem with dynamic approaches in formal semantics in which only u and u' (or corresponding sets of possible worlds) are demarcated but not c.

situation may be shared by the interlocutors in different ways and to different degrees, a possibility that is precluded by having just one entity that is also assumed to be fully shared. Partly, the difference between the two approaches may also have to do with different goals: one view is concerned with modeling a limited part of the data of communication (e.g., how the information state or common ground is updated), the other is concerned more with creating a framework and theory of communication that can accommodate a larger perspective and so needs to account for distinctions that exist in the communicative process. Some distinctions may be relevant to the narrower goal, others may just supply added penumbral description. I suspect that distinguishing between utterance and described situations is relevant to the narrower goals as well but I leave for another occasion a more detailed examination of this difference in approaches to the situation of utterance.

Some utterances u in d may also be associated with *resource* situations r that are accessed in order to locate a referent (or set of possible referents). This happens when the referent is in some perceptually salient situation v_u or some subsituation of the described situation c. That is, the referent is always in some more or less shared resource situation r, which is either perceptually shared or shared in virtue of the discourse up to that point. As d progresses, the relevant r may also change. A large situation $\mathcal{D}$ called the *discourse state* contains all the resource and described situations accessed via the utterances in d as well as other information.[37] As the name suggests, it is most relevant when considering discourse and so will not be much mentioned here.

The agents $\mathcal{A}$ and $\mathcal{B}$ have all manner of (shared) beliefs and knowledge about d and associated situations such as r, c, and $\mathcal{D}$. Some of these epistemic and doxastic states are explicitly represented mentally and some are left implicit—both can be modeled by further situations, which may partly be subsituations of the above situations, though these issues are not pursued here. The finite environment $\mathcal{E}$ contains all of the above situations and everything of interest. It is a subset of $\mathcal{O}$.

2.7 An Example

It is time to look at an example to see how the contents of a reasonably complex linguistic utterance can be rendered in situation theory. Consider

37. $\mathcal{D}$ is usually called the *discourse model*, but *discourse state* is preferred as the word "model" conjures up extraneous associations. The overall "model" is the ontology $\mathcal{O}$.

the sentence mentioned above used in some unspecified parametric utterance situation $\dot{u}$:

John saw the pretty girl with a telescope.

This sentence has at least two possible readings. One reading involves the noun phrase THE PRETTY GIRL being modified by the prepositional phrase. The other reading involves the verb SAW being modified by the prepositional phrase. The relevant infons are built up step by step, with more detail in each succeeding step.

The basic form of the infon for the first reading is ⟪see; John; the pretty girl with a telescope; l; $(t \mid t \prec t_{\dot{u}})$⟫ where the various constituents in English need to be replaced by appropriate entities. The relation $\prec$ refers to temporal precedence. We could have written ⟪$\prec$; t; $t_{\dot{u}}$⟫, but infix notation is easier to read. To make this infon unambiguous, we would write ⟪(0, see); (1, John); (2, the pretty girl with a telescope); $(-1, l)$; $(-2, (t \mid t \prec t_{\dot{u}}))$⟫, but these numerical indices will be avoided. The polarity of 1 has also been omitted here. The next step in the construction is the infon ⟪see; John; (the girl | ⟪pretty⟫ $\wedge$ ⟪with; a telescope⟫); l; $(t \mid t \prec t_{\dot{u}})$⟫. This says something like "John sees the girl such that the girl is pretty and such that the girl is with a telescope at a time such that the time precedes the time of utterance." The last step would be to replace each of the words and phrases in the infon with appropriate and precise symbols for their contents. All lexical ambiguities are removed by appropriate subscripting.

We are not in a position yet to carry out this last step, but it should be clear that each of the constituents of the infon makes a reference to the parameter $\dot{u}$: the relation "saw" refers to the time of utterance, "John" will be shown in the next chapter to require a resource situation that depends on the utterance situation, and so on. Without this parameter, the sentence is inert; it cannot cross the chasm to a referential content. The reason why the sentence appears to carry a referential meaning in vacuo is that the interpreter supplies this missing situation in the form of a parameter.

The other reading where the verb is modified is obtained as follows. We start with ⟪see with a telescope; John; the pretty girl; l; $(t \mid t \prec t_{\dot{u}})$⟫. This is then elaborated as ⟪(see | ⟪with; a telescope⟫); John; (the girl | ⟪pretty⟫); l; $(t \mid t \prec t_{\dot{u}})$⟫. The relation "see" is an implicit argument of the relation "with"; this often happens with prepositions, where a relation is an argument of another relation. The final step is once again the replacement of the various words in the infons with precise and unambiguous symbols representing their contents.

Both readings conform to the general infonic form $\langle\!\langle R \mid C_0; a_1 \mid C_1; \ldots; a_n \mid C_n; l \mid C_{-1}; t \mid C_{-2}; i \rangle\!\rangle$ and the underlying principle for constructing complex infons is to take this form and add successive refinements to its constituents. Of course, this single example cannot guarantee that something of the complexity written by Joyce or Proust can be expressed situation-theoretically but at least there is some warrant to think that if the universe of objects described falls short, it should not be too difficult to add more objects to enable the representation in question. In this book, I will stick to complexities of the kind present in sentences like the one just considered, but the epigraph by Joyce is partly meant to suggest that I have the full range of meaning that language makes possible in mind.

2.8 Language and World

Now that the monoids $(\mathcal{L}, \circ)$ and $(\mathcal{I}, \odot_u)$ have been specified, it is possible to define an *interpretation* or *content* function $\mathcal{C}_u$ for each utterance situation u that maps any expression α uttered in u to its infonic content. This content function will have a *locutionary* component and an *illocutionary* component denoted by $\mathcal{C}_u^\ell$ and $\mathcal{C}_u^\imath$, respectively, such that $\mathcal{C}_u = \mathcal{C}_u^\ell \odot_u \mathcal{C}_u^\imath$. These terms and component contents will be defined in chapter 4. For the moment, note the following assumption involving locutionary content.

Assumption 8 Given an utterance situation u, there is a map $\mathcal{C}_u^\ell : \mathcal{L} \to \mathcal{I}$ such that $\mathcal{C}_u^\ell$ is a homomorphism, $\mathcal{C}_u^\ell(0) = \mathbf{0}$, and, when uttered in u, $\mathcal{C}_u^\ell(\alpha)$ is the locutionary content of expression α in u.[38]

A homomorphism between two algebraic systems is a map that shows that the two systems have a similar structure by mirroring the results of the operations in the two systems. Specifically, by a homomorphism between two monoids, it is meant that $\mathcal{C}_u^\ell(\alpha \circ \alpha') = \mathcal{C}_u^\ell(\alpha) \odot_u \mathcal{C}_u^\ell(\alpha')$ for all

38. To guarantee that α is actually uttered in u, there must be an anchor f that anchors the parameter $\dot{\varphi}$ in u to α; that is, we must have an anchor f such that $f(\dot{\varphi}) = \alpha$. If the notation had to be made fully explicit, it would be necessary to write $u[f]$ rather than just u. To make the content function total, it could be defined as follows:

$$\mathcal{C}_{u[f]}^\ell(\alpha) = \begin{cases} \sigma & \text{if } f(\dot{\varphi}) = \alpha \\ \mathbf{1} & \text{otherwise} \end{cases} \tag{2.3}$$

where σ is some infon that is the content of α being uttered in u.

α, α' in $\mathcal{L}$ and $\mathcal{C}_u^{\ell}(e) = \mathbf{1}$ where e is the empty string. The relevance of the monoidal structure of $(\mathcal{L}, \circ)$ and $(\mathcal{I}, \odot_u)$ lies in making possible a homomorphic map between the two sets. In section 4.11, we will see that this structure is shared with a third monoid and this fact allows one to prove an important result about the universality of games of partial information.

The anchoring of $\dot{\varphi}$ in u to the expression α when considering $\mathcal{C}_u^{\ell}(\alpha)$ is left implicit.[39]

39. It is worth giving an example of the role of the anchor in some detail. Consider an utterance situation u, say, at the Capulets' ball in *Romeo and Juliet*, in which there are two utterances. Then, u will have two parameters $\dot{\varphi}$ and $\dot{\varphi}'$, one for each utterance. Let the two sentences uttered in u be "Romeo kissed Juliet" (ψ) and "Juliet kissed Romeo" (ψ'). The two anchors f and f' will have $f(\dot{\varphi}) = \psi = \text{Romeo kissed Juliet}$ and $f(\dot{\varphi}') = \psi' = \text{Juliet kissed Romeo}$. Since both sentences involve an utterance of Juliet, we have $\psi_3 = \psi_1' = \text{Juliet}$, where ψ_3 is the third word of ψ, and ψ_1' is the first word of ψ'. If j represents Juliet, the locutionary contents of the two utterances of Juliet are represented as follows:

$$\mathcal{C}_{u[f]}^{\ell}(\psi_3) = \mathcal{C}_{u[f]}^{\ell}(\text{Juliet}) = \langle\langle (2, j) \rangle\rangle$$

$$\mathcal{C}_{u[f']}^{\ell}(\psi_1') = \mathcal{C}_{u[f']}^{\ell}(\text{Juliet}) = \langle\langle (1, j) \rangle\rangle$$

Without the anchors to distinguish the two different occurrences of Juliet in the two quite different sentences ψ and ψ', the value of the content map for each utterance would be forced to be the same. The value of the first map has Juliet occupying the *second* argument role while the value of the second map has her occupying the *first* argument role, with very different meanings. Incidentally, if there were no anchor f anchoring the parameter in u to Juliet, we would have by equation 2.3:

$$\mathcal{C}_u^{\ell}(\text{Juliet}) = \mathbf{1}$$

If r stands for Romeo, the locutionary content of the first utterance would be expressed as follows:

$$\begin{aligned}
\mathcal{C}_{u[f]}^{\ell}(\psi) &= \mathcal{C}_{u[f]}^{\ell}(\psi_1 \circ \psi_2 \circ \psi_3) && (\psi = \psi_1 \circ \psi_2 \circ \psi_3) \\
&= \mathcal{C}_{u[f]}^{\ell}(\psi_1) \odot_u \mathcal{C}_{u[f]}^{\ell}(\psi_2) \odot_u \mathcal{C}_{u[f]}^{\ell}(\psi_3) && \text{(homomorphism)} \\
&= \langle\langle (1, r) \rangle\rangle \odot_u \langle\langle (0, R^{kissed}) \rangle\rangle \odot_u \langle\langle (2, j) \rangle\rangle && \text{(value of content map)} \\
&= \langle\langle (0, R^{kissed}); (1, r); (2, j) \rangle\rangle && \text{(ordinary merging)}
\end{aligned}$$

and the locutionary content of the second utterance would be expressed as follows:

$\mathcal{C}_u^\ell$ is just the standard interpretation function from model theory with the added fact that $\mathcal{C}_u^\ell(0) = \mathbf{0}$. Indeed, the space of infons $\mathcal{I}$ can be replaced by any other domain that can serve as an adequate model for natural language.[40] When an agent utters a sentence φ in a situation u, then its content will be $\mathcal{C}_u(\varphi)$ and its propositional content will be $c \models \mathcal{C}_u(\varphi)$, where c is the described situation. To allow for variations in content between interlocutors, it is necessary to distinguish such contents by appropriate superscripts: we write $\mathcal{C}_u^{\mathcal{A}}(\varphi)$ and $\mathcal{C}_u^{\mathcal{B}}(\varphi)$ for the meanings derived by $\mathcal{A}$ and $\mathcal{B}$ from the utterance.

The central problem of meaning, that is, of semantics (and pragmatics) is to give an account of these content maps from first principles for each given utterance situation u. This is what equilibrium semantics will do.

$$
\begin{aligned}
\mathcal{C}_{u[f']}^\ell(\psi') &= \mathcal{C}_{u[f']}^\ell(\psi_1' \circ \psi_2' \circ \psi_3') && (\psi' = \psi_1' \circ \psi_2' \circ \psi_3') \\
&= \mathcal{C}_{u[f']}^\ell(\psi_1') \odot_u \mathcal{C}_{u[f']}^\ell(\psi_2') \odot_u \mathcal{C}_{u[f']}^\ell(\psi_3') && \text{(homomorphism)} \\
&= \langle\!\langle (1, j) \rangle\!\rangle \odot_u \langle\!\langle (0, R^{kissed}) \rangle\!\rangle \odot_u \langle\!\langle (2, r) \rangle\!\rangle && \text{(value of content map)} \\
&= \langle\!\langle (0, R^{kissed}); (1, j); (2, r) \rangle\!\rangle && \text{(ordinary merging)}
\end{aligned}
$$

Such situations where two utterances in the same utterance situation may create a potential problem for the content map will not occur in this book, so I will leave the anchor implicit to avoid cluttering the notation. But the anchor is always available to disambiguate any potential ambiguities in the arguments to the content map.

40. I do not believe the framework of possible worlds is fine-grained enough or is able to capture partiality the way it is required for natural language, so I do not believe it can serve as an adequate model. However, it is not possible to argue for this here. See, for example, Barwise (1989c) and several other relevant references therein.

3 Situated Choice

More than any time in history mankind faces a crossroads. One path leads to despair and utter hopelessness, the other to total extinction. Let us pray that we have the wisdom to choose correctly.
—Woody Allen

Alan and Barbara, our two protagonists $\mathcal{A}$ and $\mathcal{B}$, have two young children: Caitlin, their daughter and the older of the two children, and Harvey, their son, so named because Alan is a fan of James Stewart, particularly his portrayal of Elwood P. Dowd in the film *Harvey* (1950, directed by Henry Koster). Barbara is less of a Stewart fan; she vetoed the name Elwood but accepted Harvey.

The couple are planning a night on the town. As I indicated in chapter 2, they must decide what to do for the evening. Barbara can get a pair of tickets to the symphony. Alan is less enthusiastic about this idea, preferring dinner and a movie. Obviously, they both want to go out and they prefer to be together; in fact, if they cannot agree on a joint activity, they have decided to stay at home with the kids. How should they decide?

Such a situation where one or more agents has to make a choice is called the *setting*. Game and decision theory offer us a way to represent the choices that $\mathcal{A}$ and $\mathcal{B}$ face this evening. Since our eventual interest is in analyzing utterances, for us the setting is just what was called the utterance situation u in section 2.6. u is a complex situation in which many things remain implicit and partially specifiable. It contains not just the facts pertaining to the agents' choices, but also their wider preferences and beliefs, what their children are doing, what the weather is like, the physical space they are in, and above all, a range of possibilities for action not easy to make explicit in advance. For example, in a setting or utterance situation like u, Alan may propose something entirely different from the alternatives itemized above: he may suggest an impromptu outing with friends. In other words, the agents can *change* the choices they face. Their tacit options are obviously constrained by u, but it is not possible to spell out the *boundary* of u.[1]

Real situations are almost always infinitely richer than the models we build to capture their particular aspects. Such settings are able to *support* multiple models of choice; a model's relevance is itself a feature of the situation, something the concerned agents actively seek to shape.

All actions thus occur in an environment and have to be understood against a background like u. Choice is always *situated.* The first step is to isolate certain key aspects of u as we have done in the informal description above. The next step is to build a mathematical model of the choices made explicit in u. The resulting game or decision problem then becomes a further part of the background within which the agents $\mathcal{A}$ and $\mathcal{B}$ produce and interpret utterances. $\mathcal{A}$ and $\mathcal{B}$ can say a variety of things; some to solve the identified game, others possibly to change the game or influence the possibilities, and yet others that relate to aspects of the setting not directly modeled by the game.

It is necessary to keep this layered background in mind when developing an account of communication. Only then can we hope to capture the full range of meaning that language makes possible. Many aspects of this setting can be represented mathematically, but perhaps not all. There may always remain certain residual aspects of communication that resist formalization. This should not be surprising given the infinite range and particularity of the situations we inhabit. This is yet another dimension of the partiality I have been emphasizing in chapter 2. Indeed, what is remarkable is how much the mathematical tools and framework I offer do allow us to express and encapsulate.

3.1 Choice in General

Game theory provides a mathematical way to approach Alan and Barbara's situation.[2] It provides the tools for modeling *strategic* choice, that is, choice in situations where each agent has to consider the other's possible actions. As we saw in section 2.5, the players in a game are more or

1. If this could be done in advance, there would be no scope for creativity in the world!

2. My treatment will be relatively informal throughout except for Appendix A. Formal treatments at different levels are available in game theory texts. See, for example, Watson (2002) and Myerson (1995).

less rational; they make choices based on trying to do the best they can given their preferences, their beliefs about the choice situation they face, and their capacity to reason intelligently. In the case at hand, Alan and Barbara, or $\mathcal{A}$ and $\mathcal{B}$, are the agents or players though there is no reason to restrict agents to persons in general. The game they have set up to play is one of choosing whether to go to the symphony or to dinner and a movie.

Each player clearly has a stake in the outcome. Both would prefer going out together to staying at home. $\mathcal{A}$ prefers going to dinner and a movie and he is lukewarm about the symphony. His preferences[3] might be ranked as:

dinner & a movie $\succ_{\mathcal{A}}$ symphony $\succ_{\mathcal{A}}$ home with the kids

$\mathcal{B}$, as I have suggested, has a different order of preferences since she would prefer the symphony:

symphony $\succ_{\mathcal{B}}$ dinner & a movie $\succ_{\mathcal{B}}$ home with the kids

Each preference relation above taken by itself would simply result in each agent choosing his or her top action. However, crucially, each preference depends on the other agent's choice as well: if one agent chooses dinner and a movie and the other chooses the symphony, then both have to stay at home with the kids, their worst choice. So the preference relations are more accurately written:

dinner & a movie for both $\succ_{\mathcal{A}}$ symphony for both $\succ_{\mathcal{A}}$ home for both

symphony for both $\succ_{\mathcal{B}}$ dinner & a movie for both $\succ_{\mathcal{B}}$ home for both

We can form a triple with the agents, their possible actions, and their preferences over the outcomes of these *joint* actions. Formally, a game is such a triple. It has been assumed in this game that neither player knows the other's choice when making their own choice.[4] If we use the letter G to denote this game, then we could write, by a slight abuse of notation, $u \models G$. This is because G could be expressed as a bunch of infons, though

3. I use the same symbol for an agent's preferences as I did for temporal precedence or succession in chapter 2. There should be no confusion as the context in which these symbols occur are quite different.

4. This may seem a trifle odd since they are in the same room discussing their plans for the evening, but we can still imagine that their choices are made *independently*. One way to account for this is to view the game model as abstracting from some of the details of their ongoing discussion.

I will not actually do so. We would describe this by saying that the setting u supports the game G. Just as no infon is true or false except with respect to some situation, similarly no game is actual without an embedding setting.[5]

For many games, such qualitative preference orderings suffice to determine the best choice for each agent. If both agents had identical preferences, for example, unlike the case at hand, each could choose the (common) top action. But in u, if $\mathcal{A}$ chooses his best action of going to dinner and a movie, and if $\mathcal{B}$ chooses her best action of going to the symphony, they would end up having to stay at home with the kids, their (common) worst choice, because of the way they have set up the game.[6]

There are many things they could do. One is to try and alter the game so that it is "easier" to play. This can be done by one of the agents simply suggesting a new course of action they might both prefer, such as meeting with friends instead. Or it can be done by one of the agents persuading the other to change their preferences, since such preferences are also situated. Indeed, this is how many similar games are resolved. Such alterations of the initial game are in a sense limitless, constrained only by u and the agents' imaginations.

Another possibility is to accept the game as it is and analyze it more closely. One way is to strengthen the information represented by the preferences above by making them quasi-numerical. That is, the agents assign numbers to the outcomes of their combined choices, but these numbers are taken not in an absolute sense but in a relative sense, like a temperature scale. Just as it does not matter exactly where we set the zero for a temperature scale and exactly how large a single degree is (e.g., a 30° temperature reading is meaningless without specifying whether we mean the Fahrenheit or Celsius scale), so it does not matter where the zero of the numerical encoding of an agent's preferences—called the *utility* scale—is or what the size of a single unit of utility is. Mathematically, this is described by saying that utility is invariant up to a positive affine trans-

5. Game theory does not traditionally recognize the need for such a setting for a game. A game's being actual means that it actually obtains in the relevant setting or situation, and if the setting is real and factual, then the game too is real and factual. That is, the game is not just a model in a theorist's head. Indeed, as will be seen in the following chapters and especially in Appendix A, a game is nothing but a complex collection of situations.

6. This game is an instance of the "Battle of the Sexes" game, which is widely discussed in introductory texts on game theory.

formation (i.e., a transformation of the form $v' = av + b$ with $a > 0$, where v and v' are the utility measures on two different scales and a and b are some constants).

Remarkably, there is a theorem that says that if an agent's preferences satisfy certain formal conditions of "rationality," then a utility function of the kind described above always exists such that maximizing preferences is equivalent to maximizing utility even in the presence of uncertainty. This implies that when required it is possible to replace qualitative preferences by quantitative utility functions without altering the predictions the theory makes about agents' behavior.

So, to make matters more amenable, the agents may be assumed to convert their choice situation into a quantitative problem by associating utilities with the various outcomes. Both $\mathcal{A}$ and $\mathcal{B}$ prefer going out to staying at home, so let us suppose they both assign 0 utility to the stay-at-home option although their zeroes may not be really comparable.

$\mathcal{A}$ prefers dinner and a movie to the symphony, so let us represent his utilities with the table in Figure 3.1.

Of course, $\mathcal{B}$'s preferences can be quantified in much the same way as shown in Figure 3.2.

One might object that the assignment of utility to our players' choices is rather arbitrary. Recall that these numbers are meant to be invariant up to positive affine transformations. So, to a certain degree, they *are* arbitrary. But they are not completely so, as they have to respect the preference orderings they are intended to represent. In many situations, especially economic ones, it may seem that such utilities or *payoffs* are better motivated because there are often monetary values associated with the outcomes, but this is not so clear-cut because it is often the agent's utility

Alan's Preferences	
Choice	Utility
dinner & movie for both	2
symphony for both	1
stay home for both	0

Figure 3.1
$\mathcal{A}$'s utility function

Barbara's Preferences	
Choice	Utility
symphony for both	2
dinner & movie for both	1
stay home for both	0

Figure 3.2
$\mathcal{B}$'s utility function

Alan's Preferences	
Choice	Utility
dinner & movie for both	a
symphony for both	b
stay home for both	c

Figure 3.3
$\mathcal{A}$'s utility function such that $a > b > c$

for a monetary reward that matters, and this is a subjective and often unknown function of the monetary outcome.

To avoid even this partial arbitrariness, it is possible to assume that the agents do not know their exact numerical utilities but do know which is the greater of each pair. For example, $\mathcal{A}$'s utilities may be a, b, and c instead of 2, 1, and 0, respectively, with $a > b > c$. This is certainly reasonable to assume since, if $\mathcal{A}$ prefers dinner and a movie to the symphony, then he has to know that $a > b$. For our simplified representation of their utilities, it can be assumed that $\mathcal{B}$ has similar assignments. Their utility functions can now be described as shown in Figures 3.3 and 3.4.

One way, now, to think about Alan and Barbara's problem is to combine the utility tables in an expanded table. Since disagreement about what to do results in their staying at home, it is not necessary to represent staying at home as a separate strategy; it is the natural result of their other choices.

Barbara's Preferences	
Choice	Utility
symphony for both	a
dinner & movie for both	b
stay home for both	c

Figure 3.4
$\mathcal{B}$'s utility function such that $a > b > c$

		$\mathcal{B}$	
		movie	symphony
$\mathcal{A}$	movie	$(2, 1)$	$(0, 0)$
	symphony	$(0, 0)$	$(1, 2)$

Figure 3.5
The game G

Figures 3.5 and 3.6 show Alan and Barbara's game G in *strategic normal form*. $\mathcal{A}$ is playing the rows and $\mathcal{B}$ is playing the columns. Inside each cell of the matrix is an ordered pair showing their respective payoffs; $\mathcal{A}$ gets the payoff corresponding to the first integer in the ordered pair and $\mathcal{B}$ gets the payoff corresponding to the second. Thus, if $\mathcal{A}$ chooses to go to the symphony and $\mathcal{B}$ also chooses to go to the symphony, then $\mathcal{A}$ gets 1 unit and $\mathcal{B}$ gets 2 units. Equally, if $\mathcal{A}$ chooses the dinner and a movie option and so does $\mathcal{B}$, then $\mathcal{A}$ gets 2 units and $\mathcal{B}$ gets 1 unit. Otherwise, if their choices diverge, they both get nothing since they have to stay at home. Of course, these numbers can be replaced by a, b, and c.

The game has two obvious *equilibria*, choices from which no player has any incentive to deviate *unilaterally*. The equilibria correspond to the choice to (jointly) go to the symphony or to (jointly) go to dinner and a movie. Suppose both $\mathcal{A}$ and $\mathcal{B}$ have decided to go to the symphony. $\mathcal{B}$ gets a points in this case; if she picks dinner and a movie instead, she would get c. Since $a > c$, she has no reason to defect from this choice. Equally, $\mathcal{A}$ gets b points in this case. If he had decided to go to dinner and a movie, then he, too, would get c. Since $b > c$, he, too, has no motivation to change his choice.

		$\mathcal{B}$	
		movie	symphony
$\mathcal{A}$	movie	(a, b)	(c, c)
	symphony	(c, c)	(b, a)

Figure 3.6
The algebraic version of the game G

Likewise, suppose both $\mathcal{A}$ and $\mathcal{B}$ had decided to go to dinner and a movie. Now, $\mathcal{A}$ gets a points and $\mathcal{B}$ gets b points. This case is really the same as the previous case with the agents switching roles. Neither player has any motivation to unilaterally change his or her choice since each one would be worse off if they did so.[7]

7. It is worthwhile to pause and consider how to formalize the notion of Nash equilibrium, as this kind of equilibrium is called, mathematically.

Let us suppose that each player i of n players has some set of pure strategies $Z_i = \{z_{i1}, \ldots, z_{ik}\}$, available to him, where each strategy z_{ij} is a series of actions that specify the player's behavior completely with respect to the game. In the simple game we are looking at here, a strategy is just a single action, either going to dinner and a movie or going to the symphony. In other games, a strategy can be a whole series of actions. When it is necessary to refer to a strategy generically, we will use either z_{ij} or z_i depending on the context.

A *mixed strategy* ζ_i has the form:

$$\zeta_i = \pi_1 z_{i1} + \cdots + \pi_k z_{ik}$$

where the π_j are probabilities and $\sum_{j=1}^{k} \pi_j = 1$. That is, the player chooses strategy z_{ij} with probability π_j. If all the π_j are 0 except one, then ζ_i is called a *pure strategy*; otherwise, it is a *mixed strategy*.

The vector $z = (z_1, \ldots, z_n)$ is called a pure strategy profile and the vector $\zeta = (\zeta_1, \ldots, \zeta_n)$ is called a mixed strategy profile.

Suppose, now, that $v_i(z_1, \ldots, z_n)$ is the payoff to player i when the players use one of their pure strategies. We can define the expected payoff to player i for a mixed strategy profile ζ as:

$$v_i(\zeta) = \sum_{z_1 \in Z_1} \cdots \sum_{z_n \in Z_n} \pi_{z_1} \pi_{z_2} \ldots \pi_{z_n} v_i(z_1, \ldots, z_n)$$

where we use π_{z_i} to refer to the weight of z_i in ζ_i.

Assuming that the n players are making their choices independently, we get the expected payoff of ζ by averaging the payoffs to each of the n-tuples of pure strategies.

The mismatched choices are clearly not equilibria. If one player chooses the symphony and the other chooses dinner and a movie, then each does better by unilaterally changing his or her mind.

It turns out that in addition to the obvious pure strategy equilibria identified above, there is a third mixed strategy equilibrium where $\mathcal{A}$ chooses dinner and a movie with probability 2/3 and the symphony with probability 1/3 and where $\mathcal{B}$ chooses the symphony with probability 2/3 and dinner and a movie with probability 1/3.[8]

All three Nash equilibria leave the players with no incentive to deviate unilaterally. However, since there are multiple equilibria, there is no unique way for the players to decide what to do this evening. If they choose different equilibria, they could end up with an outcome that is not an equilibrium.

Game theorists have devised a number of means to further enable the selection of one of these equilibria and we shall look at several types of equilibrium refinements in section 3.3.5. In any case, this is partly where the choice being situated comes in. Perhaps there are features of the situation u that have not been represented in this simple model: for example,

---

Now, we will say that a mixed strategy profile $(\zeta_1^*, \ldots, \zeta_n^*)$ is a *mixed strategy Nash equilibrium* if, for each player $i = 1, \ldots, n$:

$$v_i(\zeta^*) \geq v_i(\zeta_i, \zeta_{-i}^*)$$

where ζ_i is any mixed strategy for player i and ζ_{-i}^* is the equilibrium strategy choices of the players other than i.

This captures the insight that an equilibrium strategy does not permit worthwhile unilateral deviations.

Crucially, every finite game has at least one Nash equilibrium, possibly more, a point to which I will return below. In particular:

Nash Existence Theorem. If each player in an n-player game has a finite number of pure strategies, then the game has a (not necessarily unique) Nash equilibrium in (possibly) mixed strategies.

8. This equilibrium is derived as follows: let β be the probability $\mathcal{B}$ assigns to dinner and a movie at equilibrium; then, referring to Figure 3.5, since the two pure strategies of $\mathcal{A}$ must yield equal payoffs, $2\beta + 0(1-\beta) = 0\beta + 1(1-\beta)$, which implies that $\beta = 1/3$ as required. The other calculation is symmetric.

In the algebraic case, all we would be able to derive is $\beta = (b-c)/(a+b-2c)$ and in particular $\beta/(1-\beta) = (b-c)/(a-c)$, which implies $\beta < 1/2$ since $a > b > c$. Little more can be said about the mixed strategy solution without more information about the actual magnitudes of a, b, and c. On the other hand, not much more may be required if we assume that agents make only rough estimates of payoffs and probabilities.

the last time they faced such a choice, $\mathcal{A}$ and $\mathcal{B}$ may have gone to the symphony, so this time both may expect the other option to be selected based on some criterion of fairness. Such a criterion could itself be incorporated into the game by altering the payoffs suitably (or by some other means), but it is sometimes more perspicuous to leave it in the ambient situation as additional information that helps the players eliminate some of the equilibria. Like this criterion, there can be a host of other aspects of the situation u—one of the players being more altruistic than the other[9] or eliminating both pure strategy equilibria as being symmetric and therefore not salient—that can help in the selection of a single equilibrium from among these three.

We have seen that a game G is actual only with respect to an embedding setting u, and it is the two entities together that jointly determine what an agent will choose to do. This insight additionally allows us to introduce many *behavioral* modes of choice by locating them in the wider u as opposed to the narrower G. Moreover, some of these behavioral choices may lie outside the scope of strict rationality and may be better viewed as extending it.[10]

Our interest in game theory is twofold: one is to show how interdependent choices can be represented and analyzed formally; more ambitiously, it is to enable the theorist to predict what agents will do in a choice situation. The latter is not always possible to do because crucial ambient information not represented in the game but present in the setting may play a role in the choice. This does not render the analysis otiose: explanatory insight, that is, "postdiction," even though it falls short of prediction, is better than no theory at all.

I started by considering how $\mathcal{A}$ and $\mathcal{B}$ could strengthen their qualitative preferences by introducing utility functions and then showed how this led naturally to the strategic form representation of a game. There is another extremely useful representation of a game called the *extensive form* that makes the information each agent has at every stage of the game transparent, something the strategic form does not.

In Figure 3.7, letting M stand for the dinner-and-a-movie option and S stand for the symphony option gives us the extensive form for Alan and Barbara's game. The algebraic version of the payoffs has been displayed

9. This information can again be represented internally within the game by amending the payoffs or it may be left in the setting.

10. Camerer (2003) discusses several behavioral approaches that use *social* utility and learning.

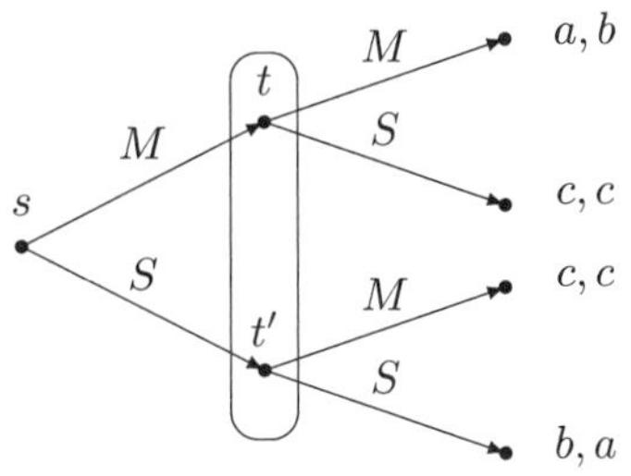

Figure 3.7
Extensive form for G

here but the letters could be replaced by the corresponding numbers if we wanted the numerical version.

One way to understand this representation is to build it up step by step. One can imagine an initial situation s represented only by a dot or node that contains the setting u together with a general intention on the part of $\mathcal{A}$ to make a choice for the evening. Since s contains u, it contains the whole rich background we have been articulating with all of its possibilities for action. Two of the actions under consideration are M and S and these are then represented by arrows issuing from s, leading to two new situations t and t', again represented by nodes. While the situation s is an actual situation existing in the world, t and t' are just *possible* situations that capture two ways s could change if the corresponding actions were chosen.

Now, $\mathcal{B}$ is assumed to make her choice independently of $\mathcal{A}$, so we assume she is ignorant of which path $\mathcal{A}$ has chosen. In other words, even though $\mathcal{A}$ may have selected an action taking him to t or t', $\mathcal{B}$ does not know exactly where she is, except that she is either in t or t'. This ignorance on $\mathcal{B}$'s part is represented by the elongated oval enclosing these two nodes and is called an *information set*. Thus, $\{t, t'\}$ is $\mathcal{B}$'s (only) information set in G. Information sets are sets of situations an agent cannot distinguish, forcing identical choices at each element of the set. This is why the same pair of actions M and S issue from both t and t', since $\mathcal{B}$ has the same options in this game as $\mathcal{A}$.[11] Incidentally, every situation where an agent has to choose an action is a member of a unique information set. Thus, $\{s\}$ is $\mathcal{A}$'s only information set in the game.

11. If some different action were to issue from either situation, then $\mathcal{B}$ could use this information to distinguish between the two situations.

After $\mathcal{B}$ makes her choice, one of four possible terminal situations ensue, though their corresponding terminal nodes have not been given names in the figure to avoid clutter. Some outcome is determined in each of these situations, essentially whether the two agents have made compatible choices or not, and this results in some utility or payoff to each agent depending on the nature of the outcome. These payoffs are tagged to the corresponding terminal situations. The reader can check that the payoffs in Figure 3.7 match those in Figure 3.6.

It should be easy to see that the two forms, the strategic form and its corresponding extensive form, represent the same choice situation. This is so even for more complex extensive forms. Of course, the extensive form additionally reveals who knows what at each stage of the game via the information sets in the game. Each form is useful in its own way when analyzing a game.

A strategy for a player is a function from each of his or her information sets to some action available from that information set. Thus, $\mathcal{A}$'s strategies are just $\{(\{s\}, M)\}$ and $\{(\{s\}, S)\}$, since these are the actions available from $\{s\}$. As the domain of the strategy is known, it can be dropped and the strategies written simply as M and S. Likewise, $\mathcal{B}$'s strategies are also $\{(\{t, t'\}, M)\}$ and $\{(\{t, t'\}, S)\}$ and can be written more simply as M and S. Each player thus has exactly two pure strategies. This shows that given an extensive form representation, we can convert it to the strategic form representation (and vice versa).

G's equilibria have already been computed, though the reader may find it useful to visually work out the pure strategy equilibria in the tree.

It is worth noting that even in this relatively simple extensive form, there could have been other variations that would have made the game different from G. For example, it need not have been assumed that $\mathcal{A}$'s and $\mathcal{B}$'s choices were independent. In this case, $\mathcal{B}$ would have made her choice after full knowledge of $\mathcal{A}$'s choice; this would have meant dropping the oval from Figure 3.8 and splitting the larger information set $\{t, t'\}$ into two information sets $\{t\}$ and $\{t'\}$ since now $\mathcal{B}$ would know exactly where she is in the tree and could choose differently in these two situations. This quite different choice situation leads to *four* pure strategies for $\mathcal{B}$ and, correspondingly, to a 2×4 matrix for the strategic form.[12]

12. $\mathcal{A}$'s two strategies are $\{(\{s\}, M)\}$ and $\{(\{s\}, S)\}$ as before; $\mathcal{B}$'s four strategies are $\{(\{t\}, M), (\{t'\}, M)\}$, $\{(\{t\}, M), (\{t'\}, S)\}$, $\{(\{t\}, S), (\{t'\}, M)\}$, and $\{(\{t\}, S), (\{t'\}, S)\}$.

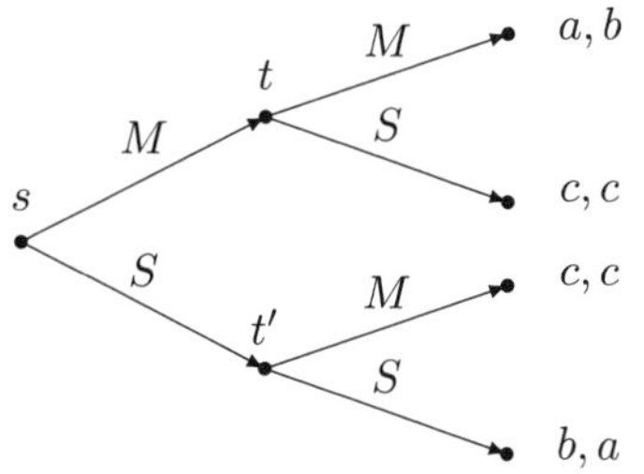

Figure 3.8
Extensive form for G'

This possibility, as well as others, are all inherent in the setting u and it really is the players who determine which game is appropriate for the joint choices they have to make in this situation. It should also be noted that more than one game may simultaneously be associated with the setting if the agents are involved in multiple aspects of it. For example, the parents may also be attending to the children as they discuss their options for the evening.

The game in Figure 3.8 is called a game of *perfect* information, while the game in Figure 3.7 is called a game of *imperfect* information—imperfect because $\mathcal{B}$ does not have full knowledge of where she is in the game tree. Both, however, are games of *complete* information because there is no uncertainty about which game is being played, that is, there is just one initial situation s. In games of *incomplete* information, there are two or more initial situations (together with certain other restrictions to be considered later).[13]

3.2 Choice in Language

As noted in chapter 1, language provides a rich locale for the study of *strategic* choice or interactive choice, where each agent takes the other agent's possible actions into account. Once we show how utterance situations can be modeled via games, the radical role of the idea of use in equilibrium semantics will become clear. No sentence by itself can ever have a content; only utterances are capable of conveying meaning.

13. Equivalently, there is an initial move of "Nature" in such games. Both imperfect information and incomplete information games have non-singleton information sets.

Communication involves interdependent choice, and choice, as we have seen in section 3.1, is inherently situated. In this chapter, we focus just on the contents of single words in an utterance. Later, the meanings of entire utterances will be considered.

Assume that $\mathcal{A}$ and $\mathcal{B}$ are in the living room while Caitlin and Harvey are playing in the family room. Suppose, in this context of u and G, $\mathcal{A}$ utters the sentence (suppressing quotation marks to heighten the ambiguity):

Harvey is playing. (φ)

All else being equal, the sentence (when spoken) is completely ambiguous. On the intended reading, $\mathcal{A}$ is noting that the movie *Harvey* is currently showing at some theater.[14] On the other reading, it could be the rather banal observation that their son Harvey is playing. All $\mathcal{A}$ and $\mathcal{B}$ share at this stage is that the first interpretation is the more likely one based on the fact that they are discussing what to do this evening. How does $\mathcal{A}$ convey the intended reading to $\mathcal{B}$ in this situation? We will see that a game can be constructed that models the communication of this content between $\mathcal{A}$ and $\mathcal{B}$ in u.

Recalling the notation of section 2.6, φ can be expressed as $\varphi_1 \circ \varphi_2 \circ \varphi_3$ with each φ_i being a word of the sentence. Remember also that φ is not directly present in u; what u contains is a parameter $\dot{\varphi}$ that gets anchored to φ. Our model will focus just on the ambiguity in $\varphi_1 = \text{H}{\small\text{ARVEY}}$, on whether $\mathcal{A}$ means the movie or the boy. Later, it will be clarified that it is generally not possible for the meanings of single uttered words to be determined in isolation—this is the reason the Fregean principle of compositionality fails in general—but I will make this simplifying assumption for now.

Since disambiguation is a selection of one meaning from many, we need to know what the possible meanings of φ_1 are in u. For this, two of the constraints mentioned in chapter 1, the Conventional Constraint **C** and the Informational Constraint **I**, are required. Here, they are mentioned only for the special case of proper names; later they will be broached more fully.

14. In this case, the utterance clearly has a conversational implicature: $\mathcal{A}$ is implying that they go to the movie (and, hence, not to the symphony). The implicature can be derived using the techniques in chapter 7 of Parikh (2001) and we will also do so in the next chapter.

3.2.1 The Conventional Constraint C

The Conventional Constraint is a map from a word β to one or more conventional meanings. Conventional meanings are just possibly indexicalized properties a word acquires by convention. A general form for this map is:

$$\beta \to P^{\beta}$$

In the case of names N, the conventionally associated property is the special property of *being named* N, written P^N.[15] This leads to the following special conventional constraint for names:

$$N \to P^N$$

3.2.2 The Informational Constraint I

This constraint takes the properties associated with a word and maps them into contextually appropriate infons. Some notation is required before I display this map.

Let $Unique(P, r_u, q_u) = \langle\!\langle = \mid r_u \subseteq q_u; \text{card}(\{y \mid r_u \models \langle\!\langle P; y \rangle\!\rangle\}); 1 \rangle\!\rangle$, an infon that expresses the information that $\{y \mid r_u \models \langle\!\langle P; y \rangle\!\rangle\}$ is a singleton. "Card" is the cardinality function and r_u, q_u are resource situations related to u.[16] Note that "$r_u \subseteq q_u$" conditions the main relation $=$ of this infon and can be taken to be true here. Recall from section 2.2 that $e(P, r_u)$ is the individual satisfying P in r_u when there is just one such individual and it is the set of such individuals otherwise. This set is just $\{y \mid r_u \models \langle\!\langle P; y \rangle\!\rangle\}$, the set in the definition of $Unique(P, r_u, q_u)$ above.

The informational map is then as follows:

$$N \to P^N \overset{u}{\to} \langle\!\langle e(P^N, r_u) \mid Unique(P^N, r_u, q_u) \rangle\!\rangle$$

The first conventional map transforms the name N into the property of being named N, and the second informational map transforms this property into the infon containing the particular individual satisfying the property of having the name N. The two maps together achieve the

15. This property has not been much used in the literature but see Kneale (1962) and Burge (1973). I use it as the conventional meaning because it avoids the kinds of criticisms made by Kripke (1972, 1980) against any Fregean (1980) two-tier theory of meaning such as Searle's (1958) *cluster theory* of sense.

16. More will be said about q_u in chapter 6.

conversion of the proper name N to the single object named N in the relevant resource situation r_u.[17]

It is instructive to see what happens when there are either no objects named N in r_u or more than one such object. As argued in sections 2.2 and 2.3.2 (see Equations 2.1 and 2.2), in both cases, the condition $Unique(P^N, r_u, q_u)$ is contradictory and equals the contradictory infon $\mathbf{0}$. In the first case, $e(P^N, r_u) = \phi$, the empty set, and in the second case, $e(P^N, r_u)$ equals a set with cardinality greater than one. By Assumption 5 in section 2.3.2 that $\langle\!\langle x \,|\, \mathbf{0} \rangle\!\rangle = \mathbf{0}$ for any x in $\mathcal{O}$, this kind of situation results in the contradictory infon $\mathbf{0}$. That is, unless there is just one object in the relevant resource situation, we get the contradictory infon because $\langle\!\langle e(P^N, r_u) \,|\, Unique(P^N, r_u, q_u) \rangle\!\rangle = \langle\!\langle e(P^N, r_u) \,|\, \mathbf{0} \rangle\!\rangle = \mathbf{0}$.

Looking ahead a bit, in an utterance involving such an infelicitous use of a name, this $\mathbf{0}$ is merged with other infons corresponding to other parts of the sentence uttered, and yields $\mathbf{0}$ as the content of the whole utterance by Fact 2 in section 2.3.3 that for all infons σ, $\sigma \odot_s \mathbf{0} = \mathbf{0} \odot_s \sigma = \mathbf{0}$. By Clause 1 of Assumption 7 in section 2.3.5 that $s \not\models \mathbf{0}$ for all situations s, this implies that all propositions expressible by such an utterance are necessarily false. For example, if there were no single object for HARVEY to refer to, this part of the utterance would result in $\mathbf{0}$, and the overall content would also be $\mathbf{0}$ and therefore necessarily false. This brief discussion foreshadows a more detailed look at "referring" noun phrases in chapter 6, especially section 6.1.1.

Having spelled out these two constraints in the case of proper names, we are now ready to look at the possible meanings of HARVEY in u. First, note that there are two distinct resource situations connected with u, one relating to the film and the second to the boy. Let us call the first r_u and the second r'_u. The film is the single object named "Harvey" in r_u and the son is the single object named "Harvey" in r'_u. Then, in the particular setting u and G, the possible meanings of φ_1 = HARVEY are as follows:

17. Note the u above the second arrow. This is meant to indicate that u is also an argument to the function that maps the property into the infon. It is not the map itself. u's being an argument allows one to access r_u and q_u. Its presence also affirms that a referent for a name is possible only when the name is actually uttered in some situation u. An unuttered name, like every other unuttered piece of language, is inert and has no reference even though it has a conventional meaning.

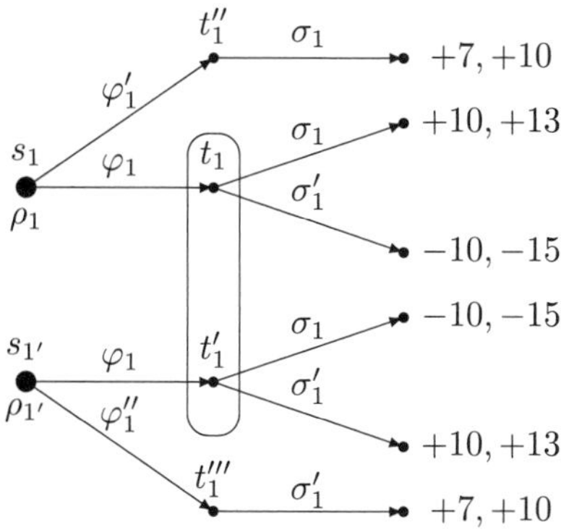

Figure 3.9
A lexical game $g_1 = g_u(\varphi_1)$

$$\varphi_1 \to P^{\varphi_1} \xrightarrow{u} \langle\langle e(P^{\varphi_1}, r_u) \mid Unique(P^{\varphi_1}, r_u, q_u) \rangle\rangle = \sigma_1$$

$$\varphi_1 \to P^{\varphi_1} \xrightarrow{u} \langle\langle e(P^{\varphi_1}, r_u') \mid Unique(P^{\varphi_1}, r_u', q_u') \rangle\rangle = \sigma_1'$$

σ_1 and σ_1' are the possible meanings of φ_1 in u. σ_1 contains the film and σ_1' contains the son. If the film is denoted by a and the boy by b, then $\sigma_1 = \langle\langle e(P^{\varphi_1}, r_u) \mid Unique(P^{\varphi_1}, r_u, q_u) \rangle\rangle = \langle\langle a \mid \mathbf{1} \rangle\rangle = \langle\langle a \rangle\rangle$ and $\sigma_1' = \langle\langle e(P^{\varphi_1}, r_u') \mid Unique(P^{\varphi_1}, r_u', q_u') \rangle\rangle = \langle\langle b \mid \mathbf{1} \rangle\rangle = \langle\langle b \rangle\rangle$ by Assumption 5 in section 2.3.2 that $\langle\langle x \mid \mathbf{1} \rangle\rangle = \langle\langle x \rangle\rangle$ for any entity x in $\mathcal{O}$.

3.2.3 The Flow Constraint F

The game that captures the communication of the partial content σ_1 is shown in Figure 3.9. $g_1 = g_u(\varphi_1)$ is an instance of the Flow Constraint **F**.

This is a game in extensive form and is called a game of partial information.[18] The node labeled s_1 represents an initial situation that contains the setting u together with $\mathcal{A}$'s intention to convey σ_1. In s_1, $\mathcal{A}$ can utter the ambiguous word φ_1 = HARVEY, this action being represented by the relevant arrow issuing from this situation. If he does, the resulting situation is t_1, where $\mathcal{B}$ has to choose an interpretation of φ_1 in u. We have seen that there are two possible interpretations, σ_1 and σ_1', each action again represented by corresponding arrows.

18. Games of partial information are in many ways similar to but slightly more general than games of incomplete information. See Parikh (2001) for a more detailed exposition and see Parikh (2006a) and Appendix A for the connection between the two types of games.

Since φ_1 is ambiguous, there is an alternative counterfactual situation $s_{1'}$ that also contains u together with the alternative possible intention to convey σ_1'. The relation of s_1 and $s_{1'}$ to u, each augmenting u with an appropriate but different intention, gives us the elementary fact that $u = s_1 \cap s_{1'}$. In $s_{1'}$, too, $\mathcal{A}$ can utter φ_1 and this results in t_1', where $\mathcal{B}$ again has the same two choices of interpretation. Indeed, $\{t_1, t_1'\}$ forms an information set for $\mathcal{B}$ because $\mathcal{B}$ is as yet unable to distinguish between the two situations.

The label φ_1' stands for an alternative locution that the speaker might have uttered but chose not to. This could be, for example, "The film *Harvey*," where $\mathcal{A}$ presumably explicitly disambiguates the noun phrase. Similarly, φ_1'' could be, "Our son Harvey," again an explicit disambiguation.

It is possible that these alternative locutions may themselves contain other ambiguities. For example, the word "film" in φ_1' is certainly ambiguous between a movie and a thin strip of a certain type of coated material. However, in the game $g_1 = g_u(\varphi_1)$, our interest is just in the ambiguity relating to φ_1, the sentence that has been uttered, not in other ambiguities that may be present in alternative locutions. The question that has to be asked is: does the phrase φ_1' disambiguate the *relevant* ambiguity? Is it something the speaker could have uttered to clear up *this* ambiguity? That is all that matters because φ_1 is the *primary* utterance in $g_u(\varphi_1)$ in a sense that will be clarified in section 3.3.6. I will thus treat phrases such as φ_1' *holophrastically* and as (relatively) unambiguous even though they may contain other ambiguities unrelated to the ambiguity being considered in the game. I will make the simplifying assumption that such unambiguous phrases are always available.[19]

Since the two locutions φ_1' and φ_1'' are unambiguous in our special relative sense, there is just one interpretation that $\mathcal{B}$ can choose after their possible utterance, either σ_1 or σ_1'.

The remaining alphabetical symbols ρ_1 and $\rho_{1'}$ are just the probabilities that $\mathcal{A}$ is conveying σ_1 and σ_1' in s_1 and $s_{1'}$. We already know that $\mathcal{A}$ and $\mathcal{B}$ share the following assumption:

$$\rho_1 > \rho_{1'}$$

We could take these probabilities to be 0.9 and 0.1, respectively, since we said the first option was highly likely. These probabilities clearly

19. Otherwise, it would be necessary to consider a more complex extensive form that is amenable to the same analysis. This is not difficult to do, but since explicit disambiguations are almost always available, the simplification is reasonable to make.

come from the entire embedding situation u (including sometimes from the language $\mathcal{L}$ itself) rather than from any fixed aspect of the utterance. Typically, when there is a commonly available referent of a term such as HARVEY in the background (i.e., the son Harvey) that is usually referred to, then a relatively *new* and unexpected referent (i.e., the film *Harvey*) is marked by intonational stress as HARV́EY. This kind of stress just adds more weight to the probability ρ_1 and reinforces the inequality above. See Clark and Parikh (2007) for more details of how stress is handled in game-theoretic interpretation.[20]

That brings us to the last labels on the figure, the payoffs. In general, payoffs are a complex resultant of positive and negative factors and we say they are made up of positive benefits and negative costs. These payoffs also come from the embedding situation u as well as from the language $\mathcal{L}$. Payoffs can depend on a very wide range of factors based on the situation the agents are in and their various characteristics—their beliefs and desires, their hopes and fears, and their concerns and inclinations. They can also depend on $\mathcal{L}$ and its associated rules.[21] The quantity of information, introduced in section 2.3.6, is only one possible component of the payoffs. While agents often prefer more information to less, what really matters is its *value*, the benefit it confers on the agents.

Perhaps it matters a great deal to $\mathcal{B}$ what $\mathcal{A}$ is conveying, so we might assign a benefit of 20 units to her of getting the right information. It may matter less to $\mathcal{A}$, so he may derive a smaller benefit of 15 units of conveying the right information.[22] Similarly, the respective costs to $\mathcal{A}$ and $\mathcal{B}$ of uttering and interpreting φ_1 may be 5 units and 7 units, respectively. And the costs of uttering and interpreting φ_1' and φ_1'' may be 8 units for each for $\mathcal{A}$ and 10 units for each for $\mathcal{B}$. Again, the numbers are quite arbitrary and the costs of these alternative locutions need not be identical—it is just a simplification. Finally, the benefit of incorrect information is, we can suppose from our story, -5 units and -7 units for $\mathcal{A}$ and $\mathcal{B}$. Adding up these benefits and costs would give us the payoffs listed in the diagram ($15 - 5 = 10$, $20 - 7 = 13$; $15 - 8 = 7$, $20 - 10 = 10$; $-5 - 5 = -10$, $-8 - 7 = -15$).

20. I would like to thank David Beaver for pointing out that stress is a likely factor in an utterance of φ in the situation described.

21. See Clark and Parikh (2007) for an example of this.

22. Note that no real interpersonal comparisons of utility are involved, this is just a manner of speaking about the situation.

As observed in Parikh (1991, 2000, 2001), it is crucial to note that, in this game and the ones to follow, we will have recourse to the "right" and the "wrong" information inferred by $\mathcal{B}$ in each situation she finds herself in. How is this correctness and incorrectness determined? $\mathcal{A}$ is conveying σ_1 or σ_1' in s_1 and $s_{1'}$ respectively and to determine the correctness of the information inferred $\mathcal{B}$'s inferences are matched against these contents being conveyed.

But it is also possible to say that the relevant inference to σ_1 or σ_1' is matched against $\mathcal{A}$'s *intention* to convey σ_1 or σ_1' in s_1 and $s_{1'}$, respectively. In other words, the payoffs implicitly include inferring $\mathcal{A}$'s possible intentions in each situation but go beyond these to also include their situationally given preferences for the information and the corresponding costs of acquiring this information. This is already a generalization of the role played by Gricean intentions since we are allowing other situational factors besides intentions to also influence payoffs. But we will see in chapter 5 that this Gricean picture of inferring intentions may be only partially correct in any case and our later discussion may force us to further generalize this picture along the lines opened up by games of partial information.

There is a certain degree of correlation between the various payoffs, and this game happens to be a pure coordination game. But there is no reason to assume that this is always the case. In ordinary communicative exchanges, the payoffs of players are not likely to be opposed; however, in many litigious and other conflictual situations, they could well represent contradictory interests. Of course, even when the overall interests are opposed, there may still be a common interest in communicating. In any case, it should be kept in mind that all benefits, costs, and payoffs could vary greatly between agents based on the situation they are in and their own varying characteristics.

The same game can also be represented in strategic form as shown in Figure 3.10, derived from the extensive form by averaging the payoffs based on the initial probabilities in the usual way. $\mathcal{A}$ has four strategies, not two, because there are two actions each at his two information sets $\{s_1\}$ and $\{s_{1'}\}$ and the strategies are labeled in terms of the actions at both of these nodes—for example, $\varphi_1\varphi_1$ represents the action φ_1 at both nodes or $\varphi_1\varphi_1''$ represents the action φ_1 at s_1 and φ_1'' at $s_{1'}$.[23]

23. $\mathcal{B}$ has no choice of action at her outlying information sets $\{t_1''\}$ and $\{t_1'''\}$ so the single actions at these sets remain implicit.

	σ_1	σ_1'
$\varphi_1\varphi_1$	8, 10.2	−8, −12.2
$\varphi_1'\varphi_1$	5.3, 8.5	7.3, 11.3
$\varphi_1\varphi_1''$	9.7, 12.7	−8.3, −12.5
$\varphi_1'\varphi_1''$	7, 10	7, 10

Figure 3.10
The lexical game g_1 in strategic form

It is easy to see the solution of the game here by inspection of the matrix. This time there are two pure strategy Nash equilibria, $(\varphi_1\varphi_1'', \sigma_1)$ and $(\varphi_1'\varphi_1, \sigma_1')$, and no mixed strategy equilibria. As there are two Nash equilibria, it is useful to define a Pareto-efficient Nash equilibrium of the game, an equilibrium among Nash equilibria where no player is worse off and at least one is better off.[24] A preference for the Pareto-Nash equilibrium could be assumed to be represented in u. We could also consider other refinements of Nash equilibrium if we wish—most standard solution concepts will predict the same outcome.[25] It is easy to see from Figure 3.10 that the payoffs for $(\varphi_1\varphi_1'', \sigma_1)$ dominate the payoffs for $(\varphi_1'\varphi_1, \sigma_1')$, so the unique Pareto-Nash equilibrium is $(\varphi_1\varphi_1'', \sigma_1)$, and so the interpretation chosen by $\mathcal{B}$ will be exactly the information $\mathcal{A}$ meant to convey, namely, σ_1, given that s_1 is factual rather than $s_{1'}$.

So I have answered the question posed at the beginning of this section—how does $\mathcal{A}$ convey σ_1 to $\mathcal{B}$—and introduced the basic model I build upon in later chapters.

It should be evident how three of the four ideas that undergird equilibrium semantics—reference, use, and equilibrium—figure even in just this partial model. The content of φ_1 has been shown to be σ_1 and this captures the idea of reference or aboutness; this content has been derived from a situated game g_1 that arises from the context u and this captures the idea of use or communication; finally, the solution process that actually gives us the meaning of φ_1 captures the idea of equilibrium. This last idea is only partially explicable at this stage since just one word of the utterance is being examined. A fuller account will appear in chapter 4.

24. See Parikh (2001) for details.

25. See section 3.3.5 for an examination of some alternatives.

It should also be possible to now appreciate how much more insight is available when we consider the game g_1 in both extensive and strategic form (Figures 3.9 and 3.10). As I remarked in section 1.4.4, Lewis (1969), inspired by Schelling (1960), used just a simple strategic form as his model and this obscures the full complexity of how the pervasive ambiguities in communication are represented and how they play out. In particular, it does not reveal the crucial role played by the sentences the speaker could have uttered but chose not to as well as the exact nature of all the information sets in the game and the role of the initial probabilities. As we will see, this applies to all aspects of meaning, whether it is literal, implicated, or related to illocutionary force.[26]

In the foregoing, the way utility numbers were assigned to payoffs may seem a little arbitrary to some readers. Instead of simply saying that the benefits are, say, 15 units or 20 units, we could try to derive them from the background game G (or the background decision problem, if that is the relevant choice situation in u) that $\mathcal{A}$ and $\mathcal{B}$ are discussing. Indeed, it was the game G that was also the source of the probabilities, because even though $\mathcal{B}$ does not know a priori what $\mathcal{A}$'s utterance is going to be about, she does know that it will be related to their effort to decide what to do this evening. Likewise, it is possible to say that the information $\mathcal{A}$ is attempting to convey has some *value* with respect to G.

We could define the value of G for $\mathcal{A}$ and $\mathcal{B}$, $v_{\mathcal{A}}(G)$ and $v_{\mathcal{B}}(G)$, to be the value each agent derives from the unique equilibrium they play. If, for example, they were to choose the mixed strategy equilibrium identified in section 3.1 based on its salience, their respective values would both be 2/3. However, if $\mathcal{A}$'s utterance is about the film, then the game G gets effectively transformed into the trivial game G'' with just one action for each agent—going to the movie—since it has the effect of eliminating the option of going to the symphony. In this case, the values of this trivial game G'' to $\mathcal{A}$ and $\mathcal{B}$ are just 2 and 1, as given in the upper left cell of Figure 3.5. Thus, the net value of $\mathcal{A}$'s utterance to both the agents is $v_{\mathcal{A}}(G'') - v_{\mathcal{A}}(G) = 2 - 2/3 = 1.33$ and $v_{\mathcal{B}}(G'') - v_{\mathcal{B}}(G) = 1 - 2/3 = 0.33$. This might be termed the *relevance* of $\mathcal{A}$'s utterance. Likewise, if $\mathcal{A}$'s utterance is about their son, then it does not change G at all and the net values of this meaning are just 0 for both. Note that the absolute numbers are not important: if required they can be scaled by positive affine transformations.

26. The extensive form representation was first developed in the context of language by Parikh (1987b) in 1985.

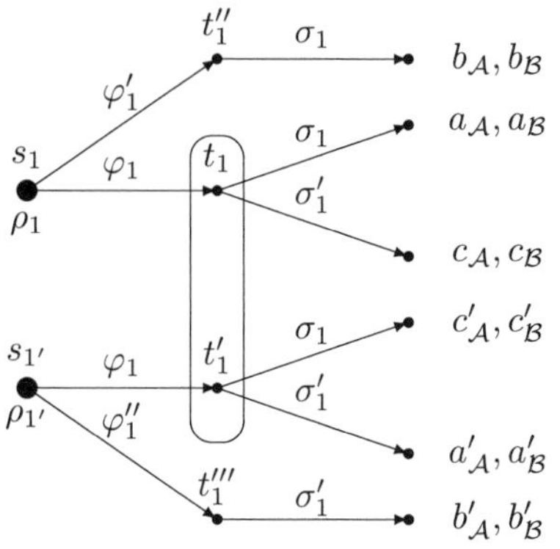

Figure 3.11
Algebraic version of lexical game $g_1 = g_u(\varphi_1)$

This then is one approach to using the setting u and the background game G to derive benefits more rigorously and less arbitrarily in the game g_1. However, this method still leaves many questions unanswered. While it gives us a way of defining *relevance* in a general setting,[27] there is no guarantee that the calculation carried out above could be carried out so smoothly in general. Will it work for all utterances φ and all games G? It may happen that the game G'' that is associated with an utterance is not so unambiguously identifiable.

There is also a certain complexity in the calculation above that we glossed over. The game G'' is really associated with both the literal *and* implicated meaning of $\mathcal{A}$'s utterance—as I said above, Alan was implying to Barbara that they go out to dinner and the film. So it is the relevance of the entire meaning that we computed, not just of the literal meaning or of the referent of the proper name.

Perhaps these problems are surmountable and perhaps it is possible to develop a rigorous account of benefits. But since we do not have such a theory yet, we choose the path already mentioned in section 3.1 when we confronted the arbitrariness of utility assignments in G—the algebraic approach.

Consider the algebraic version of g_1 in Figure 3.11.

27. See Parikh (1992, 2006b) for earlier articulations of the same idea in the context of both decision problems as well as games. See also Merin (1999) for a different formulation of relevance in terms of *amount* of information rather than value of information. And see van Rooij (2003) for a use of my idea. Incidentally, van Rooij's use of decision problems in this paper is also from the same sources.

Here, the utility numbers have been replaced by self-explanatory symbols. As discussed in some detail in Theorem 10 and section 2 of Parikh (1990), $\mathcal{A}$ and $\mathcal{B}$ may be assumed to have the following general preferences:

successful communication $\succ$ unsuccessful communication

and

less costly communication $\succ$ more costly communication

Note that these costs are different for $\mathcal{A}$ and $\mathcal{B}$: for $\mathcal{A}$ the costs are associated with anticipating $\mathcal{B}$'s interpretation and producing the utterance, and for $\mathcal{B}$ they are associated with perceiving and interpreting the utterance.

The first of the two general preference orderings rests on a minimal assumption that our agents wish to communicate and could be seen as an expression of Grice's Cooperative Principle at *one* level. The second of the two preferences depends also on a minimal assumption that our agents prefer less effort and cost to more.[28]

They may be combined by the two agents thus:[29]

successful and less costly communication

$\succ$ successful but more costly communication

$\succ$ unsuccessful communication

The two agents may not know exactly what the numerical utility encodings of their preferences are, but they do know the following as a result of these preferences:

$$a_{\mathcal{A}} > b_{\mathcal{A}} > c_{\mathcal{A}}$$

$$a'_{\mathcal{A}} > b'_{\mathcal{A}} > c'_{\mathcal{A}}$$

28. Both assumptions are distinct from the assumption of rationality, which is just the assumption mentioned in section 3.1 that agents' preferences satisfy certain formal criteria (see, e.g., Myerson, 1995).

29. Unsuccessful communication here is intended to go with less costly communication. It may happen in rare cases that unsuccessful but less costly communication is actually preferred to successful but more costly communication if the cost of unambiguous communication is unusually high and unsuccessful communication is not penalized too heavily. But because natural language is as rich as it is, such a situation is relatively unlikely, and I will simply ignore it or otherwise assume it does not occur.

	σ_1	σ_1'
$\varphi_1\varphi_1$	$\rho_1 a_A + \rho_{1'} c_A', \rho_1 a_B + \rho_{1'} c_B'$	$\rho_1 c_A + \rho_{1'} a_A', \rho_1 c_B + \rho_{1'} a_B'$
$\varphi_1'\varphi_1$	$\rho_1 b_A + \rho_{1'} c_A', \rho_1 b_B + \rho_{1'} c_B'$	$\rho_1 b_A + \rho_{1'} a_A', \rho_1 b_B + \rho_{1'} a_B'$
$\varphi_1\varphi_1''$	$\rho_1 a_A + \rho_{1'} b_A', \rho_1 a_B + \rho_{1'} b_B'$	$\rho_1 c_A + \rho_{1'} b_A', \rho_1 c_B + \rho_{1'} b_B'$
$\varphi_1'\varphi_1''$	$\rho_1 b_A + \rho_{1'} b_A', \rho_1 b_B + \rho_{1'} b_B'$	$\rho_1 b_A + \rho_{1'} b_A', \rho_1 b_B + \rho_{1'} b_B'$

Figure 3.12
The algebraic lexical game g_1 in strategic form

$a_B > b_B > c_B$

$a_B' > b_B' > c_B'$

The payoffs at the left represent successful communication with the least expensive locution, the ones in the middle represent successful communication with a more costly locution, and the ones on the right represent unsuccessful communication (with the less costly locution).

It has already been noted that $\mathcal{A}$ and $\mathcal{B}$ take $\rho_1 > \rho_{1'}$, something they share because they are contemplating G. Earlier, I assumed somewhat arbitrary values of 0.9 and 0.1 for these probablities; now these numbers can be replaced with a simple inequality.

The algebraic version of the strategic form for g_1 is shown in Figure 3.12. Close scrutiny of the matrix with the inequalities above in mind should convince the reader that these relations suffice to establish the two Nash equilibria of the game, $(\varphi_1\varphi_1'', \sigma_1)$ and $(\varphi_1'\varphi_1, \sigma_1')$.

It turns out that a unique Pareto-Nash equilibrium may not exist even when numerical utilities are assumed. It depends on the distribution of payoffs and probabilities. In the game g_1 in Figures 3.9 and 3.10, the numbers were such that a unique Pareto-Nash equilibrium did exist. When the pattern of payoffs and probabilities is not right, both the Nash equilibria are Pareto-Nash equilibria as well, and then the appropriate solution to look for is a mixed strategy equilibrium, as we did in G.

The algebraic version of g_1 allows us to examine the different cases that arise. These are based directly on the definition of a Pareto-efficient Nash equilibrium.

Case 1: Pareto-Nash Inequalities If either $\rho_1 a_A + \rho_{1'} b_A' > \rho_1 b_A + \rho_{1'} a_A'$ and $\rho_1 a_B + \rho_{1'} b_B' \geq \rho_1 b_B + \rho_{1'} a_B'$ or $\rho_1 a_A + \rho_{1'} b_A' \geq \rho_1 b_A + \rho_{1'} a_A'$ and

$\rho_1 a_B + \rho_{1'} b'_B > \rho_1 b_B + \rho_{1'} a'_B$ then $(\varphi_1 \varphi''_1, \sigma_1)$ is the unique Pareto-Nash equilibrium.

Case 2: Pareto-Nash Inequalities If either $\rho_1 a_A + \rho_{1'} b'_A < \rho_1 b_A + \rho_{1'} a'_A$ and $\rho_1 a_B + \rho_{1'} b'_B \leq \rho_1 b_B + \rho_{1'} a'_B$ or $\rho_1 a_A + \rho_{1'} b'_A \leq \rho_1 b_A + \rho_{1'} a'_A$ and $\rho_1 a_B + \rho_{1'} b'_B < \rho_1 b_B + \rho_{1'} a'_B$ then $(\varphi'_1 \varphi_1, \sigma'_1)$ is the unique Pareto-Nash equilibrium.

Case 3: Mixed Strategy Equilibria If neither Case 1 nor Case 2 hold, then $(\varphi_1 \varphi''_1, \sigma_1)$ and $(\varphi'_1 \varphi_1, \sigma'_1)$ are both Pareto-Nash equilibria and a mixed strategy equilibrium is likely to be preferred instead (on grounds of salience, for example, as we saw with G).

The first two cases impose very weak conditions for the existence of unique Pareto-Nash equilibria. If, for example, we are given that:

$$a_A - b_A \approx a'_A - b'_A \tag{3.1}$$

and

$$a_B - b_B \approx a'_B - b'_B \tag{3.2}$$

then all that is required for a unique Pareto-Nash equilibrium is that $\rho_1 > \rho_{1'}$, as it is in g_1, or we are given its inverse $\rho_{1'} > \rho_1$.[30] Moreover, in such a situation, the most likely interpretation *is* the unique equilibrium and this provides a convenient and easy way to solve many such games, both for the theorist and the agents themselves.

Each difference above just represents the additional cost of uttering or interpreting an unambiguous locution. If these additional costs are roughly equal for each agent, as they are often likely to be for a natural language, then the Pareto-Nash inequalities hold when either initial probability exceeds the other and we get a unique Pareto-Nash equilibrium. This is what happened with g_1, as can be seen from Figure 3.9.

30. The latter may occur if their discussion had been interrupted by the question of where the children were and what they were doing. In this case, the setting game would shift from G to a game about the children. Then we would have $\rho_{1'} > \rho_1$ in g_1 for both players since Alan is more likely to be talking about their son than about some vintage James Stewart movie.

As a variation on the above theme, suppose that young Harvey is playing in the room where his parents are having their discussion. The linguistic system now gives Alan a further way of indicating that their son is amusing himself: he could simply say "He is playing" where the reference of the pronoun is determined deictically. I assume here that referring to a salient object with a pronoun is preferred to using a name or some other description, as in Clark and Parikh (2007).

Of course, if the two probabilities are roughly equal instead, then we minimally require the additional cost to be sufficiently greater *on the same side* for each agent. For an example of this situation involving anaphora, see Clark and Parikh (2007).

Uniqueness can of course fail to obtain, as attested by Case 3 above. This happens when the relevant pair of inequalities work in *different* directions for $\mathcal{A}$ and $\mathcal{B}$.

It is important to note that because all these different situations can obtain, it is *not* in general possible to reduce the game simply to choosing the option with the highest probability. In any case, some simple algebra gives us the conditions for the uniqueness of Pareto-Nash equilibria. It is easy to extend these calculations to all games of partial information (where it may happen that more than two possible interpretations have to be considered).

What I have established, repeating the discussion of Parikh (1990) in more detail, is that multiple Nash equilibria are given to us in the algebraic version of a game of partial information more or less for free because the inequalities required for their derivation always hold in more or less reasonable and cooperative contexts. And beyond this, if we assume the weak inequalities above for the uniqueness of Pareto-Nash equilibria, we can dispense with actual numbers for the payoffs and probabilities altogether!

This fortunate fact about games of partial information should dispel any qualms some readers may have about the arbitrariness of the numbers involving payoffs and probabilities. By making relatively weak and natural assumptions in the form of inequalities involving algebraic symbols, it is possible to derive what $\mathcal{A}$ is communicating to $\mathcal{B}$ from first principles. We have so far seen this just in the case of the partial content of HARVEY uttered in u. But in chapter 4, more or less the full content of the utterance of φ in u will be derived in a similar but significantly more complex way involving interactions among multiple, interdependent games of partial information.

3.3 A Closer Look at Games of Partial Information

It was important to first consider the broad outlines of G and especially g_1 and their solutions in the preceding sections. We now take a closer look at some aspects of games in general as well as of games of partial information in particular.

3.3.1 The Form of the Game Tree in g_1

The game tree encodes the set of situated choices the interlocutors face during any communicative interaction.

The key organizing principle here is the paraphrase relation; when two linguistic elements are in the paraphrase relation, even if their implicatures and presuppositions differ, then the speaker and hearer face a linguistic choice. These choices can occur within a grammatical derivation or across the outputs of the grammar. The grammar makes resources available to speakers and hearers both of whom must use these resources optimally in order for communication to proceed. Games of partial information provide a general framework for studying the strategic deployment of these resources.

There are two broad ways in which we can think about how the choices are made. We could try to build choice into the grammar itself. One might consider all the forms possible by generating them and then selecting the optimal one. This choice would be considered part of the machinery of the grammar. Optimality Theory, in phonology,[31] is an example of a grammar that uses global optimization in this way.

Choice can be embedded inside the grammar in a variety of ways. To make things more concrete, let us consider a particular constraint, *superiority*. This constraint can be informally stated as:

No rule may target an element, X, if there is another candidate for the rule, Y, such that Y is superior to X.

where "superior" is interpreted in terms of syntactic prominence.[32] This principle is intended to guide the application of the grammatical machinery and, so, involves a choice between elements. Consider, for example, the following contrast:

Who saw what?

What did who see?

The intuitive judgment is that the first sentence is fine as a multiple wh-question while the second only works as an echo question. Thus, the first can be answered by:

31. See Prince and Smolensky (2004).

32. We need not tarry on a precise definition of syntactic prominence here. Superiority shows up in a variety of ways in syntactic theory: our statement is intended as a cover for superiority, "A-over-A," accessible subject, relativized minimality, "move closest," and a variety of other proposed syntactic principles.

John saw the Eiffel Tower, Bill saw the Bridge of Sighs, Mary saw the Golden Pavilion ...

while the response to the second would be the clarification:

What did **John** see?

Superiority says that the syntactically most prominent wh-phrase should count as the main wh-question operator. Thus, in WHO SAW WHAT? the wh-phrase WHO is most prominent; WHAT is less prominent, but can be interpreted as a dependent on WHO since its base position is lower than that of WHO.

If we compare this with WHAT DID WHO SEE?, superiority forces us to take WHAT as the main question operator. Since the base position of WHO is more prominent than that of WHAT, WHO cannot be interpreted as a wh-question word, but must be interpreted as an "echo" question, asking for a clarification.

I have modified the standard account of Superiority here for simplicity, but the guiding idea is that Superiority is a principle inside the grammar that guides choices made during the course of the derivation. Choice, then, is embedded inside the grammatical machinery itself.

I have presented a rather different approach to choice. Indeed, the games we have been considering involve choice at a different level. As I have been emphasizing, any complete theory of language must address the question of what role context plays in meaning. This is also the question of how speakers and hearers strategically deploy their knowledge of grammar to communicate contents. By placing these strategic decisions in the theory of situated choice, we can simplify our account of the derivational machinery required to make the basic elements of choice since questions of strategy can be factored out of our analysis of the grammatical rules and placed in the formal theory of situated choice.

More concretely, we could let the syntactic component of the grammar freely generate WHO SAW WHAT and WHAT DID WHO SEE. These two forms will be available to express a variety of meanings; the choice of association between form and meaning, however, is a strategic one, and speakers and hearers have an interest in optimizing this choice. Thus, we can think of the association of form and meaning as a game involving interactions between agents or, better, a family of games that take place at a variety of levels—lexical choice, word order, intonation, and so on. This move will, in general, simplify our theory of linguistic rules. It will also make theories of meaning ineluctably contextual as I noted in chapter 1.

A good analogy would be the rules of a board game such as Go. The rules of Go are quite simple: a stone may be placed on any empty intersection, stones that are completely surrounded are removed, Black moves first, and so on. The strategy and tactics of Go, on the other hand, are quite complex and difficult to master. Imagine that we tried to state the rules of Go in such a way as to include the strategies and tactics in the rules themselves. The various rules might then include descriptions of the state of play along with an instruction to place a stone on some particular intersection if the board was in the described state. The result would be so complex as to be useless as a description for how to play Go. It is preferable to give the simplest rules possible for a description of the rules that constitute Go and use other means to study the strategy and tactics.

Suppose, now, that we discover that certain readings of an ambiguous sentence are systematically missing in certain environments. We might try to state our rules of semantic interpretation in such a way as to guarantee that these readings are simply unavailable in these environments. On the other hand, we might note that the choices that the grammar makes available include a way of encoding the missing reading that has greater utility than the form in question would. That is, the interpretation of the form is eliminated from the Pareto-Nash strategy. The theory of situated linguistic choice would then account for why the reading is missing and we would not have to use the grammatical machinery to try to otherwise block this reading. As a result, the grammar is simplified and the distribution of possible readings would be made to follow from a general theory of situated strategic behavior. It would also allow exceptions to a putative rule to be handled naturally in terms of expected utility maximization without having to build them in explicitly. These twin benefits would be a gain both for the theory of grammar and for the theory of strategic choice, and indeed for the theoretical enterprise as such, since the theorist would be relying on weaker assumptions of a more general cognitive sort than on stronger assumptions of a specialized linguistic sort.

3.3.2 Benefits and Costs

The next ingredient in a game theoretic account is the assignment of utility to the outcomes of the players' choices.

As explained in sections 3.1 and 3.2, one starts with a preference ordering over outcomes that is then translated into a compatible real-valued utility function that is invariant up to positive affine transformations. It turns out that with the help of a few relatively weak assumptions, it is possible to take the analysis of a game fairly far with just algebraic stand-ins for numerical utilities. This is convenient because in many games including those involving communication, it is sometimes felt that the arbitrariness of payoff numbers is an obstacle to a convincing analysis.

Utility in g_1 is made up of benefits and costs. Benefits arise essentially from the players' goals broadly conceived. Some attention was given to the derivation of numerical benefits in section 3.2 and I gave an informal definition of *relevance* as the difference in values of some transformation of the setting game G based on the utterance and G.[33] Of course, it was found that merely assuming that successful communication was preferred to unsuccessful communication together with allied assumptions about costs was enough to enable the computation of Nash equilibria.

The essential element of cost is effort broadly conceived. The speaker's main effort lies in anticipating the addressee's interpretation and in producing an utterance; the addressee's main effort lies in perceiving and interpreting it. Both types of effort are linked ultimately to the language $\mathcal{L}$, but they are also connected of course to the physical makeup of human agents.

Beyond these obvious sources of effort and cost, there may be other subtler types of effort and, as more and more specific communicative phenomena are examined, more such sources are likely to come to light. Some possibilities for these are referring to a less salient discourse entity which can cost more,[34] and possibly other sociolinguistic factors such as group identity, turn taking, and politeness may also contribute to costs.

No doubt many other items are relevant in correctly framing the costs of various linguistic elements and their interpretations. The more or less rational deployment of linguistic resources will involve considerations from a wide variety of domains. Part of the job of the linguist is to develop theories (expressed in terms of utility) of these factors and an overall theory of cost.

However, I point out again that while such a numerical theory would be of immense interest, it is not strictly required since simply using the reasonable general preference that less costly actions are preferred to more costly actions with other relatively weak assumptions enables us to

33. It may be found more useful to define relevance as the absolute value of this difference.

34. See Clark and Parikh (2007) for a detailed consideration of such factors. Essentially, it is the added psychological effort involved in accessing something that is less salient.

compute the desired equilibria. Consequently, all that is really required is that both agents be able to make a rough assessment of costs so as to be in a position to decide what options are costlier than others.

3.3.3 Probabilities

Recall that g_1 involved the choice between a single, ambiguous lexical item and a more complex description. From these possibilities arises a forest of game trees that are connected by the ambiguous lexical item, as shown in Figures 3.9 and 3.11.

The probabilities associated with the roots of the various trees in the forest could stem from a variety of sources in general. One possibility is that the probability associated with the root is an objective probability, in which case it is a reflection of the frequency of the lexical senses in question. To see this more clearly, consider an utterance of a garden path sentence:

The rich man the boats. (ν)

Intuitively, the sentence is difficult because the appropriate sense of MAN, where it is a verb that denotes the act of providing personnel to operate the boat, is less frequent than the noun sense. Equally, the most frequent interpretation of RICH is its adjectival one, the noun interpretation being slightly less frequent.

If ν is represented as $\nu_1 \circ \nu_2 \circ \cdots \circ \nu_5$, with $\nu_1 =$ THE, $\nu_2 =$ RICH, $\nu_3 =$ MAN, $\nu_4 =$ THE, and $\nu_5 =$ BOATS, then the relevant lexical games $g_u(\nu_2)$ and $g_u(\nu_3)$ are shown in Figures 3.13 and 3.14 with respect to some utterance situation u.

The second of these games involves the partial contents τ_3 and τ_3' which represent the verb and noun readings of MAN respectively. I have retained the same payoff symbols as before since only the inequalities matter. Here, clearly $\rho_3 < \rho_{3'}$, since the objective probability of the verb reading is less likely. This game would have the same Nash equilibria as we had for g_1, but this time the unique Pareto-Nash equilibrium would be $(\nu_3'\nu_3, \tau_3')$, assuming of course that Case 2 of the Pareto-Nash Inequalities is satisfied. The best choice for $\mathcal{B}$ is to interpret (THE) MAN to denote some adult male human.

Likewise, the first game involves the partial contents τ_2 and τ_2' which represent the nominal and adjectival readings of RICH, respectively. Here again, $\rho_2 < \rho_{2'}$, since the objective probability of the nominal reading is less likely. The unique Pareto-Nash equilibrium would be $(\nu_2'\nu_2, \tau_2')$, and

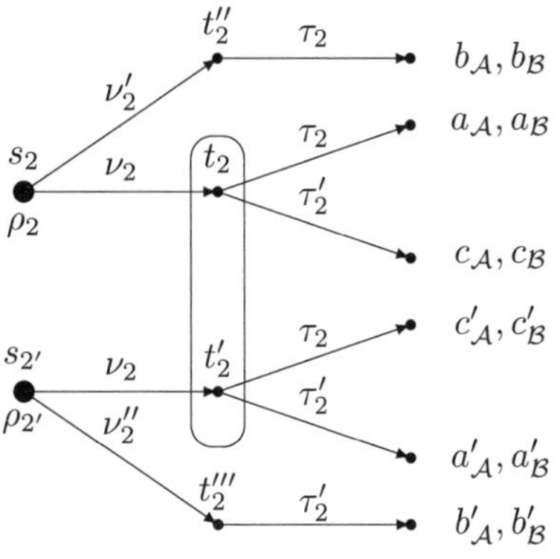

Figure 3.13
A lexical game involving a garden path effect

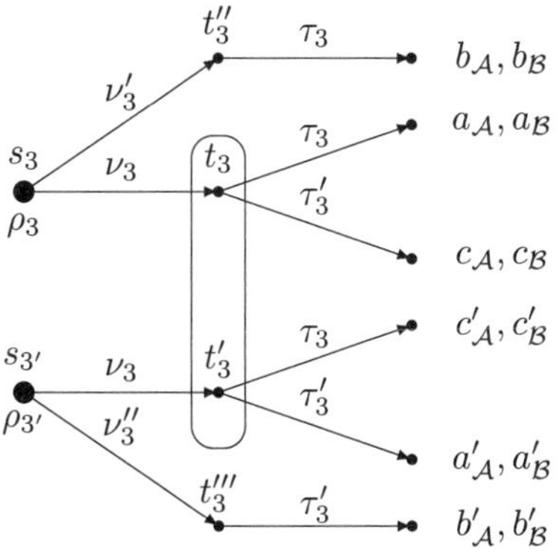

Figure 3.14
A related lexical game involving a garden path effect

the best choice for $\mathcal{B}$ is to interpret RICH in the adjectival sense of being wealthy.

In both cases, the high frequency sense dominates the optimal choice, all else being equal. Notice further that the most frequent senses reinforce each other; RICH as an adjective is an obvious modifier of MAN as a noun. This fact contributes to the severity of the garden path effect.

In order to account for such an utterance, we must include information other than raw frequencies in the assessment of probabilities. In this example, the probabilities are conditioned by syntactic information and assessments of the likelihood of various interpretations. This brings up the fact that other kinds of information than raw frequency can impact the assessment of probability. As an aside, notice that it makes sense that considerations other than raw frequency can influence lexical choice; if it were solely a matter of frequency, less frequent senses of a word would be driven out and eventually vanish.

I will return to this example in sections 4.9 and 7.1.1 where a more rigorous account will be given that involves the conventional and informational maps for v_2 and v_3 and more precise renderings for τ_2 and τ_3.

Consider the following well-known example:

The astronomer married the star.

The example is hard to process, presumably because the word ASTRONOMER *primes* (that is, makes more accessible) the wrong sense of STAR, leading to an increase in processing load. This indicates that the probability associated with an interpretation can also be influenced by subjective probabilities in addition to objective probabilities based on frequency. The probability associated with the astronomical sense of STAR increases due to the presence of ASTRONOMER. In the full theory to follow, I will account for the different degrees of influence that the noun ASTRONOMER and the verb MARRY exert. The increase in processing load, however, can be identified with the conflicting information provided by these two lexical items.

Another source of subjective and objective probability is obviously the situational context itself. As we saw with g_1, aspects of the context (e.g., attending to G) can influence the probability associated with a situation.

This assessment of subjective and objective and linguistic and contextual probabilities can affect the Pareto-Nash equilibrium and, therefore, has a profound impact on the predictions we make. Crucially, we must have a systematic way of assessing likelihood given a variety of information sources.

Just as it is unexceptionable that people have goals expressible as preferences idealized to utilities, so it is part of the basic picture of human agency that people have beliefs expressible as estimates of probabilities. Indeed, people are adept at forming rough estimates of likelihood in the course of choosing their actions based on their goals and beliefs. When these beliefs conflict, as they did with THE ASTRONOMER MARRIED THE STAR, the assessments of likelihood become more difficult. These rough estimates can be idealized to numerical probabilities when required. Given, therefore, that people have methods of assessing both objective and subjective probability, we can construct game-based models of conditioned linguistic behavior. These models should be faithful not just to our intuitions, but to empirical data gleaned from language in context. In a good model, the probabilities, utilities, and game trees should be a matter of broad agreement.

This brings us to a matter of great importance, the question of the epistemic status of these models.

3.3.4 Common Knowledge and Subjective Games of Partial Information

In classical game theory, it is always assumed that the extensive forms and strategic forms of a game are part of the common knowledge of the players of the game. Indeed, common knowledge of the choice structure is part of the formal *definition* of a game.

Common knowledge between two agents of an infon σ is equivalent to two infinite chains of knowledge of σ: $\mathcal{A}$ knows that $\mathcal{B}$ knows that $\mathcal{A}$ knows that ... σ and $\mathcal{B}$ knows that $\mathcal{A}$ knows that $\mathcal{B}$ knows that ... σ.[35] In our case, both G and g_1 would have to be assumed to be common knowledge between $\mathcal{A}$ and $\mathcal{B}$.[36] Interestingly, this notion originated in the study of convention by both Lewis (1969) and Schiffer (1972) and was subsequently taken over by game theorists for games in general.[37]

The common knowledge assumption is standard in classical game theory though it has come under attack in the last couple of decades after the advent of evolutionary game theory. Often, the point is made in an all-or-nothing way that common knowledge is impossible to achieve because of its infinitary requirement, and that human agents are, in fact, seldom able without considerable cognitive effort to go beyond just a few iterations of shared knowledge.[38] Sometimes, it is even maintained that as a result classical game theory should be abandoned in favor of evolutionary interpretations where common knowledge is not required.

I believe the general criticism that common knowledge is often difficult to achieve is fair but needs to be made in a more nuanced way. For example, if two persons are facing each other at a table in a restaurant and engaged in ordinary conversation, there should be little doubt that they

35. This characterization has a redundancy but it has the advantage of symmetry.

36. Remember that I had written $u \models G$ earlier because I had said G could be expressed as a bunch of infons. So can g_1.

37. Chapter 5 of Parikh (2001) explains in detail why common knowledge is required for (Gricean) communication and there is no point in going over the same ground here.

38. See Gintis (2000), chapter 1, page 14, for example.

possess the common knowledge that they are so engaged. More generally, if two or more people are copresent in ordinary ways in some situation, then again there is no reason to think that common knowledge among them does not obtain. Of course, it is not necessary for the human agents to *explicitly* represent the infinite chains of iterated knowledge in their heads for them to have common knowledge; given their copresence, they can derive these iterated levels of knowledge to an arbitrary degree. Thus, (situated) common knowledge *is* possible for people to achieve in fairly ordinary circumstances, even though they may not be able to explicitly represent it mentally to arbitrary degrees.

However, for many situations involving games, it seems reasonable to doubt that common knowledge of the entire game may obtain. A game involves three elements in addition to the agents themselves—the choices available to each agent, the payoffs based on the outcomes of these choices, and the probabilities of initial situations, whether singular as in G or multiple as in g_1.[39] While for both G and g_1 it is reasonable to assume that $\mathcal{A}$ and $\mathcal{B}$ have common knowledge of the players in each game (i.e., themselves), it appears unlikely that they would have common knowledge of their choice sets, their payoffs, or probabilities. Entities such as choice sets, payoffs, and (especially subjective) probabilities are abstract and invisible, although it is arguable that certain aspects of actions available to an agent are embedded in the situations themselves and, therefore, perceivable by other agents; that is part of what makes actions and choices *situated*. This relative invisibility of these entities makes it difficult to accept that agents have common knowledge of the choice structure that makes up a game in general.

One possible response to this problem is to switch to dynamic considerations and evolutionary games. While this may be a good approach for genuinely historical and evolutionary phenomena in language, it is not likely to be satisfactory in actual communicative situations like u. I have myself urged the adoption of evolutionary models for other domains; however, such models typically require noncognitive, non-intentional action, something contrary to the empirical facts about communicative behavior, and, equally importantly, require suboptimal behavior until an

39. It will be seen in the next chapter that the probabilities in g_1 are not quite the probabilities of the *initial situations* themselves, but rather of the relevant agent's referring to a partial content (viz. either σ_1 or σ_1') given the other partial contents referred to via the rest of the utterance as well as given $u = s_1 \cap s_{1'}$. This detail cannot be explained here, but I mention it just as a cautionary note.

equilibrium emerges. The latter problem renders the evolutionary model inappropriate for what are essentially one-shot situations requiring immediate resolution. One alternative is to say that solutions to such communicative problems are communally worked out in advance by evolutionary means so that in u itself the equilibrium is immediately available. However, it is not clear how this could actually be realized given the very wide range of utterance situations u that obtain. Even in our limited example, it will be seen in the next chapter that a slight change of the circumstances in u would imply the communication of the other partial content σ_1', the son Harvey. In other words, it does not appear feasible to rely on *rules* given the extreme variability of contexts.[40]

Another response is to note that the argument above against common knowledge obtaining in most games based on the invisibility and abstractness of choice sets, payoffs, and probabilities more or less dissolves if one resorts to the *algebraic* versions of G and g_1.

It seems harmless to grant common knowledge of choice sets on three grounds taken together. One is the fact that $\mathcal{L}$ and the choices it affords are shared to a reasonable degree in a linguistic community. The second is that conventional meanings are also shared to a greater or lesser degree within a community. The third ground involves a somewhat subtle observation about the special nature of g_1 that was not made explicit which, together with the first two facts, allows us to assume effective common knowledge of choice sets.

This third fact is as follows. It cannot be assumed that g_1 is common knowledge or even partially shared before $\mathcal{A}$ has actually uttered φ_1 because there is no way for $\mathcal{B}$ to know what $\mathcal{A}$ was about to say. What happens is that $\mathcal{A}$ plays g_1 in his head, solves the game, finds the unique equilibrium action he needs to perform, and then utters φ_1. (The full complexity of this seemingly simple observation will be addressed in section 3.3.6.) Once $\mathcal{B}$ perceives the utterance, she (re)constructs g_1 in her head, solves it, finds the unique equilibrium action she needs to perform, and then interprets $\mathcal{A}$'s utterance (as the film *Harvey*). I do not mean to imply that these agents are actually representing and solving games in their heads in some conscious and articulate way. More will be said about this in section 3.3.6 and section 7.4, but for now we can pretend that this is how the process works.

Given this assumption, it is not necessary for $\mathcal{A}$'s and $\mathcal{B}$'s model of $\mathcal{A}$'s choice sets to coincide exactly. Since $\mathcal{A}$ has already uttered φ_1, this

40. For more detailed discussion of this point, see Parikh (2007).

element of the speaker's choice set is already common knowledge. The other alternative utterances φ_1' and φ_1'' in Figure 3.11 are never uttered and could be taken by the two agents to be different locutions as long as they are costlier paraphrases than φ_1. That is all that is required for the payoff inequalities redisplayed below to hold—the strict identity of the alternative utterances is not required. On the addressee's side, since conventional meanings are more or less shared in general, and since the possible utterances in g_1 are more or less shared, their partial contents can also be assumed to be common knowledge.

Thus, while strict common knowledge of choice sets may not obtain, "enough" can be assumed for the moment.

Now recall the assumptions regarding payoffs in games of partial information:

successful and less costly communication

$\succ$ successful but more costly communication

$\succ$ unsuccessful communication

For g_1, these preferences imply:

$a_A > b_A > c_A$

$a_A' > b_A' > c_A'$

$a_B > b_B > c_B$

$a_B' > b_B' > c_B'$

It seems evident that such preferences could well be common knowledge as they are only based on a minimal assumption of cooperative reasonableness and common knowledge of cooperative reasonableness is then not so costly to assume, especially since people share a common physical architecture and live in the same linguistic communities. It follows, then, that common knowledge of the algebraic inequalities above for g_1, as well as similar inequalities for more general games of partial information, may be assumed without much ado.

Next, we saw earlier that numerical probabilities could be replaced by an algebraic inequality such as $\rho_1 > \rho_{1'}$ for g_1 and similar relations would hold for other such games. These inequalities come from the setting u and its associated game(s) G and possibly from $\mathcal{L}$ itself. So whether common knowledge of the inequality obtains or not depends on whether the relevant aspects of u and G are common knowledge or not. In many situations where copresence or some similar enabling facts apply, common knowledge of the inequality could easily arise. But it should be noted that such common knowledge may be quite fallible and, in many situations, may not obtain at all. Indeed, this is one of the principal ways in which *miscommunication* occurs—by the agents assuming exactly the opposite inequalities, possibly by attending to different aspects of u and the ongoing discourse.[41] Thus, assuming common knowledge of the probability inequality entails some risk, but it is a reasonable risk because when it does not hold, the communication itself may fail on account of something going awry. Of course, there is a middle ground where, in the absence of common knowledge, (Gricean) communication does not succeed but some weaker flow of information does occur.

It was also pointed out that these inequalities just yield the two Nash equilibria of g_1. To get a unique Pareto-Nash equilibrium, we need what were called the Pareto-Nash Inequalities. Since it was argued that these inequalities impose relatively weak conditions for uniqueness, it seems safe to simply take these as common knowledge when both agents feel it acceptable to assume them individually.

It appears, then, that there is roughly enough warrant for common knowledge of algebraically considered games of partial information, and when there is not it does not matter, either because knowledge of choice sets does not need to be shared exactly, or because there is miscommunication involving conflicting assumptions about probabilities, or finally because full Gricean communication does not occur, just some weaker information flow.

Despite this warrant, it is worth pushing the argument further. We can explore the consequences of common knowledge failing to hold, even just in this partial way. The inescapable conclusion one has to draw is that there just is not *one* game g_1 that $\mathcal{A}$ and $\mathcal{B}$ have common knowledge of or partially share, but rather *two* separate games, one for each agent. This observation has fascinating implications, both for language and for game theory.[42]

41. See chapter 9 of Parikh (2001) for a detailed discussion of miscommunication. Also, earlier I referred to G and to an alternative setting game about the protagonists' children. If the two agents have differing views about which setting game is the reference game, then such miscommunication may easily occur, one player thinking that $\rho_1 > \rho_{1'}$ and the other that $\rho_{1'} > \rho_1$.

42. Game theorists have avoided this implication of giving up common knowledge of games and exploring the more general *strategic interactions* that result. Because the structures are more general, solution concepts are difficult to define and there are fewer results.

The broad consequences of this separation into two choice structures are threefold. First, when there are two games (or what are better termed *strategic interactions*), say g_1^A and g_1^B, each game ceases to be common knowledge. The first choice structure is $\mathcal{A}$'s model of the strategic interaction while the second choice structure is $\mathcal{B}$'s. Now $\mathcal{A}$ merely *believes* that g_1^A is common knowledge and $\mathcal{B}$ also merely believes that g_1^B is common knowledge. In general, this is much weaker than common knowledge. But it may happen, to use Dretske's (1981) analysis of knowledge, that these respective beliefs are *informationally caused*. In this case, each agent could be said to *know* that his or her game is common knowledge and then the two games would indeed have to be identical and common knowledge. But for the most part, each agent would stay within the realm of belief, each with their separate games. Information flow would occur only when there was, in fact, sufficient overlap between g_1^A and g_1^B, a good deal of which there is some warrant for, as we have just seen.

Second, when there is just a partial overlap between g_1^A and g_1^B, we have seen that information flows that are weaker than full Gricean communication may occur. In such cases, each agent believes something weaker than common knowledge and we can call this system of beliefs an information structure $\mathcal{I}_g$. In any case, now there is a mechanism to study these flows through the medium of these strategic interactions given by the triple of the two games and the information structure.[43]

The last implication is of *indeterminacy*, the third idea of equilibrium semantics, which is considered in chapter 5.

This rounds out our discussion of common knowledge. It is reasonable to take a decent amount of the communicative interaction between $\mathcal{A}$ and $\mathcal{B}$ as common knowledge when it is viewed algebraically, but to the extent we cannot there are just two separate choice structures involved. These lead on occasion to weaker information flows and even to miscommunication.

3.3.5 Perfect Bayesian Equilibrium and Other Solution Concepts

In section 3.2, the algebraic game g_1 of Figure 3.11 was solved by looking at the strategic form in Figure 3.12 and computing the Pareto-Nash Equilibrium. It is possible to solve this game directly via the extensive form repeated below in Figure 3.15 by using the notion of a Perfect Bayesian Equilibrium. One reason for doing this is to see whether the additional in-

43. This was pursued in chapters 5 and 6 of Parikh (2001).

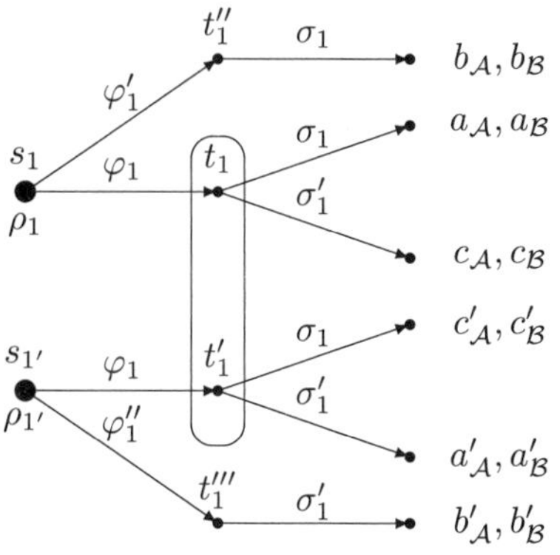

Figure 3.15
Algebraic version of lexical game $g_1 = g_u(\varphi_1)$

formation available through the explicitly represented information sets in the extensive form enables us to eliminate the unwanted Nash equilibrium $(\varphi_1'\varphi_1, \sigma_1')$. If so, it would provide an alternative to the Pareto criterion I used in section 3.2.

To describe it, the notion of a "conditional belief" at an information set is required. This is just the probability a player assigns to each node of an information set she finds herself in given that the information set has been reached. In the special case of Figure 3.15, there is just one nontrivial information set $\{t_1, t_1'\}$ where a nontrivial assignment is required. The conditional probability $\mathcal{B}$ assigns to the node t_1 given that the information set $\{t_1, t_1'\}$ was reached will be called q. Then the probability of t_1' would have to be $1 - q$. More precisely, $q = Prob(t_1 \mid \{t_1, t_1'\}) = Prob(s_1 \mid \varphi_1)$ when Bayes' rule can be applied; otherwise it can be any number between 0 and 1.

Perfect Bayesian Equilibrium is an extension of Nash Equilibrium to games of incomplete and partial information that embodies the idea of sequential rationality. It is a natural generalization of a subgame perfect equilibrium to situations where a subgame does not exist as at the nontrivial information set $\{t, t'\}$. Consider a strategy profile for $\mathcal{A}$ and $\mathcal{B}$ as well as beliefs over the nodes at all (nontrivial) information sets. Then the strategy profile together with the beliefs is called a perfect Bayesian equilibrium if each player's strategy specifies optimal actions, given his beliefs and the strategies of the other player, and all beliefs are consistent with Bayes' rule whenever possible.

Applying this criterion to the four strategies of $\mathcal{A}$, we find:

1. $(\varphi_1\varphi_1'')$: This strategy implies that $q = Prob(s_1 \mid \varphi_1) = 1$, which in turn implies that σ_1 is optimal (since $a_\mathcal{B} > c_\mathcal{B}$); finally, $(\varphi_1\varphi_1'')$ is a best response to σ_1. Thus, each strategy is optimal, given the other and given that $q = 1$, and q was also obtained via Bayes' rule. This means $(\varphi_1\varphi_1'', \sigma_1)$ together with $q = 1$ is a perfect Bayesian equilibrium.
2. $(\varphi_1'\varphi_1)$: This strategy implies that $q = Prob(s_1 \mid \varphi_1) = 0$, which in turn implies that σ_1' is optimal (since $a_\mathcal{B}' > c_\mathcal{B}'$); finally, $(\varphi_1'\varphi_1)$ is a best response to σ_1'. Thus, each strategy is optimal, given the other and given that $q = 0$, and q was also obtained via Bayes' rule. This means $(\varphi_1'\varphi_1, \sigma_1')$ together with $q = 0$ is also a perfect Bayesian equilibrium. As should be clear, this unwanted Nash equilibrium survives the perfect Bayesian equilibrium concept.
3. $(\varphi_1\varphi_1)$: This strategy implies that $q = Prob(s_1 \mid \varphi_1) = \rho_1$, which in turn implies either that σ_1 is optimal if $\rho_1 > \rho_{1'}$ or that σ_1' is optimal if $\rho_1 < \rho_{1'}$. But if $\rho_1 > \rho_{1'}$ and $\mathcal{B}$ selects σ_1, then $(\varphi_1\varphi_1'')$ is better than $(\varphi_1\varphi_1)$, so all the choices are not consistent. Likewise, if $\rho_1 < \rho_{1'}$ and $\mathcal{B}$ selects σ_1', then $(\varphi_1'\varphi_1)$ is better than $(\varphi_1\varphi_1)$, so once again the choices are not consistent. This means there is no perfect Bayesian equilibrium with $(\varphi_1\varphi_1)$.
4. $(\varphi_1'\varphi_1'')$: This strategy implies that q is arbitrary since Bayes' rule does not apply. This case is a little more involved since we have chosen to deal with algebraic payoffs, but if we made the simplifying assumption that the all primed payoffs (e.g., $a_\mathcal{A}'$) are equal to the corresponding unprimed payoffs (e.g., $a_\mathcal{A}$), then this case reduces to two subcases based on whether $q > 0.5$ or not. The reasoning is similar to the previous case. If $q > 0.5$, then σ_1 is optimal and if $q < 0.5$, then σ_1' is optimal. But if $\mathcal{B}$ selects σ_1, then $(\varphi_1\varphi_1'')$ is better than $(\varphi_1'\varphi_1'')$, so all the choices are not consistent. Likewise, if $\mathcal{B}$ selects σ_1', then $(\varphi_1'\varphi_1)$ is better than $(\varphi_1'\varphi_1'')$, so once again the choices are not consistent. Again, there is no perfect Bayesian equilibrium with $(\varphi_1'\varphi_1'')$.

It should be evident that the results are exactly the same as with the Nash equilibrium computations in section 3.2. Therefore, as before, the second of the two perfect Bayesian equilibria would have to be eliminated by the Pareto criterion to yield the same overall solution to the game.

It is possible to view the procedure described above as a kind of forward induction since the movement is from front to back—from the information sets at the beginning of the game tree to the ones at the end. Backward induction is the process of analyzing a game from back to front—from information sets at the end of the game tree to information sets at the beginning. At each information set, one strikes from consideration actions that are dominated, given the terminal nodes that can be reached. In addition to subgame perfect equilibria, backward induction can be extended to the computation of perfect Bayesian equilibria as well.

Assuming that corresponding primed and unprimed payoffs are equal, we get the two strings of *consistent* implications below:

1. $q > 0.5 \Rightarrow \sigma_1$ is optimal $\Rightarrow (\varphi_1\varphi_1'')$ is optimal $\Rightarrow q = 1$
2. $q < 0.5 \Rightarrow \sigma_1'$ is optimal $\Rightarrow (\varphi_1'\varphi_1)$ is optimal $\Rightarrow q = 0$

This is clearly the same two solutions as before. When the corresponding primed and unprimed payoffs are not the same, the number 0.5 has to be replaced by an algebraic expression based on the payoffs. This is straightforward to compute: we must have $qa_B + (1-q)c_B' > qc_B + (1-q)a_B'$, which implies $q > (a_B' - c_B')/(a_B - c_B + a_B' - c_B')$. This results in the following consistent implications as above:

1. $q > (a_B' - c_B')/(a_B - c_B + a_B' - c_B') \Rightarrow \sigma_1$ is optimal $\Rightarrow (\varphi_1\varphi_1'')$ is optimal $\Rightarrow q = 1$
2. $q < (a_B' - c_B')/(a_B - c_B + a_B' - c_B') \Rightarrow \sigma_1'$ is optimal $\Rightarrow (\varphi_1'\varphi_1)$ is optimal $\Rightarrow q = 0$

Since the equilibrium belief q is either 1 or 0, the value of the algebraic expression does not really matter as it lies between 0 and 1. Notice that when the unprimed and corresponding primed payoffs are equal, that is, when $a_B = a_B'$ and $c_B = c_B'$, the algebraic expression reduces to 0.5.

Of course, solution concepts other than these may also be used to analyze games of partial information, but they result in the same two Nash equilibria. As games go, the structure of a single partial information game is relatively *simple* (more precisely, this simplicity consists in their generally having just one nontrivial information set) and so different solution processes cannot generally produce different results. For example, the standard refinements of Nash equilibrium (sequential, perfect, and proper equilibria, [iterated] dominance, the intuitive criterion, divinity, and universal divinity) all produce the same results because they all have force by imposing *restrictions* on "out-of-equilibrium" beliefs, that is, beliefs in information sets that are off the equilibrium path. Since there is generally just one nontrivial information set in games of partial information, and since both Nash equilibria involve this nontrivial information set, it will never be off the equilibrium path. So the only information sets off the equilibrium path will be singletons and the beliefs there will always be trivial (viz. 1). This means the unintuitive Nash equilibria can never be ousted by such concepts. All the Nash equilibria are also stable.[44]

This suggests that we need to employ either the Pareto criterion or something similar to eliminate the undesirable Nash equilibria and derive the single meaning of the utterance. In section 4.11, I will show that such a map from games of partial information to an equilibrium does exist uniquely, but specifying it constructively is another issue because the Pareto criterion itself may not work under all conditions. Even so, is there a way to independently justify the Pareto-Nash equilibrium? I quote at length from section 4.4 of Parikh (2001):

> To solve this multiple equilibrium problem I will use the idea of Pareto dominance. It says simply that of two strategies in a game, if one results in higher payoffs for all players concerned, the other can be eliminated. Though this appears to make perfect intuitive sense, there is a problem with it because it implicitly assumes some degree of correlated action (correlated deviation) among players. This element of cooperation requires additional assumptions in a noncooperative game. In fact, there is often a conflict between the Nash criterion and the Pareto-dominance criterion (as shown, e.g., by the well-known Prisoner's Dilemma).
>
> To sidestep this potential conflict, and also to create a single criterion out of Nash equilibrium and Pareto-dominance, I will use Pareto-dominance as a *second-order* condition. First, we determine the set of Nash equilibria. In our case, this is $\{N_1, N_2\}$. Then we apply the Pareto criterion to this set. This ensures that all solutions satisfy the important Nash property that there is no incentive to deviate. That, after all, is what justifies calling it an "equilibrium" strategy. And this second-order way of eliminating counterintuitive Nash equilibria (and their refinements) may be easier to justify. There is also an important general point to be made in justifying this hybrid solution concept and I develop it at some length in a footnote.[45]

44. I have given a *general* reason why most refinements do not help. I have looked at the perfect Bayesian equilibrium as one alternative in detail, I urge readers to try out others. See Selten (1975), Kreps (1986), In-Koo Cho and Kreps (1987), Myerson (1978), Bernheim (1984), and Kohlberg and Mertens (1986), among others.

45. As Schelling (1960), most notably, has pointed out, noncooperative games have payoffs that can be thought of (at least loosely) as lying along a continuum ranging from games of pure coordination to games of pure conflict. Intuitively, a game of pure coordination is one in which all players have "perfectly aligned interests," and a game of pure conflict is one in which they have "strictly opposed interests." A sufficient condition for a game to be a pure coordination game is that the payoffs of all players be identical. For a game of pure conflict, it turns out that only two-person zero-sum games can have payoffs with strictly opposed interests. Most games lie in between these two extremes: their payoffs reflect a mix

of conflict and coordination, and they are, predictably, called mixed-motive games. The term *noncooperative* that is used to describe this entire class of games refers not to the "interests" of the players but to the constraints under which they have to choose a rational course of action. Noncooperative games are models of situations in which no "*binding* agreements" are possible. Cooperative games admit binding agreements between players and it is this element that makes them "cooperative" games, resulting in the possibility of coalition-based behavior (Aumann, 1976).

The evolution of game theory seems to suggest an implicit bias against an appreciation of the element of coordination that is present in most noncooperative games. All the solution concepts that have been explored appear to focus exclusively on the possibilities for conflictual behavior. Fully rational behavior should, at least intuitively, reflect both caution against possible conflictual behavior by other players as well as the extraction of possibilities for coordination. And the solution concepts we define should capture both sets of possibilities. To be sure, the recent literature shows how subtle considerations of strategic interactions can be. But I am tempted to think that most game theorists would agree that it is problematic that we do not have a solution concept that gives us the obvious unique solution to the following pure coordination game:

x, x	$0, 0$
$0, 0$	$1, 1$

$x =$ one million

Kohlberg and Mertens (1986) feel that for the game above with $x = 3$, noncooperative game theory has nothing to offer that will eliminate the equilibrium $(1, 1)$, and that such considerations should fall under the relatively restricted domain of cooperative game theory. However, at least one implication we might draw from the interest in criteria that admit correlated behavior of various sorts (Aumann, 1987; Kreps and Ramey, 1987) is that traditional views of "coordinative" behavior may not be so obviously true, even if they do turn out to be true in the end. Further, if we allow contexts to determine the appropriateness of different solution criteria for the same game, as Kreps has recommended, then there seems little doubt that there is a place for solution concepts that explicitly admit both conflictual and coordinative aspects of the game.

As a first and obvious move towards this, I will adopt the mixed "Pareto-Nash" criterion defined above. Note that the game under consideration is a pure coordination game (of partial information). In such games, the set of Pareto-dominant strategies is a subset of the set of Nash equilibria so that there is no conflict between the two solution concepts considered independently. But I will consider more general mixed-motive games below and use the same criterion for these games as well. The Pareto-Nash criterion is admittedly a rather simple concept and is unlikely to have much force. But it should be seen as a first step. The various conflictual solution concepts that have been investigated show much

Thus, what emerges from this quote is that one reason why the Pareto criterion has some (partial) force is that it uses the coordinative or "cooperative" dimensions of the payoffs in games of partial information. Since such games are never zero-sum games, there is always some coordination to exploit even when the games are not *pure* coordination games. If we interpret Grice's (1975) Cooperative Principle to stand for this kind of cooperation between players in solving games, then the use of something like the Pareto criterion seems justifiable.[46]

A refinement that I have not considered so far, one that also exploits the coordinative dimensions of a game, is Harsanyi and Selten's (1988) risk dominance criterion. Intuitively, we should also expect it to have some force like the second-order Pareto criterion because it involves an element of cooperation between the players. As we will see below, this turns out to be true. However, because of the relative simplicity of games of partial information, this time involving the pattern of payoffs, it also transpires that what I call the Pareto-Nash equilibrium concept and what Harsanyi and Selten call payoff dominance is *equivalent* to risk dominance under the assumptions I made in section 3.2 (Equations 3.1 and 3.2). These assumptions sufficed for the Pareto-Nash inequalities and I reproduce them here for ease of reference. If it is assumed that:

$$a_A - b_A \approx a'_A - b'_A$$

and

$$a_B - b_B \approx a'_B - b'_B$$

---

sophistication in exploiting the conflictual elements in games. There does not seem to be any a priori reason to limit the possibilities for sophisticated "cooperative" or coordinative behavior.

The entire discussion above is based on three imprecise but suggestive premises. The first is an intuitive notion of the degree of conflict and coordination in a game. The second is an extremely vague notion of the possibility of separating the conflictual and coordinative aspects of a game. And the third is the identification of the motivations underlying most existing solution concepts with the conflictual aspects of games. It is unclear whether any of these premises would hold up under more rigorous scrutiny. But we must leave our discussion of these issues here and return to our main story.

46. To the best of my knowledge, Parikh (1987b) was the first to use this concept, even before Harsanyi and Selten's (1988) differently named but identical concept of payoff dominance. Michael Spence (2001) also uses it in his Nobel lecture on signaling.

	σ_1	σ_1'
$\varphi_1\varphi_1$	$\rho_1 a_A + \rho_{1'} c_A'$, $\rho_1 a_B + \rho_{1'} c_B'$	$\rho_1 c_A + \rho_{1'} a_A'$, $\rho_1 c_B + \rho_{1'} a_B'$
$\varphi_1'\varphi_1$	$\rho_1 b_A + \rho_{1'} c_A'$, $\rho_1 b_B + \rho_{1'} c_B'$	$\rho_1 b_A + \rho_{1'} a_A'$, $\rho_1 b_B + \rho_{1'} a_B'$
$\varphi_1\varphi_1''$	$\rho_1 a_A + \rho_{1'} b_A'$, $\rho_1 a_B + \rho_{1'} b_B'$	$\rho_1 c_A + \rho_{1'} b_A'$, $\rho_1 c_B + \rho_{1'} b_B'$
$\varphi_1'\varphi_1''$	$\rho_1 b_A + \rho_{1'} b_A'$, $\rho_1 b_B + \rho_{1'} b_B'$	$\rho_1 b_A + \rho_{1'} b_A'$, $\rho_1 b_B + \rho_{1'} b_B'$

Figure 3.16
The algebraic lexical game g_1 in strategic form

and additionally, *beyond* the requirements for the Pareto-Nash equilibrium, that

$$b_A - c_A \approx b_A' - c_A'$$

and

$$b_B - c_B \approx b_B' - c_B'$$

and finally that

$$\rho_1 > \rho_{1'}$$

then the two criteria are equivalent. Of course, these conditions would need a slightly extended formulation for games involving more that two initial nodes.

I now show this equivalence for the two node game g_1. A general proof of this claim requires somewhat tedious but similar algebra and is omitted. I first reproduce Figure 3.12 as Figure 3.16.

The risk dominance criterion requires that the product of the losses from unilateral deviation by each player from the relevant Nash equilibrium to an alternative Nash equilibrium be the largest. In the context of our example, if $\mathcal{A}$ deviates unilaterally from the desired equilibrium $(\varphi_1\varphi_1'', \sigma_1)$ to the other unsolicited equilibrium $(\varphi_1'\varphi_1, \sigma_1')$, that is, if he deviates unilaterally from the equilibrium strategy $(\varphi_1\varphi_1'')$ to the equilibrium strategy $(\varphi_1'\varphi_1)$, his loss from this deviation is:

$$[(\rho_1 b_A + \rho_{1'} c_A') - (\rho_1 a_A + \rho_{1'} b_A')]$$

If $\mathcal{B}$ deviates unilaterally in like manner, her loss is:

$$[(\rho_1 c_B + \rho_{1'} b_B') - (\rho_1 a_B + \rho_{1'} b_B')]$$

The product of these losses is then:

$$[(\rho_1 b_A + \rho_{1'} c'_A) - (\rho_1 a_A + \rho_{1'} b'_A)][(\rho_1 c_B + \rho_{1'} b'_B) - (\rho_1 a_B + \rho_{1'} b'_B)]$$

Similarly, the respective losses for $\mathcal{A}$ and $\mathcal{B}$ from unilateral deviation from the other unwanted equilibrium $(\varphi'_1\varphi_1, \sigma'_1)$ to the favored equilibrium $(\varphi_1\varphi''_1, \sigma_1)$ are:

$$[(\rho_1 c_A + \rho_{1'} b'_A) - (\rho_1 b_A + \rho_{1'} a'_A)]$$

and

$$[(\rho_1 b_B + \rho_{1'} c'_B) - (\rho_1 b_B + \rho_{1'} a'_B)]$$

and their product is:

$$[(\rho_1 c_A + \rho_{1'} b'_A) - (\rho_1 b_A + \rho_{1'} a'_A)][(\rho_1 b_B + \rho_{1'} c'_B) - (\rho_1 b_B + \rho_{1'} a'_B)]$$

Then if the Nash equilibrium $(\varphi_1\varphi''_1, \sigma_1)$ has to (strictly) risk dominate the Nash equilibrium $(\varphi'_1\varphi_1, \sigma'_1)$, it is required that the product of the losses for deviating from the desired equilibrium be greater than the product of the losses for deviating from the undesired equilibrium:

$$\begin{aligned}&[(\rho_1 b_A + \rho_{1'} c'_A) - (\rho_1 a_A + \rho_{1'} b'_A)][(\rho_1 c_B + \rho_{1'} b'_B) - (\rho_1 a_B + \rho_{1'} b'_B)]\\&\quad > [(\rho_1 c_A + \rho_{1'} b'_A) - (\rho_1 b_A + \rho_{1'} a'_A)][(\rho_1 b_B + \rho_{1'} c'_B) - (\rho_1 b_B + \rho_{1'} a'_B)]\end{aligned}$$

This simplifies to:

$$\begin{aligned}&\rho_1[\rho_1(b_A - a_A) + \rho_{1'}(c'_A - b'_A)](c_B - a_B))\\&\quad > \rho_{1'}[\rho_1(c_A - b_A) + \rho_{1'}(b'_A - a'_A)](c'_B - a'_B)) \qquad (3.3)\end{aligned}$$

and, by assuming the above equations among payoffs, to:

$$\rho_1 > \rho_{1'}$$

which is true.

Therefore, it seems that under fairly general conditions, we may use either Pareto dominance or risk dominance for games of partial information without any change in results. In fact, the Pareto criterion is more intuitive and conceptually simpler. However, these assumptions do *not* always hold: see section 5.2, footnote 2 for a situation in which the predictions of the two solution concepts *diverge*.

The general condition under which risk dominance of a Nash equilibrium holds is given by Equation 3.3, which is clearly different from the Pareto-Nash Inequalities below:

Case 1: Pareto-Nash Inequalities If either $\rho_1 a_A + \rho_{1'} b'_A > \rho_1 b_A + \rho_{1'} a'_A$ and $\rho_1 a_B + \rho_{1'} b'_B \geq \rho_1 b_B + \rho_{1'} a'_B$ or $\rho_1 a_A + \rho_{1'} b'_A \geq \rho_1 b_A + \rho_{1'} a'_A$ and $\rho_1 a_B + \rho_{1'} b'_B > \rho_1 b_B + \rho_{1'} a'_B$ then $(\varphi_1 \varphi''_1, \sigma_1)$ is the unique Pareto-Nash equilibrium.

Case 2: Pareto-Nash Inequalities If either $\rho_1 a_A + \rho_{1'} b'_A < \rho_1 b_A + \rho_{1'} a'_A$ and $\rho_1 a_B + \rho_{1'} b'_B \leq \rho_1 b_B + \rho_{1'} a'_B$ or $\rho_1 a_A + \rho_{1'} b'_A \leq \rho_1 b_A + \rho_{1'} a'_A$ and $\rho_1 a_B + \rho_{1'} b'_B < \rho_1 b_B + \rho_{1'} a'_B$ then $(\varphi'_1 \varphi_1, \sigma'_1)$ is the unique Pareto-Nash equilibrium.

Case 3: Mixed Strategy Equilibria If neither Case 1 nor Case 2 hold, then $(\varphi_1 \varphi''_1, \sigma_1)$ and $(\varphi'_1 \varphi_1, \sigma'_1)$ are both Pareto-Nash equilibria and a mixed strategy equilibrium is likely to be preferred instead (on grounds of salience, e.g., as we saw with G).

Thus, under the most general conditions, the two solution concepts make different predictions. The uniqueness of Pareto or payoff dominance does not imply and is not implied by the uniqueness of risk dominance. Is there an a priori reason for always preferring one to the other, or should we always choose the one that gives a solution in pure strategies, or, finally, is the preference itself *situated*, depending on the ambient situation u?

It does not appear that in situations involving communication there should be an a priori preference for either solution concept over the other. Perhaps pure strategy solutions are generally preferred to mixed strategy solutions, but it is difficult to justify this in cases of communication. One possibility is to use the fact that the payoffs from a mixed strategy equilibrium are generally less than the payoffs from a pure strategy equilibrium to argue that pure strategy solutions are to be preferred. Then, whichever solution concept yields such a pure solution should be used.[47] On the other hand, as I will show in section 5.2, all communication, whether literal or implicated, may be indeterminate and probabilistic. We have to conclude that solving a game of partial information is itself a situated activity, and that pure solutions may not always be better even if they yield higher equilibrium payoffs.

47. See footnote 5 in section 5.2.

There may also be room for an evolutionary argument here. It would be interesting to see if there are conditions under which agents gravitate to one or other concept over time and whether these conditions are independently justifiable.

In the rest of the book, I will continue to use the Pareto-Nash equilibrium concept with only an occasional pointer to risk dominance.

3.3.6 The "Glocal" Game

As was noted in section 3.3.4, it cannot be assumed that $g_1 = g_u(\varphi_1)$ is common knowledge or even partially shared *before* $\mathcal{A}$ has actually uttered φ_1 because there is no way for $\mathcal{B}$ to know what $\mathcal{A}$ is about to say. This introduces a slight wrinkle in the analysis of the utterance and interpretation of HARVEY in u and requires a *prior* game to be played by $\mathcal{A}$ in his head. The lexical game g_1 analyzed so far is called the *local* game to contrast it with this prior game that was earlier called the *global* game in Parikh (2001). I now call it a *"glocal"* game because the word "global" will be reserved for other purposes to be described in chapter 4 and "glocal" is a hybrid term that serves to remind us of its connection to local games.

Once $\mathcal{A}$ utters $\varphi_1 =$ HARVEY, it is clear that g_1 emerges into the open and possibly even becomes common knowledge between $\mathcal{A}$ and $\mathcal{B}$. But how does $\mathcal{A}$ come to the decision to say φ_1 in the first place?

The language $\mathcal{L}$ makes various locutions available to $\mathcal{A}$ to convey σ_1. One, obviously, is "Harvey," another, clearly, is the paraphrase "The film *Harvey*," and there are yet others. In general, given the finite nature of our agents, only a small handful of the full set of choices the language offers is considered. Since this choice set depends on the content σ_1 to be conveyed, we call it $C(\sigma_1)$. Then for every locution $\varphi_1^y \in C(\sigma_1)$, there is a corresponding local game $g_u(\varphi_1^y)$, where y stands for zero or more primes. So for $\varphi_1 \in C(\sigma_1)$, we have the game $g_u(\varphi_1)$ that we have already seen. Likewise, for $\varphi_1' \in C(\sigma_1)$, we would have the game $g_u(\varphi_1')$, and so on. The locution φ_1^y in $g_u(\varphi_1^y)$ is called the *primary* locution of $g_u(\varphi_1^y)$ as was remarked in section 3.2.

In section 3.2, I also noted that in the locution "The film *Harvey*" the word "film" is ambiguous as is "Harvey." Indeed, as will be argued later, even "the" is ambiguous. Therefore, the game $g_u(\varphi_1')$ will be a large game that simultaneously disambiguates all three sets of ambiguities. As will become clear in chapter 4, this game is a product of three smaller lexical games, one for each word in the phrase.

Incidentally, this should make fully clear the earlier statement in section 3.2 that when alternative locutions to the primary locution are considered in a game like $g_u(\varphi_1)$, only the ambiguity relating to the primary locution—what we may call the *primary ambiguity*—needs to be dealt with in *that* game. This is because other secondary ambiguities like the one in "film" are dealt with in other local games like $g_u(\varphi_1')$.

Returning to $\mathcal{A}$'s decision to utter φ_1, what happens is this: first $\mathcal{A}$ plays the *prior* glocal game corresponding to σ_1—call it G_1—in his head. This game involves the prior choices $C(\sigma_1)$ $\mathcal{A}$ considers for conveying σ_1 to $\mathcal{B}$. Each choice in $C(\sigma_1)$ leads to a local game $g_u(\varphi_1^y)$ and each local game has a *value*. For example, the value to $\mathcal{A}$ of $g_u(\varphi_1)$ is clearly $a_{\mathcal{A}}$ because this is the payoff he would actually receive if he were to utter φ_1 in u. So what $\mathcal{A}$ does is simply to choose the utterance with the greatest value in the glocal game. To make this choice, he is forced to consider all the local games that could arise from each possible choice. In our case, if we assume that $\mathcal{A}$'s only choices in $C(\sigma_1)$ are φ_1 and φ_1', then, since the latter is costlier, it will turn out that its value is less than the value $a_{\mathcal{A}}$ of uttering φ_1. This results in $\mathcal{A}$'s decision to utter φ_1.

Once $\mathcal{B}$ perceives this utterance, she (re)constructs $g_1 = g_u(\varphi_1)$ in her head, solves it, finds the unique equilibrium action she needs to perform, and then interprets $\mathcal{A}$'s utterance (as the film *Harvey*).

The various local games arising from $\mathcal{A}$'s wanting to convey σ_1 are embedded in the glocal game G_1. There is an important asymmetry in G_1. $\mathcal{B}$ gets to consider only one local game, the one constructed from $\mathcal{A}$'s optimal choice. $\mathcal{A}$, on the other hand, has to consider all the local games issuing from his choice set $C(\sigma_1)$ and then choose the best one. It is not possible or necessary for $\mathcal{B}$ to consider $C(\sigma_1)$.

There is a great deal more that could be said about games of partial information, especially about alternative ways they may be analyzed.[48] Implicit in what has been said so far is the claim and insight that every utterance situation can be modeled as a strategic interaction and possibly as a game of partial information.[49] Now that the basic tools of situation theory and game theory are in place, I describe the framework of equilibrium semantics in the next chapter.

48. For readers interested in the issue of using numbers versus algebraic symbols to capture payoffs and probabilities, I suggest consulting especially the first chapter of Pearl (1988). In any case, game theory is not really about the numbers; it is about the structure of strategic reasoning.

49. A game of partial information is just a strategic interaction where common knowledge obtains.

4 Equilibrium Semantics

Everything should be made as simple as possible, but not simpler.
—Albert Einstein

In chapter 1 I referred to the mainstream pipeline view of meaning: semantics first yields an *underspecified*, context-free, and conventional content that is subsequently filled in contextually by pragmatics. This primarily Gricean dictum stems from the decision to try to get as far as we can with just language by itself and bring in situations only when we fail to go all the way. While conventional meaning *is* required to get semiosis off the ground once language is established (as we saw with the Conventional Constraint for the name HARVEY in section 3.2), the growing consensus[1] is that this pipeline picture is progressively being shown to be inadequate. One reason why the Gricean framework (together with its many contemporary variants) has seemed ineluctable to many is that it comes across as being the only way to combine language and context and thereby gives rise to the semantics/pragmatics distinction itself—it appears to provide the *only* possible synthesis of semantics (i.e., language) and pragmatics (i.e., context).

In stark contrast, in equilibrium semantics the context of utterance drills down into the lowest lexical levels of sentences, making even so-called *literal* content thoroughly situated. Each word of a sentence in an utterance is associated with the context u and with a corresponding game, just as HARVEY was associated with $g_u(\text{HARVEY}) = g_u(\varphi_1) = g_1$. Thus, there are games $g_u(\text{IS}) = g_u(\varphi_2) = g_2$ and $g_u(\text{PLAYING}) = g_u(\varphi_3) = g_3$; moreover, as I hinted in chapter 3, these games are *interdependent*. Besides these lexical games, there are phrasal and sentential games, all of them together called *locutionary* games and the solutions they yield

1. See, for example, Recanati (2004b) and the articles in Horn and Ward (2004).

locutionary meanings. In addition, there are *illocutionary* games at lexical, phrasal, and sentential levels to enable access to *illocutionary* meanings.

Rather than a linear view with semantic meaning as primary and pragmatic meaning as secondary, the picture suggested by equilibrium semantics is one of mereological interdependence with context inextricably mixed in. Since context is not an afterthought in this framework, there is no question of any sort of underspecification. Only individual words have conventional meanings[2] and the rest is all mutually determined by *situated* language and choice in the full sense of the term.

While some readers may feel I am just proposing yet another view of the semantics/pragmatics distinction, the pervasive role of context and the interdependence among the parts of a sentence and their corresponding games, as well as between locutionary and illocutionary meanings and games, makes it very hard to see how my view bears any resemblance to the family of distinctions that are around today. The framework is best seen as a unification of semantics and pragmatics into a single domain and discipline as I advocated in chapter 1. In this sense, while it draws upon some of Grice's ideas—after all, he was one of the first philosophers to explicitly consider context—it offers a genuine nonlinear and mathematically worked out alternative to the Gricean synthesis of semantics and pragmatics.

4.1 Aspects of Meaning

The process of inferring the content of an utterance may broadly be described as *disambiguation* in its wider preferred sense of selecting one (or more) meanings from many as I said in chapter 1. While all disambiguations involve the same type of inference called a *strategic* inference[3] required for the solution of a game of partial information, it is useful to make finer discriminations.

Consider the following processes in recovering the content of an utterance:

1. Lexical and structural disambiguation (e.g., *Harvey is playing*; Harvey saw her duck)
2. Saturation (e.g., *He* is playing; Caitlin is taller [*than Harvey*])

2. Idiomatic constructions and related phenomena are beyond the scope of the book.

3. See Parikh (1987b) for the first use of this term.

3. Concept construction (e.g., Harvey is *young*)
4. Free enrichment or expansion or completion (e.g., Harvey is playing [*in New York*])
5. Inferring implicature (e.g., Harvey is playing $\hookrightarrow$ [*Let's go see it*])
6. Deriving direct and indirect illocutionary force (e.g., Harvey is playing $\rightsquigarrow$ [*statement*]; [*Let's go see it*] $\rightsquigarrow$ [*suggestion*])

Of course, this is not an exhaustive listing of all the processes involved. I include force as a component of meaning. The strategic inference involved in each process can be thought of as generating a partial content, all of them together yielding the full content of the utterance.[4] My goal in this chapter is to derive more or less the full meaning of φ in u as described in chapter 3 from first principles.

4.2 The Four Constraints

We saw in section 1.4.4 how language and its use may be viewed as a system of four (sets of) constraints. Later, in section 3.2, we saw a particular instance of three of these constraints, **C**, **I**, and **F**. Now we consider all four constraints in light of the entire sentence φ in u.

4.2.1 The Syntactic Constraint

As noted earlier, φ is made up of individual words and may be represented as $\varphi_1 \circ \varphi_2 \circ \varphi_3$. Recall from chapter 2 that $(\mathcal{L}, \circ)$ is a monoid.

φ has the following single parse tree:[5]

$$[_S \, [_{NP} \, \varphi_1] \circ [_{VP} \, [_V \, \varphi_2] \circ [_{VP} \, \varphi_3]]]$$

I call the set of syntactic structures for the sentences of $\mathcal{L}$ the *Syntactic Constraint* and label it **S**.

4.2.2 The Conventional Constraint

I assume *every* word in $\mathcal{L}$ is associated with one or more *conventional meanings*, either a property or relation. As we saw in section 3.2, the conventional meaning of HARVEY is denoted by $P^{Harvey} = P^{\varphi_1}$ and is

4. See Parikh (2006b) for an incipient sketch of the framework.

5. Equilibrium semantics is compatible with most syntactic theories. Many competing parses are available for any given sentence and I have made a more or less arbitrary choice with help from Robin Clark. Readers are free to use their preferred parses.

simply the property of being *named Harvey*. The verb IS has at least three conventional meanings that could be denoted by $P_1^{is} = P_1^{\varphi_2} = P^{=}$, $P_2^{is} = P_2^{\varphi_2} = P^{\epsilon}$, and $P_3^{is} = P_3^{\varphi_2} = P^{aux}$, the first being the sense involved in a sentence such as "Voltaire is Arouet" or "Batman is Bruce Wayne," the second being the sense involved in a sentence such as "Harvey is young," and the third being the sense operative in our example "Harvey is playing." I will restrict attention to just the third property $P^{aux} \equiv P_3^{\varphi_2} \equiv P^{\varphi_2}$ to keep things simple. PLAYING clearly has at least two conventional meanings, which we denote $P_1^{\varphi_3}$ and $P_2^{\varphi_3}$, the first being the sense *showing* (*in a theater*), and the second being the sense of *amusing* (*himself*).[6] These conventional associations of words are also collectively called the *conventional maps.*

As the term suggests, conventional meanings are conventional, that is, they are the sorts of meanings that can largely be found in a dictionary.[7] Of course, by this I mean the corresponding properties or relations, not the words themselves. It will be assumed that they are independent of the utterance situation *u* to keep things simple. In actual communication, a subset (or slight displacement) of the full range of conventional meanings is identified contextually via the utterance situation, but I will only address this complexity in section 7.1.2.

Only words have conventional meanings; phrases and sentences are conventionally meaningless unless we simply collect the properties associated with their constituent words and call the collection the conventional meaning of the complex expression. In either case, conventional meanings of phrases and sentences, if they are defined, are not required to derive their referential meaning.

How do conventional meanings of words arise? This is a rather complex matter, one that Grice (1968) attempted to tackle informally. He saw speaker meaning as primary and saw conventional meanings (of words and sentences) emerging as uniformities across utterances. Barwise and Perry (1983) largely endorsed this view of word meaning, but did not get any further in analyzing the phenomenon. My view is that this picture is correct, but is only half the story. The other half is that speaker meaning obviously depends on conventional meaning. In other words, like much else in equilibrium semantics, the process is "circular" and is gov-

6. Actually, PLAYING has several other conventional meanings but I will just ignore them here.

7. Largely, but not entirely. See section 7.1.2 for further discussion.

erned by an equilibrium or fixed point. More will be said about this problem in section 7.1.2.

In this book, I assume that the conventional meanings of words are given and use these conventional maps to derive the referential meanings or contents of utterances. I call the set of conventional meanings or "senses" for all the words in $\mathcal{L}$ the *Conventional Constraint* and label it **C**.

4.2.3 The Informational Constraint

It is assumed next that given a set of conventional maps for a word in $\mathcal{L}$ and given an utterance of the word (typically in the context of a sentence), we can map the word's conventional meanings into one or more infons that represent the *possible* contents or (referential) meanings of the word uttered. I call these the *informational maps*, and all of them together the *Informational Constraint* and label it **I**.

We can string the conventional and informational maps together for the words in φ as follows.

HARVEY:

- Referential use: $\varphi_1 \rightarrow P^{\varphi_1} \xrightarrow{u} \langle\!\langle e(P^{\varphi_1}, r_u) \mid Unique(P^{\varphi_1}, r_u, q_u) \rangle\!\rangle = \sigma_1$
- Referential use: $\varphi_1 \rightarrow P^{\varphi_1} \xrightarrow{u} \langle\!\langle e(P^{\varphi_1}, r_u') \mid Unique(P^{\varphi_1}, r_u', q_u') \rangle\!\rangle = \sigma_1'$

As we saw in section 3.2, there are two distinct resource situations r_u and r_u' connected with u, one relating to the film and the second to the boy. The film is the single object named Harvey in r_u and the son is the single object named Harvey in r_u'. The role of q_u and q_u' will be clarified in chapter 6 in the context of noun phrases generally.

Both uses of HARVEY are called *referential* and correspond to the ontological operation of instantiation introduced in section 2.4.

IS:

- Auxiliary use: $\varphi_2 \rightarrow P^{\varphi_2} \xrightarrow{u} \langle\!\langle t \mid (t \parallel t_u) \wedge t, t_u \in [t_0, t_\infty] \rangle\!\rangle = \sigma_2$

Here $P^{\varphi_2} \equiv P^{aux}$, the preferred conventional meaning for IS, is mapped into a conditioned temporal infon. This is a special type of map that applies when auxiliary verbs are involved and so does not belong with the more general ontological maps of section 2.4. So the special name *auxiliary use* is given to this way of deploying IS. The property $P^{\varphi_2} \equiv P^{aux}$ "disappears" from the resulting infon. As we saw in section 2.3.2, $t \parallel t_u$ means that the action conveyed by the verb temporally overlaps with the time of utterance. The only constraint on t_0 and t_∞ is that t_u belong to the interval $[t_0, t_\infty]$. σ_2 is defined here just as σ_1 and σ_1' were earlier.

I will not use the other two conventional meanings of IS to simplify the analysis.[8]

PLAYING:

- Predicative use: $\varphi_3 \rightarrow P_1^{\varphi_3} \xrightarrow{u} \langle\langle P_1^{\varphi_3} \rangle\rangle = \sigma_3$
- Predicative use: $\varphi_3 \rightarrow P_2^{\varphi_3} \xrightarrow{u} \langle\langle P_2^{\varphi_3} \rangle\rangle = \sigma_3'$

Here there are two conventional senses of PLAYING, each involved in a predicative use. They correspond to the ontological operation of identity in section 2.4.

Several observations are in order. Implicit in the instances of **C** and **I** listed above is a *theory* of noun and verb phrases. I will deal with noun phrases explicitly in chapter 6; here I simply take it as a postulate that this is how these categories of words work. This is one area where variant theories are possible: this is why I said equilibrium semantics was a *framework* that was compatible with different *theories*. The important thing for the framework is that the two maps provide appropriate infons as the possible contents of the words in an utterance.

The value of the conventional map is the conventional meaning, and the value of the informational map is the referential meaning. When the latter is clear from the context, I will refer to it as just the meaning (or content). What the two maps together give us is the possible (referential) meanings of the words in an utterance. Conventional meaning and referential meaning are intended as generalizations or refinements of the traditional distinctions between intension and extension, or connotation and denotation, or sense and reference.

Some contents (like σ_1 and σ_1') make a reference to resource situations. When accessible, these situations enable the identification of the object(s) being referred to. When not accessible, all that an addressee can infer is that some inaccessible resource situation that identifies the referent(s) exists. This issue will become clearer in chapter 6.

8. I list the two omitted instances for completeness:

- Predicative use: $\varphi_2 \rightarrow P_1^{\varphi_2} \xrightarrow{u} \langle\langle P_1^{\varphi_2}; (t \mid t \parallel t_u) \rangle\rangle = \sigma_2'$
- Membership use: $\varphi_2 \rightarrow P_2^{\varphi_2} \xrightarrow{u} \langle\langle t \mid t \parallel t_u \rangle\rangle = \sigma_2''$

In the second case, which is given a special name as it identifies another special map, the relevant property also "disappears" from the resulting infon. Incidentally, these are the possible meanings of IS, something Bill Clinton wondered about during his presidency.

Lexical ambiguity can involve either the conventional map or the informational map, an important fact that is often obscured. In the case of IS and PLAYING, lexical ambiguity involves the conventional map; in the case of HARVEY, it involves the informational map. This observation plays an important role in the theory of noun phrases described later.

Note that the *u* above the second arrow in all the maps above indicates that each word has to be uttered in some situation in order for it to have one or more contents. Without being uttered, it remains inert and carries a conventional meaning but no referential meaning. As I said in chapter 1, this is a basic fact that is often simply ignored.

I now check that these lexical contents combine in the expected way. Consider the two examples below:

$$\sigma_2 \odot_u \sigma_3 = \langle\!\langle t \mid (t \parallel t_u) \wedge t, t_u \in [t_0, t_\infty] \rangle\!\rangle \odot_u \langle\!\langle P_1^{\varphi_3} \rangle\!\rangle$$

$$= \langle\!\langle P_1^{\varphi_3}; t \mid (t \parallel t_u) \wedge t, t_u \in [t_0, t_\infty] \rangle\!\rangle$$

$$\sigma^{\ell} = \sigma_1 \odot_u (\sigma_2 \odot_u \sigma_3)$$

$$= \langle\!\langle e(P^{\varphi_1}, r_u) \mid Unique(P^{\varphi_1}, r_u, q_u) \rangle\!\rangle$$

$$\odot_u \langle\!\langle P_1^{\varphi_3}; t \mid (t \parallel t_u) \wedge t, t_u \in [t_0, t_\infty] \rangle\!\rangle$$

$$= \langle\!\langle P_1^{\varphi_3}; e(P^{\varphi_1}, r_u) \mid Unique(P^{\varphi_1}, r_u, q_u);$$

$$t \mid (t \parallel t_u) \wedge t, t_u \in [t_0, t_\infty] \rangle\!\rangle$$

$$= \langle\!\langle P_1^{\varphi_3}; a; t \mid (t \parallel t_u) \wedge t, t_u \in [t_0, t_\infty] \rangle\!\rangle$$

Roughly, all the second-last complex-looking expression says is that the film *Harvey* denoted by *a* is playing at the time of utterance. Both instances of unification involved the first case of Ordinary Merging from section 2.3.3.

Where do informational maps and the Informational Constraint come from? They correspond to the ontological maps introduced in section 2.4. Each category of word is associated with certain ontological maps. Grammar and the logical structure of the world jointly constrain the uses of words in fundamental ways. However, a philosophical *theory* is required to say why a particular map occurs with a particular category of word. I take **I** as given in this book. A basic assumption of equilibrium

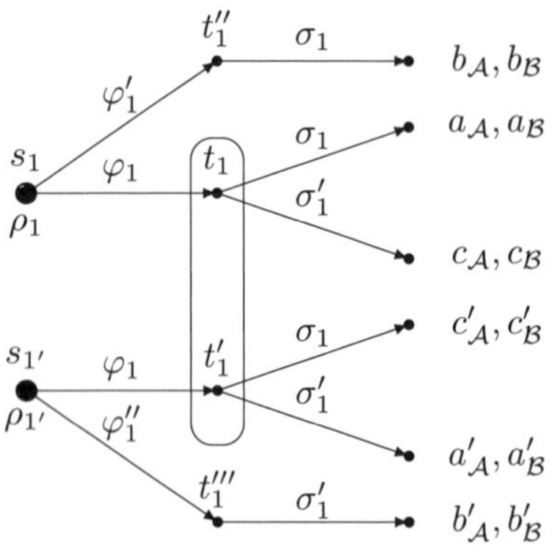

Figure 4.1
Algebraic version of lexical game $g_1 = g_u(\varphi_1)$

semantics is that **C** and **I** govern the uses of all words relative to some utterance situation u.

4.2.4 The Flow Constraint

The next constraint, labeled **F** for the *Flow Constraint*, enables us to derive games of partial information from the material obtained from the instances of **C** and **I** above and from basic principles of action and situated choice, as we saw in chapter 3.

Lexical Games Figure 3.11 is reproduced here as Figure 4.1. The emergence of this game from u and G should now be clear.

In section 3.2 where I first introduced this game, I said a little glibly that ρ_1 and $\rho_{1'}$ are the probabilities that $\mathcal{A}$ is conveying (or referring to) σ_1 and $\sigma_{1'}$ in s_1 and $s_{1'}$ but things are not quite so simple.

Let $P(x)$ be the probability that $\mathcal{A}$ is conveying the infon x. This is a slight abuse of notation since I do not mean the probability of x by $P(x)$ but the probability that $\mathcal{A}$ is conveying x (or that $\mathcal{A}$ intends to convey x).

Let x_i stand for the possible contents σ_i^y of φ_i, where y stands for zero or more primes. That is, x_1 is either σ_1 or σ_1', x_2 is just σ_2, and x_3 is either σ_3 or σ_3'. Then the probability at an initial node for a lexical game is not just $\rho_i = P(\sigma_i)$ for example,[9] as I have been pretending so far, but it is really the conditional probability $P(\sigma_i \mid x_{-i}, \overline{s_i})$, where x_{-i} are the possible contents of words in φ other than those corresponding to x_i and $\overline{s_i} =$

9. Or $\rho_{i^y} = P(\sigma_i^y)$ more generally.

$s_i \cap s_{i'} \cap s_{i''} \cap \cdots = \bigcap s_{i^y}$. Since $\bigcap s_{i^y} = u$, the conditional probability expression can be rewritten as $P(\sigma_i \,|\, x_{-i}, u)$, replacing $\bar{s_i}$ by u. In plain English, this is read as the conditional probability that $\mathcal{A}$ is conveying the content σ_i given that $\mathcal{A}$ is conveying the other possible contents x_{-i} and given the utterance situation u.

Thus, $\rho_1 = P(\sigma_1 \,|\, x_{-1}, u) = P(\sigma_1 \,|\, x_2, x_3, u)$ involves the two cases $P(\sigma_1 \,|\, \sigma_2, \sigma_3, u)$ and $P(\sigma_1 \,|\, \sigma_2, \sigma_3', u)$ based on the different possible values of the conditioning variables. So, for this sentence, under the simplifying assumptions I have made regarding the conventional meanings of IS and PLAYING, there are two possible values for ρ_1. In general, of course, $P(\sigma_1 \,|\, \sigma_2, \sigma_3, u) \neq P(\sigma_1 \,|\, \sigma_2, \sigma_3', u)$. Likewise, $\rho_{1'} = P(\sigma_1' \,|\, x_{-1}, u) = P(\sigma_1' \,|\, x_2, x_3, u)$, which involves the same two cases $P(\sigma_1' \,|\, \sigma_2, \sigma_3, u)$ and $P(\sigma_1' \,|\, \sigma_2, \sigma_3', u)$.

Needless to say, we require that $\rho_1 + \rho_{1'} = 1$, taking care to use exactly the same conditioning variables for both conditional probabilities. It may be, for example, that $P(\sigma_1 \,|\, \sigma_2, \sigma_3, u) = 0.9$. Then we must have $P(\sigma_1' \,|\, \sigma_2, \sigma_3, u) = 1 - 0.9 = 0.1$. Intuitively, the first probability is high because the content σ_1, which corresponds to the film *Harvey*, is conditioned by σ_3, which corresponds to the sense of PLAYING involving *showing in a theater*. Similarly, $P(\sigma_1 \,|\, \sigma_2, \sigma_3', u) + P(\sigma_1' \,|\, \sigma_2, \sigma_3', u) = 1$, where the first probability may be 0.2 and the second, therefore, 0.8.

Since there are two possible values for ρ_1 (either $P(\sigma_1 \,|\, \sigma_2, \sigma_3, u)$ or $P(\sigma_1 \,|\, \sigma_2, \sigma_3', u)$), *the game* g_1 *involves a choice not just of utterance and interpretation but also of the initial probability*. Indeed, it is not just that there are two possible values for ρ_1, there are two possible *initial probability distributions* for the game g_1. This is because ρ_1 and $\rho_{1'}$ together specify a distribution (their sum is 1), and since there are two values for ρ_1 and two corresponding values for $\rho_{1'}$, there are actually two distributions associated with the game g_1, with $P(\sigma_1 \,|\, \sigma_2, \sigma_3, u) + P(\sigma_1' \,|\, \sigma_2, \sigma_3, u) = 1$ for one distribution and $P(\sigma_1 \,|\, \sigma_2, \sigma_3', u) + P(\sigma_1' \,|\, \sigma_2, \sigma_3', u) = 1$ for the second. So the speaker and addressee are both faced with this additional choice, the choice of one of these distributions from the two available.

It is easy to see that $P(\sigma_1 \,|\, \sigma_2, \sigma_3, u) > P(\sigma_1' \,|\, \sigma_2, \sigma_3, u)$ because all the conditioning variables—u and σ_3 in particular—push in the same direction. u supports the background game G and in attending to this, the probability on the left is pushed upward. $\sigma_3 = \langle\!\langle P_1^{\varphi_3} \rangle\!\rangle$ also pushes upward because the interpretation of *showing in a theater* reinforces the interpretation of HARVEY as the film (i.e., σ_1) rather than as the boy (i.e., σ_1'). Since there is upward pressure from all conditioning variables (σ_2 has no effect), we can say that $P(\sigma_1 \mid \sigma_2, \sigma_3, u) > P(\sigma_1' \mid \sigma_2, \sigma_3, u)$ for the first distribution.

However, the situation is less straightforward with the other distribution. Is $P(\sigma_1 \mid \sigma_2, \sigma_3', u)$ greater or is $P(\sigma_1' \mid \sigma_2, \sigma_3', u)$? Here, it is clear that u pushes upward on the former probability as before (i.e., the interpretation σ_1 of HARVEY as the film is preferred), but now σ_3' (i.e., the meaning *amusing oneself*) pushes in the opposite direction, favoring σ_1' (i.e., the interpretation of HARVEY as the boy). Indeed, it is even arguable that this latter push outweighs the former since the combination of meanings σ_1 and σ_3' is somewhat incoherent. So we are forced to conclude that in fact $P(\sigma_1' \mid \sigma_2, \sigma_3', u) > P(\sigma_1 \mid \sigma_2, \sigma_3', u)$.

The agents therefore face a two-level optimization problem. At the first level, they either assume that $\rho_1 > \rho_{1'}$ (i.e., they consider the first distribution above) and then solve the game to get the Pareto-Nash equilibrium involving φ_1 and σ_1 (i.e., $(\varphi_1\varphi_1'', \sigma_1)$) as before *or* they assume the opposite values $\rho_1 < \rho_{1'}$ (i.e., they consider the second distribution) and then solve the game to get the Pareto-Nash equilibrium involving φ_1 and σ_1' (i.e., $(\varphi_1'\varphi_1, \sigma_1')$). Earlier in section 3.2, both these equilibria were Nash equilibria. Now, because there are two different assumptions about the initial probabilities, that is, there are two different distributions from which one has to be selected, they are both Pareto-Nash equilibria as well, each corresponding to one of the distributions. This is reasonable since, in a sense, two different versions of g_1 are being considered by the agents, one involving $\rho_1 > \rho_{1'}$ and the other involving $\rho_1 < \rho_{1'}$.

At the second level, they make a choice about which assumption or inequality is the right one, that is, they solve for the optimal probability distribution, either $P(\sigma_1 \mid \sigma_2, \sigma_3, u)$ (and its complement) or $P(\sigma_1 \mid \sigma_2, \sigma_3', u)$ (and its complement), or more crudely, they solve for whether ρ_1 is *high* or *low* (e.g., whether it is 0.9 or 0.2 in the numerical example above).[10] Of course, if both sets of conditioning variables had identical rather than opposite effects, that is, if both inequalities were identical rather than inverses, then the second level choice problem becomes trivial since it is the inequality that matters and not the precise value.

At the level of g_1 alone, there is no way for the agents to solve the second level of this problem. Locally, both equilibria are acceptable because the underlying probability distributions satisfy different inequalities. (If

10. Selecting the optimal value for ρ_1 automatically sets the value of $\rho_{1'}$ since the two form a distribution, so the agents need to select just the equilibrium value for one of these two probabilities.

both inequalities had been identical, then this problem is trivial as I said and, in this special case, it can be solved locally.)

I have simplified the foregoing analysis somewhat by focusing exclusively on the relationship between probabilities. In the most general case, the payoffs would have to be brought in and we would have to check which of the Pareto-Nash Inequalities held. Earlier, in section 3.2, I had made the simplifying assumption that $a_A - b_A \approx a'_A - b'_A$ and $a_B - b_B \approx a'_B - b'_B$ (Equations 3.1 and 3.2). If this were true, our argument above would go through without modification.

The main points being made here, however, are that a two-tier equilibrium problem is involved in solving g_1, and an equilibrium involves not two but *three* things: the equilibrium utterance, the equilibrium interpretation, *and* the equilibrium probability distribution. The fact that the initial probability distribution is a choice variable itself is a new feature of games and gives rise to an extended notion of equilibrium. We will see presently how this third variable can also be selected strategically in a way that all three choice variables—utterances, interpretations, and initial probability distributions—are in equilibrium in the extended sense we require. For the moment, I call this extended equilibrium a *global* equilibrium.

It is important to clarify that having to *choose* the equilibrium probability distribution at the initial nodes does *not* mean that these initial probabilities are arbitrary. As we saw in section 3.3.3, there are many sources of these distributions—subjective and objective, linguistic and contextual. What is being said now is that it is not the probabilities themselves that are fixed by these sources, but the *set of choices* available to the agent that is externally (i.e., with respect to g_1 and other such games) given. The strategic selection of the equilibrium probability distribution from among these choices (e.g., *high* or *low* for ρ_1) is endogenous.

Another important clarification is that since the initial probability distributions have to be optimally selected internally by the agents, there is just *one* game g_1 and not two. One way to think about it is to take g_1 as having two *versions*, as I wrote above, but even this is not fully satisfactory.

I now consider the game corresponding to the second word φ_2 in the utterance. I noted in the previous section that IS actually has three conventional meanings and therefore three possible referential meanings, but I chose to keep things simple and ignore two of them, retaining just the relevant option. This implies that there is no real choice involved as there

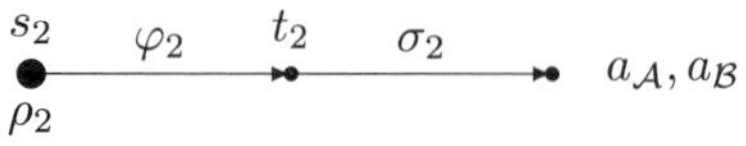

Figure 4.2
Algebraic version of lexical game $g_2 = g_u(\varphi_2)$

is only one infon to choose from and so we get the trivial game in Figure 4.2.

The initial situation in which $\mathcal{A}$ utters φ_2 is s_2, and it contains u (just as s_1 did) together with the appropriate intention to convey the meaning of φ_2 in u, namely σ_2. The situation that results from this action is t_2, and it leads to an interpretive action σ_2 by $\mathcal{B}$. Following this is the single outcome of the game. I have retained the same payoffs here as in g_1 for successful communication (with a less costly utterance). There is no reason to think the agents would have different payoffs for different parts of the utterance. After all, their goals are to convey and interpret the whole meaning.

Following our discussion above, $\rho_2 = P(\sigma_2 \mid x_{-2}, u) = P(\sigma_2 \mid x_1, x_3, u) = 1$, since it is the only initial probability. Strictly speaking, the conditioning variable should be $\overline{s_2} = s_2$ and not u, but since the only difference between the two is the intention in s_2 to convey σ_2, which is, in any case, invisible to the addressee, we can set $s_2 \approx u$ when considering such probabilities. There are actually four different combinations of conditioning variables, two for x_1 and two for x_3, resulting in four distinct probability distributions. But in this special case, they have no effect on the conditioned variable and are all identical.

This game has the obvious solution of $\mathcal{A}$ uttering φ_2 and $\mathcal{B}$ interpreting the utterance as σ_2 at the "first" level. Since the game is trivial, the choice of the initial probability distribution as a strategic variable at the "second" level is also trivial. It is because this game is special that we are able to compute its global equilibrium locally, that is, without recourse to anything outside g_2.

Incidentally, if we had taken all three possible meanings of IS into account, we would have gotten a much larger game involving *three* initial situations instead of the single situation s_2 and a correspondingly larger tree. Though, in general, the four probability distributions would then *not* have been identical, in this case, they do turn out to be the same because the favored meaning of IS remains so through all the four combinations of x_1 and x_3. Likewise, in general, the global equilibrium would *not* have been computable locally but in this case it turns out to be possible

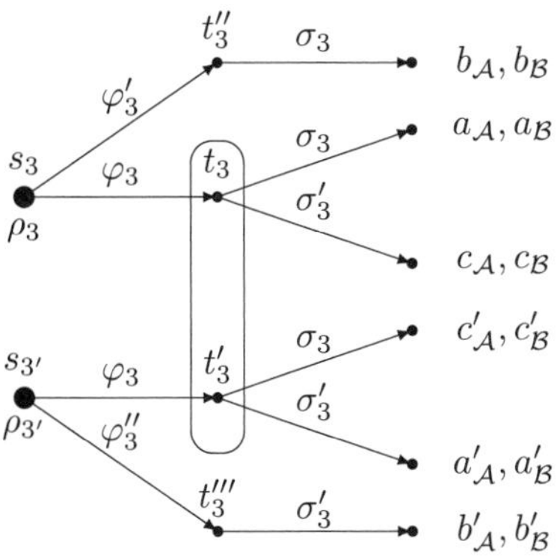

Figure 4.3
Algebraic version of lexical game $g_3 = g_u(\varphi_3)$

because the relevant initial probability ρ_2 remains the highest through all the combinations of x_1 and x_3. It is instructive to write out these four distributions explicitly for this larger game and I do so below. The number of probability distributions for g_1 and g_3 also increase because the number of combinations of conditioning variables would go up.

Since $\varphi_3 =$ PLAYING has two possible contents, σ_3 and σ_3', it should be relatively straightforward to see the genesis of $g_3 = g_u(\varphi_3)$ in Figure 4.3.

The strategic issues that arise in this game are mirror images of the ones in g_1. In particular, there is the same two-tiered equilibrium problem requiring a global solution. In addition to the choice of utterance and interpretation, the agents have to choose between two values of ρ_3, either $P(\sigma_3 \mid \sigma_1, \sigma_2, u)$ or $P(\sigma_3 \mid \sigma_1', \sigma_2, u)$, that is, they have to choose between two distributions as in g_1. In this case, too, the inequalities happen to be inverses, so the choice is not a trivial one. Again, crudely put, the agents have to make a choice between *high* and *low* for ρ_3.

Just to be certain that the presence of multiple probability distributions at the initial nodes of each lexical game is crystal clear, I display these again in a more visually accessible form. Remember that the general form of these three sets of distributions is $P(x_i \mid x_{-i}, u)$ for $i = 1, 2, 3$.

1. For g_1:

$$\rho_1 = \begin{cases} P(\sigma_1 \mid \sigma_2, \sigma_3, u) & \text{if } x_2 = \sigma_2 \text{ and } x_3 = \sigma_3 \\ P(\sigma_1 \mid \sigma_2, \sigma_3', u) & \text{if } x_2 = \sigma_2 \text{ and } x_3 = \sigma_3' \end{cases}$$

$$\rho_{1'} = \begin{cases} P(\sigma_1' \mid \sigma_2, \sigma_3, u) & \text{if } x_2 = \sigma_2 \text{ and } x_3 = \sigma_3 \\ P(\sigma_1' \mid \sigma_2, \sigma_3', u) & \text{if } x_2 = \sigma_2 \text{ and } x_3 = \sigma_3' \end{cases}$$

$\rho_1 + \rho_{1'} = 1$

$\rho_1 > \rho_{1'}$ if $x_2 = \sigma_2$ and $x_3 = \sigma_3$

$\rho_1 < \rho_{1'}$ if $x_2 = \sigma_2$ and $x_3 = \sigma_3'$

2. For g_2:

$$\rho_2 = \begin{cases} P(\sigma_2 \mid \sigma_1, \sigma_3, u) & \text{if } x_1 = \sigma_1 \text{ and } x_3 = \sigma_3 \\ P(\sigma_2 \mid \sigma_1, \sigma_3', u) & \text{if } x_1 = \sigma_1 \text{ and } x_3 = \sigma_3' \\ P(\sigma_2 \mid \sigma_1', \sigma_3, u) & \text{if } x_1 = \sigma_1' \text{ and } x_3 = \sigma_3 \\ P(\sigma_2 \mid \sigma_1', \sigma_3', u) & \text{if } x_1 = \sigma_1' \text{ and } x_3 = \sigma_3' \end{cases}$$

$\rho_2 = 1$

3. For g_3:

$$\rho_3 = \begin{cases} P(\sigma_3 \mid \sigma_1, \sigma_2, u) & \text{if } x_1 = \sigma_1 \text{ and } x_2 = \sigma_2 \\ P(\sigma_3 \mid \sigma_1', \sigma_2, u) & \text{if } x_1 = \sigma_1' \text{ and } x_2 = \sigma_2 \end{cases}$$

$$\rho_{3'} = \begin{cases} P(\sigma_3' \mid \sigma_1, \sigma_2, u) & \text{if } x_1 = \sigma_1 \text{ and } x_2 = \sigma_2 \\ P(\sigma_3' \mid \sigma_1', \sigma_2, u) & \text{if } x_1 = \sigma_1' \text{ and } x_2 = \sigma_2 \end{cases}$$

$\rho_3 + \rho_{3'} = 1$

$\rho_3 > \rho_{3'}$ if $x_1 = \sigma_1$ and $x_2 = \sigma_2$

$\rho_3 < \rho_{3'}$ if $x_1 = \sigma_1'$ and $x_2 = \sigma_2$

If we had considered the other two meanings for IS, then there would have been more combinations of *conditioning* variables to consider for g_1 and g_3 as well as more *conditioned* variables to consider for g_2 via other possibilities for x_2. I now display the distributions for the three lexical games taking the other two meanings of IS into account. The second and third initial probabilities for the second and third initial nodes in g_2 are $\rho_{2'}$ and $\rho_{2''}$ corresponding to the other two meanings σ_2' and σ_2'' for IS mentioned in footnote 8 in this chapter.

1. For g_1:

$$\rho_1 = \begin{cases} P(\sigma_1 \mid \sigma_2, \sigma_3, u) & \text{if } x_2 = \sigma_2 \text{ and } x_3 = \sigma_3 \\ P(\sigma_1 \mid \sigma_2', \sigma_3, u) & \text{if } x_2 = \sigma_2' \text{ and } x_3 = \sigma_3 \\ P(\sigma_1 \mid \sigma_2'', \sigma_3, u) & \text{if } x_2 = \sigma_2'' \text{ and } x_3 = \sigma_3 \\ P(\sigma_1 \mid \sigma_2, \sigma_3', u) & \text{if } x_2 = \sigma_2 \text{ and } x_3 = \sigma_3' \\ P(\sigma_1 \mid \sigma_2', \sigma_3', u) & \text{if } x_2 = \sigma_2' \text{ and } x_3 = \sigma_3' \\ P(\sigma_1 \mid \sigma_2'', \sigma_3', u) & \text{if } x_2 = \sigma_2'' \text{ and } x_3 = \sigma_3' \end{cases}$$

$$\rho_{1'} = \begin{cases} P(\sigma_1' \mid \sigma_2, \sigma_3, u) & \text{if } x_2 = \sigma_2 \text{ and } x_3 = \sigma_3 \\ P(\sigma_1' \mid \sigma_2', \sigma_3, u) & \text{if } x_2 = \sigma_2' \text{ and } x_3 = \sigma_3 \\ P(\sigma_1' \mid \sigma_2'', \sigma_3, u) & \text{if } x_2 = \sigma_2'' \text{ and } x_3 = \sigma_3 \\ P(\sigma_1' \mid \sigma_2, \sigma_3', u) & \text{if } x_2 = \sigma_2 \text{ and } x_3 = \sigma_3' \\ P(\sigma_1' \mid \sigma_2', \sigma_3', u) & \text{if } x_2 = \sigma_2' \text{ and } x_3 = \sigma_3' \\ P(\sigma_1' \mid \sigma_2'', \sigma_3', u) & \text{if } x_2 = \sigma_2'' \text{ and } x_3 = \sigma_3' \end{cases}$$

$$\rho_1 + \rho_{1'} = 1$$

$$\rho_1 > \rho_{1'} \quad \text{if } x_2 = \sigma_2 \text{ or } \sigma_2' \text{ or } \sigma_2'' \text{ and } x_3 = \sigma_3$$

$$\rho_1 < \rho_{1'} \quad \text{if } x_2 = \sigma_2 \text{ or } \sigma_2' \text{ or } \sigma_2'' \text{ and } x_3 = \sigma_3'$$

2. For g_2:

$$\rho_2 = \begin{cases} P(\sigma_2 \mid \sigma_1, \sigma_3, u) & \text{if } x_1 = \sigma_1 \text{ and } x_3 = \sigma_3 \\ P(\sigma_2 \mid \sigma_1, \sigma_3', u) & \text{if } x_1 = \sigma_1 \text{ and } x_3 = \sigma_3' \\ P(\sigma_2 \mid \sigma_1', \sigma_3, u) & \text{if } x_1 = \sigma_1' \text{ and } x_3 = \sigma_3 \\ P(\sigma_2 \mid \sigma_1', \sigma_3', u) & \text{if } x_1 = \sigma_1' \text{ and } x_3 = \sigma_3' \end{cases}$$

$$\rho_{2'} = \begin{cases} P(\sigma_2' \mid \sigma_1, \sigma_3, u) & \text{if } x_1 = \sigma_1 \text{ and } x_3 = \sigma_3 \\ P(\sigma_2' \mid \sigma_1, \sigma_3', u) & \text{if } x_1 = \sigma_1 \text{ and } x_3 = \sigma_3' \\ P(\sigma_2' \mid \sigma_1', \sigma_3, u) & \text{if } x_1 = \sigma_1' \text{ and } x_3 = \sigma_3 \\ P(\sigma_2' \mid \sigma_1', \sigma_3', u) & \text{if } x_1 = \sigma_1' \text{ and } x_3 = \sigma_3' \end{cases}$$

$$\rho_{2''} = \begin{cases} P(\sigma_2'' \mid \sigma_1, \sigma_3, u) & \text{if } x_1 = \sigma_1 \text{ and } x_3 = \sigma_3 \\ P(\sigma_2'' \mid \sigma_1, \sigma_3', u) & \text{if } x_1 = \sigma_1 \text{ and } x_3 = \sigma_3' \\ P(\sigma_2'' \mid \sigma_1', \sigma_3, u) & \text{if } x_1 = \sigma_1' \text{ and } x_3 = \sigma_3 \\ P(\sigma_2'' \mid \sigma_1', \sigma_3', u) & \text{if } x_1 = \sigma_1' \text{ and } x_3 = \sigma_3' \end{cases}$$

$$\rho_2 + \rho_{2'} + \rho_{2''} = 1$$

$$\rho_2 > \rho_{2'} \approx \rho_{2''} \quad \text{if } x_1 = \sigma_1 \text{ or } \sigma_1' \text{ and } x_3 = \sigma_3 \text{ or } \sigma_3'$$

3. For g_3:

$$\rho_3 = \begin{cases} P(\sigma_3 \mid \sigma_1, \sigma_2, u) & \text{if } x_1 = \sigma_1 \text{ and } x_2 = \sigma_2 \\ P(\sigma_3 \mid \sigma_1, \sigma_2', u) & \text{if } x_1 = \sigma_1 \text{ and } x_2 = \sigma_2' \\ P(\sigma_3 \mid \sigma_1, \sigma_2'', u) & \text{if } x_1 = \sigma_1 \text{ and } x_2 = \sigma_2'' \\ P(\sigma_3 \mid \sigma_1', \sigma_2, u) & \text{if } x_1 = \sigma_1' \text{ and } x_2 = \sigma_2 \\ P(\sigma_3 \mid \sigma_1', \sigma_2', u) & \text{if } x_1 = \sigma_1' \text{ and } x_2 = \sigma_2' \\ P(\sigma_3 \mid \sigma_1', \sigma_2'', u) & \text{if } x_1 = \sigma_1' \text{ and } x_2 = \sigma_2'' \end{cases}$$

$$\rho_{3'} = \begin{cases} P(\sigma_3' \mid \sigma_1, \sigma_2, u) & \text{if } x_1 = \sigma_1 \text{ and } x_2 = \sigma_2 \\ P(\sigma_3' \mid \sigma_1, \sigma_2', u) & \text{if } x_1 = \sigma_1 \text{ and } x_2 = \sigma_2' \\ P(\sigma_3' \mid \sigma_1, \sigma_2'', u) & \text{if } x_1 = \sigma_1 \text{ and } x_2 = \sigma_2'' \\ P(\sigma_3' \mid \sigma_1', \sigma_2, u) & \text{if } x_1 = \sigma_1' \text{ and } x_2 = \sigma_2 \\ P(\sigma_3' \mid \sigma_1', \sigma_2', u) & \text{if } x_1 = \sigma_1' \text{ and } x_2 = \sigma_2' \\ P(\sigma_3' \mid \sigma_1', \sigma_2'', u) & \text{if } x_1 = \sigma_1' \text{ and } x_2 = \sigma_2'' \end{cases}$$

$$\rho_3 + \rho_{3'} = 1$$

$$\rho_3 > \rho_{3'} \quad \text{if } x_1 = \sigma_1 \text{ and } x_2 = \sigma_2 \text{ or } \sigma_2' \text{ or } \sigma_2''$$

$$\rho_3 < \rho_{3'} \quad \text{if } x_1 = \sigma_1' \text{ and } x_2 = \sigma_2 \text{ or } \sigma_2' \text{ or } \sigma_2''$$

As mentioned earlier, ρ_2 dominates $\rho_{2'}$ and $\rho_{2''}$ irrespective of the values of x_1 and x_3, so g_2 is still solvable locally and yields σ_2, the expected meaning of IS, as its solution.

The circular and two-level nature of global equilibrium should now already be clearly visible: the choice of the optimal probability distribution in each game depends on which contents are optimal in the other two games as these condition the distributions, and the choice of the optimal content in each game depends on the optimal distribution in that game. This will be amplified further below.

This completes our discussion of lexical games. Similar lexical games can be formed for each word in any utterance. For a general sentence $\varphi = \varphi_1 \circ \cdots \circ \varphi_n$ uttered in some utterance situation u, the corresponding lexical games are denoted by $g(\varphi_i, u) = g_u(\varphi_i) = g_i$.

Phrasal and Sentential Games We turn now to phrasal and sentential games. These higher-level molecular games are built from atomic lexical games by defining a product operation $\otimes$ on the space of games of partial information. That is, we generate the set of partial information games $\mathcal{G}$ by starting with the set of lexical games (with a fixed u) and multiplying them with one another. This is exactly how the monoid $(\mathcal{L}, \circ)$ was generated, by concatenating words to form phrases and sentences. Indeed, I will show later in this chapter that there is an intimate connection between $(\mathcal{L}, \circ)$ and $(\mathcal{G}, \otimes)$. A relatively simple product of g_2 and g_3 is shown in Figure 4.4.

Since there is just one initial situation s_2 in g_2 and there are two initial situations s_3 and $s_{3'}$ in g_3, the product has $1 \times 2 = 2$ initial situations $s_{23} = s_2 \cup s_3$ and $s_{23'} = s_2 \cup s_{3'}$. That is, the initial situations of the prod-

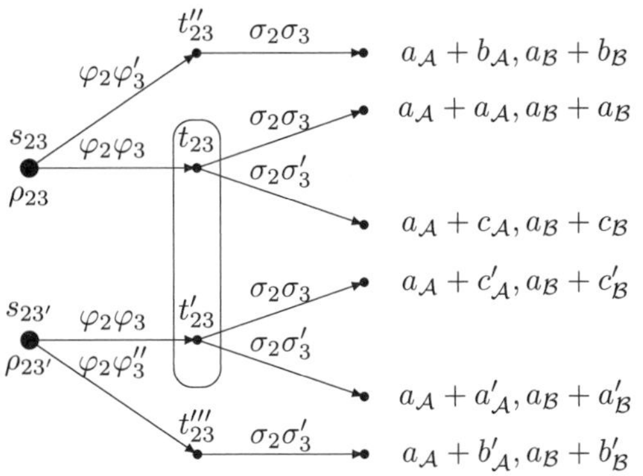

Figure 4.4
The phrasal game $g_{23} = g_2 \otimes g_3$

uct game g_{23} are just the unions of the corresponding initial situations in the component games. What these unions achieve is the combination of the intentions to convey σ_2 and σ_3 or σ_2 and σ'_3, or by distributivity, they result in the intentions to convey $\sigma_2 \odot_u \sigma_3$ or $\sigma_2 \odot_u \sigma'_3$. To save space, as we saw in chapter 2, these infon products can be abbreviated to $\sigma_2\sigma_3$ and $\sigma_2\sigma'_3$, as shown in Figure 4.4. Further, in these initial situations, the choices $\mathcal{A}$ has also combine and distribute in the right way. In s_{23}, for example, $\mathcal{A}$ can choose to utter φ_2 and φ_3 or, in other words, $\mathcal{A}$ can choose the *phrase* $\varphi_2 \circ \varphi_3 = \varphi_2\varphi_3$ as shown. $\mathcal{B}$'s choices also arise in a similar way. The shape of the tree follows in a natural way from taking all possible relevant combinations of nodes and branches into account. The payoffs involve the corresponding arithmetical sums because the agents receive the corresponding payoffs from each component game since they engage in combined actions from both games. The corresponding payoff inequalities are also preserved as follows:

$$a_{\mathcal{A}} + a_{\mathcal{A}} > a_{\mathcal{A}} + b_{\mathcal{A}} > a_{\mathcal{A}} + c_{\mathcal{A}}$$

$$a_{\mathcal{A}} + a'_{\mathcal{A}} > a_{\mathcal{A}} + b'_{\mathcal{A}} > a_{\mathcal{A}} + c'_{\mathcal{A}}$$

$$a_{\mathcal{B}} + a_{\mathcal{B}} > a_{\mathcal{B}} + b_{\mathcal{B}} > a_{\mathcal{B}} + c_{\mathcal{B}}$$

$$a_{\mathcal{B}} + a'_{\mathcal{B}} > a_{\mathcal{B}} + b'_{\mathcal{B}} > a_{\mathcal{B}} + c'_{\mathcal{B}}$$

Based on the foregoing discussion, the probabilities in the product game would be $\rho_{23} = P(\sigma_2, \sigma_3 \mid x_1, \overline{s_{23}})$ and $\rho_{23'} = P(\sigma_2, \sigma'_3 \mid x_1, \overline{s_{23'}})$. Here $\overline{s_{23}} = \overline{s_{23'}} = [s_2 \cup s_3] \cap [s_2 \cup s_{3'}] = s_2 \approx u$ as before. This allows us to replace $\overline{s_{23}} = \overline{s_{23'}}$ by u in the expressions above.[11] Since there are two possible values for the conditioning variable x_1, there are two possible values for each probability and two possible distributions, and once again, $\rho_{23} + \rho_{23'} = 1$ in each case. I display this again for clarity.

For g_{23}:

$$\rho_{23} = \begin{cases} P(\sigma_2, \sigma_3 \mid \sigma_1, u) & \text{if } x_1 = \sigma_1 \\ P(\sigma_2, \sigma_3 \mid \sigma_1', u) & \text{if } x_1 = \sigma_1' \end{cases}$$

$$\rho_{23'} = \begin{cases} P(\sigma_2, \sigma_3' \mid \sigma_1, u) & \text{if } x_1 = \sigma_1 \\ P(\sigma_2, \sigma_3' \mid \sigma_1', u) & \text{if } x_1 = \sigma_1' \end{cases}$$

$$\rho_{23} + \rho_{23'} = 1$$

$$\rho_{23} > \rho_{23'} \quad \text{if } x_1 = \sigma_1$$

$$\rho_{23} < \rho_{23'} \quad \text{if } x_1 = \sigma_1'$$

The two inequalities we get for the probabilities are again inverses as in g_3 since the presence of σ_2 as a conditioned variable does not change anything significantly. That is, $P(\sigma_2, \sigma_3 \mid \sigma_1, u) > P(\sigma_2, \sigma_3' \mid \sigma_1, u)$ but $P(\sigma_2, \sigma_3 \mid \sigma_1', u) < P(\sigma_2, \sigma_3' \mid \sigma_1', u)$. There are two Pareto-Nash equilibria as before and the game cannot be solved locally.

This phrasal game also participates in the circular two-level global equilibrium along with the three lexical games. Once again, the choice of optimal distribution in g_{23} depends on the optimal value of x_1, and the optimal value of x_1 depends on the optimal distribution in g_1, which depends on the optimal values of x_2 and x_3, which depend on the optimal distributions in g_2 and g_3 and g_{23}!

I now exhibit a more complex (sentential) product $g_1 \otimes g_{23} = g_{123}$ in Figure 4.5.

The explanation of the formation of this product follows the same pattern. This game is drawn a bit differently to conveniently accommodate the large diagram on a single page. First, the initial nodes of the game are the bolder dots in the middle rather than to the left as before. Since g_1 has two initial nodes and g_{23} also has two initial nodes, g_{123} has $2 \times 2 = 4$ initial nodes, labeled with the unions of the corresponding situations. For example, $s_{123} = s_1 \cup s_{23} = s_1 \cup s_2 \cup s_3$. The tree takes its shape from the "product" of the input trees in a natural way, though not

11. Since the only additional content in the initial situations is various invisible intentions, it is possible to use u from the start.

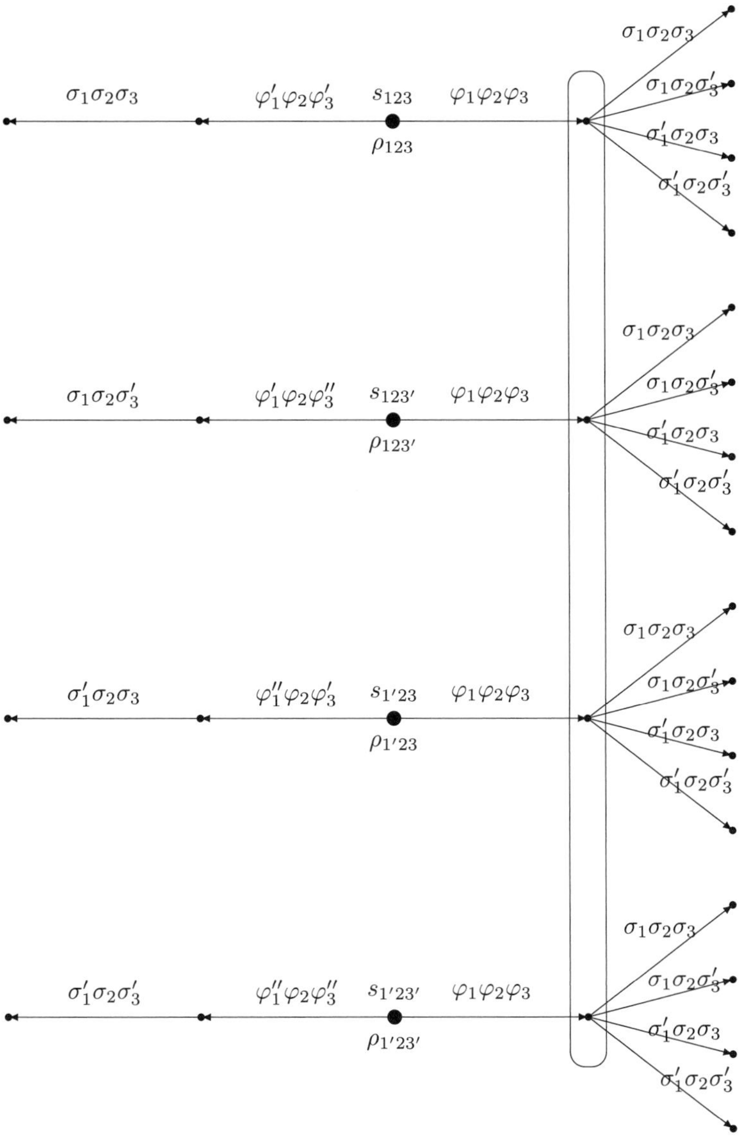

Figure 4.5
The sentential game $g_{123} = g_1 \otimes g_{23} = g_1 \otimes (g_2 \otimes g_3)$

all the branches have been shown to avoid clutter.[12] The utterances in the product involve the concatenations $\circ$ of the corresponding utterances in the multiplier and multiplicand, the contents involve the product $\odot_u$ of the corresponding infons, and the payoffs involve the corresponding arithmetical sums. Again, the payoffs have been left out to fit the diagram onto the page but they still preserve the corresponding inequalities.[13]

The probabilities in g_{123} would be $\rho_{123} = P(\sigma_1, \sigma_2, \sigma_3 \mid \overline{s_{123}})$, $\rho_{123'} = P(\sigma_1, \sigma_2, \sigma_3' \mid \overline{s_{123'}})$, $\rho_{1'23} = P(\sigma_1', \sigma_2, \sigma_3 \mid \overline{s_{1'23}})$, and $\rho_{1'23'} = P(\sigma_1', \sigma_2, \sigma_3' \mid \overline{s_{1'23'}})$. Here $\overline{s_{123}} = \overline{s_{123'}} = \overline{s_{1'23}} = \overline{s_{1'23'}} = [s_1 \cup s_2 \cup s_3] \cap [s_1 \cup s_2 \cup s_{3'}] \cap [s_{1'} \cup s_2 \cup s_3] \cap [s_{1'} \cup s_2 \cup s_{3'}] = s_2 \approx u$ as before. These four probabilities sum to 1 as they all form a single distribution.

Notice that now there is only one conditioning variable u for all the four conditional probabilities. This means there is only *one* probability distribution and *one* set of values for each of the four probabilities *in this example* because $\mathcal{A}$ and $\mathcal{B}$ are discussing their plans for the evening and are attending to G. As I said in chapter 3, they could unambiguously have been attending to their children, in which case there would also have been a single but different set of probability values. Or, interestingly, there could have been some real uncertainty about what they were attending to and this would have meant more than one set of values.

In the first case, because $\mathcal{A}$ and $\mathcal{B}$ are attending to G in u, it follows that $\rho_{123} > \rho_{1'23'} > \rho_{123'} \approx \rho_{1'23} \approx 0$. That is, both $\mathcal{A}$ and $\mathcal{B}$ share the fact that the probability associated with $\mathcal{A}$ conveying that the film *Harvey* is showing in a theater is the highest; the probability associated with $\mathcal{A}$ conveying that their son is amusing himself is next in the ranking; and the other two probabilities are almost zero because they refer to more or less incoherent contents.

In the second case, where the parents are attending to their children instead, we have the shared ranking $\rho_{1'23'} > \rho_{123} > \rho_{123'} \approx \rho_{1'23} \approx 0$.

In the last case, where there is some real uncertainty about what the agents are attending to, they must be assumed to have subjective beliefs

12. For example, the branch conjoining φ_1 with $\varphi_2\varphi_3'$ at the node s_{123} has not been shown, along with its corresponding content and payoffs. Essentially, all possible combinations need to be accounted for with respect to the tree itself, the utterances, the contents, and the payoffs and probabilities. The reader should draw the tree out to ensure the shape is clear.

13. Just as one example, the payoffs at the very top right node of the diagram are $3a_{\mathcal{A}}$, $3a_{\mathcal{B}}$. One instance of an inequality is as follows: $3a_{\mathcal{A}} > 2a_{\mathcal{A}} + b_{\mathcal{A}} > 2a_{\mathcal{A}} + c_{\mathcal{A}} > a_{\mathcal{A}} + 2c_{\mathcal{A}}$. Of course, there are actually more terms in the inequality since some branches have been deliberately omitted.

that there is common knowledge of a probability distribution over the alternative sets of probability values or rankings. Section 3.3.4 dealt with this type of situation where the extent of shared knowledge becomes tenuous.

To return to the first case and to the circumstances of our example, since there is just one distribution and one corresponding ranking $\rho_{123} > \rho_{1'23'} > \rho_{123'} \approx \rho_{1'23} \approx 0$, the second-tier equilibrium problem becomes trivial for this product game g_{123}. The reader should check that with this ranking and with the payoffs preserving the relevant inequalities, the unique Pareto-Nash solution to g_{123} is that $\mathcal{A}$ utters $\varphi_1\varphi_2\varphi_3$ and $\mathcal{B}$ interprets it as $\sigma_1\sigma_2\sigma_3$, exactly as we would expect.

I once again display the single distribution that arises corresponding to this case—which is the situation of our example—for clarity.

For g_{123}:

$$\rho_{123} = P(\sigma_1, \sigma_2, \sigma_3 \mid u)$$

$$\rho_{1'23'} = P(\sigma_1', \sigma_2, \sigma_3' \mid u)$$

$$\rho_{123'} = P(\sigma_1, \sigma_2, \sigma_3' \mid u)$$

$$\rho_{1'23} = P(\sigma_1', \sigma_2, \sigma_3 \mid u)$$

$$\rho_{123} + \rho_{1'23'} + \rho_{123'} + \rho_{1'23} = 1$$

$$\rho_{123} > \rho_{1'23'} > \rho_{123'} \approx \rho_{1'23} \approx 0$$

This sentential game is equally part of the global equilibrium as the others. Since the solutions to all the interdependent games must be simultaneously consistent, the sentential game solution $\sigma_1\sigma_2\sigma_3$ cascades down the parse tree to the phrasal and lexical games, forcing the solution to g_1 to be φ_1 and σ_1 and the *high* probability for ρ_1 (i.e., $\rho_1 = P(\sigma_1 \mid \sigma_2, \sigma_3, u)$). The same pattern holds for g_3 and g_{23} where the nontrivial two-tier problems get resolved in the same way by the requirement of internal consistency or what I called global equilibrium. This makes the global equilibrium an equilibrium among local equilibria, exactly as I adumbrated in section 1.4.4.

I urge the reader to go back to all the displayed probability distributions and check that the choices of utterance, of interpretation, and of probability distribution in each of the five games considered—g_1, g_2, g_3, g_{23}, and g_{123}—are internally consistent.

To repeat, each of g_1, g_3, and g_{23} have two local Pareto-Nash equilibria (including the selection of initial probability distributions), as we saw above. Under our special assumption of a single conventional meaning for IS g_2 has just one such local equilibrium but it is compatible with all the pairs of equilibria of g_1, g_3, and g_{23}. The sentential game g_{123}, however, turns out to have just one local equilibrium $\sigma_1\sigma_2\sigma_3$ which is compatible with only one of the local equilibria of g_1, g_3, and g_{23} (and g_2)—those corresponding to σ_1, (σ_2), and σ_3. This local equilibrium of g_{123} eliminates the incompatible local equilibria of g_1, g_3, and g_{23}—those corresponding to σ_1' and σ_3'—and forces the selection of unique local equilibria (including the choice of initial probability distributions). That is, all the local equilibria have to be in equilibrium and this is what is meant by an equilibrium among equilibria, a *global* equilibrium.

Thus, the solutions to the family of games in the Flow Constraint **F** are obtained globally. g_{123} was built up from g_1 and g_{23}, and g_{23} from g_2 and g_3, and then the solution to g_{123} enabled the solution to the atomic games. The key upshot of all the initial probabilities in various games being conditioned by the contents or solutions of other games is that the meanings of the words in an utterance are interdependent and influence each other. As we have seen, each probability in a game affects the interpretation of the part of the utterance in that game. But each such probability is itself affected by the interpretations of other parts of the utterance. Thus, the interpretations of the parts of the utterance affect each other. Put differently, the solutions of the different games affect each other. This is what was meant by *mereological* interdependence. In our example, σ_1 reinforces the choice of σ_3 and $\sigma_2\sigma_3$, and vice versa. Likewise, σ_1' reinforces the choice of σ_3' and $\sigma_2\sigma_3'$, and vice versa. These influences are not direct but indirect, via the initial probabilities in the corresponding games.

These probabilities can be more compactly expressed by leveraging the notation: write $P_i(x \mid u) = P(x_i \mid x_{-i}, u)$, where x is the vector (x_i) and u is an approximate stand-in for the intersection of the situations at all the initial nodes in g_i. It is always possible to use the subscript of the ρ's or the P's to figure out which variables are the conditioned random variables and which ones are the conditioning random variables. For example, $P_{23}(x \mid u)$ would be identical to $P(x_2, x_3 \mid x_{-23}, u)$, where x_{-23} is just the contents left out, namely, x_1. The key is the subscript of ρ or P that allows anyone to unambiguously determine the position of the arguments. This notation enables a compact representation of the fundamental equation of equilibrium semantics in the next section.

This long discussion shows how games of partial information can be set up to model the context of utterance u in order to derive the *actual* content of each word, phrase, and the entire sentence from the various *possi-*

ble contents (obtained from **S**, **C**, and **I**) as the solution to the relevant game. This fourth Flow Constraint **F** is in some sense the main constraint of the framework.

4.3 SCIF: Equilibrium Semantics and Locutionary Meaning

Locutionary meaning is the part of literal meaning that is conveyed linguistically (or locutionarily). Even locutionary meaning is thoroughly contextual and situated.

Equilibrium semantics is a generalization of model theory and draws upon four central ideas: reference, use, indeterminacy, and equilibrium. It involves combining the four constraints I have introduced into a single framework. Indeed, the last constraint itself begins to slide into it.

The framework consists essentially of the two *homomorphic* maps shown below:

$$(\mathcal{L}, \circ) \xrightarrow{g_u} (\mathcal{G}, \otimes) \xrightarrow{f_u} (\mathcal{I}, \odot_u)$$

These maps connect three monoids[14] and take us from words and phrases via their embedding situations and corresponding games to their

14. We already know that the identity of $\mathcal{L}$ is the empty string e and the identity of $\mathcal{I}$ is the supremum of the infon lattice **1**. The identity of $\mathcal{G}$ is the empty game g_e, which is just the trivial game with a single initial node (with initial probability 1) and a branch labeled with e issuing from it, a further branch labeled **1** issuing from the node that ends the first branch, and any terminal payoff, preferably 0. The reader should check that for any game $g \in \mathcal{G}$, we get $g \otimes g_e = g_e \otimes g = g$ and that $g_u(e) = g_e$ and $f_u(g_e) = \mathbf{1}$. There is also a similar zero game g_0 with a single branch labeled 0 and a further branch labeled **0** such that $g \otimes g_0 = g_0 \otimes g = g_0$ for all $g \in \mathcal{G}$ and that $g_u(0) = g_0$ and $f_u(g_0) = \mathbf{0}$. To summarize:

- Identity of $\mathcal{L}$: e
- Zero of $\mathcal{L}$: 0
- Identity of $\mathcal{I}$: **1**
- Zero of $\mathcal{I}$: **0**
- Identity of $\mathcal{G}$: g_e

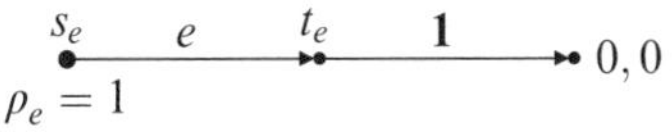

- Zero of $\mathcal{G}$: g_0

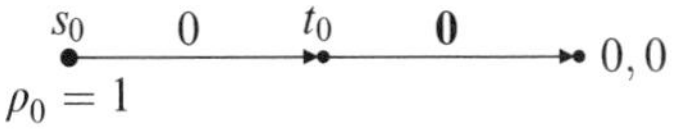

locutionary contents. As we could have anticipated from the foregoing, the locutionary content or meaning $C_u^{\ell} = f_u \circ g_u$ where $\circ$ now stands for function composition. This content function is not yet the full content $C_u : \mathcal{L} \to \mathcal{I}$ defined in section 2.8, but it is a significant part of it. For example, $C_u^{\ell}(\varphi) = (f_u \circ g_u)(\varphi) = \sigma^{\ell} = \sigma_1\sigma_2\sigma_3 = \langle\!\langle P_1^{\varphi_3}; e(P^{\varphi_1}, r_u) \mid Unique(P^{\varphi_1}, r_u, q_u); t \mid (t \parallel t_u) \wedge t, t_u \in [t_0, t_\infty] \rangle\!\rangle$, the last long expression recalled from section 4.2.3.

These two maps essentially involve maps from the parse trees of the sentence to corresponding "trees of games" and further to trees of contents (or infons). That is, g_u maps a word or expression into a corresponding game, relative to the context of utterance u. These games are embedded in an *isomorphic* tree of games, that is, a tree with the same structure as the parse tree. And f_u maps each game into its unique solution, which is its corresponding locutionary content.[15]

We have already seen the parse tree in **S**:

$$[_S\ [_{NP}\ \varphi_1] \circ [_{VP}\ [_V\ \varphi_2] \circ [_{VP}\ \varphi_3]]]$$

The isomorphic tree of games based on **C**, **I**, and **F** and obtained via the map g_u is as follows:

$$[_S\ [_{NP}\ g_1] \otimes [_{VP}\ [_V\ g_2] \otimes [_{VP}\ g_3]]]$$

The phrasal and sentential games g_{23} and g_{123} are implicitly present in the tree above, as should be evident.

The third corresponding tree obtained via the map f_u is the contents tree that is isomorphic to the first two.

$$[_S\ [_{NP}\ \sigma_1] \odot_u [_{VP}\ [_V\ \sigma_2] \odot_u [_{VP}\ \sigma_3]]] \qquad (4.1)$$

The phrasal and sentential contents $\sigma_2\sigma_3$ and $\sigma_1\sigma_2\sigma_3$ are also implicitly present in the tree above. This becomes clearer in Figure 4.6 below.

These three trees give us the full solution to the problem of deriving the locutionary meaning of φ from first principles. There are five nodes in each tree and there are correspondingly five expressions, five games, and five contents. The second tree is obtained from the first via g_u and the third tree is obtained from the second via f_u. Notice how the ideas of generativity and (global) equilibrium *combine* in these trees, especially in the latter two.

15. The map f_u is not to the whole solution or strategy profile, just to that part of the profile corresponding to the addressee's interpretation.

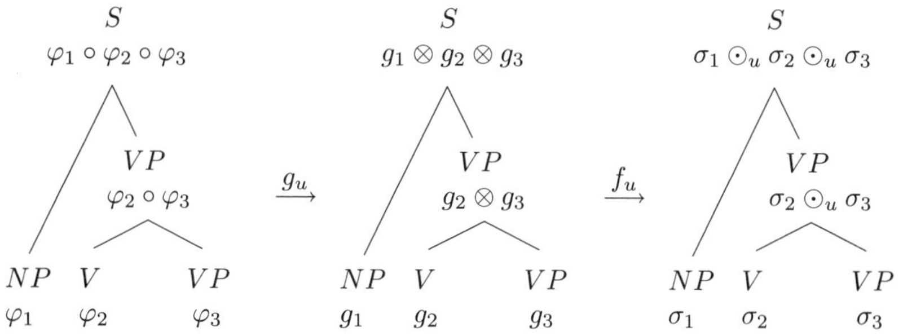

Figure 4.6
The three isomorphic trees

Clearly, the two maps have not been formally defined, but we have seen several instances of both in chapters 3 and 4. Giving a formal definition requires an elaborate prior specification of various constituent concepts since a game is a complicated entity involving not just players but also choice sets, payoffs and probabilities, and information sets. Moreover, in our case, the games are *situated* and this requires embedding them in situations and constructing them from the building blocks of situation theory, just as numbers can be constructed from the elements of set theory.[16] It should be intuitively clear that this can be carried out and the two maps defined, so I have relegated it to Appendix A.

If we make explicit the dependence of the map $g_u(\alpha_i)$ on the initial probabilities that come from u and other conditioning variables, we can write this as $g_u(\alpha_i, P_i(x \mid u))$. Here α_i is any constituent of φ and i naturally ranges from 1 to the number of nodes in the parse tree. This then allows us to write $C_u^\ell(\alpha_i) = f_u[g_u(\alpha_i, P_i(x \mid u))]$, which is equal to x_i in global equilibrium. So if we express this in vector notation by including all the i's, we get a compact and elegant vector fixed point equation:

$$C_u^\ell(\alpha, P(x \mid u)) = f_u[g_u(\alpha, P(x \mid u))] = x \tag{4.2}$$

Fully spelled out, this equation is as follows:

$$\begin{bmatrix} f_u[g_u(\alpha, P_1(x_1 \mid x_2, x_3, u))] \\ f_u[g_u(\alpha, P_2(x_2 \mid x_1, x_3, u))] \\ f_u[g_u(\alpha, P_3(x_3 \mid x_1, x_2, u))] \\ f_u[g_u(\alpha, P_{23}(x_2, x_3 \mid x_1, u))] \\ f_u[g_u(\alpha, P_{123}(x_1, x_2, x_3 \mid u))] \end{bmatrix} = \begin{bmatrix} x_1 \\ x_2 \\ x_3 \\ x_2 \odot_u x_3 \\ x_1 \odot_u (x_2 \odot_u x_3) \end{bmatrix} \tag{4.3}$$

16. An earlier version was presented in the appendix to Parikh (2001).

This is the equation[17] we have to solve to compute the locutionary meaning of an utterance. It nicely captures the idea of global equilibrium or what could also be called a *double* fixed point, local at one level and global at the second. The reader can verify that the solution to this equation is precisely the product of the infons in Equation 4.1.

Thus, equilibrium semantics combines the constraints **SCIF** via two homomorphic maps g_u and f_u into a new theory and framework for locutionary meaning. It should be clear how this new semantics is a generalized model theory that incorporates the ideas of reference, use, and equilibrium and how it fuses the basic ideas of semantics and pragmatics into a single discipline. Henceforth, I will consign the term "pragmatics" itself to the dustbin![18]

Of course, many things in equilibrium semantics still remain to be described: for example, how other categories of words are handled, how structural ambiguity, incompleteness in sentences, implicature, and illocutionary force are accommodated, and so on. An account of most of these will be given later.[19]

I now point out a fundamental consequence of equilibrium semantics: because the Pareto-Nash equilibrium involves a set of numerical or algebraic simultaneous linear equations and inequalities, what we have achieved is to transform words and phrases together with the ambient circumstances into a system of simultaneous linear equations and inequalities. Thus, to figure out the locutionary meaning of *any* utterance (in principle) all that is required is the solution of this system. We have metamorphosed words into numbers!

As remarked above, the solution of this system of simultaneous equations is a *double* fixed point: the Nash equilibrium is itself a fixed point but because the probabilities in each game are interdependent, so are the games; thus the overall global solution to all the interdependent games in the tree of games *simultaneously* considered is a fixed point among fixed points, or a *double* fixed point.

Another somewhat startling consequence of this framework mentioned in section 1.4.1 is that the hallowed Fregean principle of compositionality

17. Note that "P" is doing double duty: in Equation 4.2 it stands for the vector (P_i); each P_i is a probability also denoted by P.

18. Of course, distinctions can still be made between different aspects of content, putting one part in semantics and another in pragmatics, but the motivation for this kind of demarcation no longer exists.

19. Incidentally, I do not say anything about conventional implicature in this book.

does not hold in general for referential meanings. The interdependence of the meanings of words and phrases arises from the interdependence of probabilities and the concomitant interdependence of the corresponding games. This means we no longer have the compositional principle that the meaning of a composite expression is a function of the meanings of its component parts *given independently*. This is because the meanings of the component parts in turn depend on the meanings of the other parts and the whole. In our simple example "Harvey is playing," we may write:

$$C_u^\ell(\text{Harvey is playing}) = h(C_u^\ell(\text{Harvey}), C_u^\ell(\text{is playing}))$$

$$C_u^\ell(\text{Harvey}) = h(C_u^\ell(\text{Harvey is playing}), C_u^\ell(\text{is playing}))$$

$$C_u^\ell(\text{is playing}) = h(C_u^\ell(\text{Harvey is playing}), C_u^\ell(\text{Harvey}))$$

and more generally, we may write:

$$C_u^\ell(S) = h(C_u^\ell(NP), C_u^\ell(VP))$$

$$C_u^\ell(NP) = h(C_u^\ell(S), C_u^\ell(VP))$$

$$C_u^\ell(VP) = h(C_u^\ell(S), C_u^\ell(NP))$$

where h is a suitable function derived from Equation 4.2. Of course, the noun phrase NP and verb phrase VP can be further broken down into their constituents in these equations. It is the presence of the second and third equations in each set above that disqualifies the Fregean principle of compositionality since the principle requires the meanings of the component parts to be determined independently and directly.

Only in the special case where there are no lexical ambiguities will the Fregean principle work. In general, we will have to resort to the double fixed point computation to determine the meanings of composite expressions. This is a complex process of simultaneous interaction among the potential meanings of each component part and whole which results in the actual (optimal) meanings of the parts and the whole. Thus, the *principle of compositionality* has to be replaced by the more general *fixed point principle*. The latter reduces to the former when no lexical ambiguities are present.

Also, since there are no conventional meanings at the level of phrases or sentences, Frege's principle automatically fails to hold at the level of conventional meaning.

The *locutionary proposition* expressed by the utterance of φ in u would be $c \models \sigma^\ell$ where c is the described situation introduced in section 2.8 and $\sigma^\ell = \sigma_1\sigma_2\sigma_3$ is the full locutionary content derived from the vector equation above. More will be said about propositions and the determination of c in section 4.7.

As I mentioned in section 2.8 and in section 3.3.4, it is possible for $\mathcal{A}$ and $\mathcal{B}$ to have different subjective models of their strategic interaction when common knowledge does not obtain. When this happens, it is necessary to form games $g_i^\mathcal{A}$ and $g_i^\mathcal{B}$ (i.e., one for each agent in the interaction) in the setup above. This yields *two* content functions $C_u^{\ell,\mathcal{A}} = f_u \circ g_u^\mathcal{A}$ and $C_u^{\ell,\mathcal{B}} = f_u \circ g_u^\mathcal{B}$ and two locutionary meanings and propositions, one for each agent. Incidentally, this separation into subjective games clarifies that the selection of optimal initial probabilities in the various games is a choice problem for *both* agents, each in his or her own subjective game. In the case where there is just one game rather than two subjective games, this choice problem is also faced by both agents but the presence of common knowledge renders their solutions identical.

The reader should apply the analysis in the foregoing to the example from section 3.3.3:

The astronomer married the star.

As we saw in that section, the conflicting influence of the meanings of ASTRONOMER and MARRIED on the interpretation of STAR makes the selection of strategic probability assessments more difficult.

4.4 S(C)IF: Equilibrium Semantics and Illocutionary Meaning

Illocutionary meaning is the part of the full meaning of an utterance that is conveyed entirely via context (or illocutionarily). There is nothing in the sentence that directly indicates its presence. It builds upon locutionary meaning by adding appropriate material obtained from the utterance situation. Some part of it may be literal and the rest implicated. We can write the general relationship:

full meaning = literal meaning $\odot_u$ implicature $\odot_u$ force

= locutionary meaning $\odot_u$ illocutionary meaning

$\approx$ aspects of meaning in section 4.1

The distinction between literal and implicated meaning is fuzzy because whether a particular partial content is literal or implicated may be *inde-*

terminate. It may be possible to break each component meaning down further into the various aspects of meaning discussed in section 4.1, but indeterminacies lurk here as well.

Locutionary meaning is always a part of literal meaning. Illocutionary meaning, on the other hand, straddles literal meaning, implicature, and force.

Lexical disambiguation, saturation, and concept construction, all partial contents in our system, are commonly treated as part of literal meaning because they are *linguistically and conventionally mandated* meanings. That is, even though they may not be directly represented unambiguously in the uttered sentence, it is some aspect of the sentence that mandates that the addressee attend to the context of utterance for their disambiguation.[20] Free enrichment is *not* linguistically mandated and yet is part of literal meaning and this is the standard argument made by radical pragmaticists for the need to introduce such contextual elements even in the determination of literal meaning. I agree with their argument but go further, maintaining again that all of semantics is thoroughly situated.

20. Barwise (1989a) called such constituents of content its articulated constituents. Phenomena of lexical and structural disambiguation, saturation including the resolution of referring expressions, and concept construction are largely seen (Recanati, 2004c; Cappelen and Lepore, 2004) as not compromising the claim that conventional meaning determines truth conditions, since recourse to context for such phenomena is directed and restricted by conventional meaning alone.

This seems like a somewhat arbitrary and externally motivated decision because "direction and restriction" are by no means enough to actually fix the content, and I find it surprising that Carston (2004) and Recanati (2004c) appear to have accepted this reasoning. I do not dwell on this further here except to say that even in the case of a "pure" indexical such as "I," no rule may suffice and a full recourse to context may be required—certainly, on stage and in movies, an actor typically represents the character he or she is playing rather than himself or herself; this can also happen when a person is in disguise—Varol Akman (2002) gives the example of the doubles of Boris Yeltsin, where Boris Yeltsin would in certain situations refer to one of his doubles by uttering "I" rather than to himself. In this latter case, even the apparently trivial sentence "I am here now" may not be true because the double may be elsewhere.

In general, the sentence may offer no sufficiently restrictive clues about which features of the context are relevant for the interpretation. These features are the part that contributes the *unarticulated non-constituents* of the content (Barwise, 1989a). As should be clear, even though recourse to context may be indicated by conventional meaning alone, the actual resolution of such contextual factors may not be possible through the medium of conventions and rules at all. For more about this issue, see Parikh (2006b, 2007). Also see footnote 22 in this chapter.

My distinction between locutionary and illocutionary meaning is in a sense more "literal-minded" than is the notion of literal meaning itself, although both distinctions are valuable and capture different slices of meaning, the traditional one from the vantage point of content (or *what* was said) and mine from a derivational viewpoint (or *how* it is derived). In general, how we divide and subdivide the full content may be partly arbitrary and may partly depend on our point of view and extraneous interests.

Lexical disambiguation is obviously a part of locutionary meaning, but saturation may be locutionary (e.g., "*He* is playing)" or illocutionary (e.g., "Caitlin is taller [*than Harvey*]). Concept construction (or the interpretation of vague terms) is locutionary whereas free enrichment, implicature, and force are all illocutionary. As I said in section 4.1, these subtypes of meaning do not exhaust the varieties of meaning but do constitute a large part of what would be the full meaning of an utterance.

In my terms, all these components, including the top-level ones in the equation above, are just instances of disambiguation since they all involve selecting the optimal meaning from among a range of possible meanings. As anticipated in Parikh (2006b), the key point of equilibrium semantics is that all these types of meaning are uniformly amenable to modeling by situated games of partial information.

In this section, I show how to derive the enrichment of φ to "Harvey is playing [*in New York*])" as well as its implicature "Harvey is playing $\hookrightarrow$ [*Let's go see it*]."

4.4.1 Enrichment

I start with aspects of (literal but illocutionary) content that are not linguistically mandated. First consider the following examples from Recanati (2004b):

1. I've had breakfast.
2. You are not going to die.

If the first sentence is uttered in response to someone asking the speaker if she is hungry, its literal content would be that the speaker has had breakfast *that morning*. If the second sentence is uttered in response to a child crying from a minor cut, its literal content would be that the child is not going to die *from that cut*.

These examples clearly show there is nothing in the sentences themselves that indicates whether and how their literal contents need enrichment in different situations. Not only is context required for content, the need for further contextual determination is itself contextual. This is evident enough with implicature, where it is patently the purposes of the participants that result in implicatures being licensed.[21] But it is also equally true of literal content. Once one notices this phenomenon, it begins to seem that practically every sentence is radically incomplete: the full literal content is seldom linguistically mandated but comes from the embedding discourse situation.[22]

Consider possible completions for an utterance of φ in u. The sentence by itself does not tell us whether the film *Harvey* is playing:

1. Issue of location
a. in New York
b. nearby
c. at a convenient location
d. in Manhattan
e. in midtown Manhattan
f. downtown
g. uptown
h. within ten blocks of the apartment
2. Issue of time
a. this evening
b. tonight
c. after 8 p.m.
d. at a convenient time

There are literally an infinite number of possible completions—even when constrained by u! The first thing that should strike the reader is that there may be no exact completion that either agent constructs and that the enrichment is *indeterminate*. Indeed, B could even respond by

21. Of course, equilibrium semantics holds that the purposes of the interlocutors are relevant throughout in all aspects of meaning.

22. Barwise (1989a) identified this incompleteness through what he called the *unarticulated constituents* of the content because these constituents are not indicated by anything in the sentence. Recanati (2004b) uses the notion of unarticulated constituent to refer only to those constituents of literal content that are linguistically mandated but that do not appear explicitly in the surface syntax of the sentence uttered. There are actually two cases: unarticulated but linguistically and conventionally mandated and unarticulated and also not linguistically mandated. Recanati may be right about his interpretation of the term "unarticulated constituent" but I will not discuss this further here. Two terms are probably required to mark the distinction. Refer also to footnote 20 in this chapter.

saying "Where is it playing? I don't mind going if it is convenient." It may be that the film is showing in more than one location in the city and the agents have different preferences about which location to choose. Some completions may even be difficult to render in language at all and yet may either be perfectly or partially grasped by *B*. For example, it may be that Alan and Barbara frequent a certain set of theaters in the city. In such a case, the relevant enrichment would be that *Harvey* is showing in one of those theaters, something more awkward to render linguistically. Temporally, it may appear that there are fewer possibilities but even here the options are infinite.

We might try to bring some order to the proliferation of possible completions[23] by separating the problem into two levels. The first level is the level of possible *issues* raised by the utterance, whether, for example, *Harvey's* location is uptown or downtown. The second level is how the issue in question is resolved by the context.

In principle, if reflected on in vacuo, even the number of possible issues could be infinite. This is important because it should pretty much dash any hope of capturing such completions in deeper levels of representations as Cappelen and Lepore (2004) and others have tried to suggest in order to rescue the mainstream view and traditional semantics/pragmatics distinction.

In addition, the number of ways an issue might be resolved might also be indeterminate. Indeed, these numbers—how many issues and how many ways each issue can be resolved—depend on how the agents individuate them, which may itself be context-dependent. For example, the agents might individuate just the two issues above with choices between *in New York* and *nearby* for location and only *this evening* for time, but clearly there are other ways to classify even this short list.

The moment a context is specified, as I did briefly for Recanati's (2004b) two examples above, the issues raised seem to become fairly definite and certainly finite. Location and time appear to be the only issues that matter in *u*. However, it is not at all obvious that these issues are in fact always absolutely clear and determinate even when a context is supplied. In some contexts, they may well be clear and determinate while in

23. Incidentally, essentially the same problem occurs with saturation and concept construction. For example, an utterance of "Caitlin is taller" could be completed by *than Harvey* or by *than her brother* or by *than her friends*, and so on. Likewise, an utterance of "Harvey is young" could be specified to varying levels of precision for "young."

others, there may just not be enough ambient information for a hearer to know exactly what issues were intended to be resolved.

All of this discussion suggests that such contextually supplied content may be fundamentally *indeterminate*. Since the role of context is ubiquitous, indeterminacy is ubiquitous as well and not just confined to enriched content. In particular, literal content is indeterminate, a startling fact that runs contrary to almost all twentieth century linguistics and philosophy!

To address these problems, I approach them in reverse order, level two before level one; that is, the resolution of issues before the identification of issues.

4.4.2 The Resolution of Issues

For the moment, let us allow that we are given an issue with a determinate number of ways of resolving it. Consider the issue of the film's location and permit just two possibilities: *in New York* and *nearby*. How should **SCIF** be modified to enable the resolution of this issue?

The Syntactic Constraint **S** is the same as in section 4.2.1:

$[_S [_{NP}\ \varphi_1] \circ [_{VP} [_V\ \varphi_2] \circ [_{VP}\ \varphi_3]]]$

The Conventional Constraint There is no direct need for any kind of conventional meaning since free enrichment does not directly involve the sentence φ, it just supervenes on it via the locutionary meaning $\sigma_1\sigma_2\sigma_3$ that was computed in the previous section. Thus, there is no counterpart to conventional maps for free enrichment and illocutionary meaning. Since its role is indirect, I parenthesize it in the abbreviation **S(C)IF**.

The Informational Constraint The role of this constraint is to capture the possible meanings involved as before and it can be represented by the following informational maps:

- Enrichment with respect to issue of location: $\varphi_4 = \varphi_2\varphi_3 \stackrel{u}{\rightarrow} \sigma_2\sigma_3 \stackrel{u}{\rightarrow} \sigma_4$
- Enrichment with respect to issue of location: $\varphi_4 = \varphi_2\varphi_3 \stackrel{u}{\rightarrow} \sigma_2\sigma_3 \stackrel{u}{\rightarrow} \sigma_4'$

where σ_4 and σ_4' represent the two ways—*in New York* and *nearby*—of resolving the issue. I do not bother to explicitly express these infons in terms of their constituents as it would lead to an unnecessary digression about how prepositions are best represented. This time u plays a role in both stages of the map from the phrase $\varphi_4 = \varphi_2\varphi_3 =$ IS PLAYING to the

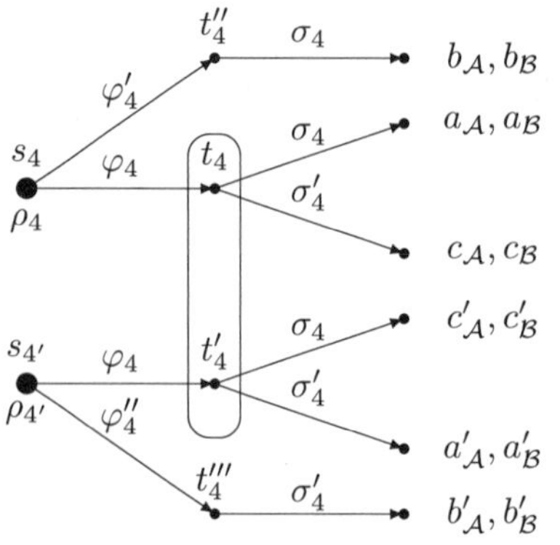

Figure 4.7
Resolving the issue of location with game g_4

locutionary phrasal content $\sigma_2\sigma_3$, and from this content to the enriched contents.

The phrase $\varphi_4 = \varphi_2\varphi_3 =$ IS PLAYING is called the *support* for the completion. As the term suggests, it is the shortest expression in the sentence that "supports" the enrichment or to which the enrichment can be appended. The entire sentence also supports the same expansion but we single out the shortest expression for the appellation. The enrichment σ_4 or σ'_4 is added not to the linguistic expression $\varphi_2\varphi_3$ but to the content of the linguistic expression $\sigma_2\sigma_3$, the expanded content being $\sigma_2\sigma_3\sigma_4$ or $\sigma_2\sigma_3\sigma'_4$. However, it is more convenient to refer to the corresponding linguistic expression $\varphi_2\varphi_3$ as the support.

The Flow Constraint **F** does its work at the outer node *VP* where the support is attached in **S** above. This constraint again involves a game of partial information, as shown in Figure 4.7. In this figure, φ'_4 stands for some alternative phrase such as "is playing in New York" and φ''_4 stands for some alternative phrase such as "is playing nearby."

The same symbols as before have been used for the payoffs to avoid multiplying the number of symbols in the text. All that is really required of the payoffs is that they satisfy the basic inequalities mentioned earlier. In this context, either of two assumptions may be made about u and these payoffs. The first is that neither agent has any particular preference between σ_4 and σ'_4, suggesting that the primed payoffs are the same as the corresponding unprimed payoffs. The second is that both agents prefer σ_4 to σ'_4, making the unprimed payoffs greater than the corresponding primed payoffs.[24] I will adopt the first assumption of equality and leave the other cases to the reader. This makes the payoffs completely symmetric with respect to the upper and lower halves of the game tree.

In the setting u and G where $\mathcal{A}$ and $\mathcal{B}$ are deciding what to do in the evening, it could be further assumed that it is their general practice to see movies anywhere in the city and not just those showing near their residence. In such a situation, it would follow that $\rho_4 > \rho'_4$. Alternatively, it could be assumed that there is no information about where they generally see movies. In this latter situation, it would follow that $\rho_4 \approx \rho'_4$.

In the first case the only Pareto-Nash equilibrium is σ_4 (more completely, $(\varphi_4\varphi''_4, \sigma_4)$), exactly what we would predict intuitively. In the second, where there is complete symmetry between payoffs and probabilities, the solution would involve a range of mixed strategy equilibria, also an expected result. That is, since there is nothing to indicate a choice between σ_4 and σ'_4, both are possible with the full range of probabilistic weights.

Thus, once an issue and its possible resolutions are determined, a game of partial information provides the appropriate solution—either σ_4 or a mixture of σ_4 and σ'_4—based on the ambient information that informs equilibrium selection. In other words, the agents select either *in New York* as the equilibrium completion or they select a probabilistic combination of the two possibilities. It is entirely possible that one agent selects one equilibrium and the second agent picks another based on different underlying assumptions about the payoffs and probabilities derived from different situational information. This is fully consonant with the discussion of subjective games of partial information in section 3.3.4 and with the discussion of *indeterminacy* in sections 5.2 and 5.3. Common knowledge frequently does not obtain, especially with illocutionary meaning where overt linguistic evidence is scarce, resulting in the agents playing somewhat different strategic interactions and arriving at different solutions. This is just another aspect of the indeterminacy of meaning and communication, something I take up more fully in the next chapter.

Equilibrium Semantics The illocutionary framework consists of two similar maps:

$$(\mathcal{L}, \circ) \xrightarrow{g_u} (\mathcal{G}, \otimes) \xrightarrow{f_u} (\mathcal{I}, \odot_u)$$

24. Of course, the two agents may have different preferences resulting in four cases rather than two, but this does not make any difference to the analysis.

g_u and f_u should perhaps be superscripted with ℓ and $\imath$ to distinguish between the *locutionary* and *illocutionary* maps, but I will leave the disambiguation to the context to avoid cluttering the notation. The illocutionary map g_u fully written out for the instance of completion considered here is $g_4 = g_u(\varphi_4) = g_u(\varphi_2\varphi_3)$. Note that g_{23} is also expressible as $g_u(\varphi_2\varphi_3)$. In the locutionary case, $\varphi_2\varphi_3$ is the phrase uttered; in the illocutionary case, it is the support of the enrichment.

The form the four constraints **S(C)IF** take in the equilibrium semantics of illocutionary meaning is shown below. **S** yields the same tree as before:

$$[_S\ [_{NP}\ \varphi_1] \circ [_{VP}\ [_V\ \varphi_2] \circ [_{VP}\ \varphi_3]]]$$

The isomorphic tree of games based on **(C)**, **I**, and **F** and obtained via g_u is as follows:

$$[_S\ [_{NP}\ g_e] \otimes [_{VP}\ [_V\ g_e] \otimes [_{VP}\ g_e] \otimes g_4] \otimes g_e]$$

Here, g_4 has been *directly* attached to the intermediate node corresponding to the verb phrase IS PLAYING and the empty game g_e has been inserted at all the other nodes of the tree. This direct attachment is very important because the relevant illocutionary game at a node may no longer be derivable from games at corresponding constituent nodes. This implies that the illocutionary g_u is *not* a homomorphism.

The reason g_4 was attached to *this* node is that it is this node that represents the *support* of this illocutionary meaning.

So far, I have considered just this one issue of location and so just one nontrivial game has been inserted into the tree. In general, multiple nonempty games can be attached to each node based on the illocutionary contents being derived, whether they come from free enrichment, implicature, illocutionary force, or some other illocutionary content. For example, both the games corresponding to the issues of location and time get attached to the same node—IS PLAYING.

The third corresponding tree obtained via the map f_u is the contents tree which is isomorphic to the first two.

$$[_S\ [_{NP}\ \mathbf{1}] \odot_u [_{VP}\ [_V\ \mathbf{1}] \odot_u [_{VP}\ \mathbf{1}] \odot_u \sigma_4] \odot_u \mathbf{1}]$$

If properly interpreted to allow for the possibility of multiple games (and therefore contents) at a single node, f_u can be viewed as a homomorphism.

In the equilibrium semantics of locutionary meaning, the initial probabilities of all the locutionary games turned out to be strategic variables that were interdependent and were part of the equilibrium selection process resulting in a two-level *global* equilibrium. In general, the initial probabilities of the different games that may arise in the context of illocutionary meaning will similarly also be interdependent and involve strategic selection, though the various issues may in actual practice often be independent. In our setting, for example, the issues of location and time may be resolved independently. In any case, these do not pose any new problems and can be handled exactly as they were in locutionary games via an *illocutionary* global equilibrium.

Recall that the locutionary global equilibrium involved a double fixed point among a system of simultaneous linear equations and inequalities. Likewise, I am saying here that the illocutionary global equilibrium involving all the illocutionary games (so far, I have considered just g_4, but one can imagine more such games for the resolution of the temporal issue and the implicature and the force and so on) is a similar double fixed point, although often the various games will be independent and so the local fixed points will trivially yield the global fixed point. These two global equilibria correspond to interdependencies within locutionary meanings considered separately and illocutionary meanings considered separately.

Now consider the map $g_u(\alpha_i)$ where α_i is again a constituent of φ. Strictly speaking, this map is not a function but a correspondence since it may happen that more than one game is associated with a single constituent or node of the parse tree. As we have seen, both the issues of time and location attach to the same node corresponding to the same expression $\alpha_j = \varphi_4 = \varphi_2\varphi_3$ for some j.

As was done earlier, I will make explicit the dependence of this map on the initial probabilities in the various illocutionary games. We can express this again as $g_u(\alpha_i, P_i(x \mid u))$ where now the vector x is the vector of all the *illocutionary* contents, each component x_i representing a *set* of issues (e.g., location and time for x_j corresponding to α_j above) each of which can be resolved in a number of ways (e.g., σ_4 or σ_4' for the issue of location). This then allows us to write $C_u^\imath(\alpha_i) = f_u[g_u(\alpha_i, P_i(x \mid u))]$, which is equal to x_i in (illocutionary) global equilibrium. So if we express this in vector notation by including all the i's, we get another similar vector fixed point equation for illocutionary meaning:

$$C_u^\imath(\alpha, P(x \mid u)) = f_u[g_u(\alpha, P(x \mid u))] = x \tag{4.4}$$

Looking ahead, this is the equation that has to be solved to get the entire illocutionary meaning of an utterance. Of course, so far we have seen just one example of this in the guise of free enrichment and the game g_4. It should be clear in any case that this equation extends our generalized model theory into an illocutionary realm where conventional model theory has nothing to offer. It also shows how the ideas of reference, use (indeterminacy), and equilibrium are incorporated in a natural way and how semantics and pragmatics are further fused into a single discipline.

This completes our discussion of the resolution of the issue of location. Once an issue is identified along with possible ways of resolving it, it can readily be disambiguated by our system of constraints **S(C)IF** and the two maps g_u and f_u of illocutionary equilibrium semantics.

The partial *illocutionary proposition* expressed via free enrichment would then be $c \models \sigma_4$.

4.4.3 The Identification of Issues

Now we come to the first level of how issues are identified. Consider the following questions and corresponding answers:

- How do we know what issues are "raised" by an utterance in a particular context? We tackle this by saying that different issues are more or less *relevant* and that the more relevant an issue is, the more important it will be for an agent to resolve it through a game. In practice, the relevance of an issue would be determined from the embedding situation including the prior discourse.
- How do we determine the relevance of issues? I said something about this in a preliminary way in section 3.2 where relevance was taken to be the difference between the value of an initial background game or decision problem and the value of the resulting game or decision problem once some information (or possible information based on some prior probability distribution) has been received. In other words, relevance is just the "value of information" in decision theory or a suitable generalization of it in the context of multi-person games.[25] The intuitive idea behind this definition is as follows: we assume that agents are frequently in situations that involve making a choice either in the presence or absence of other agents and often in the presence of uncertainty. Thus, agents frequently face one or more decision problems or games. Externally supplied information may be more or less useful to them in solving these choice problems. This enables us to identify the *relevance* of information with the value this externally supplied information might have for them. Prior

25. See footnote 27 in chapter 3.

to having this information, they might have received a certain expected payoff from their decision problem or game; now, armed with this information, they are in general able to secure a different expected payoff, and the difference between these two expected payoffs should give us the relevance of the information. Relevance is therefore also a fully situated concept based on the choice problems faced by an agent in a particular situation. In our example, the issues of location and time will then have some identifiable relevance for the participants that may be different for the two agents. If this relevance is high, perhaps the agents will hasten to play the corresponding illocutionary game and resolve the issue; if not, they may not bother.

- How are issues and their ways of resolution individuated? There is no easy answer to this but perhaps it does not really matter as far as the content is concerned exactly how they are individuated—each agent need consider just some particular way for the various illocutionary games to be set up.
- Should the game g_4 above be viewed in exactly the same way as the various locutionary games? Not quite. The idea is that in different contexts different issues will be raised (i.e., be more or less relevant). The agents might consider some of these issues explicitly. But others will remain implicit. For example, the issue of location may be explicitly considered by $\mathcal{A}$ and $\mathcal{B}$ because it may matter to them where in New York the film is playing; on the other hand, the issue of time may remain implicit because no alternatives need be entertained. If the issue of time is raised explicitly by either of the agents later (or even by an observing ethnographer), then the agents would play the corresponding game and resolve it in favor of *this evening*. Thus, while these illocutionary games are formally similar, a key difference lies in whether they are considered explicitly by agents or not.

In other words, the picture that emerges is that when communication occurs, not everything may get explicitly represented either in the sentence uttered or in peoples' heads (the speaker's and the hearer's), unless for whatever reason it needs to be explicitly considered. That is, when $\mathcal{A}$ utters φ to $\mathcal{B}$, perhaps just the explicitly represented part of the content (i.e., *Harvey* is playing) gets explicitly intended and inferred by $\mathcal{A}$ and $\mathcal{B}$; the remainder—*Harvey's* location and time of playing—may or may not be explicitly intended and inferred. Other issues would be treated similarly. The games that model each issue therefore may or may not get played at the time of utterance and reception, but possibly only later if that particular issue comes to be reflected upon. Also, because whether something is an issue may itself be uncertain, the literal and implicated contents may be indeterminate. Further, $\mathcal{A}$ and $\mathcal{B}$ may differ in what they consider relevant and what they consider explicitly and may also arrive at somewhat different resolutions of the same issue.

This should reinforce the view that the literal content of an utterance may not always be a sharply definable entity and may also differ from agent to agent. For both these reasons it may not always be clear how to go about identifying an objective content as *the* literal content. But more about this later.

4.4.4 Implicature

Now that one type of illocutionary meaning has been accounted for, the others follow readily even though the topic of implicature has traditionally been a weighty one. This is part of the power of the framework of equilibrium semantics: the uniform treatment it makes possible for all aspects of locutionary meaning and illocutionary meaning as well as *across* these domains, as evinced by the similar fixed point equations that capture the essence of both realms of meaning. In section 4.6 I will add a completely new conceptual and empirical dimension to implicature but for now I simply show that its derivation follows the same pattern as the derivation of free enrichment.

As before, there are two levels that need to be addressed in explaining implicature. The first is the level of what issues are raised in the context of implicature and the second is the resolution of these issues. In our example of $\mathcal{A}$ uttering φ to $\mathcal{B}$ in u, the only implicature appears to be the one mentioned in section 4.1: Harvey is playing $\hookrightarrow$ [*Let's go see it*]. There is no natural name for the corresponding issue like *location* or *time*, so let us just call it the *implicature issue*. There are then at least two obvious ways of resolving it as follows:

Implicature issue

- *Let's go see it*
- **1**

The second item, **1**, just represents the empty infon that indicates, in this instance, an empty implicature. As Grice (1975) had observed, there is some indeterminacy about the precise rendering of an implicature but, as should now be apparent, this is a part of all illocutionary meaning, not just implicature.

Once again, we have to identify the contributions of the four constraints. **S** is the same as before and **C** has its parenthetical role.

The Informational Constraint The possible meanings involved can be represented by the following informational maps:

- Implicature with respect to implicature issue: $\varphi_5 = \varphi = \varphi_1\varphi_2\varphi_3 \stackrel{u}{\rightarrow} \sigma_1\sigma_2\sigma_3 \stackrel{u}{\rightarrow} \sigma_5$
- Implicature with respect to implicature issue: $\varphi_5 = \varphi = \varphi_1\varphi_2\varphi_3 \stackrel{u}{\rightarrow} \sigma_1\sigma_2\sigma_3 \stackrel{u}{\rightarrow} \sigma_5'$

where σ_5 and σ_5' represent the two implicatures, *Let's go see it* and **1**, that resolve the implicature issue. Again, I do not bother to explicitly express these infons in terms of their constituents. As with enrichment, u plays a role in both stages of the map from the sentence $\varphi_5 = \varphi = \varphi_1\varphi_2\varphi_3 =$ HARVEY IS PLAYING to the locutionary content $\sigma^\ell = \sigma_1\sigma_2\sigma_3$ and from this content to the implicatures.

This time the entire sentence is the *support* for the implicature. Like free enrichments, implicatures can have any support in general and so implicatures can be added to any part of the sentence in general.[26]

The Flow Constraint Since the support of the implicature is the entire sentence, the relevant game of partial information g_5 is attached to the top-level sentential node of the parse tree.

Essentially, the same game as in Figure 4.7 (with all the subscripts 4 changed to 5) is required to disambiguate between the two possible implicatures. The alternative utterances could be "Let's go see it" and the empty string e. Since the same type of game is relevant for the derivation of the implicature, the analysis also follows the same pattern and I leave it to readers to work their way through it.

Once an issue and its possible resolutions are identified, a game of partial information provides the appropriate solution—either σ_5 or a mixture of σ_5 and σ_5'—based on the ambient information that informs equilibrium

26. This flexibility to add implicatures to any node of the parse tree becomes very important when there are subsentential clauses that carry implicatures as in the standard view of "It is better to get married and have children than to have children and get married." In general, it is *not* necessary to compute the entire literal content before computing implicatures. See Chierchia (2004), Sauerland (2004), and Ross (2006). I have shown an example of a free enrichment occurring at a subsentential node; the procedure for working out a subsentential implicature is similar.

selection. In other words, the agents select either *Let's go see it* as the equilibrium implicature or they select a probabilistic combination of the two possibilities. Again, owing to indeterminacy, it is entirely possible that one agent selects one equilibrium and the second agent picks another based on different underlying assumptions about the payoffs and probabilities derived from different situational information. This again fits with our discussion of subjective games of partial information in section 3.3.4. Common knowledge frequently does not obtain, especially with illocutionary meaning where overt linguistic evidence is scarce, resulting in the agents playing somewhat different strategic interactions and arriving at different solutions. This just serves to reinforce the third key attribute of equilibrium semantics, the *indeterminacy* of meaning and communication.

Equilibrium Semantics The form the four constraints **S(C)IF** take in the equilibrium semantics of implicature is shown below. **S** yields the same tree as before:

$$[_S\ [_{NP}\ \varphi_1] \circ [_{VP}\ [_V\ \varphi_2] \circ [_{VP}\ \varphi_3]]]$$

The isomorphic tree of games based on **(C)**, **I**, and **F** and obtained via g_u is as follows:

$$[_S\ [_{NP}\ g_e] \otimes [_{VP}\ [_V\ g_e] \otimes [_{VP}\ g_e] \otimes g_e] \otimes g_5]$$

Here g_5, the implicature game, is attached to the sentential node and the empty game g_e has been inserted at all the other nodes of the tree. Again, the illocutionary map g_u is *not* a homomorphism.

The third corresponding tree obtained via the map f_u is the contents tree which is isomorphic to the first two.

$$[_S\ [_{NP}\ \mathbf{1}] \odot_u [_{VP}\ [_V\ \mathbf{1}] \odot_u [_{VP}\ \mathbf{1}] \odot_u \mathbf{1}] \odot_u \sigma_5]$$

As before, f_u can still be viewed as a homomorphism.

Since all the illocutionary games are interdependent, we can combine the trees for enrichment and implicature as follows:

$$[_S\ [_{NP}\ g_e] \otimes [_{VP}\ [_V\ g_e] \otimes [_{VP}\ g_e] \otimes g_4] \otimes g_5]$$

$$[_S\ [_{NP}\ \mathbf{1}] \odot_u [_{VP}\ [_V\ \mathbf{1}] \odot_u [_{VP}\ \mathbf{1}] \odot_u \sigma_4] \odot_u \sigma_5]$$

One can now appreciate how, as more illocutionary contents are considered, more nodes of the trees get filled in with appropriate games and contents.

Equation 4.4 was meant to apply to all illocutionary meanings, so nothing more needs to be said about how implicatures fall out directly through the solution of this illocutionary fixed point equation. Now we have two games, g_4 and g_5, playing a role in the equation. Note, in particular, that different illocutionary meanings can influence one another just as earlier we had different locutionary meanings affecting one another. In the example at hand, the enrichment σ_4 influences the implicature σ_5 since it is the fact that the film is playing *in New York* that enables the implicature. Likewise, σ_5 reinforces σ_4.

The partial *illocutionary proposition* expressed via implicature is $c \models \sigma_5$.

As I did with enrichment, I initially just assumed that the implicature issue was raised by the utterance and then resolved via g_5. The identification of this issue and its modes of resolution follow the same method as developed in section 4.4.3, based on the idea of relevance as the value of information.

Since all illocutionary meanings follow the same pattern of identification of issues raised and then their resolution via a game, I have moved somewhat briskly through the determination of the implicature of φ in u. Illocutionary force can also be derived in exactly the same way. Usually, force is regarded as separate from meaning or content, but there seems to be no particular reason to exclude it from the larger import of an utterance.

4.5 Meaning and the Gricean Properties

Grice and others identified certain key properties that could serve as necessary conditions for implicature. These attributes are: existence, calculability, cancelability or defeasibility, indeterminacy, nondetachability, and reinforceability. Parikh (2001) considered these properties in detail in the context of the game-theoretic analysis of implicature, so I do not repeat that discussion here. The equilibrium semantics account would be roughly the same.

My first observation is that existence and calculability apply to all meanings, locutionary and illocutionary. Grice believed that literal meanings were given by convention so the questions of existence and calculability never arose. But in my framework, where everything has to be inferred relative to a context, whether it is literal or implicated, locutionary or illocutionary, the twin questions certainly do arise and are answerable in the affirmative. Since all our meanings emerge ultimately as Nash equilibria, and since we have the Nash Existence Theorem cited in section

3.1, our meanings all exist and are calculable since Nash equilibria are also calculable.

Next, cancelability and reinforceability also apply to *all* meanings but only in the presence of *ambiguity*. They do not apply just to implicature, as Grice and others following him have often believed. By "ambiguity" I mean my preferred general sense of the term indicating the presence of multiple possible meanings. This is a surprising observation but one that is naturally accommodated in the framework presented here.

The reader can verify this directly. In an utterance of the sentence "Harvey liked the ball," if the equilibrium meaning in the relevant utterance situation involved the spherical toy and not the formal dance, the speaker could still go on to say "I mean the dance, not the spherical toy" (cancelation) or "I mean the spherical toy, not the dance" (reinforcement). In other words, where there are two or more candidates for a (partial) meaning, one can always cancel or reinforce the equilibrium meaning without contradiction. This is due to the context-dependence of all meaning. Only in the rare situations when there is no ambiguity, that is, only when the relevant Flow Constraint involves trivial games with a single initial node, do cancelability and reinforceability fail to hold. Another pithy way of saying this is that almost no sentence is literally literal.

Finally, indeterminacy and nondetachability hold for all *illocutionary* meanings, not just for implicature. This insight is less surprising because the context dependence is more obvious. I will be taking a closer look at indeterminacy in the next chapter but suffice it to say here that it sometimes also applies to locutionary meanings, especially in the presence of vagueness. Nondetachability holds for all illocutionary meanings because other ways of conveying the same locutionary meaning (e.g., "Harvey is showing") continue to raise the same issues as before which have to be resolved in the same way as before, whether they are issues related to saturation or free enrichment or implicature.

Such observations extend to the Gricean maxims as well. In Parikh (2001), it was argued that the maxims are superfluous once one has the game-theoretic apparatus since expected payoff maximization adequately captures and generalizes the work done informally by the maxims. On the other hand, if desired, the maxims can be derived as ceteris paribus rules from the game-theoretic setup. Moreover, once again, the domain of application of the maxims is much wider than that of implicature—they apply to *all* meanings and especially when ambiguity is present. This is because expected utility maximization and equilibrium computation—

the route to deriving meaning—are required for *all* meanings, not just for implicature.

Likewise, related pragmatic rules like the Horn rules for marked expressions and the Levinson rules for scalar implicature, discussed in Parikh (2007), are all derivable from equilibrium semantics. They are as superfluous as the maxims, but can also be shown to hold in limited contexts as ceteris paribus rules.

Even the Cooperative Principle, which I assumed in chapter 3 when I introduced the various payoff inequalities to develop the algebraic versions of our games, turns out not to be fully general. It is possible for agents not to cooperate when communicating and, if payoffs arise situationally in noncooperative ways, these can be naturally accommodated in the wider range of payoff structures that games of partial information make available.

Assume a person works at a company and his boss stops by at his office to ask about the whereabouts of a coworker. If the coworker has gone fishing at a nearby river bank, the worker could well say to the boss, "He has gone to the bank," knowing that the boss will understand him to mean that the coworker is at a financial bank, a legitimate location for an office employee. So the agent has in a sense protected himself by uttering the literal component of a truth by taking advantage of and manipulating the context in which the literal component is evaluated. The boss takes the context to be one thing, the employee another; the games the two play are importantly different, resulting in different meanings for the utterance. Of course, the employee is also aware of the meaning the boss will derive so, objectively viewed, this is a case of deception, though the boss would find it hard to make a charge of lying stick. The employee could always deny that he had the second meaning in mind.

This kind of example and others suggest that the Cooperative Principle plays a *double* role, with respect to the background game *G* as well as with respect to the payoff inequalities in the various local games and their corresponding solution.

There is not much more that needs to be said about the Gricean framework for implicature except perhaps to repeat that the more general framework of equilibrium semantics accommodates the relevant facts and principles more precisely and derives them from more basic assumptions and that these facts and principles apply more or less to the entire domain of locutionary and illocutionary meaning, not just to implicature.

Indeed, the mainstream view blocked these new observations but they flow in a natural way from this new way of computing the meaning of an utterance.

4.6 The Interdependence of Locutionary and Illocutionary Meanings

The interesting question that arises now is whether there are interactions and interdependencies of meaning between and across the realms of locutionary and illocutionary meanings requiring an interdependence among both locutionary and illocutionary games. So far, I have assumed that these realms are separate with distinct fixed point equations for each domain and the only interactions that occur are those that lie *within* each type of meaning, locutionary or illocutionary.

Certainly, with regard to enrichment, the issues of location and time for IS PLAYING are issues based on the disambiguation of the verb phrase, so there is a dependence of illocutionary meaning on locutionary meaning. If the other meaning for the verb phrase *is amusing himself* had been the locutionary global solution, then the issues raised would have been correspondingly different. The same holds for the implicature issue: if the literal meaning had been different, if it had been that Alan and Barbara's son is amusing himself, a different issue would have been raised for resolution. Both instances of the dependence of illocutionary meaning on locutionary meaning are just an extension of the Gricean observation that implicature depends upon literal meaning.[27] This one-way dependence could be explicitly inscribed in the probability notation as $\rho_4 = P(\sigma_4 \mid \sigma_2\sigma_3\sigma_5, u)$ and $\rho_5 = P(\sigma_5 \mid \sigma_1\sigma_2\sigma_3\sigma_4, u)$, where ρ_5 is the corresponding initial probability in the game g_5.[28] This does not cause any substantive change or revision in our understanding of the two global equilibria, locutionary and illocutionary. All that is required is a small change in the illocutionary fixed point equation where the various conditional probabilities are additionally conditioned by the locutionary contents correspond-

27. As I said in section 4.4.4, in equilibrium semantics, illocutionary meanings including implicatures can in general be attached to any appropriate node of the parse tree, that is, they can have any appropriate support, so in particular they do not need to depend on the *entire* literal content, just a part of it.

28. Note that the probability of conveying the implicature σ_5 is also conditioned by the enrichment σ_4, not just by the locutionary content $\sigma_1\sigma_2\sigma_3$, and vice versa. This is just the interdependence of illocutionary meanings already discussed.

ing to the relevant support of the illocutionary content being determined, that is, of the independent variable in the conditional probability, as I have indicated above.

So the real question is whether it is possible for the dependence to go the other way, for locutionary meaning to be influenced by illocutionary meaning (or analogously, in Gricean terms, for literal meaning to depend on implicature). It has always been assumed since Grice that there is no such dependence, that literal meaning *had* to be computed before implicature.[29] This is just the basic assumption of the linear *pipeline* view of semantics determining pragmatics but not the other way around. But from the point of view of equilibrium semantics, such a two-way dependence, *if* empirically required, could be seamlessly accommodated within the framework: two relatively separate sets of simultaneous linear equations and inequalities would just become one integrated set yielding an overall global equilibrium that transcends the locutionary/illocutionary distinction. Mathematically, this is painless to do although notationally it becomes a little cumbersome.

Just as the speaker's conveying the optimal meaning of HARVEY as the film reinforced the speaker's conveying the optimal meaning of IS PLAYING as *is showing* and vice versa, so it is possible that each locutionary meaning is interdependent with each illocutionary meaning, making their individual determination nonlinear and circular. Of course, in neither case is the circularity of a vicious sort, just the harmless *codetermination* of variables in a linear system of simultaneous equations and inequalities.

For example, it is entirely possible to allow that the completion σ_4 influences and reinforces the selection of the optimal locutionary meaning $\sigma_1\sigma_2\sigma_3$ just as this locutionary meaning enables the completion. The other locutionary meaning of the son's amusing himself would raise other possible issues and their corresponding resolution would in turn push in favor of this alternative but suboptimal locutionary meaning, just as the alternative and suboptimal lexical meanings buttress each other.

Likewise, consider the case of the utterance's implicature derived in section 4.4.4: $\sigma_1\sigma_2\sigma_3 \hookrightarrow \sigma_5$. In this context, the question becomes: is it *required* that we may also have σ_5 reinforcing $\sigma_1\sigma_2\sigma_3$? That is, just as the literal meaning enables the implicature to be inferred, does the implicature enable the literal meaning to be inferred?

29. I am not referring just to subsentential implicatures but also to full sentential implicatures.

Since the entire framework of equilibrium semantics is radically probabilistic—not only do the various games and their solution processes involve conditional probabilities, but the solutions can themselves be probabilistic when they involve mixed strategies—this question has to be seen probabilistically. Mereological circularity and the idea and image of equilibrium offer the possibility that various (partial) meanings, whether locutionary or illocutionary, get *further* bolstering *or* undermining from one another than when considered linearly and sequentially. It is easy to see that the implicature $\sigma_5 = [Let's\ go\ see\ it]$ is the main *point* of $\mathcal{A}$'s communication in the setting u. Without it, the literal meaning that the film is showing in New York this evening is pointless. Indeed, Grice introduced the maxims of conversation precisely to permit the derivation of implicatures and would have said for this example that the implicature in question is a result of flouting the maxim of relevance. But he failed to notice that the implicature *in turn* helps to justify (or at least strengthen) the corresponding literal meaning as well! That is, the speaker's conveying σ_5 gives a further reason (or probabilistic underpinning) for the optimal literal meaning $\sigma_1\sigma_2\sigma_3$ I have derived in sections 4.2 and 4.3 as opposed to the competing meaning that the boy Harvey is amusing himself.

Thus, it seems entirely reasonable that locutionary meaning influences and is influenced by illocutionary meaning just as the two types of meaning have internal interdependencies. This is an *empirical* fact, one that was invisible because the sequential Gricean framework had no means to allow its manifestation. On the other hand, as I have been emphasizing, this extraordinary fact is something that naturally suggests itself based on the interactive idea of equilibrium!

Indeed, it now becomes clearer that illocutionary meanings may generally interact with one another via locutionary meanings rather than directly, as distinct illocutionary meanings may not possess the kind of internal unity that locutionary meanings possess. That is, the enrichment $\sigma_4 = in\ New\ York$ and the implicature $\sigma_5 = [Let's\ go\ see\ it]$ connect with each other only in the presence of the locutionary content $\sigma^\ell = Harvey\ is\ playing$, making the illocutionary content $\sigma^\imath$ a somewhat artificial construct.

It may be difficult to construct an empirical test for this kind of interdependence between locutionary and illocutionary meanings because it is difficult to isolate just the effect of the speaker's conveying one illocutionary meaning on the speaker's conveying the optimal locutionary meaning—there are so many factors simultaneously pushing and jostling in one direction or another to generate the full meaning of an utterance.

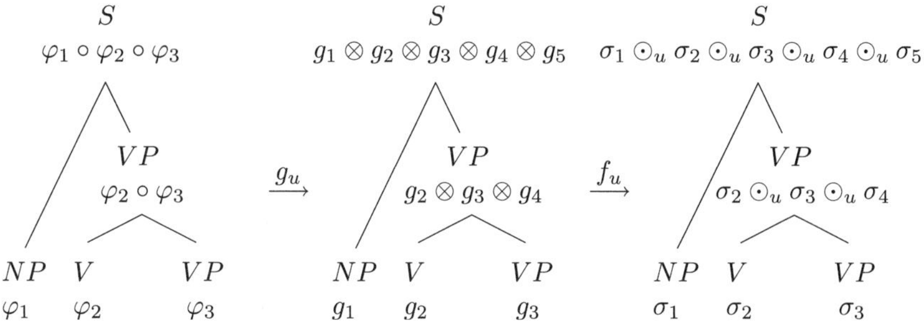

Figure 4.8
The three isomorphic trees with the full content

But once one has accepted the basic ideas of equilibrium semantics, the interdependence appears obvious and indispensable.

So far, I have derived seven partial contents σ_1, σ_2, σ_3, $\sigma_{23} = \sigma_2\sigma_3$, $\sigma_{123} = \sigma_1\sigma_2\sigma_3$, σ_4, and σ_5, either via **SCIF** or via **S(C)IF**. The initial probabilities $P_i(x \mid u) = P(x_i \mid x_{-i}, u)$ in the various games have to be reinterpreted to include all the locutionary and illocutionary contents in the vector x with the range of the index i being adjusted accordingly. Earlier, we had $x = (x_1, x_2, x_3, x_{23}, x_{123})$ for locutionary meaning and we had $x = (x_4, x_5)$ for illocutionary meaning. Now, $x = (x_1, x_2, x_3, x_{23}, x_{123}, x_4, x_5)$ and the various conditional probabilities involve all these seven sets of contents.[30]

The combined equilibrium semantics of locutionary and illocutionary meanings may be expressed via the following isomorphic trees:

$[_S\ [_{NP}\ \varphi_1] \circ [_{VP}\ [_V\ \varphi_2] \circ [_{VP}\ \varphi_3] \circ e] \circ e]$

$[_S\ [_{NP}\ g_1] \otimes [_{VP}\ [_V\ g_2] \otimes [_{VP}\ g_3] \otimes g_4] \otimes g_5]$

$[_S\ [_{NP}\ \sigma_1] \odot_u [_{VP}\ [_V\ \sigma_2] \odot_u [_{VP}\ \sigma_3] \odot_u \sigma_4] \odot_u \sigma_5]$

Visually displayed, the trees look as in Figure 4.8.

We get the same fixed point equation as before, but suitably extended to include the interdependencies of both locutionary and illocutionary meaning.

$$C_u(\alpha, P(x \mid u)) = f_u[g_u(\alpha, P(x \mid u))] = x \tag{4.5}$$

30. Of course, I have made the simplifying assumption that these seven sets of contents exhaust the full meaning of the utterance, but it is easy to extend the vector x to include more contents.

Just to be crystal clear what this equation is, I will spell it out below:[31]

$$\begin{bmatrix} f_u[g_u(\alpha, P_1(x_1 \mid x_2, x_3, x_4, x_5, u))] \\ f_u[g_u(\alpha, P_2(x_2 \mid x_1, x_3, x_4, x_5, u))] \\ f_u[g_u(\alpha, P_3(x_3 \mid x_1, x_2, x_4, x_5, u))] \\ f_u[g_u(\alpha, P_{23}(x_2, x_3 \mid x_1, x_4, x_5, u))] \\ f_u[g_u(\alpha, P_{123}(x_1, x_2, x_3 \mid x_4, x_5, u))] \\ f_u[g_u(\alpha, P_4(x_4 \mid x_1, x_2, x_3, x_5, u))] \\ f_u[g_u(\alpha, P_5(x_5 \mid x_1, x_2, x_3, x_4, u))] \end{bmatrix} = \begin{bmatrix} x_1 \\ x_2 \\ x_3 \\ x_2 \odot_u x_3 \\ x_1 \odot_u (x_2 \odot_u x_3) \\ x_4 \\ x_5 \end{bmatrix} \tag{4.6}$$

Since the locutionary meaning is σ^ℓ and the illocutionary meaning is $\sigma^\imath$, the full meaning is given by $\mathcal{C}_u(\varphi) \equiv \mathcal{C}_u(\varphi, P(x \mid u)) = \sigma^\ell \odot_u \sigma^\imath = \sigma_1\sigma_2\sigma_3\sigma_4\sigma_5 = \sigma$. Of course, in this larger globally interactive model, σ^ℓ and $\sigma^\imath$ also codetermine each other. Alternatively, the speaker's conveying all the seven contents σ_1, σ_2, σ_3, $\sigma_2\sigma_3$, $\sigma_1\sigma_2\sigma_3$, σ_4, and σ_5 simultaneously codetermine one another.

Thus, as promised, I have derived the full meaning of the utterance of φ in u from first principles involving nothing but basic assumptions about ontology and action! Such a system of linear simultaneous equations and inequalities was hinted at over twenty years ago in Parikh (1987b) and later publications by the author. It has now been realized.

The full proposition expressed by the utterance is of course $c \models \sigma$.

4.7 Propositions

Just as infons are partial and quantized, so are propositions. But they are so in a completely derivative way that supervenes on the partiality of infons.

The partial propositions derived so far were $c \models \sigma_i$ for $i = 1, \ldots, 5$, the locutionary proposition was $c \models \sigma^\ell$, the illocutionary proposition was $c \models \sigma^\imath$, and the full proposition just derived was $c \models \sigma$. It is straightforward to see how more complete propositions are built up from their proper parts.

Once c is determined, it tells us whether the utterance is true or false based on whether c really does support σ or not. When statements are not involved, it would tell us whether the utterance is appropriate or not, or, to use Austin's (1975) expression, whether it is *felicitous* or not.

31. I have deliberately left out some components of the vector such as x_{234}, x_{1234}, and x_{12345} to keep things simple.

For the example at hand, c could well be taken to be the rather large situation of New York this evening. Then the first four contents σ_1, σ_2, σ_3, and σ_4 expressing the statement that the film *Harvey* is playing in New York (this evening) would be true with respect to c if the film is in fact playing in New York this evening. Without a situation c to compare the infons against, there is no way to determine the truth of the utterance.

I will address the question of how c is identified and discuss truth at greater length in the next chapter. This will lead us to a further analysis of free enrichment or completion.

4.8 Computing Meaning

Since the vector fixed point Equation 4.5 is a system of simultaneous linear equations and inequalities, it can be reexpressed more simply as a family of linear systems thus:

$$A_j v_j \geq b_j$$

where the matrices A_j and vectors v_j and b_j contain appropriate numerical (or algebraic) constants ultimately derivable from all the payoffs and probabilities in each of the many games (e.g., g_1, g_2, g_3, g_{23}, g_{123}, g_4, g_5 in our example). The reason why our fixed point equation translates into a *family* of linear systems, rather than just one system, is that the fixed point equation itself compactly represents *all* the possible cases that arise based on one possible solution set or another. For example, if a set of contents including σ_1 is a possible solution, then it corresponds to one set of inequalities and to one system out of the whole family of linear systems. If instead the set of contents including σ_1' is a possible solution, then that set corresponds to a different set of inequalities and to a different system in the family, and so on. Usually, a small subset of the possible systems will be valid (i.e., will be true and internally consistent) and the contents corresponding to this subset will then represent the optimal meanings of the utterance. It would be an instructive exercise for the reader to write down the many equations that make up the family of linear systems for our example. Basically, each system is just a permutation of the same linear expressions representing the expected payoffs for different strategies.

I show a few of these equations to get the reader started. Consider the equations corresponding to the game g_1 for the instance of x_1 where σ_1 is the solution. These are derived from the game shown earlier in Figures 3.12 and 3.16 and shown again for convenience in Figure 4.9.

	σ_1	σ_1'
$\varphi_1\varphi_1$	$p_1a_A + p_{1'}c_A', p_1a_B + p_{1'}c_B'$	$p_1c_A + p_{1'}a_A', p_1c_B + p_{1'}a_B'$
$\varphi_1'\varphi_1$	$p_1b_A + p_{1'}c_A', p_1b_B + p_{1'}c_B'$	$p_1b_A + p_{1'}a_A', p_1b_B + p_{1'}a_B'$
$\varphi_1\varphi_1''$	$p_1a_A + p_{1'}b_A', p_1a_B + p_{1'}b_B'$	$p_1c_A + p_{1'}b_A', p_1c_B + p_{1'}b_B'$
$\varphi_1'\varphi_1''$	$p_1b_A + p_{1'}b_A', p_1b_B + p_{1'}b_B'$	$p_1b_A + p_{1'}b_A', p_1b_B + p_{1'}b_B'$

Figure 4.9
The algebraic lexical game g_1 in strategic form

The first inequality corresponding to g_1 for the instance σ_1 of x_1 relates to the choice of initial probability as a strategic variable in the global equilibrium:

$$p_1 \geq p_{1'}$$

The next set of inequalities relates to the choices of utterance $\varphi_1\varphi_1''$ and interpretation σ_1 as a Nash equilibrium. They are derived by comparing the appropriate expected utilities shown in the cells in Figure 4.9:

$$p_1a_A + p_{1'}b_A' \geq p_1a_A + p_{1'}c_A'$$

$$p_1a_A + p_{1'}b_A' \geq p_1b_A + p_{1'}c_A'$$

$$p_1a_A + p_{1'}b_A' \geq p_1b_A + p_{1'}b_A'$$

$$p_1a_B + p_{1'}b_B' \geq p_1c_B + p_{1'}b_B'$$

The third set of inequalities relates to the choices of utterance $\varphi_1'\varphi_1$ and interpretation σ_1' as the other (inferior) Nash equilibrium extracted in the same way:

$$p_1b_A + p_{1'}a_A' \geq p_1c_A + p_{1'}a_A'$$

$$p_1b_A + p_{1'}a_A' \geq p_1c_A + p_{1'}b_A'$$

$$p_1b_A + p_{1'}a_A' \geq p_1b_A + p_{1'}b_A'$$

$$p_1b_B + p_{1'}a_B' \geq p_1b_B + p_{1'}c_B'$$

Finally, the equations relating to the choice of $(\varphi_1\varphi_1'', \sigma_1)$ as the Pareto-Nash equilibrium obtained by comparing the expected payoffs for the two Nash equilibria are as follows:

$$\rho_1 a_A + \rho_{1'} b_A' \geq \rho_1 b_A + \rho_{1'} a_A'$$

$$\rho_1 a_B + \rho_{1'} b_B' \geq \rho_1 b_B + \rho_{1'} a_B'$$

We get these eleven inequalities for g_1 and the instance σ_1 of x_1. For a different smaller or larger game, there would be a different number. Notice that all eleven equations can be expressed in terms of the vector $(\rho_1, \rho_{1'})$, so this can be a part of the vector v_j in one member of the family $A_j v_j \geq b_j$. The matrix A_j can then be filled in appropriately with combinations of payoffs. The column vector b_j would just be the zero vector.

We have to consider similar sets of inequalities for the remaining games g_2, g_3, g_{23}, g_{123}, g_4, and g_5 as they relate to the different instantiations for x_2, x_3, x_{23}, x_{123}, x_4, and x_5. All of these inequalities *together* for σ_1 as an instance of x_1 and for other contents as instances of x_2, x_3, x_{23}, x_{123}, x_4, and x_5 constitute just *one* member of the family of linear systems referred to above. There are different such linear systems for each possible candidate for x in the global fixed point Equation 4.4.

The inequalities obtained from the other games can then fill in the rest of the linear system $A_j v_j \geq b_j$ in the same way as was done for g_1 and σ_1 as an instance of x_1. This gives us a block diagonal matrix for A_j consisting of combinations of payoffs. It gives us $v \equiv v_j = (\rho_1, \rho_{1'}, \rho_2, \rho_3, \rho_{3'}, \ldots, \rho_5, \rho_{5'})$ for all j and it gives us $b \equiv b_j = 0$ for all j. The family of linear systems thus simplifies to:

$$A_j v \geq 0$$

The solution of this set of equations is not like the usual mode of solution involved with a linear system. The unknown x is not directly present in the equations. Each candidate for x simply corresponds to a set of numerical (or algebraic) inequalities. Since we already have the entire space of possible solutions from the constraints **C** and **I**, all that has to be done is to *check* whether the linear system corresponding to a set of contents is valid or not (i.e., contains true inequality statements or not). When it is, those contents can jointly be said to be one of the full meanings of the utterance.[32] Even though the satisfaction of various inequalities is trivial

32. I am deliberately allowing for the case where an utterance has multiple meanings, as in a pun.

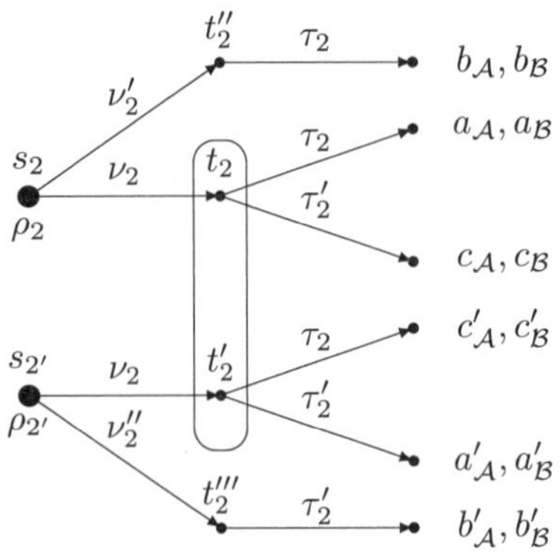

Figure 4.10
A lexical game g_2 involving a garden path effect

to check by hand—indeed, the reader can check the eleven inequalities above by inspection—the number of linear systems in the family and the number of equations in each linear system can be large, so the most convenient way to compute the meaning of an utterance is to use a digital computer to check which linear systems are valid and which are not.

Thus, I have, modulo certain basic assumptions and first principles, reduced the problem of deriving the full meaning of an utterance of φ in the situation u to a numerical computational task! It seems reasonable to think that all natural language utterances can be brought within the ambit of this framework by proceeding in a similar way.

4.9 A Garden Path Sentence

Recall the garden path sentence of section 3.3.3 uttered in an appropriate situation u:

The rich man the boats. (ν)

ν was represented as $\nu_1 \circ \nu_2 \circ \cdots \circ \nu_5$, where $\nu_1 = $ THE, $\nu_2 = $ RICH, $\nu_3 = $ MAN, $\nu_4 = $ THE, and $\nu_5 = $ BOATS. Two of the relevant lexical games are displayed in Figures 4.10 and 4.11.

To avoid multiplying symbols, I use $g_2 = g_u(\nu_2)$ and $g_3 = g_u(\nu_3)$ to stand for these two games.

Figure 4.10 involves the partial contents τ_2 and τ_2' which represent the nominal and adjectival readings of RICH respectively. Earlier, I assumed that $\rho_2 < \rho_{2'}$, since the objective probability of the nominal reading is

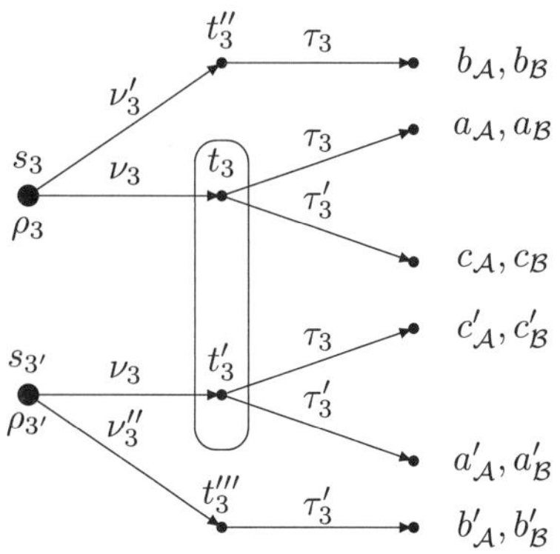

Figure 4.11
A related lexical game g_3 involving a garden path effect

less likely. The unique Pareto-Nash equilibrium would then be $(\nu_2'\nu_2, \tau_2')$, assuming that Case 2 of the Pareto-Nash Inequalities is satisfied, and the best choice for $\mathcal{B}$ would be to interpret RICH in the adjectival sense of being wealthy.

Figure 4.11 involves the partial contents τ_3 and τ_3' which represent the verb and noun readings of MAN, respectively. Here, I assumed that $\rho_3 < \rho_{3'}$, since the objective probability of the verb reading is less likely. This game would have the unique Pareto-Nash equilibrium $(\nu_3'\nu_3, \tau_3')$ and the best choice for $\mathcal{B}$ would be to interpret (THE) MAN to denote some adult male human.

In both cases, the high frequency sense appears to dominate the optimal choice, all else being equal. Notice further that the most frequent senses reinforce each other; RICH as an adjective is an obvious modifier of MAN as a noun. This fact contributes to the severity of the garden path effect.

Of course, all else is *not* equal, as I proceed to show.

There are two ways to look at the communication involved in this utterance: from a psycholinguistic perspective and from a semantic perspective. The psycholinguistic viewpoint shows how we actually interpret an utterance in real time, going from left to right in the sentence, using the information gleaned from the first word to help us interpret the second, simultaneously reinforcing our conjecture about the meaning of the first word, then using the information gleaned from the first two words to help us interpret the third, with the third hopefully reinforcing and confirming our hypotheses about the first two words, and so on. The garden path effect reveals precisely this temporal and therefore *partial* process of interpretation and simultaneously reveals its pitfalls because not all of the information provided by the utterance has been absorbed *in parallel* until we reach the end of the sentence. When studying the utterance of φ from a semantic viewpoint, we had every atomic and molecular content influencing every other atomic and molecular content *simultaneously*, since from this perspective we abstract from the temporal process and take all the information provided by the utterance as given *together*. When the end of the sentence is reached, all the information does become available, and then our psycholinguistically derived interpretation changes dramatically.

Let us look at these two viewpoints in some detail as they show the versatility of equilibrium semantics in handling both vantage points in a natural way.

4.9.1 The Syntactic Constraint

From an abstract semantic viewpoint, **S** is clear:

$$[_S\,[_{NP}\,[_{Det}\,v_1] \circ [_N\,v_2]] \circ [_{VP}\,[_V\,v_3] \circ [_{NP}\,[_{Det}\,v_4] \circ [_N\,v_5]]]]$$

However, from a more concrete psycholinguistic standpoint, **S** progresses through five stages as follows:

Stage 1

$$[_S\,[_{NP}\,[_{Det}\,v_1] \ldots] \ldots]$$

Stage 2

$$[_S\,[_{NP}\,[_{Det}\,v_1] \circ [_N\,v_2]] \ldots]$$

or

$$[_S\,[_{NP}\,[_{Det}\,v_1] \circ [_{NP}\,[_{Adj}\,v_2] \ldots]] \ldots]$$

Stage 3

$$[_S\,[_{NP}\,[_{Det}\,v_1] \circ [_N\,v_2]] \circ [_{VP}\,[_V\,v_3] \ldots] \ldots]$$

or

$$[_S\,[_{NP}\,[_{Det}\,v_1] \circ [_{NP}\,[_{Adj}\,v_2] \circ [_N\,v_3]]] \ldots]$$

Stage 4

$$[_S\,[_{NP}\,[_{Det}\,v_1] \circ [_N\,v_2]] \circ [_{VP}\,[_V\,v_3] \circ [_{NP}\,[_{Det}\,v_4] \ldots]] \ldots]$$

or

$[_S [_{NP} [_{Det}\ v_1] \circ [_{NP} [_{Adj}\ v_2] \circ [_N\ v_3]]] \circ [_{NP} [_{Det}\ v_4] \ldots] \ldots]$

Stage 5

$[_S [_{NP} [_{Det}\ v_1] \circ [_N\ v_2]] \circ [_{VP} [_V\ v_3] \circ [_{NP} [_{Det}\ v_4] \circ [_N\ v_5]]]]$

or

$[_S [_{NP} [_{Det}\ v_1] \circ [_{NP} [_{Adj}\ v_2] \circ [_N\ v_3]]] \circ [_{NP} [_{Det}\ v_4] \circ [_{NP}\ v_5]] \ldots]$

At the first stage, there is only one possible beginning of the parse. In the second, third, and fourth stages, there are two possible incomplete parses with the first being much *less* likely than the second, given the objective frequencies referred to above. In the last stage, when all seemed to be going well for the more likely second parse, there are no further words to help complete it. The ellipsis in this parse indicates that more material is expected, but the sentence ends abruptly, creating the garden path effect. In the case of the less likely first parse in the last stage, no more material is expected and a satisfactory parse of the words is achieved and the addressee is forced to switch to this parse. What happens psycholinguistically is that the addressee is unable to hold both parses in her head simultaneously and so simply ignores the less likely parse until the end of the sentence when she is forced to come up with it. The constraint **S** explains the syntactic aspect of the garden path effect, the inability to achieve a complete parse with what seemed like more likely partial parses. Clearly, this occurs because the addressee does not have access to the words that appear later in the sentence, that is, the addressee does not have access to the whole sentence together and so is forced to go by what seems like the most likely parse based on the objective frequencies of the syntactic categories for the words in the sentence.

4.9.2 The Conventional Constraint

There are four distinct words in v—THE, RICH, MAN, and BOATS. Of these, RICH has many conventional meanings, though I will simplify and consider just one, namely $P^{rich} = P^{v_2}$, which is just the property of being wealthy. Likewise, I will assume MAN and BOATS are associated with just one property each, $P^{man} = P^{v_3}$ and $P^{boats} = P^{v_5}$, respectively. Finally, I will be analyzing the definite article in detail in chapter 6, so here I take THE to be conventionally associated with the single property $P^{the} = P^{v_1} = P^{v_4}$. More will be said about this special property later.

4.9.3 The Informational Constraint

Here we look at **I** just for RICH and MAN since these are the words that create the garden path effect.

RICH:

- Referential use: $v_2 \to P^{v_2} \xrightarrow{u} \langle\!\langle e(P^{v_2}, r_u) \rangle\!\rangle = \tau_2$
- Predicative use: $v_2 \to P^{v_2} \xrightarrow{u} \langle\!\langle P^{v_2} \rangle\!\rangle = \tau_2'$

Technically, the first referential use ought to be a predicative use but I identify it as a referential use because I consider the noun phrase THE RICH as a shortcut to avoid having to deal explicitly with the definite article in this chapter. It picks out the extension of the property of being wealthy relative to an appropriate resource situation r_u. The second predicative use simply singles out the property itself. As shown in Figure 4.10, these are the two possible contents of v_2 in u.

MAN:

- Predicative use: $v_3 \to P^{v_3} \xrightarrow{u} \langle\!\langle P^{v_3} \rangle\!\rangle = \tau_3$
- Referential use: $v_3 \to P^{v_3} \xrightarrow{u} \langle\!\langle e(P^{v_3}, r_u') \mid Unique(P^{v_3}, r_u', q_u') \rangle\!\rangle = \tau_3'$

The first constraint is straightforward and refers to the predicative use of MAN as a verb. The second should also be just a predicative use but, as before, I have combined it with the effect of THE and take it as the content of the combined phrase THE MAN. Again, these are the two possible contents of v_3 in u as shown in Figure 4.11.

4.9.4 The Flow Constraint

As was done with **C** and **I**, I will omit consideration of the lexical games corresponding to v_1, v_4, and v_5 and look more closely at the games $g_2 = g_u(v_2)$ and $g_3 = g_u(v_3)$ shown in Figures 4.10 and 4.11.

The key thing to take note of is the initial probabilities. From the abstract semantic viewpoint where all the information is simultaneously available, these are $\rho_2 = P(\tau_2 \mid x_{-2}, u) = P(\tau_2 \mid x_1, x_3, x_4, x_5, u)$ and $\rho_3 = P(\tau_3 \mid x_{-3}, u) = P(\tau_3 \mid x_1, x_2, x_4, x_5, u)$. In this situation, the reader can check that $\rho_{2'} = P(\tau_2' \mid x_{-2}, u) = P(\tau_2' \mid x_1, x_3, x_4, x_5, u) \approx 0 \ll \rho_2$ and likewise $\rho_{3'} = P(\tau_3' \mid x_{-3}, u) = P(\tau_3' \mid x_1, x_2, x_4, x_5, u) \approx 0 \ll \rho_3$ because when the whole sentence is taken into account it becomes clear to the addressee that $\rho_{2'}$ and $\rho_{3'}$, the likelihood that $\mathcal{A}$ is conveying the adjectival sense of RICH or the nominal sense of MAN, are both just zero. Earlier, I included just the objective high frequencies of these senses, but when the addressee takes all the conditioning information into account—in particular, the fact that no complete parse is achievable—these high frequencies are *overridden* by the rest of the information. In the semantic view, all this information *is* available and so there is no garden path effect. The global solutions to the two games are $(v_2 v_2'', \tau_2)$ rather than $(v_2' v_2, \tau_2')$, and $(v_3 v_3'', \tau_3)$ rather than $(v_3' v_3, \tau_3')$, with ρ_2 and ρ_3 as the high probabilities rather than the other way around.

However, from the psycholinguistic viewpoint, all the conditioning information is *not* simultaneously available. Each conditioning variable makes its appearance only as the utterance progresses. So when only the first two words v_1 and v_2 have been uttered, the probability $\rho_{2'} = P(\tau_2' \mid x_{-2}, u) = P(\tau_2' \mid x_1, u) \gg \rho_2$ because there is only the high frequency of this adjectival sense of v_2 and the conditioning by x_1 and u. The conditioning variables x_3, x_4, and x_5 are absent. As a result, the solution to the game is $(v_2' v_2, \tau_2')$ as I had noted earlier and the addressee is already on the garden path. Then, as the next word v_3 appears, we get $\rho_{2'} = P(\tau_2' \mid x_{-2}, u) = P(\tau_2' \mid x_1, \tau_3', u) \gg \rho_2$ and, of course, $\rho_{3'} = P(\tau_3' \mid x_{-3}, u) = P(\tau_3' \mid x_1, \tau_2', u) \gg \rho_3$. Notice that $\rho_{2'}$ changes dynamically as $x_3 = \tau_3'$ gets introduced as one more conditioning variable. This new conditioning variable in the case where $x_3 = \tau_3'$ and not $x_3 = \tau_3$ in fact *reinforces* the adjectival high frequency sense, just as $x_2 = \tau_2'$ reinforces the nominal sense τ_3' of v_3. This takes $\mathcal{B}$ further along the garden path. But then v_4 and v_5 appear, and though the garden path continues because a coherent parse is still available, the addressee's confidence in the interpretation begins to diminish since the difference between ρ_2 and $\rho_{2'}$ and ρ_3 and $\rho_{3'}$ is no longer as great. Then $\mathcal{B}$ comes to the end of the sentence and her hypothesis collapses since no parse is possible; now all the conditioning variables are present as we had in the semantic viewpoint and, most critically, the information that there is no complete parse for the adjectival and nominal readings of v_2 and v_3 becomes available through the conditioning variable u.[33] Earlier, u did not contain this information because the utterance was still in progress; now it does since the utterance has ended. This can be seen more perspicuously by breaking down u into the sequence of subsituations u_1, u_2, u_3, u_4, and u_5. This leads $\mathcal{B}$ to turn to the other parse and essentially to the semantic solution above.

The full equilibrium semantics of this sentence with respect to the three isomorphic trees makes the situation even clearer.

33. In section 7.1.1, I show how to represent this information explicitly via the conditioning variables.

4.9.5 The Equilibrium Semantics of the Garden Path Sentence

From an abstract semantic viewpoint, the locutionary semantics for v uttered in u is no different in essence from that of φ:

$$[_S\ [_{NP}\ [_{Det}\ v_1] \circ [_N\ v_2]] \circ [_{VP}\ [_V\ v_3] \circ [_{NP}\ [_{Det}\ v_4] \circ [_N\ v_5]]]]$$

$$[_S\ [_{NP}\ [_{Det}\ g_1] \otimes [_N\ g_2]] \otimes [_{VP}\ [_V\ g_3] \otimes [_{NP}\ [_{Det}\ g_4] \otimes [_N\ g_5]]]]$$

$$[_S\ [_{NP}\ [_{Det}\ \tau_1] \odot_u [_N\ \tau_2]] \odot_u [_{VP}\ [_V\ \tau_3] \odot_u [_{NP}\ [_{Det}\ \tau_4] \odot_u [_N\ \tau_5]]]]$$

Here $g_1 = g_u(v_1)$, $g_2 = g_u(v_2)$, $g_3 = g_u(v_3)$, $g_4 = g_u(v_4)$, and $g_5 = g_u(v_5)$ and τ_1, τ_2, τ_3, τ_4, and τ_5 are their equilibrium contents.

However, from a more concrete psycholinguistic standpoint, the trees progress through five stages as follows:

Stage 1

$$[_S\ [_{NP}\ [_{Det}\ v_1] \ldots] \ldots]$$

$$[_S\ [_{NP}\ [_{Det}\ g_1] \ldots] \ldots]$$

$$[_S\ [_{NP}\ [_{Det}\ \tau_1] \ldots] \ldots]$$

Stage 2

$$[_S\ [_{NP}\ [_{Det}\ v_1] \circ [_N\ v_2]] \ldots]$$

$$[_S\ [_{NP}\ [_{Det}\ g_1] \otimes [_N\ g_2]] \ldots]$$

$$[_S\ [_{NP}\ [_{Det}\ \tau_1] \odot_u [_N\ \tau_2]] \ldots]$$

or

$$[_S\ [_{NP}\ [_{Det}\ v_1] \circ [_{NP}\ [_{Adj}\ v_2] \ldots]] \ldots]$$

$$[_S\ [_{NP}\ [_{Det}\ g_1] \otimes [_{NP}\ [_{Adj}\ g_2] \ldots]] \ldots]$$

$$[_S\ [_{NP}\ [_{Det}\ \tau_1'] \odot_u [_{NP}\ [_{Adj}\ \tau_2'] \ldots]] \ldots]$$

Stage 3

$$[_S\ [_{NP}\ [_{Det}\ v_1] \circ [_N\ v_2]] \circ [_{VP}\ [_V\ v_3] \ldots] \ldots]$$

$$[_S\ [_{NP}\ [_{Det}\ g_1] \otimes [_N\ g_2]] \otimes [_{VP}\ [_V\ g_3] \ldots] \ldots]$$

$$[_S\ [_{NP}\ [_{Det}\ \tau_1] \odot_u [_N\ \tau_2]] \odot_u [_{VP}\ [_V\ \tau_3] \ldots] \ldots]$$

or

$$[_S\ [_{NP}\ [_{Det}\ v_1] \circ [_{NP}\ [_{Adj}\ v_2] \circ [_N\ v_3]]] \ldots]$$

$[_S\ [_{NP}\ [_{Det}\ g_1] \otimes [_{NP}\ [_{Adj}\ g_2] \otimes [_N\ g_3]]] \ldots]$

$[_S\ [_{NP}\ [_{Det}\ \tau'_1] \odot_u [_{NP}\ [_{Adj}\ \tau'_2] \odot_u [_N\ \tau'_3]]] \ldots]$

Stage 4

$[_S\ [_{NP}\ [_{Det}\ v_1] \circ [_N\ v_2]] \circ [_{VP}\ [_V\ v_3] \circ [_{NP}\ [_{Det}\ v_4] \ldots]] \ldots]$

$[_S\ [_{NP}\ [_{Det}\ g_1] \otimes [_N\ g_2]] \otimes [_{VP}\ [_V\ g_3] \otimes [_{NP}\ [_{Det}\ g_4] \ldots]] \ldots]$

$[_S\ [_{NP}\ [_{Det}\ \tau_1] \odot_u [_N\ \tau_2]] \odot_u [_{VP}\ [_V\ \tau_3] \odot_u [_{NP}\ [_{Det}\ \tau_4] \ldots]] \ldots]$

or

$[_S\ [_{NP}\ [_{Det}\ v_1] \circ [_{NP}\ [_{Adj}\ v_2] \circ [_N\ v_3]]] \circ [_{NP}\ [_{Det}\ v_4] \ldots] \ldots]$

$[_S\ [_{NP}\ [_{Det}\ g_1] \otimes [_{NP}\ [_{Adj}\ g_2] \otimes [_N\ g_3]]] \otimes [_{NP}\ [_{Det}\ g_4] \ldots] \ldots]$

$[_S\ [_{NP}\ [_{Det}\ \tau'_1] \odot_u [_{NP}\ [_{Adj}\ \tau'_2] \odot_u [_N\ \tau'_3]]] \odot_u [_{NP}\ [_{Det}\ \tau'_4] \ldots] \ldots]$

Stage 5

$[_S\ [_{NP}\ [_{Det}\ v_1] \circ [_N\ v_2]] \circ [_{VP}\ [_V\ v_3] \circ [_{NP}\ [_{Det}\ v_4] \circ [_N\ v_5]]]]$

$[_S\ [_{NP}\ [_{Det}\ g_1] \otimes [_N\ g_2]] \otimes [_{VP}\ [_V\ g_3] \otimes [_{NP}\ [_{Det}\ g_4] \otimes [_N\ g_5]]]]$

$[_S\ [_{NP}\ [_{Det}\ \tau_1] \odot_u [_N\ \tau_2]] \odot_u [_{VP}\ [_V\ \tau_3] \odot_u [_{NP}\ [_{Det}\ \tau_4] \odot_u [_N\ \tau_5]]]]$

or

$[_S\ [_{NP}\ [_{Det}\ v_1] \circ [_{NP}\ [_{Adj}\ v_2] \circ [_N\ v_3]]] \circ [_{NP}\ [_{Det}\ v_4] \circ [_{NP}\ v_5]] \ldots]$

$[_S\ [_{NP}\ [_{Det}\ g_1] \otimes [_{NP}\ [_{Adj}\ g_2] \otimes [_N\ g_3]]] \otimes [_{NP}\ [_{Det}\ g_4] \otimes [_{NP}\ g_5]] \ldots]$

$[_S\ [_{NP}\ [_{Det}\ \tau'_1] \odot_u [_{NP}\ [_{Adj}\ \tau'_2] \odot_u [_N\ \tau'_3]]] \odot_u [_{NP}\ [_{Det}\ \tau'_4] \odot_u [_{NP}\ \tau'_5]] \ldots]$

This progression of trees should require no explanation. Remember that each tree of games is obtained from the corresponding parse tree via the map g_u and each contents tree is obtained from the corresponding tree of games via the map f_u. The key point to note is that whenever there are two sets of trees in a single stage, the initial probabilities are different in each set because they are conditioned by different contents and they play a strategic role in the global equilibrium in that stage. In the last (fifth) stage, the second parse fails as there is no more material forthcoming, and so we are left with just the solutions desired. This gives us a full explanation of the psycholinguistic garden path effect. It should be clear from the analysis that the fundamental reason why the garden path effect exists is that the interpretive process is embedded in *time* and that this constrains the nature of our access to the sentence. If we wish, this can be considered a kind of bounded rationality that arises as a result of our bounded perceptual powers (and when speech is involved, then our bounded powers of production), although a Kantian may prefer to see temporality as a precondition and part of rationality and therefore not a way of bounding rationality.

4.10 Structural Ambiguity

In the previous section, there were two competing parses until the very end when one of the parses failed. Frequently, however, there are multiple parses for a sentence and the selection of the meaning corresponding to a favored parse becomes a further factor in eliciting the content of an utterance.

Suppose, for example, that Harvey is playing with his sister Caitlin, and the father Alan, observing them, says to the mother Barbara in a new utterance situation also denoted by u:

Harvey saw her duck. (μ)

Here the background game G need not be spelled out, although it is about the parents observing the children play. Let $\mu_1 = $ HARVEY, $\mu_2 = $ SAW, $\mu_3 = $ HER, and $\mu_4 = $ DUCK. Notice that μ has two legitimate parses.

The Syntactic Constraint:

S is now:[34]

$$[_S\, [_{NP}\, \mu_1] \circ [_{VP}\, [_V\, \mu_2] \circ [_{VP}\, [_{NP}\, \mu_3] \circ [_{VP}\, [_V\, \mu_4]]]]]$$

or

$$[_S\, [_{NP}\, \mu_1] \circ [_{VP}\, [_V\, \mu_3] \circ [_{NP}\, [_{Det}\, \mu_3] \circ [_N\, \mu_4]]]]$$

If the children are playing, Caitlin could actually have ducked or Harvey might have seen her toy duck or perhaps even a real duck. To simplify things, I will assume there is no duck of any kind in the apartment, and so the probability that Alan is referring to an animal of some kind, whether real or toy, is low.

The first parse involves an attitude report with an embedded tenseless sentence HER DUCK. I want to avoid such constructions here that require

34. I am using somewhat old-fashioned parses.

a complicating factor since their content involves a relation between an individual and a *situation* that supports the content of the embedded sentence. In the example being considered, the content would be a relation between Harvey and a situation in which Caitlin ducked. This is a point made in chapter 8 of Barwise and Perry (1983).

To avoid this complication here because it would take us on an unnecessary detour, I do not go into a detailed analysis of this utterance but focus just on the issue of interest, namely, how equilibrium semantics deals with structural ambiguity.

Assume that υ_1 (i.e., the Greek letter upsilon, not the English letter "v") is the infon representing the equilibrium content of the lexical game involving HARVEY and υ_2 is the infon representing the equilibrium content of the lexical game involving SAW. These two infons are the same for both readings of the utterance. Let υ_3 and υ_3' represent the two infons capturing the equilibrium content of the lexical game involving HER, the former for the first parse and the latter for the second parse. Likewise, let υ_4 and υ_4' represent the two infons capturing the equilibrium content of the lexical game involving DUCK, again the former for the first parse and the latter for the second parse. These six contents are intuitively obvious but I will not write them out via the Conventional and Informational Constraints. For the curious, the third and fourth former contents would require infons of the form $\upsilon_3^s = \langle\langle \models; s; \upsilon_3 \rangle\rangle$ and $\upsilon_4^s = \langle\langle \models; s; \upsilon_4 \rangle\rangle$ where s is the situation seen by Harvey. These more complex infons, rather than υ_3 and υ_4, would enter into the corresponding contents tree.

The method of equilibrium semantics dictates that the function g_u would map each parse tree into a corresponding tree of games and the function f_u would then map these trees of games into corresponding content trees as before. So far, everything would be as we have seen with the earlier examples except for the complicating situational factor.

This gives us two candidates for the meaning of the utterance as we would expect, $\upsilon_1\upsilon_2\upsilon_3^s\upsilon_4^s$ and $\upsilon_1\upsilon_2\upsilon_3'\upsilon_4'$. Structural disambiguation now requires a further game of partial information involving two initial nodes, one for each reading, with these two contents as the possible interpretations of μ. It would be solved in the usual way with the desired meaning $\upsilon_1\upsilon_2\upsilon_3^s\upsilon_4^s$ as the equilibrium of the game. This would follow essentially from the probability of a reference to a duck being remote, other things being equal.

This treatment is a little rushed but the reader should be sufficiently familiar with equilibrium semantics by now to be able to supply the missing details. As it stands, this method of handling structural ambiguity works but it lacks elegance. The creative solution to this problem, revealed in section 7.1.1, yields a system of vast power and beauty.

In section 4.1, I listed several of the key aspects of meaning and have shown explicitly how many of these can be handled by my framework. It seems reasonable to expect that the *full* meaning of an utterance can be recovered in the same way.

4.11 The Universality of Games of Partial Information

I now state and prove a basic theorem that establishes the universality of games of partial information for the semantics of natural language. This result is so basic that from the standpoint of equilibrium semantics it could well be called "The Fundamental Theorem of Semantics." Universality is a concept from algebra and is commonly found in category-theoretic contexts. My treatment remains elementary; I do not venture into category-theoretic realms but restrict my considerations to basic algebra.

Fix a parameter u for the utterance situation. As explained in section 2.6, u contains a parameter $\dot{\varphi}$ that can be anchored to any expression that is uttered in u.

As before, the vocabulary $\mathcal{V}$ is a finite set of words. A special concatenation operation $\circ$ is defined on it and it is used to generate the set $\mathcal{L}$, which contains all the words, phrases, and sentences of the language together with the empty and zero strings. $\circ$ is associative and with the empty string makes $\mathcal{L}$ a monoid.

Again, $\mathcal{I}$ is the set of infons with the operation $\odot_u$. Recall from Fact 1 in section 2.3.3 that $\mathcal{I}$ is also a monoid with $\mathbf{1}$ as identity. C_u^ℓ is the interpretation function from $\mathcal{L}$ to $\mathcal{I}$. As a result, C_u^ℓ is a homomorphism.

Let $\mathcal{G}$ be the set of games of partial information derived from $\mathcal{L}$ with respect to u via the game map g_u. This map is an elaborate construction given in Appendix A. As we have seen, we can define an operation $\otimes$ on $\mathcal{G}$ that, together with the empty game g_e, makes $\mathcal{G}$ a monoid.

Proposition 1 $g_u : \mathcal{L} \to \mathcal{G}$ is an isomorphism.

Proof g_u is a surjection because every game $g \in \mathcal{G}$ is defined in terms of some string $\alpha \in \mathcal{L}$.

$g_u(\alpha_1) = g_u(\alpha_2)$ implies that $\alpha_1 = \alpha_2$ by the construction of g_u and the fact that $\circ$ is associative. So g_u is an injection.

Thus, g_u is a bijection.

From the construction of g_u in Appendix A (see section A.5) it also follows that $g_u(\alpha_1 \circ \alpha_2) = g_u(\alpha_1) \otimes g_u(\alpha_2)$.

Finally, g_u maps the empty string e onto the empty game g_e, that is, $g_u(e) = g_e$.

Thus, $\mathcal{L} \cong \mathcal{G}$ and g_u is an isomorphism. □

Note that the definition of g_u makes a reference to $\odot_u$, the third operation.

Theorem 2 Given an interpretation function $\mathcal{C}_u^\ell : \mathcal{L} \to \mathcal{I}$ that is a homomorphism and given the game function $g_u : \mathcal{L} \to \mathcal{G}$, there is a unique homomorphism $f_u : \mathcal{G} \to \mathcal{I}$ such that $\mathcal{C}_u^\ell = f_u \circ g_u$.

Proof By Proposition 1, g_u is an isomorphism.

This allows us to define $f_u : \mathcal{G} \to \mathcal{I}$ such that $f_u = \mathcal{C}_u^\ell \circ g_u^{-1}$.

Clearly, $f_u \circ g_u = (\mathcal{C}_u^\ell \circ g_u^{-1}) \circ g_u = \mathcal{C}_u^\ell \circ (g_u^{-1} \circ g_u) = \mathcal{C}_u^\ell$.

Also, any composition of homomorphisms is a homomorphism, so f_u is a homomorphism. In any case, this can be shown as follows.

Let $\alpha_1 = g_u^{-1}(g_1)$ and $\alpha_2 = g_u^{-1}(g_2)$.

Now $f_u(g_1 \otimes g_2) = f_u[g_u(\alpha_1) \otimes g_u(\alpha_2)] = f_u[g_u(\alpha_1 \circ \alpha_2)] = f_u \circ g_u(\alpha_1 \circ \alpha_2)$ $= \mathcal{C}_u^\ell(\alpha_1 \circ \alpha_2) = \mathcal{C}_u^\ell(\alpha_1) \odot_u \mathcal{C}_u^\ell(\alpha_2) = f_u \circ g_u(\alpha_1) \odot_u f_u \circ g_u(\alpha_2) = f_u[g_u(\alpha_1)]$ $\odot_u f_u[g_u(\alpha_2)] = f_u(g_1) \odot_u f_u(g_2)$ as required.

Suppose there is another function f_u' that is also a homomorphism such that $\mathcal{C}_u^\ell = f_u' \circ g_u$.

Then $\mathcal{C}_u^\ell = f_u \circ g_u = f_u' \circ g_u$, which implies that $f_u = f_u'$ because g_u is invertible.

Thus, f_u is unique. □

Mathematically, this result is trivial to establish, but it has profound implications. I represent it visually in the commutative diagram of Figure 4.12.[35]

First, the fact that $\mathcal{L} \cong \mathcal{G}$ says something interesting in itself because strings and games are very different objects and *look* relatively different. Essentially, strings *are* games (of partial information built to model communication). This provides insights that go in both directions, as isomorphisms always do. For example, in Appendix A I will use the fact that it is not sentences but utterances that are relevant in the communication of meaning to suggest that games are similar in requiring contexts in order to produce solutions. Just as meanings are the result of sentences uttered in situations, so solutions to games are the result of games played in contexts. And just as changing the context changes the meaning of a sentence, so changing the context changes the solution of a game. This is an

35. The diagram's being commutative means that we can get from $(\mathcal{L}, \circ)$ to $(\mathcal{I}, \odot_u)$ either directly via $\mathcal{C}_u^\ell$ or indirectly via g_u and f_u with the same result.

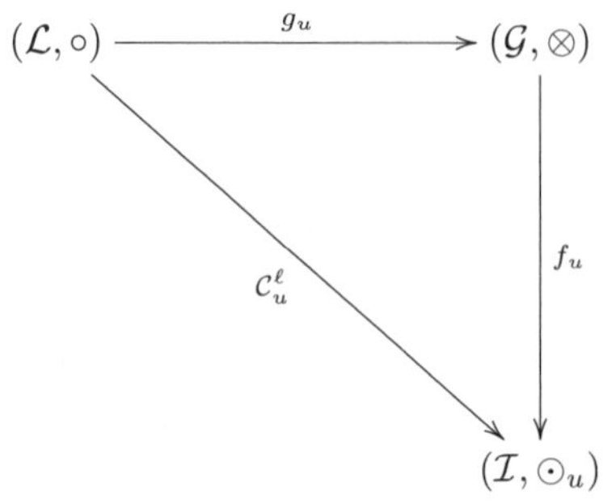

Figure 4.12
The commutative diagram: $\mathcal{C}_u^\ell = f_u \circ g_u$

insight that is absent from game theory because game theorists have tried to solve games entirely on the basis of only the game model itself just as earlier semanticists tried to derive the meanings of sentences entirely on the basis of only the sentence itself, completely ignoring the situation of utterance. In other words, just as a shift from sentences to utterances suggests itself in semantics, so a shift from games to "contextual games" is required in game theory. To go in the opposite direction, an insight from game theory that is transferable to semantics is that just as a game model can be made more or less encompassing and can capture different levels of detail of the situation being modeled, so a sentence (or string) is like a model of a content that can be made more or less detailed and explicit in its attempt to capture the content. That is, it is up to the speaker how elaborate a sentence he chooses to utter in getting at the content he wants to convey just as it is up to the players (and the game theorist) how elaborate a game model they choose to use to get at the situation being modeled.

The fact that the set $\mathcal{I}$ is a set of infons was not used anywhere in establishing the universality result, so it can be replaced by any other suitable ontology as long as $\mathcal{C}_u^\ell$ is a homomorphism. In other words, situation theory is not indispensable; alternative frameworks that capture the informational space would do as well. Of course, my opinion is that no other current account of information exists that meets the twin demands of partiality and fine-grainedness that situation theory accommodates so naturally. But those with different tastes are free to adopt their favored ontologies.[36]

36. See footnote 40 in section 2.8.

This result involving the universality of g_u and therefore of games of partial information has the following fundamental consequence: if there is *any* other theory (e.g., mainstream rule and convention based semantical theory, optimality theory, relevance theory, etc.) that succeeds in providing an account of the locutionary interpretation function C_u^ℓ, the theorem says that it *has* to be essentially equivalent to the map f_u. Thus, I have proved that games of partial information are essential to interpretation or are "universal."

This result is statable in directly category-theoretic terms once one notices that the three monoids can be viewed as categories and the three maps as functors. In fact, there should be a natural transformation from the functor C_u^ℓ to the functor f_u. The existence of such a natural transformation underscores the above-mentioned universality.

Since the parameter u contains a parameter $\dot{\varphi}$ that can be anchored to any sentence or expression, the result holds for all expressions in $\mathcal{L}$. It should be borne in mind that all illegitimate strings 0 are mapped into the zero game g_0 and then into the contradictory infon $\mathbf{0}$. In addition, even meaningless but grammatical strings are mapped via various games into $\mathbf{0}$.

What the result also means is that *some* equilibrium solution exists if C_u^ℓ exists. This is because I have proved that f_u, the solution to the game, must exist. In some cases this may coincide with the Pareto-Nash equilibrium, in others it may not. But our first concern is with existence, then with construction of a specific solution concept. From a theoretical standpoint, all that matters is existence. To *compute* meanings, one needs a particular solution concept like the Pareto-Nash equilibrium or the risk dominant equilibrium.

Not only does the theorem establish the existence of f_u, it also gives us its uniqueness. This means that there is a unique solution for the relevant games of partial information corresponding to the utterance, which in turn means that while particular solution concepts like the Pareto-Nash equilibrium may sometimes yield multiple equilibria for our games and thereby fall short of our requirements, a unique solution does exist. We may not know what it is and therefore may not be able to derive or compute the meaning of the utterance, but the framework tells us that it exists *uniquely*.

It should be noted that this result does *not* capture the entire problem of natural language semantics—there still remain the issues of free enrichment, implicature, and illocutionary force. The theorem needs to be extended to these aspects of meaning as well. This can be readily carried out following the same pattern of proof, although we lose the property that C_u^z and g_u are homomorphisms. In any case, the universality of games of partial information for the locutionary level of meaning is established, which implies that these games are an essential and indispensable part of semantics.

4.12 Strategic Inference

The concept of strategic inference was first introduced in Parikh (1987b). It was used to describe the processes involved in communication that enable an addressee to infer the full meaning of an utterance. It primarily includes its strategic aspects requiring each agent to take account of the other agent's possible actions, which in turn involve the various probabilistic and Bayesian inferences that we have seen are necessary to take account of the interactions between and among the partial meanings of an utterance. Remember that the interactions among the various conditional probabilities $P(x_i \mid x_{-i}, u)$, which result in the inferential pushes and pulls on the various partial meanings, are in fact pushes and pulls among the speaker $\mathcal{A}$ *conveying* these meanings rather than direct interactions among abstract contents. That presence of the speaker's possible actions—conveying this or that meaning—and corresponding actions by the addressee is what makes all the component inferences *strategic* and the overall inference also strategic, resulting in a *global* equilibrium involving choices of initial probabilities, utterances, and interpretations. Basically, the reasoning involves thinking of the following kind: if the speaker is conveying this partial meaning, it is more likely that he is also conveying that meaning and less likely that he is conveying this other meaning, and so on in a self-confirming spiral that is optimal. Talk about direct interactions between meanings is just a convenient shorthand. As should now be clear, it is this very different conception of a *situated* inference that is required to give an account of inference for a situated language like English. The existence of *indeterminacy*, only partially considered so far, makes this probabilistic reasoning even more ineluctable.

Such an account will naturally look quite different from the conventional model-theoretic account of inference where there are two parallel sides to inference, one carried out syntactically with sentences and the other carried out semantically with their contents, resulting in the twin concepts of soundness and completeness. In general, the syntactic shape of a sentence no longer suffices to tell us what inferences and inference rules are acceptable, since the utterance situation u that accompanies it plays a crucial part in the inference, and u is a part of the world and not a part of language. Indeed, as I had said in chapter 1, without u there is no utterance and without an utterance there is no content.

At this stage, it is not clear what an appropriate theory of inference based on equilibrium semantics would look like. Presumably, it would have to be embedded in a wider theory of situated inference. I suspect that altogether different types of mathematics may be involved in such a theory, possibly drawing upon stochastic optimization theory conceived as encompassing the narrower field of game theory. That is, an inference in the traditional sense would have to be recast as an optimization problem of some sort, probably involving a theory of global equilibrium. It is known that the inferences of ordinary propositional logic can be so recast,[37] so there is some warrant to hope that a general theory of situated inference based on the ideas of optimization and equilibrium could be created. I leave this as an open problem.

For the present, I remark that there *is* a notion of *form* in a strategic inference just as there is with an ordinary inference rule like *modus ponens*. It is possible to abstract from the particular sentences involved and look at modus ponens formally: one can say "from α and $\alpha \rightarrow \beta$, infer β" without specifying what particular sentences α and β stand for.

Now refer to all the games with two initial nodes in chapter 4. These may be found in Figures 4.1, 4.3, 4.4, 4.7, 4.9, 4.10, and 4.11. It should be obvious that all these games have the same overall form independent of the particular locutions and contents being considered. Prima facie, it ought to be possible to say: "from a game of partial information with two initial nodes involving primary locution α and (primary) content σ, infer σ. But the matter is slightly more complicated.

While the game diagrams in the figures listed above *look* identical and while these diagrams are *part* of the form of the strategic inference involved, they are *not* the *whole* form. What matters is also the algebraic relationships between and among the payoffs and probabilities. Look at the three cases that arise (mentioned in section 3.2) again:

Case 1: Pareto-Nash Inequalities If either $\rho_1 a_A + \rho_{1'} b'_A > \rho_1 b_A + \rho_{1'} a'_A$ and $\rho_1 a_B + \rho_{1'} b'_B \geq \rho_1 b_B + \rho_{1'} a'_B$ or $\rho_1 a_A + \rho_{1'} b'_A \geq \rho_1 b_A + \rho_{1'} a'_A$ and $\rho_1 a_B + \rho_{1'} b'_B > \rho_1 b_B + \rho_{1'} a'_B$ then $(\varphi_1 \varphi''_1, \sigma_1)$ is the unique Pareto-Nash equilibrium.

37. See Chandru and Hooker (1999).

Case 2: Pareto-Nash Inequalities If either $\rho_1 a_A + \rho_{1'} b'_A < \rho_1 b_A + \rho_{1'} a'_A$ and $\rho_1 a_B + \rho_{1'} b'_B \leq \rho_1 b_B + \rho_{1'} a'_B$ or $\rho_1 a_A + \rho_{1'} b'_A \leq \rho_1 b_A + \rho_{1'} a'_A$ and $\rho_1 a_B + \rho_{1'} b'_B < \rho_1 b_B + \rho_{1'} a'_B$ then $(\varphi'_1 \varphi_1, \sigma'_1)$ is the unique Pareto-Nash equilibrium.

Case 3: Mixed Strategy Equilibria If neither Case 1 nor Case 2 hold, then $(\varphi_1 \varphi''_1, \sigma_1)$ and $(\varphi'_1 \varphi_1, \sigma'_1)$ are both Pareto-Nash equilibria and a mixed strategy equilibrium is likely to be preferred instead (on grounds of salience, for example, as we saw with G).

Thus, each diagram of a game with two initial nodes splits into *three* possible forms leading to three possible strategic inferences:

1. From a game of partial information with two initial nodes and primary locution α with possible contents σ and σ', if Case 1 applies, infer σ.
2. From a game of partial information with two initial nodes and primary locution α with possible contents σ and σ', if Case 2 applies, infer σ'.
3. From a game of partial information with two initial nodes and primary locution α with possible contents σ and σ', if Case 3 applies, infer an appropriate mixture of σ and σ'.

Of course, even this finer view is not quite the whole story because, as has been amply argued, the equilibrium meaning or inference is determined by a *global* and not a local equilibrium, and the probabilities are themselves *strategic* variables. That is, a single game of partial information cannot be solved in isolation from the other games that arise across the entire utterance. So the form of the strategic inference involved in a game of two initial nodes has to be complicated by the forms of all these other games. One theme of this book, the presence of "circularity," appears inescapable.

In any case, the initial feeling of puzzlement that may have been experienced at the repetition of the "same" games for many of the different examples examined in this chapter should now disappear. Just as we are not puzzled when someone points out that the inferences involved in "from smoke, and smoke implies fire, infer fire" and in "from black clouds, and black clouds imply rain, infer rain" are the same, so we should not be puzzled that all the games with two initial nodes (i.e., with two possible interpretations for an utterance) represent roughly the same strategic inference whatever the particular locutions and contents may be.

This discussion should suffice to show the general way in which the form of a strategic inference may be obtained. With larger games involving more than two initial nodes, the inferences naturally become more complex combinatorially.

It should also be clear that there is a close interplay between the solution process for an utterance and the strategic inferences that correspond to it. This is why it was said that the ideas of optimization and equilibrium may be the right ones to formulate an account of strategic and situated inference.

5 Indeterminacy

"The question is," said Alice, "whether you *can* make words mean so many different things."
—Lewis Carroll, *Through The Looking Glass*

We have already encountered indeterminacy, the fourth idea in the quartet of ideas undergirding equilibrium semantics, especially in the previous chapter. As mentioned in section 1.4.3, three questions that raise the specter of indeterminacy in the meanings of utterances are:

1. Is content always intended?
2. Is content always deterministically given?
3. Is content always the same for speaker and addressee?

It was pointed out in that section that the answer to all three questions is a definite no, sometimes even for the simplest of utterances. Yet overwhelmingly in the literature of the last century, both in linguistics and in the philosophy of language, a positive answer to these questions has been the shared assumption. Even Wittgenstein, Austin, and Grice, three philosophers who were very sensitive to aspects of the use of language, have made this assumption. Perhaps the emphasis on *clarity* in the underlying analytic tradition—despite the ubiquity of vagueness in natural language—made indeterminacy too outré to contemplate. In this chapter, I continue to depart from Gricean thinking and, indeed, from both traditions—ideal language and ordinary language philosophy and their offshoots—in fundamental ways.

Beyond these general questions, there are specific questions related to equilibrium semantics as well:

4. Are the issues invoked in deriving illocutionary content always clear?
5. Are the games based on these issues always explicitly played by speaker and addressee?

As discussed in section 4.4 and especially in section 4.4.3, the answer to these questions is also a definite no.

Each of these questions is now examined in turn. Then I look at a further general source of indeterminacy related to my favored Austinian conception of truth. Next, the key question of why texts often have multiple interpretations is addressed. Then phonologically based indeterminacies are briefly mentioned. Finally, I give rigorous formal definitions of the fundamental semantic concepts involved in language and communication, showing how they can be reduced to psychological notions, something Grice and many others have attempted over the past half-century.

5.1 The Role of Intentions

It was noted briefly in section 3.2 that the Gricean picture of inferring intentions to derive the payoffs in a local game and through the payoffs the content conveyed may be only partially correct. Even if it were fully correct, recall that payoffs are determined not just from intentions but also from the larger utterance situation as well as from language. That is, inferring intentions cannot be the whole story because while the structure of payoffs (and probabilities) in the game tree yield the meaning of the utterance, the payoffs themselves are determined by intentions *as well as* other situational and language-related factors.

But now we have to countenance the further fact that not all of the locutionary and illocutionary content may be explicitly represented mentally and therefore intended by a speaker. For example, the illocutionary content *this evening* that would attach to the locutionary content *Harvey is playing* (i.e., σ^{ℓ}) may be left implicit by the speaker or addressee or both. Thus, on the one hand, the payoffs in local games are determined only *partly* through a recognition of speaker intentions. On the other, all of the content conveyed in an utterance is often not explicitly represented and therefore cannot be said to be intended. How does one reconcile these conflicting thrusts and understand the diminished role of intentions?

It seems clear enough that at least part of the content is explicitly represented and intended by speakers because they are engaged in purposive activity. Indeed, as emphasized earlier, there are corresponding intentions on the side of the hearer as well.[1] Whatever their scope, intentions are invisible to addressees, so the interlocutors must in any case rely on publicly available evidence to infer content.

1. See Strawson (1964) and Parikh (2001).

In **F**, it was more or less assumed that the speaker $\mathcal{A}$ had an intention to convey a content σ in u. However, it was the public evidence that was used to set up the game, including the initial situations at its initial nodes. So, *at a purely formal level*, we could dispense with the situated intentions and say there are two ways of resolving the possible contents of the utterance given the evidence—this would lead to the same game tree, the same payoffs, the same probabilities, and therefore, the same results. And the situations s_i and $s_{i'}$ would simply carry the information that $\mathcal{A}$ was conveying σ_i or σ_i' instead of the information that $\mathcal{A}$ *intended* to convey σ_i or σ_i'. This is a seemingly small but crucial change, especially from a philosophical standpoint.

In other words, the model is not dependent on any particular way of construing intentions and their recognition. We could say either that the evidence leads to a recognition of speaker intentions and this leads to the content, or we could skip the intermediate step and go directly from the evidence to the content—all this via the entire game-theoretic model of course!

This flexibility is desirable precisely because intentions are themselves *situated* so that speakers do not need to explicitly intend everything. For example, did James Joyce explicitly intend the entire literal and implicated content of *Finnegan's Wake*? It is perhaps even physically impossible to do so because, even minimally, there would be so much implicit information being conveyed, as already seen with simpler examples.

What the formal flexibility provides is an additional degree of freedom to model intentions more or less *independently* so that we can use them just as much as may be required for accuracy without forcing them into unrealistic roles. This flexibility also allows us to think of intentions in other ways, as postdictive or implicit or unconscious or hypothetical, for example.

The way to think about content is to allow for some of it not to be explicitly intended, but to see if the speaker might assent to the particular part of the content in question. As just suggested above, Alan is not likely to have *explicitly* intended that the film *Harvey* was playing *this evening*, but if asked if this was part of what he meant, he would assent to it. Likewise, Barbara could be asked if a particular content (again, the film's playing *this evening*) was what she understood from the utterance, even if she may not have explicitly played the game related to that issue.

Unlike Alan and Barbara who are always available for such questions, one is seldom in a position to ask most speakers and addressees about their utterances and interpretations, and so one has to reconcile oneself to saying that the content is partly indeterminate in this sense, since it may have partly not been explicitly intended. It would be very interesting to carry out actual experiments to examine these and related hypotheses.

Perhaps Grice (1989), who first introduced intention-based derivations of content, expected too much to be resolved by intentions. Schiffer (1972) even referred to Grice's program as "Intention Based Semantics" (IBS). It appears that the actual picture is both simpler and more complex—simpler because we can bypass intentions in deriving content, and more complex because some partial contents *are* intended while others are not.

5.2 Probabilistic Communication

Grice was probably the first philosopher to allow that content may be partly indeterminate, but he restricted this indeterminacy just to implicature, assuming that the literal content was always determinately given in communication. Chapter 7 of Parikh (2001) looked at this aspect of the indeterminacy of implicature by modeling such indeterminacy as probabilistic content. Parikh (2006a, 2006b) and Clark and Parikh (2007) then extended this kind of probabilistic indeterminacy to all content.

Recall the three cases for Nash equilibria introduced in sections 3.2, 3.3.5, and 4.12 and repeated below for convenience.

Case 1: Pareto-Nash Inequalities If either $\rho_1 a_A + \rho_{1'} b'_A > \rho_1 b_A + \rho_{1'} a'_A$ and $\rho_1 a_B + \rho_{1'} b'_B \geq \rho_1 b_B + \rho_{1'} a'_B$ or $\rho_1 a_A + \rho_{1'} b'_A \geq \rho_1 b_A + \rho_{1'} a'_A$ and $\rho_1 a_B + \rho_{1'} b'_B > \rho_1 b_B + \rho_{1'} a'_B$ then $(\varphi_1 \varphi''_1, \sigma_1)$ is the unique Pareto-Nash equilibrium.

Case 2: Pareto-Nash Inequalities If either $\rho_1 a_A + \rho_{1'} b'_A < \rho_1 b_A + \rho_{1'} a'_A$ and $\rho_1 a_B + \rho_{1'} b'_B \leq \rho_1 b_B + \rho_{1'} a'_B$ or $\rho_1 a_A + \rho_{1'} b'_A \leq \rho_1 b_A + \rho_{1'} a'_A$ and $\rho_1 a_B + \rho_{1'} b'_B < \rho_1 b_B + \rho_{1'} a'_B$ then $(\varphi'_1 \varphi_1, \sigma'_1)$ is the unique Pareto-Nash equilibrium.

Case 3: Mixed Strategy Equilibria If neither Case 1 nor Case 2 hold, then $(\varphi_1 \varphi''_1, \sigma_1)$ and $(\varphi'_1 \varphi_1, \sigma'_1)$ are both Pareto-Nash equilibria and a mixed strategy equilibrium is likely to be preferred instead (on grounds of salience, for example, as we saw with G).

So far it has been assumed in all the games examined that the Pareto-Nash Inequalities held for our payoffs and probabilities—that is, either

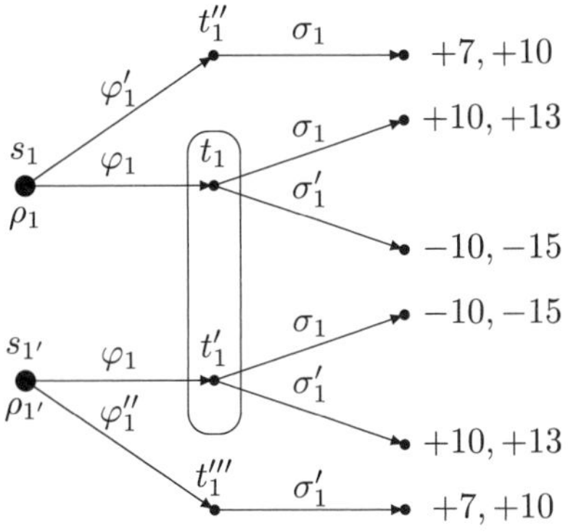

Figure 5.1
A lexical game $g_1 = g_u(\varphi_1)$

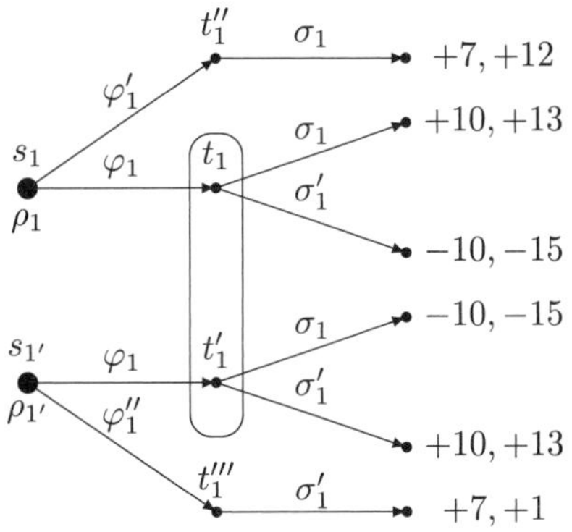

Figure 5.2
The game for probabilistic communication $g_1' = g_u'(\varphi_1)$

Case 1 or Case 2. But what if Case 3, the case of "Mixed Strategy Equilibria," were to hold in a game? In this event, there would be more than one Pareto-Nash equilibrium and therefore a mixed strategy equilibrium in that game.

Reconsider the example of the game g_1 of Figure 3.9 repeated as Figure 5.1 with slightly modified payoffs in Figure 5.2.

The only difference between g_1 and g_1' is that the payoffs to $\mathcal{B}$ when φ_1' and φ_1'' are uttered have been changed from +10 to +12 and from +10 to +1, respectively. Everything else is identical, including the initial probabilities of $\rho_1 = 0.9$ and $\rho_{1'} = 0.1$. Notice that the primary payoff inequalities, encoded in the following algebraic forms, still hold as before.

$a_A > b_A > c_A$

$a'_A > b'_A > c'_A$

$a_B > b_B > c_B$

$a'_B > b'_B > c'_B$

How precisely does one account for this slight change in payoffs that preserve the primary inequalities but switch the game from the Pareto-Nash Inequalities to the case of Mixed Strategy Equilibria? Some alternative story could be told. Perhaps the cost of perceiving and interpreting φ'_1 is relatively reduced, thereby increasing the payoff from +10 to +12. Likewise, perhaps the cost of perceiving and interpreting φ''_1 is relatively increased, thereby reducing the payoff from +10 to +1. Since payoffs are made up of benefits and costs and both components are situationally based, in practice, a variety of stories could be told, each appropriate to a different situation.

The corresponding strategic forms for g_1 (repeated from Figure 3.10) and g'_1 are given in Figure 5.3 and Figure 5.4.

	σ_1	σ'_1
$\varphi_1\varphi_1$	8, 10.2	−8, −12.2
$\varphi'_1\varphi_1$	5.3, 8.5	7.3, 11.3
$\varphi_1\varphi''_1$	9.7, 12.7	−8.3, −12.5
$\varphi'_1\varphi''_1$	7, 10	7, 10

Figure 5.3
The lexical game g_1 in strategic form

	σ_1	σ'_1
$\varphi_1\varphi_1$	8, 10.2	−8, −12.2
$\varphi'_1\varphi_1$	5.3, 9.3	7.3, 12.1
$\varphi_1\varphi''_1$	9.7, 11.8	−8.3, −13.4
$\varphi'_1\varphi''_1$	7, 10.9	7, 10.9

Figure 5.4
The probabilistic communication game g'_1 in strategic form

The key thing to notice about the numbers in the second strategic form is that there are now two Pareto-Nash equilibria rather than a unique one because neither of the two Nash equilibria dominates the other. We could do the same thing with other solution concepts as well. The point being made is not about a particular solution concept but rather about mixed strategy solutions whatever solution concept is used. Because this solution concept and perhaps other solution concepts one might use do not yield a unique outcome in pure strategies, the players of the game might reasonably look to mixed strategies for a solution. This is a standard motivation for considering mixed strategies.[2]

There are an infinite number of mixed strategy equilibria but one plausible one is where $\mathcal{A}$ mixes just his second and third strategies and $\mathcal{B}$ mixes her two strategies.[3] This yields an equilibrium probability of 0.78 for σ_1.[4] This means that the relevant information that $\mathcal{A}$ is referring to the film is interpreted with a probability of 0.78 and that $\mathcal{A}$ is referring to the son is interpreted with a probability of 0.22.

There are many possible interpretations of mixed strategies, one or more of which may be relevant to a particular context. Osborne and Rubinstein (1994) discuss many options and a more thorough analysis would go through each of these and see whether or not it was a possible interpretation in our type of game. For our purposes, however, the simplest option that the players explicitly randomize may be quite

2. Note, however, that because Equations 3.1 and 3.2 in sections 3.2 and 3.3.5 do not hold for g_1' in Figure 5.2, $a_{\mathcal{B}} - b_{\mathcal{B}} = 13 - 12 = 1$ and $a_{\mathcal{B}}' - b_{\mathcal{B}}' = 13 - 1 = 12$ and so $a_{\mathcal{B}} - b_{\mathcal{B}} \not\approx a_{\mathcal{B}}' - b_{\mathcal{B}}'$, the results of Pareto-Nash equilibrium and risk dominance *diverge*. Referring to Figure 5.4, it turns out that the Nash equilibrium $\varphi_1\varphi_1''$ risk dominates the Nash equilibrium $\varphi_1'\varphi_1$ because $(5.3 - 9.7)(-13.4 - 11.8) > (-8.3 - 7.3)(9.3 - 12.1)$, the left-hand side being 110.88 and the right-hand side being 43.68. Thus, even though we do not get a unique Pareto-Nash equilibrium, we do get a unique risk-dominant Nash equilibrium. Can we justify using the pure strategy solution afforded by risk dominance? It appears that all we can say is that it would depend on the precise circumstances that obtain in u that led to the payoffs and probabilities in the first place. See section 3.3.5 for further discussion.

3. One reason it is compelling is that these pure strategies are the components of the two Nash equilibria in the game.

4. The calculation is as follows: If $\pi_{\mathcal{B}}$ is the unknown equilibrium probability of σ_1 that $\mathcal{B}$ uses to mix her two strategies, then it must satisfy $5.3\pi_{\mathcal{B}} + 7.3(1 - \pi_{\mathcal{B}}) = 9.7\pi_{\mathcal{B}} - 8.3(1 - \pi_{\mathcal{B}})$, which yields $\pi_{\mathcal{B}} = 0.78$. Similarly, if $\pi_{\mathcal{A}}$ is the unknown equilibrium probability of $\varphi_1'\varphi_1$ that $\mathcal{A}$ uses to mix his two relevant strategies, then it must satisfy $9.3\pi_{\mathcal{A}} + 11.8(1 - \pi_{\mathcal{A}}) = 12.1\pi_{\mathcal{A}} - 13.4(1 - \pi_{\mathcal{A}})$, which yields $\pi_{\mathcal{A}} = 0.9$.

acceptable. This does not mean that more involved interpretations may not also be suitable, but for the purposes here, the direct option suffices.

Explicit randomizing would mean here that $\mathcal{A}$ chooses his two strategies $\varphi_1'\varphi_1$ (i.e., choose φ_1' in s_1 and φ_1 in s_1') and $\varphi_1\varphi_1''$ (i.e., choose φ_1 in s_1 and φ_1'' in s_1') with probabilities $\pi_{\mathcal{A}} = 0.9$ and $(1 - \pi_{\mathcal{A}}) = 0.1$ (i.e., since the initial situation that is factual is s_1 and not $s_{1'}$, he says φ_1' with probability $\pi_{\mathcal{A}}$ and φ_1 with probability $(1 - \pi_{\mathcal{A}})$ in s_1) and this would further mean that he is initially undecided about the optimal locution to utter in s_1 and chooses one or the other with the given probabilities.

Similarly, $\mathcal{B}$ too is initially undecided between σ_1 and σ_1', and in her case she may never need to make a decision. She may just keep all the information about σ_1, σ_1' and their respective probabilities $\pi_{\mathcal{B}} = 0.78$ and $(1 - \pi_{\mathcal{B}}) = 0.22$ as part of her interpretation of the utterance.[5]

The principal insight here is that communication and information flow can be probabilistic, something I believe was first noted in this general form in Parikh (2001, 2006a) and was implicit in Parikh (1987b).

I have considered just g_1 rather than all the interdependent games required for deriving the meaning of the whole utterance. But such indeterminacies can afflict any game of partial information and therefore the entire content conveyed. I also cheated a little and analyzed g_1 in isolation from all the other games by assuming the initial probabilities ρ_1 and $\rho_{1'}$ were given and the mixed strategy equilibrium was derivable locally. This is not true in general and mixed strategy equilibria, like their pure strategy counterparts, have to be computed globally with the initial probabilities being strategic variables. Finally, the payoffs and probabilities in g_1' were interpreted numerically rather than algebraically to enable the derivation of point probabilities rather than inequalities for the probabilities, as discussed in section 3.1.

In any event, it has been shown that probabilistic communication is important in the determination of both literal content and implicature, that is, in all aspects of meaning. Once we take note of this fact, we begin to

5. Earlier, in g_1 shown in Figure 3.9, since s_1 is factual, $\mathcal{A}$ would have received $+10$ and $\mathcal{B}$ $+13$ under the unique Pareto-Nash equilibrium strategy $(\varphi_1\varphi_1'', \sigma_1)$. Now, in g_1', under the mixed strategy equilibrium just derived, $\mathcal{A}$ would receive $+3.54$ and $\mathcal{B}$ $+6.23$ in the factual situation s_1. These reduced payoffs can be interpreted as a cost of the uncertainty imposed by a mixed strategy equilibrium. It may be possible to use the fact that the payoffs from a mixed strategy equilibrium are generally less than the payoffs from a pure strategy equilibrium to argue that pure strategy solutions are to be preferred and whichever solution concept yields such a solution should be used.

see it everywhere, even in the simplest information flows—as just seen with the interpretation of the utterance of "Harvey." This makes the need for probabilistic approaches to communication and interpretation like game and decision theory even more compelling.

As Clark and Parikh (2007) make clear, such initial uncertainties in communication sometimes get cleared up in subsequent discourse. To quote from that paper:

> John's spaghetti spilled on Bill's jacket. He didn't notice.
>
> Either John or Bill can be taken as the antecedent for the pronoun in the second clause.... Neither John nor Bill is more prominent than the other, so the payoffs are entirely symmetrical. Since neither possible antecedent for the pronoun can be ranked and the lexical semantics provides no clues, we assume that the probability of information state s and the probability of information state s' are essentially indistinguishable. This in turn suggests that the best that the players can do is to adopt a mixed strategy so that the anaphor is truly indeterminate and the sentence is truly ambiguous. Notice that the indeterminacy could be resolved by a further sentence:
>
> John's spaghetti spilled on Bill's jacket. He didn't notice. His jacket, however, was ruined.
>
> Although the second sentence is indeterminate, the third sentence entirely resolves the ambiguity. This happens without any sense of a garden path, indicating that both possibilities were available (via a mixed strategy).

At other times, the uncertainties may remain, with the addressee left dangling indeterminately with a probability distribution on a set of contents rather than a single meaning. Incidentally, in such a symmetrical situation, risk dominance would be equivalent to the Pareto criterion and would also yield a mixed solution.

Thus, this establishes conclusively that all aspects of content may be probabilistic and indeterminate and that an addressee may infer not just propositions from an utterance but also the probabilities with which they are being communicated.

5.3 Speaker Meaning and Addressee Meaning

In much of the literature of the last century it has been assumed that communication (and more generally, the transmission of information that may not be communicative in the Gricean sense) consists in just an identity between a proposition conveyed and a proposition grasped. Closer examination of this assumption shows that this is just the simplest case.

Formally, the key point is that the situation u contains two choice situations $c^{\mathcal{A}}$ and $c^{\mathcal{B}}$, one for $\mathcal{A}$'s utterance, the other for $\mathcal{B}$'s interpretation, and each choice situation contains a model of their interaction. That is, there is not one game model but two, not just g_i for various values of i but $g_i^{\mathcal{A}}$ and $g_i^{\mathcal{B}}$, as argued in section 3.3.4, and these two models may differ in minor or major ways depending on the kind of information each possesses about their interaction. So there is a whole infinity of possible models ranging from common knowledge of a single game structure to no overlap between the game models of $\mathcal{A}$ and $\mathcal{B}$. Which model obtains depends on the system of beliefs about their interaction encoded in the information structure $\mathcal{I}_g$.

Because there are different models of their interaction, the interlocutors will also have different solutions to their models in general, and different probabilities corresponding to propositions when the equilibria are mixed. Thus, it is often not a question of whether communication occurred or not or whether a flow of information occurred or not, but rather a question of the degree of overlap between the speaker's meaning and the addressee's meaning. This is why the largely universal model of communication which assumes an identity between meaning conveyed and meaning grasped is just an ideal case seldom realized in practice.

It should now be easy to see how, if the payoffs and probabilities were different for $\mathcal{A}$ and $\mathcal{B}$, they would arrive at different views on the meaning of the utterance. As an instance of this, I consider partial or what may be termed *mis*communication as discussed in chapter 9 of Parikh (2001).

5.3.1 An Example

In her book, Tannen (1990) has the following example of a conversation between a couple in their car:

> The woman had asked, "Would you like to stop for a drink?" Her husband had answered, truthfully, "No," and they hadn't stopped. He was later frustrated to learn that his wife was annoyed because she had wanted to stop for a drink. He wondered, "Why didn't she just say what she wanted? Why did she play games with me?" The wife was annoyed not because she had not gotten her way, but because her preference had not been considered.

Tannen's suggestion that the husband and wife had different (but equally valid) styles can be easily understood from the perspective of subjective games. There are two possible meanings—illocutionary forces in particular—of the question the woman asked. The miscommunication occurs because both play different games, resulting in different partial interpretations. In order to communicate, it is necessary to be playing the same game. This is just one more instance of the pervasive ambiguity in language we have encountered throughout and it is ambiguity that is primarily responsible for partial communication.

The husband sees the game as quite straightforward. For him "Would you like to stop for a drink?" is just a yes/no question. This is for him the illocutionary force of the question. Since he interprets his wife as asking him a direct question, he responds equally directly with his answer to the question. A simple "No" seems absolutely appropriate to him. And he is right. He did not want to stop, so he just has to say so. So the game that he plays out partly in his head puts a greater probability on the direct intention, or equivalently on the "informational" yes/no force.

The problem is, however, that the wife sees her question as not about seeking a yes or no from her husband, but about starting a negotiation about what both would like. The game she expects her husband to play is the question she has asked, followed by some negotiational or, we might say, indirect interpretation. This negotiational or indirect interpretation is another possible illocutionary force of the question. If her husband had understood the question this way, he might have responded, "No, do you?" and the game would have gone on.[6]

5.3.2 Subjective Games

Let $\mathcal{A}$ be the wife and $\mathcal{B}$ the husband (for a change). Figures 5.5 and 5.6 show their subjective games. The key for Figures 5.5 and 5.6 is as follows:

Utterances:

ψ: "Would you like to stop for a drink?"
ψ': "I mean this negotiationally: would you like to stop for a drink?"
ψ'': "I mean this informationally: would you like to stop for a drink?"

Contents:

υ (i.e., the Greek letter upsilon): the indirect reading
υ': the direct reading

The only difference between the two games is in the distribution of initial probabilities. For $\mathcal{A}$ the indirect mode is more probable; for $\mathcal{B}$ it is the direct mode that seems likely. In this situation, as was mentioned in section 3.3.4, each agent merely *believes* that his or her subjective game is

6. There is even a third "suggestive" reading, whereby the wife *suggests* that she would like a drink, and asks if he would, but I will ignore it. This suggestion is not an illocutionary force, but falls outside Gricean communication, as explained in chapter 6 of Parikh (2001). It is a different type of information flow with a different information structure $\mathcal{I}_g$ involving something weaker than common knowledge. So the full example is a hybrid example with two possible illocutionary forces within a communicative information flow and a third possibility within a "suggestive" information flow.

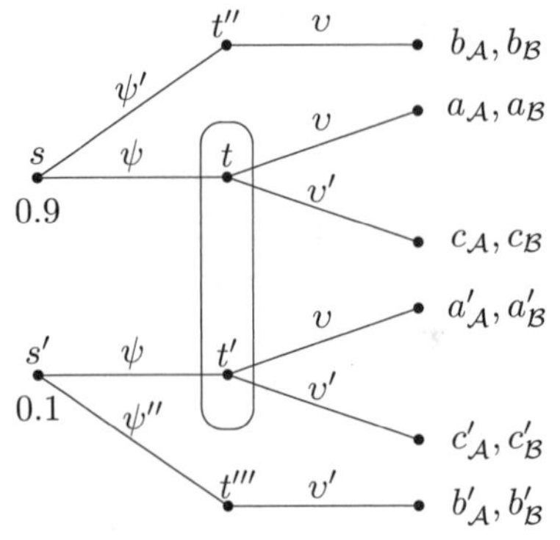

Figure 5.5
$g_u^{\mathcal{A}}(\psi)$: $\mathcal{A}$'s subjective game

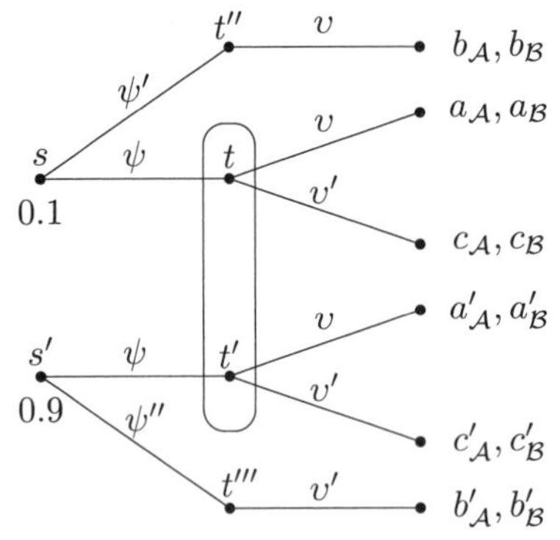

Figure 5.6
$g_u^{\mathcal{B}}(\psi)$: $\mathcal{B}$'s subjective game

common knowledge: these games are not, in fact, common knowledge. This is a situation in which $g^{\mathcal{A}}$'s solution is υ, the indirect reading, whereas $g^{\mathcal{B}}$'s solution is the direct interpretation υ', the other Nash equilibrium owing to the reversed probabilities.

It is now obvious why the husband and wife were annoyed at their interaction. The wife intended the negotiational force to be the right one and the husband expected the informational force to be the right one. They were playing different games with different solutions and so their exchange got blocked.

Why do they pick different games? This is where Tannen's suggestion of different styles comes in. Both husband and wife have different communicative styles. It appears in this case that the husband has a more direct communicative style, while the wife has a more indirect style. That is why the husband assigned a greater probability to the direct reading and the wife chose the indirect reading.[7]

This example shows that the communication between $\mathcal{A}$ and $\mathcal{B}$ was partial. The husband did understand part of the question about whether they should stop for a drink;[8] he just did not get the intended negotiational force. This kind of situation of overlapping but distinct meanings is commonplace.

Is it right to identify the *correct* meaning of this utterance with the wife's intended interpretation? In fact, as we saw in section 5.1, this indirect force may not even have been explicitly intended by $\mathcal{A}$. Since *style* or something similar is a situational variable, it is difficult to defend the view that the speaker's meaning is necessarily the right one. Indeed, it may happen that the wife may not even have realized explicitly what she was communicating in its entirety and therefore why she got annoyed when her husband reacted differently from her expectations. Moreover, no external observer can adjudicate between the two interpretations, as this *situated* ethnographer would need to construct a *third* game with its *own* payoffs and probabilities. At best, a theorist may be able to model each subjective game accurately and on this basis explain why the information flowed only partially from $\mathcal{A}$ to $\mathcal{B}$.

Incidentally, the same sort of analysis can also be given for the husband's response "No" to the wife's question, something Tannen does not pursue. Again there are two forces, a force in which the response is negotiable and one in which it is not.[9] This time, instead of a question, we have a statement. But the rest of the analysis carries through in exactly the same way. The miscommunication can go on indefinitely, possibly with comic effects. This is exactly what happens in the parlor game "Chinese Whispers" where you have miscommunication compounded over a chain of communicators. The various contents bear a family resemblance to each other in Wittgenstein's (1953/1968) sense. This is also what happens in some absurdist plays like Ionesco's *The Chairs*.

7. The issue of style is likely to be more complex than this simple example suggests. I suspect that style is also situated, and changes even for the same person from context to context.

8. This part of the content would be handled by the apparatus I have already shown how to build.

9. This very response in another context is a not infrequent matter of doubt when people are dating.

All of the foregoing raises the question of what the model for meaning ought to be. It is possible to identify one subjective (or, more correctly, intersubjective) content for each participant in a conversation. Moreover, there is no content that is the interlocutor-independent "objective" content of the utterance in question, even for the simplest utterance. This is because each game model and its solution depends integrally on the information and preferences of the relevant participant; there is no "objective" game that can provide an "objective" content. Thus, this fact introduces yet another aspect of indeterminacy into meaning.

5.4 The Indeterminacy of Issues

As explained in section 4.4, illocutionary meanings are meanings that are not directly triggered by the locutionary aspects of an utterance, that is, by the sentences uttered, but rather by the situations in which sentences are uttered. As such, the range of possible illocutionary meanings of an utterance cannot be generated via the Conventional Constraint **C** as with locutionary meanings, but via *issues* that are raised jointly by the sentence uttered *in a particular context*. This mechanism of the invocation and resolution of issues has been discussed in detail in connection with enriched content and implicature in chapter 4 and applies to *all* illocutionary meaning uniformly.

Here my purpose is merely to point out again that issues are raised by whether they are more or less relevant in a setting, a measure that may differ for speaker and addressee. There is no sharp cutoff beyond which an issue is deemed relevant. So the issues raised by an utterance are in general indeterminate and may differ for the speaker and addressee. This makes the equilibrium content derived from the issues also indeterminate and agent-relative. Part of this illocutionary content is literal and part of it is implicated, so both literal content and implicature are indeterminate in general.

5.5 Implicit Illocutionary Games

Just as the issues raised by an utterance are indeterminate, the illocutionary games that are induced by them can be explicitly considered by either agent or may remain implicit, as I said in section 4.4. When they remain implicit, they do not get played by the relevant agent at the time of utterance and interpretation and so that part of the content also remains implicit for that agent. This is therefore a further source of indeterminacy.

5.6 Meaning and Truth

I discussed free enrichment as a process that enables the completion of linguistically incomplete utterances in section 4.4.

Cappelen and Lepore (2004), Carston (2004), Recanati (2004b), and many others view the data discussed there simply as the incompleteness of linguistic representations that need contextually mandated enrichment to get one to the full literal content expressed on an occasion. This is because they all share the same concept of truth, whether it is on the side of truth-conditional semantics or truth-conditional pragmatics. While incompleteness certainly appears to be undeniable (the only defense against it might be some deep representational articulation), there appears to be another, apparently fundamental and perhaps more radical, dimension of this incompleteness that may not be incorporable within either truth-conditional semantics or truth-conditional pragmatics because it requires, as Travis (1996) has argued, another, Austinian (1979a, 1979c) conception of truth. In discussing Travis (1996), Cappelen and Lepore (2004) do not seem to address this dimension squarely, instead interpreting the data of incompleteness exclusively through the lens of literal content.

Consider the following example from Travis (1996):

The oven is hot. (ζ)

Imagine that $\mathcal{A}$ and $\mathcal{B}$ are making a pizza and, at some suitable point, $\mathcal{A}$ utters ζ to $\mathcal{B}$. Now if the oven's temperature is in fact just 100°C, then while it might be judged hot in some situations, $\mathcal{B}$ is likely to complain that $\mathcal{A}$ was wrong.

From what we have seen about incompleteness, we might want to say that what $\mathcal{A}$ literally expressed was that the oven was hot *for baking pizza*. This certainly seems possible. But Travis, following Austin, suggests that the situated purposes for which the oven was judged hot, form another dimension relative to which the content that the oven is hot be judged. That is, the context of utterance u not only provides the means to infer the content expressed by the utterance, it also provides the standard by which that content is to be judged. This provides another way to view the data, where truth is Austinian rather than Tarskian.

Consider another example:

The book is on the table. (η)

Imagine a situation where Austin's *Philosophical Papers* is lying on top of his *How to Do Things with Words* which in turn is on top of a table. If

$\mathcal{B}$ asks $\mathcal{A}$ where the book is, then, assuming that they both know they are referring to the first book, there will be certain contexts where an utterance of η by $\mathcal{A}$ would be true and others false because the standards of judgment would be different. In one ordinary context where $\mathcal{B}$ is looking for the book and does not know where it is, the statement would be judged true; in another context where they are stacking objects on top of one another, it would be judged false because it is on top of *How to Do Things with Words* and not on the table. Notice also that it is difficult to offer natural enrichments of the literal content relative to such contexts.

Even in cases where there is just one book lying directly on a table, the relevant utterance could have different truth values. Imagine a situation involving orientation inside a spaceship in outer space and another with how the center of mass of the two objects under consideration might momentarily reverse their relative positions if viewed quantum mechanically; for these contexts, the standards of judgment would be different because the purposes of the participants might be quite different and might render an utterance of η false even if in ordinary contexts the book is in fact on the table relative to most purposes. It also seems more difficult to offer more complete literal contents according to the first strategy above—at the very least it would be rather awkward.

Perhaps even some ordinary sentences of the differential and integral calculus might be judged differently by quite different standards in the eighteenth and nineteenth centuries because Cauchy and others invented the (almost) modern tools of analysis in the first half of the nineteenth century.

Even our earlier sentence φ could be assessed in these two alternative ways relative to u.

Harvey is playing. (φ)

Is the fact that the film is playing *in New York* a possible enrichment of the content or is it in fact a standard of judgment by which the truth of φ is to be assessed?

A final example:

Snow is white. (η')

Surely there are circumstances in which one would judge snow that has turned to slush as still being white and other circumstances in which one would come to exactly the opposite conclusion. It may not be enough to say that "snow is white" is true if and only if snow is white. It may be possible to view this example and the others above as instances of vagueness or ambiguity, but it is far from obvious that this is a sound strategy.

My opinion is that many such examples are compelling for the Austinian strategy and a different conception of truth. Barwise (1989d) and Barwise and Seligman (1997) are instructive in this regard. The account of propositions in chapter 2 and the proposition expressed by φ in section 4.7 allow us to accommodate this Austinian conception in a natural way. It is the described situation c first identified in section 2.6 that contains information about the standards by which the truth of a proposition is to be judged. For example, it was said in section 4.7 that c could be the relatively large situation of New York this evening. If this is so, then the completion *in New York* is not required. It is enough to leave the literal content just as $\sigma^{\ell} = \sigma_1\sigma_2\sigma_3$ and leave out σ_4, because the literal content would be judged by the standards of c, *not* against the whole world. If the film were playing in Mumbai, for instance, it would not count, because the film's showing is being evaluated vis-à-vis New York. Of course, there would be nothing wrong with treating σ_4 as part of the literal content; it would just be redundant.

This ambivalence about whether to treat information as part of the infonic meaning or whether to treat it as part of the described situation that makes it a standard of evaluation is yet another source of indeterminacy, albeit of a technical kind since the information is available *somewhere* in the proposition. That is, the indeterminacy pertains to which side of $c \models \sigma_1\sigma_2\sigma_3$ the partial content σ_4 belongs to—the side of c or the side of the infons.

This equivocation about where to place certain contextually derived information means there are two fundamentally different ways of dealing with the incompleteness of linguistic representations, one offering an enriched content based on issues raised, the other a standard of judgment also derived from the same issues and located in the described situation. Indeed, there may be no fact of the matter and each interlocutor is free to make his or her own decisions in this regard and place some of the information so derived on the side of infons and the rest on the side of the described situation.

When an agent decides to place certain information on the side of c, the relevant issues and corresponding games of partial information would need to be relocated. This is part of the process by which c is determined, a matter left unfinished in section 4.7. For example, if one of our interlocutors decides to place the partial information *in New York* in the enriched content, then c could be left as unconstrained as the whole wide world; on the other hand, if this partial information were placed in c, then c is constrained to be the situation in New York. If the issue in question had been resolved differently, say as the partial infon *nearby*, and if this information were made part of *c*, then *c* would be even more narrowly fixed to be a location near the home of $\mathcal{A}$ and $\mathcal{B}$.

In addition to such determinations of *c*, the described situation could also contain part of the earlier content conveyed in an ongoing discourse.

5.7 The Ambiguity of Texts

This brings us to a seventh source of indeterminacy. In all of the foregoing chapters, it has been shown how the pervasive ambiguity in language—in the extended sense of "ambiguity" I am using—can be more or less (i.e., modulo various indeterminacies) *eliminated* to enable a derivation of what a speaker communicates to an addressee. In a sense, the central problem of semantics can be stated as the problem of computing the meaning of an utterance from first principles or commensurately as the problem of first generating and then reducing the multivalence of an utterance to a single content (unless, of course, multiple contents are part of the communication as with puns). This is the problem the *general* framework of equilibrium semantics has addressed and, I hope, solved—at least in principle and modulo the specification of the constraints **C** and **I** for all classes of words.

Yet, a profound mystery remains. We have all read texts—novels, for example—where our interpretation differs from that of others, and literary critics, especially Continental ones, have delighted in reminding us of the multiplicity of readings of a given text. Can *Waiting for Godot*, for example, be tied to a single meaning? It seems impossible to do so and it would greatly reduce the richness of the play were we to so tether it by applying some semantical framework. But then how are we to account for this ambiguity of texts if we have succeeded in reducing single utterances to single meanings and therefore a longer text to a concatenation of single meanings?[10] How, in other words, is it possible to go from ambiguity to disambiguation and then back to ambiguity?

A key factor in solving this mystery is the indeterminacy of *contexts*. Throughout, I have maintained the fiction that the utterance situation and its concomitant setting games were more or less clearly *given* to the interlocutors and even shared by them. In ordinary and relatively simple communication, especially when the interlocutors are copresent, this can be a reasonable assumption to make, although even here the agents need

10. The meaning of a text is not just a conjunction of the meanings of its constituent utterances but I make this simplification here.

to single out the same very small set of features of a rich, visually shared scene. But when larger texts like plays are involved, readers and viewers bring a wide range of contexts to bear upon the sentences uttered. Critics, moreover, even bring imaginative theoretical frameworks to the interpretive task and these frameworks also become part of the context of interpretation. Indeed, it is arguable that a single context just does not exist in such cases, because there is necessarily an irreducible subjective element that every addressee brings to the task, making the context partly relative to that addressee. In ordinary information flows, if an interlocutor mistakes the utterance situation for something different, we are liable to call it an instance of miscommunication; with especially literary texts (and other symbol systems), this mismatch of contexts can in fact be quite productive and yield fresh and interesting meanings.

In the short story *Pierre Menard, Author of the* Quixote, Jorge Luis Borges underscores this fertility of context in light of an identical *Quixote* produced by the protagonist:

> It is a revelation to compare Menard's *Don Quixote* with Cervantes'. The latter, for example, wrote (part one, chapter nine):
>
> ... truth, whose mother is history, rival of time, depository of deeds, witness of the past, exemplar and adviser to the present, and the future's counselor.
>
> Written in the seventeenth century, written by the "lay genius" Cervantes, this enumeration is a mere rhetorical praise of history. Menard, on the other hand, writes:
>
> ... truth, whose mother is history, rival of time, depository of deeds, witness of the past, exemplar and adviser to the present, and the future's counselor.
>
> History, the *mother* of truth: the idea is astounding. Menard, a contemporary of William James, does not define history as an inquiry into reality but as its origin. Historical truth, for him, is not what has happened; it is what we judge to have happened. The final phrases—*exemplar and adviser to the present, and the future's counselor*—are brazenly pragmatic.
>
> The contrast in style is also vivid. The archaic style of Menard—quite foreign, after all—suffers from a certain affectation. Not so that of his forerunner, who handles with ease the current Spanish of his time.

What Borges does in the story is to artificially change the context of *Quixote* without changing the text and thereby changes its meaning in a startling way.

The central problem of semantics referred to above assumes that both the sentence *and* its embedding context are given and known to all the interlocutors, as I said in section 2.8. When this is the case, the key component of the solution is the reduction of ambiguity—made possible through games of partial information via constraint **F**. That is, *disambiguation* in the *general* sense I have in mind is the *heart* of the solution to the problem of meaning—relative, of course, to *some* account of the constraints **S**, **C**, and **I**. *This* is the large and difficult problem that is the primary focus of this book.

It needs to be distinguished clearly from the second and, in some sense, even larger and more difficult problem of semantics where it *cannot* be assumed that the context is given and known.[11] This latter problem is typically the one literary critics and some philosophers address.

In the second problem, the context u changes from addressee to addressee for one reason or another, and so the content necessarily changes as well. To repeat, this change in u lies *outside* the definition of our first central problem. Since the content is a function of both the context u and the sentence φ, altering u naturally alters the content and thus makes it indeterminate.

It is important to be clear that the unavailability of context in the latter problem is not just some messy pragmatic factor that can be assumed away for the purposes of theory-building. This is a kind of *second-order* context-dependency: at the first level—something that still remains the dominant view in linguistics and philosophy—utterances are ignored in favor of sentences, supposing that theory-building always involves some idealizing and so we can largely ignore context or build in its influence into the sentence itself. At the second level, where virtually all of us in the relative minority who want to take context seriously belong, the utterance situation is allowed a clear presence in one way or another *but*—most significantly—the assumption is almost universally made that this context can be taken as given and shared. Perhaps the Relevance Theorists (1986a, 1986b, 2004) are the ones who have been the most aware of this issue, as they have tried to come to grips with it by assuming that there is some *method* that agents can follow to compute the relevance of ambient contextual features.

The rather dramatic fact is that often there simply *is* no single context for a more or less complex text as explained above. Thus, at the first level, we need to recognize that the problem of meaning is ineluctably context-dependent. At the second, we need to recognize that there are times when the context itself is not given—that is, in some sense, is context-dependent. Thus, there is a kind of first-order and then a second-order

11. The sentence or text can usually be taken to be given in both problems. There are, of course, naturally occurring situations like trying to interpret a damaged historical text when even the full text is not available. This happened recently with the discovery of one of Archimedes's texts on the calculus. Or it may be that **S** and **C** are initially unavailable, as happened with the Rosetta Stone.

kind of situatedness in meaning. When the second-order issue arises, then there simply is no *fact* of the matter about the meaning of a text.

This is certainly part of what Derrida (1988) and other Continental writers are referring to when they say language is inherently ambiguous or that it is impossible to fix the meaning of an utterance. But they in turn appear to have erred in two ways.

First, they seem not to have made a clear distinction between the two problems of meaning—one where *u* is given and the other where it is not—and so they have not known how to pinpoint the precise source of this indeterminacy. If they had, they would have made more nuanced statements about when the meanings of utterances can be reasonably fixed and when they cannot.

Second, what Derrida has often done, as in his take on Austin, is to be deliberately perverse in his interpretations. If one's goals are to interpret another's statements, then it is not legitimate to *willfully* distort meanings. This is what leads to the outlandish conclusions of deconstructionists, something only the true believer—for whom believing is seeing—can accept.

The only response that critics such as Hirsch (1988), who want to defend a unitary meaning for texts, have had recourse to is to identify authorial intention as the source of objective meaning. We have already seen some of the pitfalls of relying on intention in this chapter. To repeat, first, there is the invisibility of intentions. We can access only publicly available evidence to infer meaning. A rejoinder to this argument is that we may never know if we have the right meaning, but such a meaning nevertheless exists. A further argument then is that intention is itself partial and situated: an author seldom intends the entire meaning completely and this meaning depends not only on the explicit intention but also on the implicit situated intention; if the latter is indeterminate and unfixed, then the meaning will also vary.

One reason why these relatively straightforward matters have remained obscure is that the first and second order ways in which the second input to meaning—the utterance situation—influences content appear not to have been made explicit. If the discussion is carried on purely with just the sentence uttered, with one side implicitly assuming the invisible context is fixed and the other implicitly assuming it is variable, then there can be no meeting of minds. Once the utterance situation is introduced clearly and explicitly, it is easy to see that both sides have a point: if *u* is held constant and is assumed to be accessible, it is possible to fix the meaning of an utterance (modulo the other indeterminacies), and if it is not, then it is impossible!

This kind of indeterminacy exists along a continuum with no sharp demarcation between utterance situations that are fully knowable and given and those that are not. On average, simpler utterances will result in communication and more complex texts will not.

In any case, equilibrium semantics enables the computation of meaning with respect to both inputs, the sentence and the context. Changing u would just mean that the setting game G would most likely change from agent to agent and the games of partial information that follow would also change, leading to different locutionary and especially illocutionary meanings for the utterance.

It is this *variation* in the context of utterance—whether deliberate, accidental, or on account of its inaccessibility and indeterminacy and partial subjectivity—that is the major source of the ambiguity of texts and their multiple readings. Indeed, coming up with appropriate contexts is half the battle in interpreting a literary (or art) work. This is a key source of the richness of language and meaning. Equilibrium semantics, with its account of meaning that makes both context and linguistic representation amenable to analysis, provides a natural way to understand this mystery.

5.8 Phonological Indeterminacy

A fifth set of phonological constraints **P** was mentioned briefly in section 1.4.4. The tone involved in uttering an expression often has a semantic value but this value is typically indeterminate. It may be impossible for both the speaker and the addressee to precisely specify the content of a tone. An example of this will be seen in chapter 6, although an examination of **P** is beyond the scope of this book.

Phonologically based meanings lie somewhere between locutionary and illocutionary meanings and so have the Gricean properties discussed in section 4.5 in a middle-of-the-road way.

In addition to semantic values, **P** is also responsible for phonological content, of course, but this dimension of language cannot be dealt with here. However, see section 7.1.1 for a way of handling this aspect of language.

5.9 Generalized Content

Having identified various sources of indeterminacy, the earlier formulation of content is now generalized to reflect the pervasive presence of probabilistic communication.

Recall from earlier chapters that I defined the content of an expression α in a situation u to be given by a map $\mathcal{C}_u : \mathcal{L} \to \mathcal{I}$ and this was shown to be equivalent to the composition of two maps $g_u : \mathcal{L} \to \mathcal{G}$ and $f_u : \mathcal{G} \to \mathcal{I}$. That is, $\mathcal{C}_u = f_u \circ g_u$.

Since I have argued in this chapter and earlier chapters that content is agent-dependent and subjective in general, the first change in the formulation above is to add superscripts for each agent in the conversation, something that has already been done. Thus, $\mathcal{C}_u$ becomes $\mathcal{C}_u^{\mathcal{A}}$ and $\mathcal{C}_u^{\mathcal{B}}$.

All that is required now is to allow pairs of infons and probabilities to be the contents as opposed to just infons as before. That is, the content function now becomes $\mathcal{C}_u^{\mathcal{A}} : \mathcal{L} \to \mathcal{I} \times [0,1]$ and $\mathcal{C}_u^{\mathcal{B}} : \mathcal{L} \to \mathcal{I} \times [0,1]$ for the two agents $\mathcal{A}$ and $\mathcal{B}$. The interval $[0,1]$ allows expressions to be mapped to ordered pairs of infons and probabilities. The general notation for such probabilistic contents will be (σ, π) where σ is the infon conveyed as before and π is the probability with which it is conveyed. That is, the mixed strategy solution (on the addressee's side) of the game corresponding to the utterance in question is (σ, π). For example, based on the discussion in section 5.2, the interpretation by $\mathcal{B}$ of $\varphi_1 =$ HARVEY with respect to the modified game g_1' would be $(\sigma_1, 0.78)$. Of course, this implies that the interpretation can also be described as $(\sigma_1', 0.22)$.

These definitions of content involve both locutionary and illocutionary contents, the latter involving the solutions to relevant issues raised by the utterance. Since content now includes probabilities as well, it becomes necessary to extend the operation $\odot_u$ on $\mathcal{I}$ to combine not just infons but also probabilities. For more details, see Parikh (2006b) where probabilistic contents are considered more fully. Incidentally, the function f_u may also be defined probabilistically as $f_u : \mathcal{G} \to \mathcal{I} \times [0,1]$. The proof of the universality result in section 4.11 then goes through without any other changes and now applies to probabilistic meanings as well.

How should this generalized formulation be interpreted intuitively? What does it tell us about the nature of content?

First, the content of an utterance is not just a single infon (or proposition) as is usually assumed, but rather a collection of infons, possibly infinite in number, relative to a described situation. Second, each of these infons is just *partially* present as a member of the content through a probability attached to it. Third, not every component of the content may be explicitly intended by the speaker or explicitly inferred and represented by the addressee. And lastly, the content may be different for the speaker and the addressee—there is no "objective" content. This lack of objectivity is reinforced by the various sources of indeterminacy mentioned above. Thus, in general, the flow of information is also a partial affair, determined by the degree of overlap between the speaker's meaning and the addressee's interpretation.

A visual image one might draw of content is as follows. Given a space of points representing the entire class of infons (i.e., a lattice as assumed in chapter 2), the content for each agent would be a subspace with each point assigned a number representing its probability. Then each agent involved would have his or her subspace and the overlap between them would determine the degree and nature of the flow of information that took place between them.

In chapter 4 I considered several ways of dividing the content of an utterance—into locutionary and illocutionary, into literal and implicated, and into further subdivisions of these—and it was said there that different classifications are suitable for different purposes. Beyond this, it is possible that the distinctions between some of the classes of content may not be quite as sharp as often assumed (even the distinction between literal content and implicature, for example) and we may have to be content with rough distinctions relative to the purposes at hand.

5.10 Defining Communication and Speaker Meaning

Parikh (2001) had defined a variety of notions, some Gricean and some extensions of them, like communication, speaker meaning, and information flow. How should these definitions be generalized to account for the picture of meaning drawn by equilibrium semantics? In this section, I look principally at the concept of communication and also some related concepts of speaker meaning and information flow.

The definition of communication given earlier in the book cited above is displayed first so that the modifications required in light of the expanded framework presented in this book can be discussed.

Definition 1 $\mathcal{A}$ communicates p to $\mathcal{B}$ by producing φ if and only if

1. $\mathcal{A}$ intends to convey p to $\mathcal{B}$.
2. $\mathcal{A}$ utters φ.
3. Condition 2 is common knowledge between $\mathcal{A}$ and $\mathcal{B}$.
4. $\mathcal{B}$ intends to interpret φ.
5. $\mathcal{B}$ interprets φ.
6. Condition 5 is common knowledge between $\mathcal{A}$ and $\mathcal{B}$.
7. $p \in m(\varphi)$.
8. Condition 7 is common knowledge between $\mathcal{A}$ and $\mathcal{B}$.
9. $g(\varphi)$ has the unique solution $\langle \varphi, p \rangle$ for $\mathcal{A}$ and $\mathcal{B}$.

There is no mention of the utterance situation u in this definition. Although u was omnipresent throughout in Parikh (2001), it was deliberately left out in the definitions presented there. I have now made it explicit. Situation theory had been minimally presented in that book and so propositions were used in the definition. Here propositions are replaced by infons (with their probabilities), although a definition could be framed in terms of propositions as well, since both types of entities are transmitted in communication. As discussed in this chapter, not all infons communicated are intended, so it becomes messier to accommodate this partial intention. I have chosen to leave this clause as before with the understanding that intentions may be explicit or implicit. The same applies to $\mathcal{B}$'s intentions, as the matter is symmetric. The two separately stated common knowledge conditions involving $\mathcal{A}$'s uttering φ and $\mathcal{B}$'s interpreting it are combined into one.

The key change required is with condition 7 above. Earlier, the system of constraints **SCIF** was not available explicitly and so it was necessary to assume that a function m establishing a connection between an utterance and a finite set of propositions containing its possible meanings was given. Now that **C** and **I** are given, the set of possible meanings of an utterance is automatically generated from first principles. Nothing further needs to be assumed. So it becomes possible to drop condition 7 (and its derivative, condition 8) altogether. It should be remembered, however, that **SCIF** forms a background for the definition.

Finally, the last and, in a sense, the main condition is stated more compactly. I now present the new definition.

Definition 2 $\mathcal{A}$ communicates (σ, π) to $\mathcal{B}$ by producing φ in u if and only if

1. $\mathcal{A}$ (explicitly or implicitly) intends to convey (σ, π) to $\mathcal{B}$ in u.[12]
2. $\mathcal{A}$ utters φ in u.

12. As with the earlier definition, "convey" merely signifies a transfer of information (or misinformation), as from one computer disk to another. We could replace "convey" with "bring about a transfer of."

One approach to the definition would include other attitudes to (σ, π) than the having of information by $\mathcal{B}$. For example, $\mathcal{A}$ might intend to cause an activated belief that (σ, π) in $\mathcal{B}$. Or he might intend to get $\mathcal{B}$ to do something. Or he might intend anything else for $\mathcal{B}$. If this approach is adopted, we can think of this definition as focusing on the case of pure information transfer. Other possibilities are then easy to define.

I prefer the second approach. Transferring information or misinformation is a prerequisite for having other attitudes to (σ, π), or doing something, so that one can circumvent having to specify the other possibilities by simply using "convey." This seems like a better approach because it does not require us to specify all the possible responses of $\mathcal{B}$ for a complete definition. The response is left open.

3. $\mathcal{B}$ (explicitly or implicitly) intends to interpret φ in u.
4. $\mathcal{B}$ interprets φ in u.
5. Conditions 2 and 4 are common knowledge between $\mathcal{A}$ and $\mathcal{B}$ in u.
6. $f_u[g_u(\varphi)] = (\sigma, \pi)$.

A few comments are in order. As noted in section 5.9, (σ, π) stands for the generalized content conveyed, with π being the probability with which σ is communicated.

As in section 4.11 on the universality of games of partial information, we need to say here what $g_u(\varphi)$ is precisely, and I do so in Appendix A. A key difference from the earlier definition of communication given above is that earlier it was necessary to say explicitly in condition 9 that the game had the appropriate solution *uniquely*. This is because both Nash and Pareto-Nash equilibria, as well as other solution concepts that may be used, are often not unique. However, the universality result of section 4.11 gives us not only the existence but also the uniqueness of the map f_u that transforms games into their solutions, one of its many nice payoffs. This allows condition 9 in Definition 1 to be restated more simply as condition 6 in Definition 2.

Interpretive acts are usually not observable externally, let alone being publicly observable. Yet the definition of communication requires that $\mathcal{B}$'s interpretive act be common knowledge. This explains the fundamental fact that we seldom have communication in practice with single utterances. Most of the time the speaker simply does not know if the addressee interpreted the utterance correctly. However, with an extended conversation or actions interspersed with dialogue, it is possible to approximate communication, if not actually reach it. This is because more and more possibilities get eliminated resulting in an increasing probability of communication.[13]

As Strawson (1964) and Clark (1996) have pointed out, there is a certain symmetry between speaker and addressee and, as should be obvious, this is perfectly captured by the definition. That is why communication is a *joint* act like, for example, the joint act of two or more people pushing a cart uphill.[14]

13. In sitcoms, one often gets two parallel interpretations going for some time until the ambiguity is finally resolved publicly.

14. This suggests that the concept of a joint act may also be defined in terms of games, with individual acts being present, common knowledge of individual acts, and perhaps an n-person game with an appropriate solution. In other words, such a definition would be a generalization of the definition of communication above.

One fact slurred over in light of section 5.6 is that since some illocutionary meanings may be placed on the side of the described situation c, it is actually necessary to consider the whole proposition and not just the infon conveyed when defining communication. This needlessly complicates the definition notationally without adding any illumination, so I have elected to leave it out.

Communication requires that both agents access the same u. Without this shared context, there is no communication, as discussed in section 5.7.

Earlier, φ was not restricted to sentences of a language. It could be any utterance—a gesture, showing a photograph, a pictorial action, Herod presenting St. John the Baptist's severed head on a charger to Salome, saying "grr" and the like—whether it is ambiguous or not. In other words, φ included "natural" and "nonnatural" actions and both could communicate in the right circumstances, which included common knowledge of $m(\varphi)$. The actions could exploit all sorts of connections with the meaning, whether resemblance or something else. All that was required was that there be *some* connection (i.e., some function m) between the utterance and its meaning.

Now, since the function $m(\varphi)$ has been replaced by the constraints **C** and **I**, we need to restrict the new definition to language since these two constraints apply just to language. Equivalent constraints for other symbol systems or, alternatively, the function m would be required to extend the definition beyond language.

This restriction to $\mathcal{L}$ and the definition's implicit dependence on **C** (embedded in the construction of g_u in Appendix A) hides an extremely important fact about *symbolic* communication. In chapter 1, I referred to the difference between a sign and a symbol and said it was based on human intention and agency. Many writers have noted the special nature of the aboutness of human language, its special way of connecting with reality that distinguishes it from much animal communication. Some of the unique features noted have been the noncausal nature of the link and the arbitrariness of conventional meaning, as I noted in section 1.4. Terrence Deacon (1997), building on Peirce's (1867–1913/1991) triad of icon, index, and symbol, has emphasized the *systemic* nature of language and other symbol systems, that is, the mediation of connections between symbol and referent by connections between symbol and symbol (e.g., word and word) to distinguish language from the calls of vervet monkeys and other animals that also communicate. All three factors—noncausality, arbitrariness, and systematicity (in the specific sense of symbol-symbol links)—are nicely captured by the constraint **C**, as explained in a simplified form in section 7.1.2 as well as in Parikh (1987a) in a more general setting. I will expand on this in section 7.1.2 but suffice it to say here that Definition 2 not only characterizes linguistic communication, it identifies its specific systemic nature as well. This becomes especially clear if we expand the definition to include nonsymbolic communication, as in Definition 1. There, the function m that established a connection between an utterance and a finite set of propositions played a crucial role. This function m is *not* always noncausal, arbitrary, and systemic as **C** is, and so fails to capture the uniqueness of human language and communication and reference.

If we wish to extend this definition beyond language to other modes of communication, then it would be necessary to replace the conventional and informational maps from **C** and **I** with their composition m_u, which is analogous to the function m that was dropped from Definition 1. And just as the conventional and informational maps provide a *theory* of m_u for language, so a corresponding theory of m_u would be required for other types of communication.

In Parikh (2001), several related concepts were defined after the core definition of communication. In particular, the one-sided concepts of speaker meaning and addressee interpretation were defined, and so were more general concepts relating to information flow where common knowledge of the interaction between speaker and addressee may not obtain. Indeed, three infinite lattices of concepts were identified, one for two-sided concepts like communication and information flow, and the other two for parallel one-sided concepts for the speaker and addressee.

It is easy to extend the new definition given above for communication to the entire range of these related concepts. Additionally, as mentioned in section 1.4, the concept of reference can also be defined in an analogous way. These definitions would all be fully *symbolic* in the sense identified above. I give below definitions of a few of these concepts so the idea of the three lattices becomes clear. I start with the concept of speaker meaning that Grice (1989) had attempted to define over a period of five decades.

We can now see why "natural" and "nonnatural" are perhaps not the best terms to distinguish between types of information flow. Both natural and nonnatural features are involved in the definition of communication for one thing. For example, reception of an utterance involves some prior mode of physical transmission of the information (like sound waves) and also some mode of sensory excitation (like aural stimulation). But more importantly, communication covers cases of natural utterances such as Herod's action above, for example, as well as nonnatural utterances such as saying "Hello." Any action can be used to communicate as long as the speaker is able to exploit the connection m. It is therefore better to use "communicative" and "noncommunicative," or "mean$_C$" and "mean$_{NC}$," instead of "mean$_{NN}$" and "mean$_N$" as Grice did. The definition of "means$_C$" in Parikh (2001) was as follows:

Definition 3 $\mathcal{A}$ means$_C$ p by producing φ if and only if there is an agent $\mathcal{B}$ such that

1. $\mathcal{A}$ intends to convey p to $\mathcal{B}$.
2. $\mathcal{A}$ utters φ.
3. $\mathcal{A}$ believes that condition 2 is common knowledge between $\mathcal{A}$ and $\mathcal{B}$.
4. $p \in m(\varphi)$.
5. $\mathcal{A}$ believes that condition 4 is common knowledge between $\mathcal{A}$ and $\mathcal{B}$.
6. $\mathcal{A}$ believes that $g(\varphi)$ has the unique solution $\langle \varphi, p \rangle$ for $\mathcal{A}$ and $\mathcal{B}$.[15]

Schiffer's (1972) definition,[16] like Grice's (1989) and Strawson's (1964), seems like a fixed-point definition just like mine, but it is couched in language that makes it difficult to determine its exact meaning and boundaries. My definition may have roughly the same scope, but it is more precisely stated, its meaning is clearer, and the outcome in a particular case can be calculated. These advantages of clarity and calculability are formidable and outweigh the costs of using the apparatus of game theory. I now update this definition to bring it in line with equilibrium semantics.

15. We would have to replace this with a more general clause if we were considering strategic interactions rather than games. This clause is as follows:

6′. $g^{\mathcal{A}}(\varphi)$ has the solution $\langle \varphi, p \rangle$ and $\mathcal{A}$ believes that $g^{\mathcal{B}}(\varphi)$ also has the solution $\langle \varphi, p \rangle$.

16. $\mathcal{A}$ meant that p by uttering x iff $\mathcal{A}$ uttered x intending thereby to realize a certain state of affairs E which is such that E's obtaining is sufficient for $\mathcal{A}$ and a certain audience $\mathcal{B}$ mutually knowing that E obtains and that E is conclusive evidence that $\mathcal{A}$ uttered x with the primary intention

1. That there be some ρ such that $\mathcal{A}$'s utterance of x causes in $\mathcal{B}$ the activated belief that $p/\rho(t)$;

and intending

2. Satisfaction of condition 1 to be achieved, at least in part, by virtue of $\mathcal{B}$'s belief that x is related in a certain way R to the belief that p;
3. To realize E.

Definition 4 $\mathcal{A}$ means$_C$ (σ, π) by producing φ in u if and only if there is an agent $\mathcal{B}$ such that

1. $\mathcal{A}$ (explicitly or implicitly) intends to convey (σ, π) to $\mathcal{B}$ in u.
2. $\mathcal{A}$ utters φ in u.
3. $\mathcal{A}$ believes that condition 2 is common knowledge between $\mathcal{A}$ and $\mathcal{B}$ in u.
4. $\mathcal{A}$ believes that $f_u[g_u(\varphi)] = (\sigma, \pi)$.

The same observations that were made above with respect to communication apply, mutatis mutandis, to speaker meaning. The key difference between the definitions of communication and speaker meaning is that in the former the conditions for a communicative flow of information actually obtain and so the flow actually occurs, whereas in the latter these conditions are merely *believed* and so need not occur. I now define the symmetric concept of addressee interpretation of interprets$_C$.

Definition 5 $\mathcal{B}$ interprets$_C$ φ as conveying (σ, π) in u if and only if there is an agent $\mathcal{A}$ such that

1. $\mathcal{A}$ utters φ in u.
2. $\mathcal{B}$ believes that condition 1 is common knowledge between $\mathcal{A}$ and $\mathcal{B}$ in u.
3. $\mathcal{B}$ intends to interpret φ in u.
4. $\mathcal{B}$ interprets φ in u.
5. $\mathcal{B}$ believes that conditions 3 and 4 are common knowledge between $\mathcal{A}$ and $\mathcal{B}$ in u.
6. $\mathcal{B}$ believes that $f_u[g_u(\varphi)] = (\sigma, \pi)$.

Note that "interpret" is different from "interpret$_C$." The first word merely signifies $\mathcal{B}$'s actual choice of interpretation without implying the full process required by the technical term "interpret$_C$." The former is just the counterpart of "utters." The symmetry between speaker meaning and addressee interpretation ought to be apparent. These two concepts are one-sided, whereas the concept of communication is two-sided in that it involves both speaker and addressee in reciprocal relations.

In all the foregoing definitions, $\mathcal{A}$ and $\mathcal{B}$ have only the simple intention to convey or interpret rather than the extremely complex intentions proposed by Grice, Strawson, and Schiffer. This is obviously a distinct advantage. There is a division of labor between the interlocutors and the game, and the ambient game does much of the work.

Additionally, we can more or less immediately deduce some intuitive facts about these concepts.

Fact 1 The following facts follow from the properties of common knowledge:

1. Communication implies meaning$_C$.
2. Communication implies interpretation$_C$.
3. Meaning$_C$ and interpretation$_C$ do not together imply communication.

Common knowledge of a fact implies belief that there is common knowledge of the fact. (In fact, it implies knowledge of common knowledge of the fact.) This is an interesting property of common knowledge that results from its infinite string involving knowledge. A solution of a game is common knowledge and as such implies belief. Contrariwise, belief that there is common knowledge does not imply common knowledge. This is an obvious property of belief. The facts above follow from these observations, and are just as they should be, given our intuitive understanding of them.

We also have two other consequences:

Fact 2 The following facts relate communication to the content of communication:

1. Communication implies that it is (becomes) common knowledge that $\mathcal{B}$ has (the information or misinformation that) (σ, π).
2. Communication implies that the $\mathcal{A}$'s (explicit or implicit) intention to convey (σ, π) to $\mathcal{B}$ is (becomes) common knowledge.

These consequences are immediate. Meaning$_C$ and interpretation$_C$ do not have these implications because they involve *belief*.

All these definitions are quite general and capture the intuitive concepts we all share. They are not stipulative definitions. I now address the question of the three lattices of concepts mentioned above.

To suggest something,[17] to imply something, to send a fax or e-mail—all violate the requirement of common knowledge. While using language involves making information flow, communication is only the main type of flow. Having defined communication and having built up a mathematically solid, philosophically sound, and even computationally tractable account of it, we now go beyond its confines and see what makes information flow in general. As we have already seen in section 3.3.4 and section 5.3, the way to do this is to generalize game theory to strategic interactions.

17. See footnote 6 in section 5.3.1.

At one level, this is very easy to do as was shown in section 3.3.4. The key is to introduce information structures in an explicit way and to allow for multiple extensive forms or normal forms. An n-person strategic interaction in extensive form is just the tuple $\langle g^{A_1}, g^{A_2}, \ldots, g^{A_n}, \mathcal{I}_g \rangle$ where each g^{A_i} is a *set* of tuples or extensive forms.[18] $\mathcal{I}_g$, the information structure, is a set of nested beliefs that the agents have about their own extensive forms and the extensive forms of others. The various tuples one gets can be completely independent of each other as long as the information structure is internally consistent. If there is no overlap at all, no solution is possible of course, no matter what the solution concept.

The interesting cases arise when there is sufficient overlap to allow a solution concept to do its work.[19] But it is not easy to define solution concepts. The information structure vastly complicates things, because it can be quite complex. It allows all manner of knowledge and beliefs about each agent.[20]

With this in mind, I will define what it is to make information flow.

Definition 6 $\mathcal{A}$ makes (σ, π) flow to $\mathcal{B}$[21] by producing φ in u if and only if

1. $\mathcal{A}$ intends to convey (σ, π) to $\mathcal{B}$ in u.
2. $\mathcal{A}$ utters φ in u.
3. $\mathcal{B}$ intends to interpret φ in u.
4. $\mathcal{B}$ receives and interprets φ in u.
5. $\mathcal{I}_g$, the information structure of g^A and g^B, is empty.
6. $f_u[g_u^A(\varphi)] = f_u[g_u^B(\varphi)] = (\sigma, \pi)$.

18. In this book, I have considered the simplest case where there was just one extensive form per interlocutor. In general, there can be more, depending on the information structure $\mathcal{I}_g$. See chapters 5 and 6 of Parikh (2001) for details.

19. Solutions are not necessarily common knowledge in this context.

20. This is analogous to the situation in mathematics where a statement may be easy to prove for small values such as 0 or 1 and also for a value of infinity, but nontrivial for intermediate values because extremal properties are often "nicer." The nested beliefs themselves are easy to describe, but the extensive forms that form the contents of these beliefs may be quite varied and complicated. Analogously, economic forms like pure competition where there is no information sharing and games where the structures are common knowledge are the easiest to tackle. The "intermediate" information structures are fortunately likely to be only of academic interest, except for certain special cases such as the structures of e-mail and suggestion. Nested beliefs of up to three or four levels may not be uncommon as Grice's (1969) many examples show.

21. It is possible to suitably amend this definition by replacing $\mathcal{B}$ with a group of agents of which $\mathcal{B}$ is a member. This would extend the definition to situations where the mass media are involved in flows of information.

The empty information structure just means that neither agent has any information about the other's model of the strategic interaction. Intermediate concepts between communication and making information flow require intermediate information structures lying between full common knowledge and zero information. This is what makes information flows weaker than communication so tantalizing at times. If something is suggested, for example, neither party knows if the other actually meant it or actually understood the message. Now we know precisely why.

There is a difference between information flow in general and making information flow. Information flow in general does not require agents. This is the delicate difference between making information flow and intending to *convey* information. To convey is to bring about a pure transfer of information, like a transfer from one computer disk to another.

It is of course possible to give definitions of making information flow in all specific cases simply by taking the details of the information structure into account. Thus, it is possible to give definitions for sending a fax or e-mail, for suggesting, hinting, and implying, and for all other types of flow. This should now be relatively easy to do. Indeed, there are an infinite number of such notions with communication the narrowest and making information flow the broadest and the rest all lying somewhere in between, forming an infinite lattice.[22]

Just as meaning$_C$ and interpretation$_C$ are the two one-sided notions corresponding to communication, we can define two one-sided notions meaning$_F$ and interpretation$_F$ corresponding to the two-sided notion of "making information flow." And, of course, there would be two one-sided notions for each of the noncommunicative (but information flow enabling) notions of suggesting, sending e-mail, and the like, that is, for each specific information structure that may arise. Meaning$_C$ and interpretation$_C$ would then be the narrowest of these notions, and meaning$_F$ and interpretation$_F$ would be the broadest of these notions, and the rest would all lie somewhere in between, forming two infinite lattices, one for meaning and the other for interpretation.

I do not tarry to define these here. For a full account of these notions, see my earlier book. In any case, we immediately get the two sets of results below.

22. In fact, there are an infinite number of infinite lattices, because there is an infinite number of game trees and an infinite number of levels of knowledge. We can formulate this as a cross product but I will not go into this construction here. I will talk about it as if it were a single lattice for convenience.

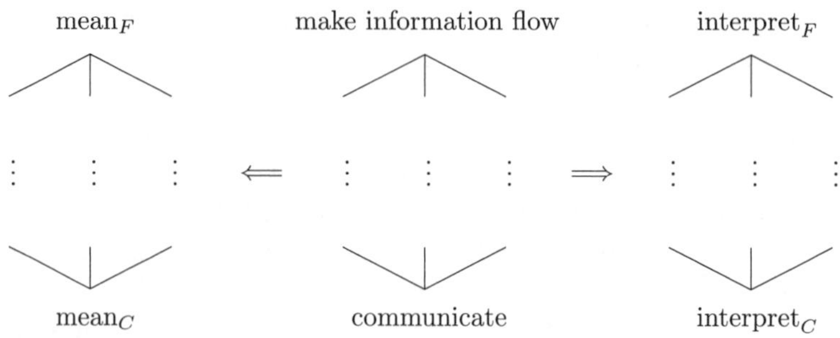

Figure 5.7
The three infinite lattices

Fact 3 The following facts obtain:

1. Making information flow implies meaning$_F$.
2. Making information flow implies interpretation$_F$.
3. Meaning$_F$ and interpretation$_F$ do not together imply making information flow.

and

4. Communication implies making information flow.
5. Meaning$_C$ implies meaning$_F$.
6. Interpretation$_C$ implies interpretation$_F$.

I have thus replaced the "nonnatural" side of Grice's "natural/nonnatural" distinction between types of information flow by an infinite lattice. It is possible to think of the case of "natural" flows (of the "smoke means fire" kind) as a single point on top of the supremum of the lattice, which is the point where an agent makes information flow or where an agent means$_F$ something. This makes the case of "natural" meaning the new supremum of the lattice.[23] This integrates the whole picture of information flow (both "natural" and "nonnatural" or "noncommunicative" and "communicative") into one structure, whether it is the two-sided information flow lattice, or the one-sided meaning lattice or interpretation lattice. The three infinite lattices are pictured in Figure 5.7.[24]

23. We no longer have an agent $\mathcal{A}$ communicating something or meaning something at this point but rather an infon (σ, π) meaning something. A full account of these notions can be found in Parikh (2001).

24. The case of natural meaning is not shown in the diagram: the three subcases sit on top of the three suprema.

The notion of reference mentioned in section 1.4 and elsewhere is analogous to these notions but applies even to parts of utterances and therefore also to partial infons.

5.11 Recapitulation

The *general* side of equilibrium semantics has now been described, showing in particular how it rests on the four fundamental ideas of reference, use, indeterminacy, and equilibrium. The way these four ideas find their way into the system of four constraints **SCIF** has been developed in detail in the context of some simple examples.

If the reader looks back to chapter 1 and to section 1.4, it should be possible to see how the desiderata for a theory of meaning laid out there have been met in subsequent chapters. Not only has a unified account of meaning that integrates semantics and pragmatics into a single whole been given, it has been articulated at three levels. At the first level of a theory of meaning, a general way to compute the meaning of a simple utterance from first principles has been described. This can be readily extended to more complex utterances. At the second level of a framework for meaning, it will be argued in the next chapter that variant theories of meaning may be produced by giving different accounts of particular phenomena within the general framework developed here. I will give my own preferred accounts of descriptions, names, and generalized quantifiers, but it will be clear that alternative explanations are also possible within equilibrium semantics. These alternatives arise from constructing different theories of **C** and especially of **I**, which together determine the possible meanings of words and therefore of phrases and sentences, possibilities that are then whittled down by a fixed **F**. Of course, not all accounts of meaning will be compatible with the constraints in **SCIF**, but many theories could be recast to fit their mold. Finally, at the third level of a paradigm for meaning, the idea and image of equilibrium as it pervades the domain of meaning has been amply shown. My claim in chapter 1 of its commensurability with the idea of generativity should now be convincing. Since my focus has been on meaning, I have deliberately not tried to discuss my larger conception that *all* aspects of language are united by interdependence and equilibrium, thus making this central idea even more paradigmatic.[25] Indeed, it is the "circularity" inherent in this idea, where there is no beginning and no end, that lay behind my choice of the epigraph from *Finnegans Wake*.

25. This is something I will address in section 7.1.1.

6 Noun Phrases

At rest, however, in the middle of everything is the sun.
—Nicolaus Copernicus

Equilibrium semantics is now applied to a variety of noun phrases. There is a truly *vast* literature on this topic, in philosophy and in linguistics. The focus here will be just on my preferred accounts of these phenomena within the system of constraints **SCIF** and the undergirding frameworks of situation theory and game theory. Alternative theories of **C** and **I** compatible with **F** are quite possible and my own views are advanced tentatively.

In developing these accounts, I have held to the belief that the ideas of reference, use, indeterminacy, and equilibrium have to play a *crucial* role in any theory aspiring to explain the behavior of noun phrases just as with all other expressions. Indeed, many competing theories prove to be unsatisfactory because they recognize these four factors inadequately. For example, as argued below, Russell's illustrious theory of definite descriptions fails to be as natural and commonsensical primarily on account of its not being referential in the required way and not accommodating the other three ideas.

I present a uniform theory of noun phrases. As a result, the distinction Frege introduced between referring expressions and quantified noun phrases turns out not to be so fundamental. In my expanded sense of reference, all noun phrases when uttered appropriately refer to *some* entity in the ontology $\mathcal{O}$ and all noun phrases also take on some attributes of quantifiers. As will be shown, the former move does not require the introduction of nonexistent entities.

The related Fregean distinction between grammatical and logical form will correspondingly also appear not to be so fundamental.

It is most convenient to start with definite descriptions, then consider indefinite descriptions briefly, go on to names, and end with generalized quantifiers. The essence of my view is that when the idea of use is taken seriously, as Strawson (1956) was the first to do in this context, a relatively straightforward account that accords with ordinary pretheoretic intuitions becomes possible.

Some of the notable work in the area of definite descriptions has been collected in Martinich (1985), Davis (1991), and Ostertag (1998). Stalnaker (1970) was perhaps the first to recognize referential and attributive uses for *all* singular terms, not just descriptions. Bach (2004) is a recent discussion of a Russellian view of definite descriptions. See Lyons (1999) for a discussion of the linguistic problems posed by definiteness and definite descriptions. The papers collected in Reimer and Bezuidenhout (2004) give a general overview of current thinking in linguistics and philosophy on definite descriptions.

Much recent work, forced to face the facts of use in response to Strawson (1956), Donnellan (1966), and others, has resorted to Grice's (1989) way of viewing semantics and pragmatics as the only way to accommodate this key facet of meaning. The general strategy of such approaches, exemplified by Kripke (1977) and Neale (1990), has been to stick to a use-independent, context-free, and conventionally given semantics and then relegate all use-based, contextual, and inferential aspects of meaning to a Gricean pragmatics.

As the preceding chapters have tried to show, this linear pipeline view of meaning is inadequate because the context of an utterance permeates all aspects of content, both literal and implicated, locutionary and illocutionary.[1] That is why I have advocated a unification of semantics and pragmatics via equilibrium semantics. If the argument has merit, then one can no longer adopt such composite strategies (e.g., Russell + Grice).

In addition, the usual focus of such syncretic approaches is on the "semantic," literal, or truth-conditional content. In a sense, the actual information conveyed in an utterance is simply transferred to Gricean pragmatics, as if it were more or less plainly available through that mechanism. As a large body of linguistic work on Grice in the last few decades has shown, deriving an implicature using the Gricean maxims is not at all a clear-cut matter. Indeed, something like a game-theoretic approach first suggested in Parikh (1987b, 1992, 2001) and refined here in chapter 4 may be the only way to make such strategic inferences precise. The Relevance

1. The reader is urged to review the opening paragraphs of chapter 4.

Theorists (1986a, 1986b, 2004), also post-Gricean in their orientation, have offered a different approach to such inferences but one that is marred by its relative imprecision and consequent unfalsifiability despite my general sympathy with its goals.

The challenge, therefore, is to give an account that is natural, intuitive, and rigorous on the one hand and also meets the criticisms of the opposition on the other.

6.1 Definite Descriptions

Most people asked to identify the content of a more or less commonplace utterance of, say, "the boy" in some situation would report that the definite description was simply used to pick out some boy who was saliently available to the interlocutors as a referent. For example, Alan may say to Barbara in u relative to some shared resource situation r where Harvey is playing:

The boy is playing.

It seems unexceptionable, on grounds of pre-theoretic common sense, to claim that $\mathcal{A}$ has said to $\mathcal{B}$ that Harvey is playing and that $\mathcal{A}$ has referred to Harvey with his use of "the boy." It is this most basic of intuitions about definite descriptions that my account tries to preserve. When exceptional situations arise, like the absence of a referent for a description or some other error,[2] they need to be treated as exceptions and handled in a way that smoothes out the scientific theory without sacrificing this basic intuition.

Neale (1990), in his able defense of Russell's theory of descriptions, describes Russell's very different approach to such unusual situations:

> According to Russell, if a putative referring expression '*b*' can be supposed not to refer, yet a sentence containing '*b*' still be supposed to express a determinate thought, then '*b*' cannot be a genuine referring expression. Whenever we encounter such a situation, the *Theory of Descriptions* is to be wheeled out and the sentence given a logical parsing in which there is no genuine "subject." For the whole purpose of the Theory of Descriptions is to make available a special class of *object-independent* thoughts. A genuine referring expression '*b*' may be combined with a (monadic) predicate expression to express an *object-dependent* thought, a thought that simply could not be expressed or even entertained if the object referred to by '*b*' did not exist. A definite description "the *F*," by contrast, although it *may* in fact be satisfied by a unique object *x*, can be combined with a (monadic)

2. For example, if Alan mistakes Harvey for someone else.

predicate to express a thought that is not contingent upon the existence of *x*. For descriptions, on Russell's account, belong with the quantifiers—what he calls denoting phrases—and not with the referring expressions.

Rather than give up the basic intuition that many ordinary uses of definite descriptions simply refer to an appropriate object and literally convey an *object-dependent* proposition, my approach is to account for cases where there is no referent and yet *a determinate thought* is expressed by what seems to me a natural but technical ironing out of such wrinkles. That is, rather than radically alter the basic theory to fit the anomaly, it is simpler to treat it by a slight extension of the basic theory.

Moreover, it is not uncommon to refer with the quantifiers as well:

Some boys are playing.
Many boys are playing.
Most boys are playing.
Every boy is playing.

Appropriately used, such quantified expressions can pick out a set of boys relative to some resource situation and literally convey that the boys in that set are playing. Thus, the contrast between referring expressions and quantified expressions is not so sharp.

This intuition is reinforced when anaphora are considered:

The boy is playing. He looks happy.
The boys are playing. They look happy.
Some boys are playing. They look happy.
Many boys are playing. They look happy.
Most boys are playing. They look happy.
Every boy is playing. They look happy.

It is as important to be able to give a natural account of such anaphorically used pronouns. This appears possible only when there is literal reference to an individual or set of individuals so that such entities are available later to be picked out anaphorically.[3]

Beyond this most basic referential intuition, further reflection may reveal other ways of using definite descriptions (and noun phrases generally) where entities other than individuals are pinpointed. This equally basic fact also needs to be accommodated in any theory. In this context, Neale (1990) goes on to say:

3. See the arguments in section 6.1.2, which apply to anaphora as well.

No one, I take it, contests the phenomenon of referential usage. But there is considerable disagreement as to the *significance* of this phenomenon when it comes to the construction of a semantical theory. A number of philosophers have argued that where a description is used referentially, we must reject Russell's object-independent truth conditions. On Russell's account, an utterance of "the *F* is *G*" is true just in case there is some entity *x* such that *x* is uniquely *F* and *x* is *G*. But according to Russell's opponent, when "the *F*" is being used referentially, the truth-conditions make no mention of any uniquely descriptive condition. In such a case "the *F*" is functioning as a singular referring expression: it is being used to refer to some particular individual *b*; and the utterance is therefore true just in case *b* is *G*. It is suggested, in short, that descriptions are *semantically ambiguous* between quantificational and referential *interpretations*.

Ever since Grice's (1989) exhortation to use a modified Occam's razor to minimize semantic ambiguity, many philosophers have been inclined to explain the meanings of utterances by passing the buck to pragmatics. Neale (1992) describes the historical motivation underlying Grice's move: influenced by the later Wittgenstein, ordinary language philosophers such as Austin, Ryle, and others attempted to undercut a philosophical position or dispose of a philosophical problem by pointing to a misuse of some expression playing an essential role in the presentation of the position or problem. This was done essentially through exploiting putative semantic ambiguities in the expression.

Grice's injunction needs to be revisited but this is not the place for such a re-examination. Suffice it to say here that such a strategy often needlessly complicates the resulting theory, often conflicts with our ordinary intuitions, and, as I have just noted above, simply relocates the problem without actually solving it. In a word, it misapplies the intuition behind Occam's razor, simplifying one part of the theory while complexifying the overall theory. It also ends up making semantics a somewhat strange no-man's-land, largely unmoored from the embedding flows of information from which all meaning arises. Equilibrium semantics tries to countenance the facts squarely and, in particular, to accept whatever semantic ambiguities appear to exist empirically at face value without a priori commitments of principle (such as Grice's modified Occam's razor) that become unquestioned dogma.

This issue will be addressed in section 6.1.6 in the context of my account and Kripke's (1977) arguments. For the moment, I will take it that there should be no such *theoretical* reason to oppose semantic ambiguities in definite descriptions and elsewhere, especially when empirical evidence and common sense intuitions suggest otherwise.

I start by presenting my core account of definite descriptions informally. It will be clear how my broad sympathies lie with those who have defended the original intuitions of Frege, Strawson, Donnellan, Stalnaker, and others. The account is also influenced by the particular theory in Barwise and Perry (1983).

6.1.1 The Core Account

By now, the evening has advanced and Alan and Barbara have opted for dinner and a movie: they have just been to the film *Harvey*, Alan's choice, and are at Cafe Boulud, the French restaurant Barbara preferred to Alan's predilection for Nobu.[4]

Assume they have interrupted placing their order and $\mathcal{A}$ says to $\mathcal{B}$ in a new utterance situation that I will continue to call u for convenience:

The waiter is rude. (ω)

As will be seen fully later, each of the four words in ω is ambiguous, resulting in multiple ambiguities in the overall utterance. But most overhearers of this conversation would agree, as would $\mathcal{A}$ and $\mathcal{B}$, that $\mathcal{A}$ has *literally* conveyed to $\mathcal{B}$ that the waiter taking their order was rude and that $\mathcal{A}$ has *literally* referred to that waiter with his use of "the waiter." How can this fundamental intuition be preserved against the unintuitive argument that the reference is merely pragmatic and achieved via a Gricean implicature and the semantic or literal content merely asserts the Russellian object-independent proposition that there is one and only one waiter and everything that is a waiter is rude?

To avoid premature complications arising from the multiple ambiguities in ω, I focus in this section just on clearing up this core problem. Once it is dealt with and the "Russell–Grice" argument averted, then the full equilibrium semantics account of this ambiguous utterance is developed from scratch, as with the other examples in earlier chapters.

Let $\omega_1 = \text{THE}$, $\omega_2 = \text{WAITER}$, $\omega_3 = \text{IS}$, and $\omega_4 = \text{RUDE}$. Let $P_1^{waiter} = P_1^{\omega_2}$ be the intended conventional meaning of $\omega_2 = \text{WAITER}$, which is just *a*

4. Incidentally, this second-order compromise following the representation G of their first-order alternatives of dinner and a movie or the symphony shows how agents not only play games but also negotiate what games to play. G may itself have been refined to include both their first- and second-order possibilities, or the players may have first arrived at a solution to G and then have played a new game to identify what movie they would see and where they would eat. All of this has taken place in the setting u as it is this situation that provided the range of options they contemplated.

person who serves customers in a restaurant. Other conventional meanings of WAITER are *a small tray or salver* and even *someone who waits for some future event*. Likewise, let $P_1^{rude} = P_1^{\omega_4}$ be the intended conventional meaning of $\omega_4 = $ RUDE, which is just *impolite*. Another conventional meaning is *roughly made* or *unsophisticated* (as in "a rude salver").

Now recall that in sections 2.2 (Equation 2.1) and 2.3.2 $e(P, s)$ was taken to be the individual $a = (x \mid s \models \langle\langle P; x\rangle\rangle)$ when the condition $s \models \langle\langle P; x\rangle\rangle$ yields just one object and the set $\{x \mid s \models \langle\langle P; x\rangle\rangle\}$ otherwise. Clearly, when *no* object has the property P in s, $e(P, s)$ will just be the empty set ϕ.

Let r_u be the resource situation relative to the utterance situation u. This is the situation just elapsed at Alan and Barbara's table with the waiter being rude.

In the case where $P_1^{\omega_2}$ is the property under consideration and r_u the situation against which it is being extensionalized, $e(P_1^{\omega_2}, r_u)$ is just the single waiter a picked out in r_u if there was just one waiter (as there was, in truth). If there had been no waiter or multiple waiters in r_u, then $e(P_1^{\omega_2}, r_u)$ would have been the corresponding *set* of waiters, either the empty set or a set with cardinality greater than one. For example, if there had been two waiters a_1 and a_2 in r_u, then $e(P_1^{\omega_2}, r_u) = \{a_1, a_2\}$.

A first stab at the *literal* content of the utterance of ω in u with respect to the resource situation r_u is as follows:

$$C_u^{\ell}(\omega) = \langle\langle P_1^{\omega_4}; e(P_1^{\omega_2}, r_u); 1\rangle\rangle = \langle\langle P_1^{\omega_4}; e(P_1^{\omega_2}, r_u)\rangle\rangle = \langle\langle P_1^{\omega_4}; a\rangle\rangle$$

One advantage of my view is that the literal content of just the description can be readily represented thus:

$$C_u^{\ell}(\text{THE WAITER}) = C_u^{\ell}(\omega_1\omega_2) = \langle\langle e(P_1^{\omega_2}, r_u)\rangle\rangle = \langle\langle a\rangle\rangle$$

The importance of this latter partial content cannot be overemphasized. If Alan had been interrupted after saying "The waiter" and was not able to complete the sentence, we would still be able to characterize the content of his incomplete utterance. It is simply not true that nothing was expressed.

What happens to the former content when no waiter is available in r_u to serve as the referent? We get:

$$C_u^{\ell}(\omega) = \langle\langle P_1^{\omega_4}; e(P_1^{\omega_2}, r_u)\rangle\rangle = \langle\langle P_1^{\omega_4}; \phi\rangle\rangle$$

This is a perfectly intelligible infon that says that nothing has the property $P_1^{\omega_4}$ in the described situation but it is not what we want as this is not the intuitive content of a vacuous definite description.

Likewise, when there are two waiters in r_u the content is:

$$\mathcal{C}_u^\ell(\omega) = \langle\langle P_1^{\omega_4}; e(P_1^{\omega_2}, r_u)\rangle\rangle = \langle\langle P_1^{\omega_4}; \{a_1; a_2\}\rangle\rangle$$

which says that a_1 and a_2 are rude, again not what is intuitively expressed. In both these cases, the *uniqueness* of the referent is lost.

To repair this, recall from section 3.2 that $Unique(P, r_u, q_u)$ was defined to be $\langle\langle = \mid r_u \subseteq q_u; \text{card}(\{y \mid r_u \models \langle\langle P; y\rangle\rangle\}); 1\rangle\rangle$, an infon that expresses the information that $\{y \mid r_u \models \langle\langle P; y\rangle\rangle\}$ is a singleton. "Card" is the cardinality function and r_u, q_u are resource situations related to u.[5] "$r_u \subseteq q_u$" conditions the main relation $=$ of this infon and can be assumed to be true by taking $q_u = r_u$ here. Notice that the set $\{y \mid r_u \models \langle\langle P; y\rangle\rangle\}$ is just the set $\{x \mid r_u \models \langle\langle P; x\rangle\rangle\}$ when $e(P, r_u)$ does not yield a single object.

For the moment, I will assert that the (determinate) literal content of ω in u is just:

$$\mathcal{C}_u^\ell(\omega) = \langle\langle P_1^{\omega_4}; e(P_1^{\omega_2}, r_u) \mid Unique(P_1^{\omega_2}, r_u, q_u)\rangle\rangle \quad (6.1)$$

That is, the constituent $e(P_1^{\omega_2}, r_u)$ is not simply unconditioned as suggested earlier, but is conditioned by $Unique(P_1^{\omega_2}, r_u, q_u)$. This conditioning infon $Unique(P_1^{\omega_2}, r_u, q_u)$ introduces precisely the Russellian uniqueness condition in a slightly different form, something that was missing from the first attempt above.

When there is exactly one waiter in r_u:

$$\begin{aligned} Unique(P_1^{\omega_2}, r_u, q_u) &= \langle\langle = \mid r_u \subseteq q_u; \text{card}(\{y \mid r_u \models \langle\langle P_1^{\omega_2}; y\rangle\rangle\}); 1\rangle\rangle \\ &= \langle\langle = \mid r_u \subseteq q_u; \text{card}(\{a\}); 1\rangle\rangle \\ &= \langle\langle = \mid r_u \subseteq q_u; 1; 1\rangle\rangle \\ &= \mathbf{1} \quad \text{since } r_u \subseteq q_u \text{ is assumed to hold.} \end{aligned}$$

and so holds in any (described) situation by Clause 1 of Assumption 7 in section 2.3.5 that $s \not\models \mathbf{0}$ and $s \models \mathbf{1}$ for all situations s. This results in the following content:

$$\begin{aligned} \mathcal{C}_u^\ell(\omega) &= \langle\langle P_1^{\omega_4}; e(P_1^{\omega_2}, r_u) \mid Unique(P_1^{\omega_2}, r_u, q_u)\rangle\rangle \\ &= \langle\langle P_1^{\omega_4}; a \mid \mathbf{1}\rangle\rangle \\ &= \langle\langle P_1^{\omega_4}; a\rangle\rangle \quad \text{by Assumption 5 in section 2.3.2} \end{aligned}$$

5. More will be said about q_u when generalized quantifiers are addressed later in this chapter.

This is exactly what should be obtained intuitively as the literal content of ω in u when there is just one waiter in r_u, since the infon identifies the individual a as having the property $P_1^{\omega_4}$ or, in other words, says that the waiter is rude.

As discussed in section 3.2, when there is no waiter:

$$
\begin{aligned}
Unique(P_1^{\omega_2}, r_u, q_u) &= \langle\!\langle = \mid r_u \subseteq q_u; \mathrm{card}(\{y \mid r_u \models \langle\!\langle P_1^{\omega_2}; y\rangle\!\rangle\}); 1\rangle\!\rangle \\
&= \langle\!\langle = \mid r_u \subseteq q_u; \mathrm{card}(\phi); 1\rangle\!\rangle \\
&= \langle\!\langle = \mid r_u \subseteq q_u; 0; 1\rangle\!\rangle \\
&= \mathbf{0} \quad \text{since } r_u \subseteq q_u \text{ is assumed to hold.}
\end{aligned}
$$

and so the resulting content is:

$$
\begin{aligned}
C_u^{\ell}(\omega) &= \langle\!\langle P_1^{\omega_4}; e(P_1^{\omega_2}, r_u) \mid Unique(P_1^{\omega_2}, r_u, q_u)\rangle\!\rangle \\
&= \langle\!\langle P_1^{\omega_4}; \phi \mid \mathbf{0}\rangle\!\rangle \\
&= \langle\!\langle P_1^{\omega_4}; \mathbf{0}\rangle\!\rangle \quad \text{by Assumption 5 in section 2.3.2} \\
&= \mathbf{0}
\end{aligned}
$$

by Fact 2 in section 2.3.3 that for all infons σ, $\sigma \odot_s \mathbf{0} = \mathbf{0} \odot_s \sigma = \mathbf{0}$ (so $\langle\!\langle P_1^{\omega_4}; \mathbf{0}\rangle\!\rangle = \langle\!\langle P_1^{\omega_4}\rangle\!\rangle \odot_u \langle\!\langle \mathbf{0}\rangle\!\rangle = \langle\!\langle P_1^{\omega_4}\rangle\!\rangle \odot_u \mathbf{0} = \mathbf{0}$ since $\langle\!\langle \mathbf{0}\rangle\!\rangle = \mathbf{0}$ by Assumption 6 in section 2.3.2).

Likewise, when there are two waiters:

$$
\begin{aligned}
Unique(P_1^{\omega_2}, r_u, q_u) &= \langle\!\langle = \mid r_u \subseteq q_u; \mathrm{card}(\{y \mid r_u \models \langle\!\langle P_1^{\omega_2}; y\rangle\!\rangle\}); 1\rangle\!\rangle \\
&= \langle\!\langle = \mid r_u \subseteq q_u; \mathrm{card}(\{a_1, a_2\}); 1\rangle\!\rangle \\
&= \langle\!\langle = \mid r_u \subseteq q_u; 2; 1\rangle\!\rangle \\
&= \mathbf{0} \quad \text{since } r_u \subseteq q_u \text{ is assumed to hold.}
\end{aligned}
$$

and so the resulting content is again:

$$
\begin{aligned}
C_u^{\ell}(\omega) &= \langle\!\langle P_1^{\omega_4}; e(P_1^{\omega_2}, r_u) \mid Unique(P_1^{\omega_2}, r_u, q_u)\rangle\!\rangle \\
&= \langle\!\langle P_1^{\omega_4}; \{a_1, a_2\} \mid \mathbf{0}\rangle\!\rangle \\
&= \langle\!\langle P_1^{\omega_4}; \mathbf{0}\rangle\!\rangle \quad \text{by Assumption 5 in section 2.3.2} \\
&= \mathbf{0}
\end{aligned}
$$

The preceding two determinate contents are also what one should get intuitively, as something has gone wrong and the failure of the uniqueness condition leads to the contradictory infon **0**.

The revised literal content of just the description is as follows:

$$C_u^{\ell}(\omega_1\omega_2) = \langle\!\langle e(P_1^{\omega_2}, r_u) \mid Unique(P_1^{\omega_2}, r_u, q_u)\rangle\!\rangle \tag{6.2}$$

$$= \begin{cases} \langle\!\langle a \mid \mathbf{1}\rangle\!\rangle = \langle\!\langle a\rangle\!\rangle & \text{when there is one waiter} \\ \langle\!\langle \phi \mid \mathbf{0}\rangle\!\rangle = \mathbf{0} & \text{when there is no waiter} \\ \langle\!\langle \{a_1, a_2\} \mid \mathbf{0}\rangle\!\rangle = \mathbf{0} & \text{when there are two waiters} \end{cases} \tag{6.3}$$

This is what the content of Alan's utterance would be if he had stopped after saying THE WAITER.

The key technical innovation here is that there is a single infon $\langle\!\langle P_1^{\omega_4}; e(P_1^{\omega_2}, r_u) | Unique(P_1^{\omega_2}, r_u, q_u)\rangle\!\rangle$ (or $\langle\!\langle e(P_1^{\omega_2}, r_u) | Unique(P_1^{\omega_2}, r_u, q_u)\rangle\!\rangle$ when the utterance is partial) which can be either object-dependent or object-independent based on whether the uniqueness condition is satisfied or not. To Russell and his followers, it seems to have appeared that a proposition (i.e., infon in our sense) has to be either always one or the other, independent of circumstances. This is precisely the strength of the *situated* approach that has been advocated throughout. It allows us to have our cake and eat it too. Russell's main worry, the positing of non-existent objects, has been avoided.

Assuming the described situation is c, the proposition (in my sense) expressed will be $c \models \langle\!\langle P_1^{\omega_4}; e(P_1^{\omega_2}, r_u) \mid Unique(P_1^{\omega_2}, r_u, q_u)\rangle\!\rangle$. When there is just one waiter, this will reduce to $c \models \langle\!\langle P_1^{\omega_4}; a\rangle\!\rangle$ and will be true; when there is either no waiter or too many waiters, it will reduce to $c \models \mathbf{0}$ and will be false by Clause 1 of Assumption 7 in section 2.3.5 (which says that $s \not\models \mathbf{0}$ and $s \models \mathbf{1}$ for all situations s). However, it is not just false: because the content is contradictory, it *could not possibly be true if there is no unique waiter*.

Russell believed and his analysis predicts that when there is no waiter, the utterance is simply false. Strawson's view is that there is a truth-value gap because the presupposition that there is a unique waiter does not hold and so the question of its truth or falsity does not arise. To quote Strawson (1956):

> Now suppose someone were in fact to say to you with a perfectly serious air: "The king of France is wise." Would you say, "That's untrue"? I think it is quite certain that you would not. But suppose he went on to *ask* you whether you thought that what he had just said was true, or was false; whether you agreed or disagreed with what he had just said. I think you would be inclined, with some hesitation, to

say that you did not do either; that the question of whether his statement was true or false simply *did not arise*, because there was no such person as the king of France.

What my account predicts, interestingly, is something that is *in between* Russell's and Strawson's predictions. Being contradictory and therefore necessarily false—given the absence of a unique waiter or a king of France—can be said to occupy a middle ground between being just false and being neither. It is at least arguable that Strawson's sentence above could be completed in the following way: "the question of whether his statement was true or false simply *did not arise*, because there was no such person as the king of France, and so the statement could not *possibly* be true *in such circumstances*." That is, the *universal* intuition that something has gone wrong when there is a failure of unique existence can be articulated either in terms of a truth value gap, as Strawson chose to do, or in terms of contradictoriness, which my theory entails—both fit perfectly with the quote above. A person asked whether the statement "The king of France is wise" is true or false would not simply agree or disagree *either* because of a truth value gap *or* because it is *contradictory*—because it *cannot* be true in the relevant circumstances. Logically, the statement's being neither simply true nor simply false does not imply that there is a truth value gap. A contradictory proposition is also not either simply true or simply false.[6]

My account thus agrees with Russell but goes beyond him in recognizing a certain failure in the utterance and so is able to differentiate between utterances that are merely false and utterances that are necessarily so in the relevant circumstances; additionally—and happily—there is no need for awkward truth-value gaps.

It appears then that I have succeeded in preserving the basic referential intuition in referential uses of definite descriptions with a technical maneuver that forestalls the problems that have plagued such attempts. Of

6. I am inclined to agree with von Fintel (2004) that there is a presupposition involved in *all* utterances involving definite descriptions, whether a bald assertion like "The king of France is wise" or "My friend went for a drive with the king of France last week." My conclusion from both such cases is that the resulting utterance is just necessarily false, although such a judgment requires a more sophisticated intuition than a layperson is likely to have. However, it seems undeniable that there is a *universal* intuition of *oddity* or *some kind of failure* and that is all I need to argue that it is plausible that the utterance is, in fact, contradictory. By the way, my use of *conditions* captures the role played by presuppositions in a natural way. See footnote 29 in chapter 2.

course, this is just the barest sketch of how definite descriptions work: there has been no mention of how such contents are to be derived from first principles, something that will need access to the other ideas of use, indeterminacy, and equilibrium encoded in the **SCIF** constraints.

It should be pointed out that the step from Equation 6.2 to Equation 6.3, that is, the step from the content of the definite description to its *evaluation* in particular circumstances requires that the addressee (and speaker) be able to access the resource situation r_u and make the relevant determination with respect to r_u. This is not automatic. If the addressee does not have this access, then all she would know is that there is some particular resource situation possibly available to the speaker with respect to which such an evaluation can be carried out. Alan may say "The waiter who served me the last time I was here was exceedingly nice." Here, it may happen that only the speaker knows the relevant resource situation and therefore has access to the individual object in it; the addressee cannot go from Equation 6.2 to Equation 6.3. It is this epistemic fact that preempts the Fregean problem of informative identities.

Though I do not consider belief and other propositional attitudes, I mention in passing that when we say something such as A believes that the waiter is rude, the content of the belief (or other attitude) has the familiar dual nature characteristic of intensional constructions: it is given by Equation 6.1, which when evaluated with respect to different resource situations—going from Equation 6.2 to Equation 6.3—yields different results. My particular way of construing definite descriptions does not introduce anything new here; it is just the well-known consequence of the intensionality of belief. How such duality is best handled in equilibrium semantics is beyond the scope of this book.

The problem of incomplete definite descriptions that plagues the Russellian account is very naturally solved with the device of resource situations. Descriptions are evaluated with respect to a limited part of the world rather than the whole world. More will be said about resource situations at the end of the chapter.

I will attend to the multiple uses of definite descriptions and to the more complete derivation of the meaning of ω in u presently. Once this is done, it will also be necessary to counter Kripke's (1977) arguments against semantic ambiguities in descriptions, especially those arising from cases of misdescription of the kind Donnellan (1966) introduced. But, first, I note that what has been accomplished is a prima facie case for a literal and semantic theory that is referential. The position of Russellians is weakened somewhat as any locutionary or literal account that is referential is intuitively more appealing. I now briefly compare some predictions of the two views with respect to the Gricean properties discussed in section 4.5.

6.1.2 Comparing Russell + Grice with My Account

A traditional way of stating the difference between the Russellian account and my account is as follows: for the Russellian, the truth conditional or "semantic" content of an utterance involving a "referential" use of a definite description is just the unique existence of an object satisfying certain properties; for me it is that some particular object a, when it exists uniquely, has these properties. The latter implies the former but not the other way around.

More specifically, both the Russellian account and my account share the fact that a so-called referential use of a definite description expresses the unique existence of an object *literally* (or "semantically") relative to a resource situation.[7] Where they differ is in the status of the referent: for me it is literal or indeed locutionary in utterances like the ones above but for Russellians (those espousing Russell + Grice in particular) it is implicated (or "pragmatic"). This is the essence of the difference and it is easy to use it to educe different predictions from the two theories.

Refer back to section 4.5 where the Gricean properties were discussed in the context of equilibrium semantics. These properties are: existence, calculability, cancelability or defeasibility, indeterminacy, nondetachability, and reinforceability.

Since existence and calculability apply to all meanings tout court, locutionary and illocutionary, these attributes do not help us to distinguish between the two views of the status of the referent.

Next, consider the property of cancelability and the following famous example of Donnellan's (1966): Smith has been found foully murdered and Jones is on trial and is behaving oddly. In this situation u, the speaker $\mathcal{A}$ utters:

The murderer is insane. (ξ)

In the composite Russell + Grice view advanced by Kripke (1977) and Neale (1990), Jones is not the "semantic" referent but the "pragmatic" or speaker referent. Now let the speaker utter:

The murderer is insane but Jones is not insane. (ξ_1')

7. While the pure Russellian account does not involve resource situations, it can be extended to include such a reference as Recanati (2004a) has shown.

This cancelation does not result in a contradiction because ξ_1' merely entails that Jones is not the murderer. If in fact Jones is the murderer, ξ_1' is false; otherwise it is true. The upshot of this is that for the Russell + Grice view, the referent is cancelable.

In my view, the referent is "semantic" or, as I would say, literal and locutionary. This makes ξ_1' contradictory which implies that the referent is not cancelable.

Is there a way to tell, independent of any theory, whether the referent is cancelable or not? That is, is there a way to tell whether the referent is literal or implicated? Unfortunately, it does not appear possible to test this difference in predictions empirically because there is a subtle shift in the intention of the speaker when considering ξ_1' from the Russell + Grice standpoint. Earlier, in uttering ξ, it was possible to say that the speaker had Jones *in mind* and that the utterance was about Jones; with ξ_1', this is no longer true. Thus, the two situations are not directly comparable because for Russell + Grice the intended (speaker) referent changes with ξ_1' whereas for me it remains the same across ξ and ξ_1'. To make the two predictions commensurable, it would be necessary to allow the intended literal or "semantic" referent in my account to change as well, in which case cancelability would hold for me as well. So it seems that both accounts are internally consistent with respect to cancelability.

The same holds, mutatis mutandis, for reinforceability. In the same circumstances, let $\mathcal{A}$ utter:

The murderer is insane, I mean Jones is insane. (ξ'')

Now, there is no anomaly in the Russell + Grice view, though there is in my account, again because a shift in intention accompanies the reinforcement in the former theory.

Though the two theories make different predictions, cancelability and reinforceability do not tell us which one is correct. This appears to be an interesting fact about these properties.

The property of indeterminacy may give us an entering wedge. Implicatures are always somewhat indeterminate but referents seldom are. Even if a description is lexically vague, its referent is usually quite determinate. With most uses of definite descriptions, the interlocutors know with reasonable certainty which entity they are talking about. Indeed, something like legal discourse depends on this determinateness of the referent.

The Russell + Grice pragmatic account requires indeterminacy and this contradicts the facts. In my view, (especially when there is no lexical ambiguity in the description and when there is just one salient possible referent), the referents of descriptions are quite determinate and this agrees with the facts. Perhaps, then, this property of implicatures weakens the former account considerably.

Nondetachability does not provide a way to distinguish between the two strategies because it applies to both locutionary and illocutionary meanings.

Now consider the following use of an anaphoric pronoun.

The hadron traced a parabolic path through the collider. The standard model in physics also predicts it should have done this.

The same argument above about indeterminacy applies to the pronoun IT as well. The reference to the elementary particle is not indeterminate. This reinforces the case for the "semantic" or literal nature of the referent.

6.1.3 The Multiple Uses of Definite Descriptions

Consider Alan's utterances of the following sentences at Cafe Boulud this evening in successive situations.

1. The waiter is rude (ω in u)
2. The waiter will take the order (λ in u')
3. The waiter is meant to serve customers in a restaurant (θ in u'')
4. This is the waiter (κ in u''')

Imagine an extended discourse situation d at Cafe Boulud starting with u, and going on to u', u'', and u''' such that $u \cup u' \cup u'' \cup u''' \subseteq d$. The discourse starts out as we saw with Alan and Barbara trying to order their dinner with the initial waiter a in the resource situation r_u. Alan finds a rude, utters ω to Barbara in u, and complains to the maître d' who looks for another waiter to serve them. As they wait, Alan utters the second sentence λ in u', the succeeding situation. Then Alan says θ in u'', the third situation, as the discourse evolves. And, finally, Alan utters κ in the last situation u''' as a new waiter approaches their table.

The same singular definite description THE WAITER is used quite differently and has quite different semantic values in each of the utterance situations described above. The first is a *referential* use as discussed and refers to a, the rude waiter in r_u, the second is an *attributive* use, picking out some waiter, whoever he turns out to be, the third is a *generic* use about waiters generally, and the last is a *predicative* use that predicates *waiterhood* of some person identified by the demonstrative pronoun THIS. Strawson (1956), in his response to Russell's (1905) classic paper a century ago, appears to have been the first philosopher to discuss in detail that the same description may be used in different ways in different circumstances.[8]

As I argue below, these uses represent semantic ambiguities in the definite article.[9] It should be evident that the referential use is the most common, given the frequent need to refer to individual objects in our environment.[10]

In the equilibrium semantics account that follows, I will specify not only the composite content of the phrase THE WAITER in each different use, but also the different meanings of THE, the different meanings of WAITER, and how these individual meanings combine to produce the composite content that becomes a constituent of the infon and proposition expressed by the utterance.

6.1.4 Deriving the Content of Definite Descriptions

I am now ready to develop the theory of definite descriptions from first principles within the full framework of equilibrium semantics.

The Syntactic Constraint ω has the following parse tree:

$$[_S\ [_{NP}\ [_{Det}\ \text{THE}][_N\ \text{WAITER}]][_{VP}\ [_V\ \text{IS}][_{Adj}\ \text{RUDE}]]]$$

or:

$$[_S\ [_{NP}\ [_{Det}\ \omega_1][_N\ \omega_2]][_{VP}\ [_V\ \omega_3][_{Adj}\ \omega_4]]]$$

As observed earlier, the grammatical categories listed above are important in determining how the *Informational Constraint* works and therefore the kinds of games we get. For example, the category *Det* leads to four possible ontological maps and the category *N* to just the identity map.

The Conventional Constraint Some conventional meanings have already been noted in section 6.1.1. To repeat, $P_1^{waiter} = P_1^{\omega_2}$ is the intended conventional meaning of $\omega_2 =$ WAITER, which is just the property of being a person who serves customers in a restaurant. Other conventional meanings of WAITER are the properties of being a small tray or salver, denoted

8. Moore (1944) may have been the first to notice this fact.

9. Not all languages have definite articles; this does not pose any special problems for my account, but I ignore these matters here.

10. Certain sentences may, by the very words they contain, make some uses awkward, so that it may not be possible to put every sentence to each of the four uses. Note that ω may be used generically as well.

by $P_2^{waiter} = P_2^{\omega_2}$, and of being someone who waits for some future event. This third meaning will be ignored to keep the number of nodes in the corresponding lexical game that ensues manageable. Likewise, $P_1^{rude} = P_1^{\omega_4}$ is the intended conventional meaning of $\omega_4 =$ RUDE, which is just the attribute of being impolite. Another conventional meaning is the attribute of being roughly made or unsophisticated (as in "a rude salver") and is denoted by $P_2^{rude} = P_2^{\omega_4}$.

As described in section 4.2.2, the verb IS has at least three conventional meanings, which could be denoted by $P_1^{is} = P_1^{\omega_3} = P^{=}$; $P_2^{is} = P_2^{\omega_3} = P^{\epsilon}$; and $P_3^{is} = P_3^{\omega_3} = P^{aux}$. The first denotes the sense involved in a sentence such as "Voltaire is Arouet," the second the sense involved in a sentence such as "Harvey is young" or "The waiter is rude," and the third the sense operative in "Harvey is playing." I will restrict my attention to just the second property $P^{\varepsilon} \equiv P^{\omega_3} \equiv P_2^{\omega_3}$ to keep the relevant lexical game simple.

This accounts for three of the four words in ω. For the moment, I simply assert that the single conventional meaning of $\omega_1 =$ THE is $P^{the} = P^{\omega_1} = \hat{P}(\dot{P} \mid Unique(\dot{P}, \dot{r}_{\dot{u}}, \dot{q}_{\dot{u}}))$.[11] Notice that everything in $Unique(\dot{P}, \dot{r}_{\dot{u}}, \dot{q}_{\dot{u}})$ is a parameter, even $\dot{u}$, since no particular utterance situation or resource situations can be specified at the level of conventional meaning. It will presently be shown how this interesting property can be inferred by recourse to the operation $\odot_u$.

In section 4.2.3, the *Informational Constraint* **I** was discussed with respect to the sentence $\varphi =$ HARVEY IS PLAYING. I quote from a paragraph in that section:

> It should be easy to see that lexical ambiguity can involve either the conventional map or the informational map, an important fact that is often obscured. In the case of IS and PLAYING, lexical ambiguity involves the conventional map; in the case of HARVEY, it involves the informational map.

This will be important when the "semantic" ambiguity of THE is discussed in section 6.1.6 below. For now, I note that THE is not conventionally ambiguous since it is associated conventionally with just the one property $\hat{P}(\dot{P} \mid Unique(\dot{P}, \dot{r}_{\dot{u}}, \dot{q}_{\dot{u}}))$. It turns out the ambiguity in THE involves the informational map.

The Informational Constraint Now that a set of conventional maps for each word in ω is given, we can map each word's conventional meanings

11. See section 2.2 for a discussion of conditioned properties and individuals.

into one or more infons that represent the *possible* contents or meanings of the word uttered. These are the *informational maps* and all of them together form the *Informational Constraint.*

We can string the conventional and informational maps together for the words in ω as follows:

THE

- Referential use: $\omega_1 \rightarrow P^{\omega_1} \xrightarrow{u} \langle\!\langle \hat{P}(e(\dot{P}, r_u) \mid Unique(\dot{P}, r_u, q_u)) \rangle\!\rangle = \sigma_1$

Here the informational map transforms the property $P^{\omega_1} = \hat{P}(\dot{P} \mid Unique(\dot{P}, \dot{r}_{\dot{u}}, \dot{q}_{\dot{u}}))$ into the conditioned infon $\langle\!\langle \hat{P}(e(\dot{P}, r_u) \mid Unique(\dot{P}, r_u, q_u)) \rangle\!\rangle$. Since the informational map involves a specific u and therefore specific resource situations r_u and q_u, the parameters in the conventional meaning $P^{\omega_1} = \hat{P}(\dot{P} \mid Unique(\dot{P}, \dot{r}_{\dot{u}}, \dot{q}_{\dot{u}}))$ get anchored to these specific situations. As a result, one input to $e(\dot{P}, r_u)$ is the parameter $\dot{P}$ and the other is the particular resource situation r_u relative to the utterance situation u. The latter is not a parameter but an actual situation at Alan and Barbara's table in the restaurant. This informational map corresponds to the ontological map of instantiation introduced in section 2.4. The same thing happens to the conditioning infon $Unique(\dot{P}, r_u, q_u)$ where again there is a parametric property and actual resource situations as inputs. The example of this use was the sentence $\omega =$ THE WAITER IS RUDE in u.

- Attributive use: $\omega_1 \rightarrow P^{\omega_1} \xrightarrow{u} \langle\!\langle \hat{P}(e(\dot{P}, \dot{r}_u) \mid Unique(\dot{P}, \dot{r}_u, \dot{q}_u)) \rangle\!\rangle = \sigma_1'$

The only difference between the referential and attributive uses is that in the latter the resource situations $\dot{r}_u$ and $\dot{q}_u$ remain as parameters. That is, these situations are not fixed by the utterance situation u. This explains why it is possible to say, "The waiter, whoever he is, ..." or "The waiter, whatever the resource situation, ..." when the definite article is used attributively. This informational map corresponds to the ontological operation of parametrization and this use may also be called the *indeterminate* use of the definite article since the single object picked out remains indeterminate. The example of this use was the sentence $\lambda =$ THE WAITER WILL TAKE THE ORDER in u'.

- Generic use: $\omega_1 \rightarrow P^{\omega_1} \xrightarrow{u} \langle\!\langle \hat{P}[\dot{x} \mid r_u'' \models \langle\!\langle \dot{P}; \dot{x} \rangle\!\rangle] \rangle\!\rangle = \sigma_1''$

This informational map corresponds to the operation of reification where the relevant property is transformed into the *type* of object that has the property relative to some *grounding* situation r_u''. Since the example given of such a use involved the sentence $\theta =$ THE WAITER IS MEANT TO SERVE CUSTOMERS IN A RESTAURANT in u'', the grounding situation r_u'' could be taken to be the whole world $\mathcal{W}$. No particular or indeterminate waiter is identified in this use, just the type of object that is a waiter. Notice that the entire sentence $\omega = $ THE WAITER IS RUDE could also be used generically.

How would such a generic use work in a description like "The grouchy waiter who served us yesterday"? As the use selects a type rather than an individual, this requirement conflicts with the rest of the description since it is relatively improbable to have such a type. This would mean that the conditional probability $\rho_{1''} = P(\sigma_1'' \mid \sigma_{-1}'', u)$ corresponding to this generic interpretation in the full lexical game $g_1 = g_u(\omega_1)$ would be relatively low (almost zero) for all values of the conditioning variables σ_{-1}''.[12] This would result in this interpretation being dropped from the local and global equilibrium. However, it is important to observe that a generic reading for THE is always available in isolation and its compatibility with the rest of the noun phrase is a matter of degree that accordingly pushes the relevant conditional probability higher or lower.

- Predicative use: $\omega_1 \to P^{\omega_1} \xrightarrow{u} \langle\langle \hat{P}(\dot{P} \mid Unique(\dot{P}, r_u, q_u)) \rangle\rangle = \sigma_1'''$

This is just the identity map. The example of this use was the sentence $\kappa = $ THIS IS THE WAITER in u'''. Strawson's (1956) example of the predicative use was "Napoleon was the greatest French soldier" where the description is used to predicate something of Napoleon. Incidentally, the verb "was" in this sentence is being used to pick out the conventional meaning $P^{\omega_3} = P_2^{is} = P_2^{\omega_3} = P^{\epsilon}$ rather than $P_1^{is} = P_1^{\omega_3} = P^{=}$ or $P_3^{is} = P_3^{\omega_3} = P^{aux}$, exactly as in the example $\omega = $ THE WAITER IS RUDE being analyzed here.

WAITER

- Predicative use: $\omega_2 \to P_1^{\omega_2} \xrightarrow{u} \langle\langle P_1^{\omega_2} \rangle\rangle = \sigma_2$
- Predicative use: $\omega_2 \to P_2^{\omega_2} \xrightarrow{u} \langle\langle P_2^{\omega_2} \rangle\rangle = \sigma_2'$

$P_i^{\omega_2}$ for $i = 1, 2$ are just the conventional meanings of WAITER mentioned under **C** above. The informational maps involved are the identity map. The kind of lexical ambiguity present here is conventional and not informational as with THE above.

IS

- Membership use: $\omega_3 \to P^{\omega_3} \xrightarrow{u} \langle\langle (t \mid t \parallel t_u) \rangle\rangle = \sigma_3$

12. The lexical game $g_1 = g_u(\omega_1)$ shown in Figure 6.1 is not the full lexical game and so does not show this conditional probability. The generic and predicative uses have been omitted for convenience.

Here $P^{\omega_3} = P_2^{\omega_3} = P^{\epsilon}$, the intended conventional meaning for IS, is transformed into a conditioned temporal infon just as with the auxiliary verb sense of IS in chapter 4. As we saw in section 2.3.2 and section 4.2.3, $t \parallel t_u$ means that the property of being rude attributed to the waiter temporally overlaps with the time of utterance. The name *membership use* was introduced in section 4.2.3. Just for completeness, I list the two omitted instances of IS even though they will not be used in what follows:

- Predicative use: $\omega_3 \to P_1^{\omega_3} \xrightarrow{u} \langle\!\langle P_1^{\omega_3}; (t \mid t \parallel t_u) \rangle\!\rangle$
- Auxiliary use: $\omega_3 \to P_3^{\omega_3} \xrightarrow{u} \langle\!\langle t \mid (t \parallel t_u) \wedge t, t_u \in [t_0, t_\infty] \rangle\!\rangle$

In the predicative use, the property remains, but, as with the membership use, the property disappears in the auxiliary use. Note that the ambiguity in IS is conventional.

RUDE

- Predicative use: $\omega_4 \to P_1^{\omega_4} \xrightarrow{u} \langle\!\langle P_1^{\omega_4} \rangle\!\rangle = \sigma_4$
- Predicative use: $\omega_4 \to P_2^{\omega_4} \xrightarrow{u} \langle\!\langle P_2^{\omega_4} \rangle\!\rangle = \sigma_4'$

$P_i^{\omega_4}$ for $i = 1, 2$ are just the conventional meanings of RUDE mentioned under **C** above. The informational maps involved are again the identity map. The kind of lexical ambiguity present here is also conventional and not informational as with THE above.

Implicit in the instances of **C** and **I** above is a *theory* of noun and verb phrases. This theory is something that has simply been asserted, not argued for. This is one area where variant theories are possible: this is why equilibrium semantics is a *framework* compatible with different *theories*. The important thing for the framework is just that the two maps provide appropriate infons as the possible contents of the words in an utterance.

Some contents (like σ_1, σ_1', and σ_1'') involve either resource situations or parameters for resource situations. When accessible, as often with the definite article, these situations enable the identification of the object being referred to. When not accessible, as with some uses of the definite article and also with the indefinite article to be considered later in this chapter, all that an addressee can infer is that some inaccessible resource situation that identifies the referent exists. In the example sentence ω in u, r_u is accessible, enabling the identification of the rude waiter. There is no question of the accessibility of a parameter for a resource situation.

For each word, the source of its lexical ambiguity has been pinpointed. Except for THE, where the ambiguity is informational, all the words are conventionally ambiguous. It should be noted that informational ambiguities may themselves be of two distinct types: one involves distinct informational or ontological maps, the other involves distinct resource situations relative to the same informational map as was seen in the case of HARVEY in chapter 3. If two waiters had initially served Alan and Barbara, there would have been two different resource situations relative to the same referential use and ontological map of instantiation.

The presence of *u* above the second arrow in all the maps indicates that each word has to be uttered in some situation in order for it to have one or more contents. Without being uttered, it remains inert and carries just a conventional meaning but no referential meaning. As I said in chapter 1, this is a basic fact that is often simply ignored.

We now check that these lexical contents combine in the expected way.

$$\sigma_1 \odot_u \sigma_2 = \langle\!\langle \hat{P}(e(\dot{P}, r_u) \mid Unique(\dot{P}, r_u, q_u)) \rangle\!\rangle \odot_u \langle\!\langle P_1^{\omega_2} \rangle\!\rangle$$

$$= \langle\!\langle e(P_1^{\omega_2}, r_u) \mid Unique(P_1^{\omega_2}, r_u, q_u) \rangle\!\rangle$$

$$= \langle\!\langle a \rangle\!\rangle \quad \text{when there is one waiter}$$

$$\sigma_1' \odot_u \sigma_2 = \langle\!\langle \hat{P}(e(\dot{P}, \dot{r}_u) \mid Unique(\dot{P}, \dot{r}_u, \dot{q}_u)) \rangle\!\rangle \odot_u \langle\!\langle P_1^{\omega_2} \rangle\!\rangle$$

$$= \langle\!\langle e(P_1^{\omega_2}, \dot{r}_u) \mid Unique(P_1^{\omega_2}, \dot{r}_u, \dot{q}_u) \rangle\!\rangle$$

$$= \langle\!\langle \dot{a} \rangle\!\rangle \quad \text{when uniqueness holds}$$

$$\sigma_1'' \odot_u \sigma_2 = \langle\!\langle \hat{P}[\dot{x} \mid r_u'' \models \langle\!\langle \dot{P}; \dot{x} \rangle\!\rangle] \rangle\!\rangle \odot_u \langle\!\langle P_1^{\omega_2} \rangle\!\rangle$$

$$= \langle\!\langle [x \mid r_u'' \models \langle\!\langle P_1^{\omega_2}; x \rangle\!\rangle] \rangle\!\rangle$$

$$\sigma_1''' \odot_u \sigma_2 = \langle\!\langle \hat{P}(\dot{P} \mid Unique(\dot{P}, r_u, q_u)) \rangle\!\rangle \odot_u \langle\!\langle P_1^{\omega_2} \rangle\!\rangle$$

$$= \langle\!\langle P_1^{\omega_2} \mid Unique(P^{\omega_2}, r_u, q_u) \rangle\!\rangle$$

The first content above is nothing but the content of the description identified in Equation 6.2. This shows that we have been able to derive this composite content from more basic assumptions involving **C** and **I** for the individual words making up the definite description. Incidentally, all the composite infons were obtained via the unification operation of Hat Merging in section 2.3.3.

The second content represents the attributive use of definite descriptions. The key difference between this content and that of referential uses is the presence of a *parametric* resource situation $\dot{r}_u$. This parameter implies that the function $e(P_1^{\omega_2}, \dot{r}_u)$ is evaluated parametrically and so does not refer to a particular individual but merely picks out an individual $\dot{a}$ *indeterminately*. When Alan says, "The waiter (whoever he is) will take the order," no particular waiter is identified relative to a particular resource situation, just an indeterminate person $\dot{a}$ relative to a parametric resource situation $\dot{r}_u$ assuming the uniqueness condition is satisfied.

The generic use results in a type and the predicative use in a property. These contents have been less studied though they also represent possible uses of definite descriptions.

In section 2.4, five possible ontological transformations were identified—instantiation and extensionalization, parametrization, reification, and identity. The first two of these correspond to the referential use, the third to the attributive use, the fourth to the generic use, and the last to the predicative use. It is interesting that such a one-to-one correspondence exists between the uses of THE and the ontological maps. One may speculate that since the ontological transforms represent a fundamental aspect of the logical structure of the world, allowing only five transmutations of properties into other objects (individuals and sets, parameters, types, and properties themselves), they must constitute the entire space of possible uses of the definite article (or any other word for that matter). In other words, it should not be possible to find any more uses of definite descriptions by looking at more examples. This is a fundamental ontological constraint on the uses of words given that each word is conventionally associated with a property (or relation) and each property is then transformed into some other entity (individuals and sets, parameters, types, and properties themselves) in $\mathcal{O}$. Alternatively, if a new use is found, it would probably mean that a new type of entity must exist in $\mathcal{O}$.

It is possible to confirm that these four contents merge with the contents of the verb phrase IS RUDE correctly. I show this for the first case.

$$\sigma_1 \odot_u \sigma_2 = \langle\!\langle \hat{P}(e(\dot{P}, r_u) \mid Unique(\dot{P}, r_u, q_u)) \rangle\!\rangle \odot_u \langle\!\langle P_1^{\omega_2} \rangle\!\rangle$$

$$= \langle\!\langle e(P_1^{\omega_2}, r_u) \mid Unique(P_1^{\omega_2}, r_u, q_u) \rangle\!\rangle$$

$$= \langle\!\langle a \rangle\!\rangle \quad \text{when there is one waiter}$$

$$\sigma_3 \odot_u \sigma_4 = \langle\!\langle (t \mid t \parallel t_u) \rangle\!\rangle \odot_u \langle\!\langle P_1^{\omega_4} \rangle\!\rangle$$

$$= \langle\!\langle P_1^{\omega_4}; t \mid t \parallel t_u \rangle\!\rangle$$

$$(\sigma_1 \odot_u \sigma_2) \odot_u (\sigma_3 \odot_u \sigma_4) = \langle\!\langle a \rangle\!\rangle \odot_u \langle\!\langle P_1^{\omega_4}; t \,|\, t \,\|\, t_u \rangle\!\rangle$$

$$= \langle\!\langle P_1^{\omega_4}; a; t \,|\, t \,\|\, t_u \rangle\!\rangle$$

The composite infons in the second and third arrays above are obtained via the case of Ordinary Merging in section 2.3.3. When there is not exactly one waiter, $\langle\!\langle a \rangle\!\rangle$ may be replaced by $\langle\!\langle e(P_1^{\omega_2}, r_u) \,|\, Unique(P_1^{\omega_2}, r_u, q_u) \rangle\!\rangle = \mathbf{0}$ and so the whole infon will be $\mathbf{0}$ on account of Fact 2 in section 2.3.3, which says that for all infons σ, $\sigma \odot_s \mathbf{0} = \mathbf{0} \odot_s \sigma = \mathbf{0}$.

Earlier, the conventional meaning of $\omega_1 =$ THE was simply asserted to be $P^{the} = P^{\omega_1} = \hat{P}(\dot{P} \,|\, Unique(\dot{P}, \dot{r}_{\dot{u}}, \dot{q}_{\dot{u}}))$. Now, we can see how this may be inferred by making intuitive judgments about the composite contents of the four uses of definite descriptions. That is, these composite contents can be expressed intuitively and the conventional meaning of ω_1 inferred. Let this conventional meaning be x. Then, noting that the predicative use involves the identity map $x \xrightarrow{u} \langle\!\langle x \rangle\!\rangle$, we get the equation:

$$\langle\!\langle x \rangle\!\rangle \odot_u \langle\!\langle P_1^{\omega_2} \rangle\!\rangle = \langle\!\langle P_1^{\omega_2} \,|\, Unique(P^{\omega_2}, r_u, q_u) \rangle\!\rangle$$

Solving this equation, we get $x = \hat{P}(\dot{P} \,|\, Unique(\dot{P}, r_u, q_u))$. This solution can then be checked against the other three contents to see whether it works. Of course, there is a kind of circularity here, since we are using $\hat{P}(\dot{P} \,|\, Unique(\dot{P}, \dot{r}_{\dot{u}}, \dot{q}_{\dot{u}}))$ to derive the composite contents and using the composite contents to derive $\hat{P}(\dot{P} \,|\, Unique(\dot{P}, \dot{r}_{\dot{u}}, \dot{q}_{\dot{u}}))$. Ultimately, $\hat{P}(\dot{P} \,|\, Unique(\dot{P}, \dot{r}_{\dot{u}}, \dot{q}_{\dot{u}}))$ has to be *assumed*, or derived from other more basic assumptions; it is the composite contents that have to be derived from $\hat{P}(\dot{P} \,|\, Unique(\dot{P}, \dot{r}_{\dot{u}}, \dot{q}_{\dot{u}}))$. The equation in the unknown x is merely a means to guess what this conditioned property is.

The Flow Constraint As there are four words in the sentence $\omega = \omega_1\omega_2\omega_3\omega_4$, there are four lexical games to consider. To make the figures manageable, only the referential and attributive uses for THE will be included, as this will restrict the corresponding lexical game to two—instead of four—initial nodes. Likewise, just one conventional meaning of IS will be taken into account so that a game with just one initial node—instead of three—results.

The four lexical games are shown in Figures 6.1, 6.2, 6.3, and 6.4. These games ought to be quite familiar by now. The reader should refer back to the various contents listed in the preceding section on the *Informational Constraint* to check the accuracy of the figures.

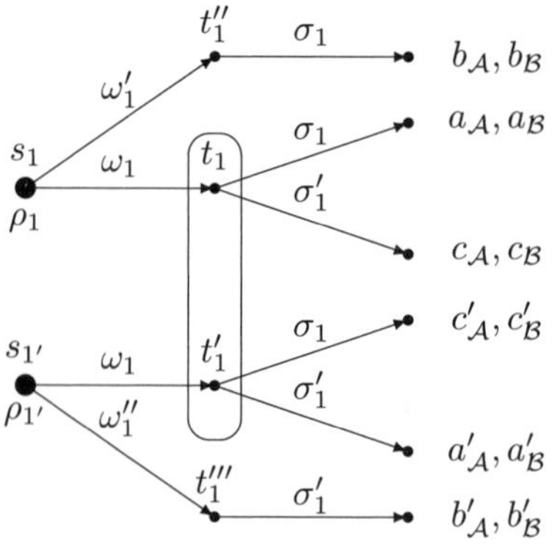

Figure 6.1
Algebraic version of lexical game $g_1 = g_u(\omega_1)$

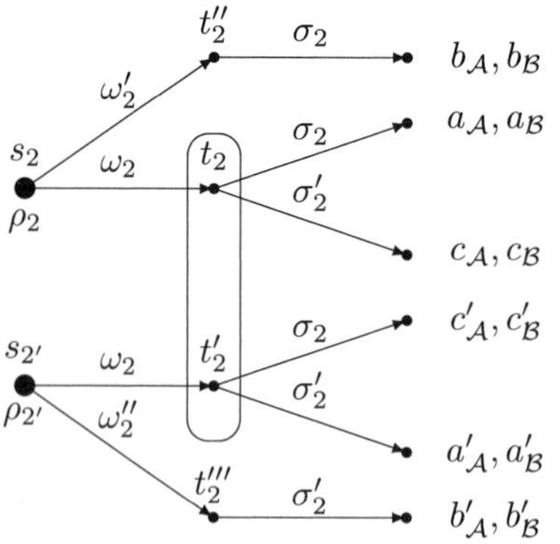

Figure 6.2
Algebraic version of lexical game $g_2 = g_u(\omega_2)$

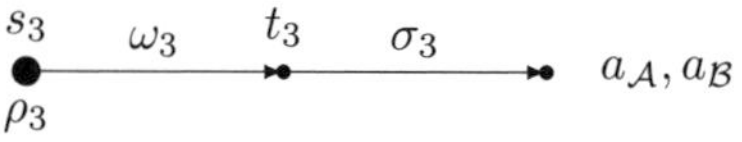

Figure 6.3
Algebraic version of lexical game $g_3 = g_u(\omega_3)$

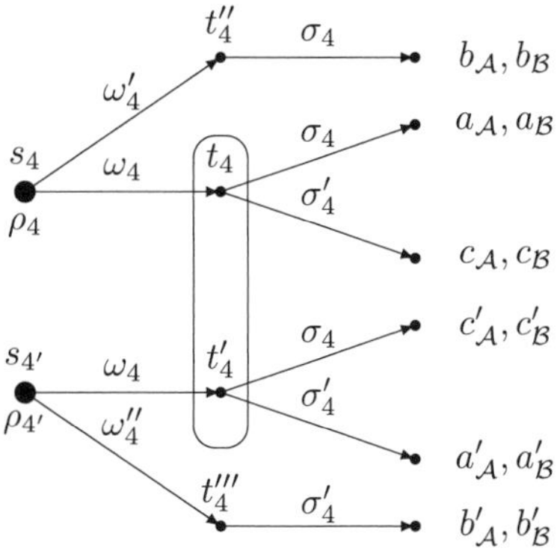

Figure 6.4
Algebraic version of lexical game $g_4 = g_u(\omega_4)$

In g_1 in Figure 6.1, ω'_1 may be taken to be something equivalent to "Referentially, the," for example, or "the" accompanied with pointing, and ω''_1 may be taken to be something equivalent to "Attributively, the" or "The, whatever the resource situation." In all these cases, the alternatives are costlier than the *primary* locution THE.[13]

In g_2 in Figure 6.2, the alternatives ω'_2 and ω''_2 may be something like "person serving us" and "small tray" or "salver." Why is the second option ω''_2 costlier than ω_2? In the first case, it involves two words "small" and "tray" instead of the single word WAITER; in the second, a less frequently used word "salver."

There are no alternatives to consider in g_3 in Figure 6.3 as it is a trivial game based on the decision to ignore the other two conventional meanings of IS.

In g_4 in Figure 6.4, the alternatives ω'_4 and ω''_4 may be something like "impolite" and "crude" or "unsophisticated."

Since the single parse tree of ω is:

$$[_S\ [_{NP}\ [_{Det}\ \omega_1] \circ [_N\ \omega_2]] \circ [_{VP}\ [_V\ \omega_3] \circ [_{Adj}\ \omega_4]]]$$

the next step is to form the phrasal products $g_1 \otimes g_2$ and $g_3 \otimes g_4$ and finally the sentential product $(g_1 \otimes g_2) \otimes (g_3 \otimes g_4)$. I present the first product $g_1 \otimes g_2$ as our primary interest is in the definite description. It is shown in Figure 6.5.

13. See section 3.3.6 for the definition of "primary."

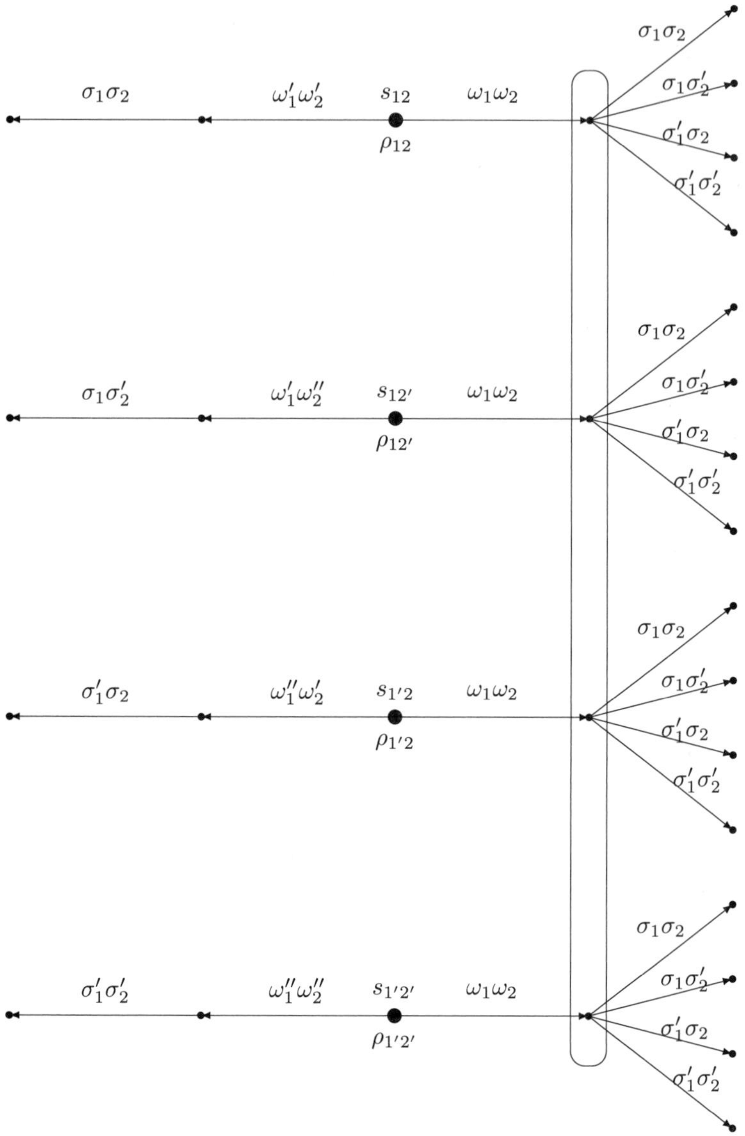

Figure 6.5
The definite description game $g_{12} = g_1 \otimes g_2$

If the full game g_1 had been drawn with four initial nodes corresponding to the four uses of THE, the game $g_{12} = g_1 \otimes g_2$ would have had $4 \times 2 = 8$ initial nodes. It was to accommodate the picture that I dropped the generic and predicative uses. This results in a game with $2 \times 2 = 4$ nodes.[14] As before with Figure 4.5 in section 4.2.4, the payoffs are not shown for convenience but they are just the additive counterparts of the payoffs of the multiplicands and obey the same inequalities. Following the discussion of *form* in section 4.12, it should be evident that the form of this game is roughly the same as that of the game in Figure 4.5.

Some suitable circumstantial assumptions about the initial probabilities need to be made in order to compute the global equilibrium of these interdependent games. These come in part from the utterance situation and a new setting game in which Alan and Barbara were trying to place their order with the first rude waiter. Since this kind of analysis has been extensively carried out in section 4.2 and in section 4.2.4 in the context of HARVEY IS PLAYING, it seems unnecessary to repeat this exercise. I urge the reader to reason through it, trying out alternative assumptions. For example, it may be assumed—as I have—that Alan is responding to a resource situation (and setting game) where the waiter has been rude. Or it may be a generic statement that Alan makes as they enter the restaurant.

It is possible that Alan intends a generic interpretation even in response to the resource situation after the rude behavior of the waiter. He may be reacting generically rather than particularly. In such a case, Barbara may well be unsure which of the referential and generic interpretations to infer, and she may model the payoffs in a way that results in a mixed strategy equilibrium. In this event, the two will have different subjective games of partial information they will be playing with only partial communication between them. This is part of the natural indeterminacy of all communication as we have seen in sections 5.2 and 5.3. This indeterminacy may get cleared up as their conversation progresses.

The other readings are less plausible for ω as it seems difficult to find circumstances where they may come into play. Of course, apart from situational assumptions, there are also the pushes and pulls from the possible meanings of the four words: WAITER interpreted in the usual way raises the conditional probability of RUDE as *impolite* rather than *crudely made* and vice versa.

14. Just for clarity, I point out that the full sentential game taking all alternatives into account for all four words would have $4 \times 2 \times 3 \times 2 = 48$ initial nodes. Even this calculation assumes that WAITER and RUDE have just two conventional meanings each.

SCIF and Equilibrium Semantics As we saw in chapter 4, the locutionary framework consists of the two *homomorphic* locutionary maps:

$$(\mathcal{L}, \circ) \xrightarrow{g_u} (\mathcal{G}, \otimes) \xrightarrow{f_u} (\mathcal{I}, \odot_u)$$

connecting three monoids that take us from words and phrases via their embedding situations and corresponding games to their *locutionary* contents. That is, the locutionary content or meaning $C_u^\ell = f_u \circ g_u$ where $\circ$ stands for function composition.

These two maps essentially involve maps from the parse trees of the sentence to corresponding "trees of games" and further to trees of contents (or infons). The first map g_u maps a word or expression into a corresponding game, relative to the context of utterance u. These games are embedded in an isomorphic tree of games. And f_u maps each game into its unique solution, which is its corresponding locutionary content.[15]

We have already seen the parse tree in **S**:

$$[_S\, [_{NP}\, [_{Det}\, \omega_1] \circ [_N\, \omega_2]] \circ [_{VP}\, [_V\, \omega_3] \circ [_{Adj}\, \omega_4]]]$$

The isomorphic tree of games based on **C**, **I**, and **F** and obtained via the map g_u is as follows:

$$[_S\, [_{NP}\, [_{Det}\, g_1] \otimes [_N\, g_2]] \otimes [_{VP}\, [_V\, g_3] \otimes [_{Adj}\, g_4]]]$$

The phrasal and sentential games g_{12}, g_{34}, and g_{1234} are implicitly present in the tree above.

The third isomorphic tree obtained via the map f_u is the contents tree below:

$$[_S\, [_{NP}\, [_{Det}\, \sigma_1] \odot_u [_N\, \sigma_2]] \odot_u [_{VP}\, [_V\, \sigma_3] \odot_u [_{Adj}\, \sigma_4]]] \tag{6.4}$$

The phrasal and sentential contents $\sigma_1\sigma_2$, $\sigma_3\sigma_4$, and $\sigma_1\sigma_2\sigma_3\sigma_4$ are also implicitly present in the tree above.

These three trees give us the full solution to the problem of deriving the locutionary meaning of ω and of the definite description $\omega_1\omega_2$ from first principles. We can write:

$$\begin{aligned} C_u^\ell(\omega) &= (f_u \circ g_u)(\omega) \\ &= \sigma^\ell \\ &= \sigma_1\sigma_2\sigma_3\sigma_4 \end{aligned}$$

15. The map f_u is not to the whole solution or strategy profile, just to that part of the profile corresponding to the addressee's interpretation.

$$= \langle\langle P_1^{\omega_4}; e(P_1^{\omega_2}, r_u) \mid Unique(P_1^{\omega_2}, r_u, q_u); t \mid t \parallel t_u) \rangle\rangle$$

$$= \langle\langle P_1^{\omega_4}; a; t \mid t \parallel t_u) \rangle\rangle$$

When the content $C_u^\ell(\omega)$ was first specified in Equation 6.1 in section 6.1.1, only a *partial* locutionary content was made explicit. The temporal part of the infon was deliberately omitted to simplify the argument. But it has now been included and the full locutionary content has been spelled out.

There are seven nodes in each tree and there are correspondingly seven expressions, seven games, and seven equilibrium contents. Notice again how the ideas of generativity and (global) equilibrium *combine* in these trees, especially in the latter two. The two maps are formally defined in Appendix A.

It is also possible to simply solve the vector fixed point equation discussed earlier to derive all the seven equilibrium contents in one shot.

$$C_u^\ell(\alpha, P(x \mid u)) = f_u[g_u(\alpha, P(x \mid u))] = x \tag{6.5}$$

As before, the equation captures the idea of a global equilibrium or what was called a *double* fixed point, local at one level and global at the second. The reader should verify that the solution to this equation is precisely the product of the infons in Equation 6.4.

Thus, as before, we see that equilibrium semantics combines the constraints **SCIF** via two homomorphic maps g_u and f_u into a new theory and framework for locutionary meaning and for definite descriptions in particular. This new semantics is a generalized model theory incorporating the ideas of reference, use, indeterminacy, and equilibrium in a way that fuses the basic ideas of semantics and pragmatics into a single discipline.

As argued in chapter 4, this framework can be extended to illocutionary meanings as well. In addition, it can also account for phonological aspects of an utterance governed by the constraint **P** mentioned in sections 1.4.4 and 5.8. If, for example, Alan had uttered ω in a certain tone, he would have been able to convey the additional presence of some unsavory epithet for the waiter, an epithet that would have remained indeterminate.

6.1.5 Misdescription

Donnellan (1966), Kripke (1977), Searle (1991), and a host of other writers have used examples involving misdescription to argue for or against a "semantic" ambiguity between *referential* and *attributive* uses of definite descriptions. In my view, misdescription is a second-order phenomenon: it should not be the primary evidence for or against such views and Donnellan's premature introduction of such cases into the argument has unfortunately confused the issue.

Donnellan (1966) considers two broad cases of misdescription and primarily uses such cases to advance his arguments for a semantic ambiguity. The two extreme cases of misdescription in an infinite range of cases may be labeled thus:

- Error
- Collusion

Most of Donnellan's (1966) (as well as Kripke's 1977) examples involve cases of error, perhaps the most famous of which is an utterance of:

Smith's murderer is insane.

The circumstances involving this utterance are as follows: Smith has been found foully murdered and Jones is on trial and is behaving oddly.

To avoid unnecessary complications, assume the same circumstances u of Smith's body being found dead and Jones's odd deportment at the trial but consider instead:

The murderer is insane. ($\xi = \xi_1\xi_2\xi_3\xi_4$)

It is worth noting that if Jones is in fact the murderer and there is no misdescription, the method by which I derived the content of THE WAITER would apply here.

However, Donnellan argues that even if there had been no murderer, even if in fact Smith's death was, say, a suicide or an accident, the speaker could still refer to Jones if the use of the definite description THE MURDERER was referential. On the other hand, in an attributive use (say, where no one had yet been apprehended), there would be no object satisfying the Russellian existential proposition or our corresponding infon involving a parametrized resource situation. Based on this, Donnellan has argued further that the description in a referential use is *inessential* because the reference goes through even though Jones is not a murderer.

This further argument requires some qualifications. Notice that $\xi_2 =$ MURDERER is not completely idiosyncratic—it (or the property P^{ξ_2} that is its conventional meaning) bears a close relationship to Jones, since even if he is not guilty, he still is on trial for the murder in the situation described. This is what makes the misdescription *slight*: the word MURDERER is not entirely irrelevant and plays some role in the communication even though it does not fit exactly. This can be seen by considering an utterance of the following sentence in exactly the same situation *u*:

The waiter is insane (ξ')

Here, the addressee is likely to ask who the speaker is referring to because, even though there is a salient object to refer to, and even though the use is referential, and even though the attribute of insanity appears to fit the salient object, the description $\xi_2' = \text{WAITER}$ (or the property $P_1^{\xi_2'}$) is just so *unrelated* to this object that the addressee is likely to be in real doubt about what was being said. It is possible to make the infelicity of $\xi_2' = \text{WAITER}$ even sharper by assuming that it is well known in *u* that Jones is a banker and that there is no possibility of his being a waiter.

This means that in a referential use, the description is not completely inessential, but some circumstantially delimited tolerance for error exists. And this tolerance for error is not confined just to referential uses of definite descriptions but can be widely observed across all of language—including with attributive uses. For example, it is quite possible in some circumstances to ask for the waiter (whoever he is) even though one really wants the sommelier.

It is not terribly important to know how a semantical theory enables the computation of the referent in such second-order situations of error, but here is one possibility. Since equilibrium semantics involves a fixed point computation requiring the *simultaneous* satisfaction of multiple equations, it is possible to get situations where some constraint is partially met, as with ξ, but, as demonstrated with ξ', the constraint cannot be flagrantly flouted. A kind of limited principle of charity may be said to operate in such cases.

Searle's (1991) suggestion is that in a referential use the property P^{ξ_2} is *secondary* and dispensable whereas there is some *primary* property that the interlocutors have recourse to and which they can fall back upon. This explanation fails to take into account examples like ξ' which make it clear that not any arbitrary secondary attribute will do: one needs something that is relatively closely related to (some property of) the referent.

Incidentally, the same analysis appears to work with proper names. Consider Kripke's (1977) example:

Jones is raking the leaves (ξ'')

Here, if it is Smith and not Jones who is raking the leaves but it is otherwise clear from the utterance situation that the interlocutors are looking at a man raking the leaves and that the utterance is about him, then it will usually not matter if P^{Jones}, that is, the property of being *named Jones*, does not fit the man. But, here again, not any name will do: it is not possible in most such contexts to utter, for example, "Obama[16] is raking the leaves" and say that Smith is raking the leaves.

One reason why a limited principle of charity can operate is as follows. In equilibrium semantics, the meanings of words are interdependent and this implies a certain redundancy or *overdetermination* of content. This allows addressees to sometimes figure out the content of an utterance even if a word or two is missing. From IS RAKING THE LEAVES and from the resource situation where the interlocutors have witnessed the act itself, the addressee could have inferred the relevant content even if a thunderclap had obscured JONES, simply in virtue of its overdetermination.

Once cases of error are explained as in the foregoing, it is a straightforward matter to handle the infinity of cases represented by the extreme case of collusion. This is because speakers and addressees are aware of how errors work via either related properties or overdetermination or both and they are then able to deliberately exploit this in their communications. The extreme case of collusion where everyone publicly knows that a certain person is not the king but is still referred to as such can easily be accounted for by bringing in the kinds of issues of common knowledge (and less than full common knowledge) amply detailed in Parikh (2001) and section 3.3.4.

In summary, I note again that misdescription is a second-order phenomenon and is not required to provide a basis for the distinction between referential and attributive uses of definite descriptions. As we have seen in the previous section, the distinction can be independently motivated and is, in fact, a fourfold one, including generic and predicative uses as well.

6.1.6 Kripke's Arguments Against Donnellan

Kripke's (1977) methodological and substantive arguments against the "semantic ambiguity" view advanced by Strawson and Donnellan are among the most persuasive. I now consider them.

First, Kripke says:

> If someone alleges that a certain linguistic phenomenon in English is a counterexample to a given analysis, consider a hypothetical language which (as much

16. That is, Barack Obama.

as possible) is like English except that the analysis is stipulated to be correct. Imagine such a hypothetical language introduced into a community and spoken by it. *If the phenomenon in question would still arise in a community that spoke such a hypothetical language (which may not be English), then the fact that it arises in English cannot disprove the hypothesis that the analysis is correct for English.*

In section 6.1.2, I argued that the Gricean property of indeterminacy allows us to weaken the Russell + Grice analysis.

In "Russell English" the reference secured by a definite description would be "pragmatic" and would therefore always be indeterminate. If the phenomenon we cite as a counterexample to this analysis is the relative determinacy of referents in English, then this phenomenon would *not* arise in Russell English by stipulation: in this hypothetical language, definite descriptions (and corresponding anaphoric pronouns) would also be indeterminate in their references. So this counterexample to the Russellian analysis appears to stand intact and it is arguable that the analysis is therefore disproved or at least considerably weakened.

Next, consider Kripke's example modifying Linsky's. Someone sees a woman with a man. Taking the man to be her husband, and observing his attitude toward her, he says, "Her husband is kind to her," and someone else may nod, "Yes, he seems to be." Suppose the man in question is not her husband. Suppose he is her lover, to whom she has been driven precisely by her husband's cruelty. Call the implied resource situation v_u, the visual scene the interlocutors are looking at.

Whereas Kripke finds Donnellan ambiguous on exactly how the first utterance has to be interpreted, my account is very clear: if the use is referential and if the resource situation is v_u, then a literal truth referring to the lover and not the husband has been expressed; if the use is referential and if the resource situation is some other situation involving the husband that is available to the addressee, then a literal falsehood has been expressed; and if the use is attributive, then again a literal falsehood has been expressed.[17]

In such cases of misdescription and especially of error, the most important point to take note of is that something has gone awry in the utterance even though the communication may succeed. As a result, one should expect certain other regularities to fail.

17. Misdescription is possible with attributive uses as well so it is possible to express a literal truth with an attributive use if "husband, (whoever he is)" is taken as meaning *lover, whoever he is.*

Assume the resource situation v_u is salient for both the speaker and addressee. There are at least two cases to consider:

1. Counterfactually, if the addressee is better informed than the speaker and knows the referent is not the woman's husband, she would realize the error but also know that the speaker was referring to the lover. This is because, on the one hand, the resource situation is salient, and, on the other, the addressee knows that the referent is not the husband. This is a commonplace occurrence when a description is incorrectly used. The regularity that fails because of the error is that *two* propositions rather than one may come to the addressee's mind, even though the salience of the resource situation and other commonly shared facts from the utterance situation would lead the addressee to drop the second interpretation involving the husband. Kripke himself suggests two possible dialogues in this case:

Dialogue 1
A: "Her husband is kind to her."
B: "No, he isn't. The man you're referring to isn't her husband."

Dialogue 2
A: "Her husband is kind to her."
B: "He is kind to her, but he isn't her husband."

Both dialogues appear acceptable on both the Russellian and equilibrium semantics accounts. For the Russellian account, there are two referents, both "pragmatic," and both are available for pronominalization. In my case, the error brings two propositions to the addressee's mind, and so again two distinct referents, both "semantic," are available. Given the ambient facts, the addressee knows the speaker was trying to convey something about the visually shared scene, so there is no confusion in her mind about which of the two propositions is the intended one. In the first dialogue, the pronoun refers to the husband, obtained from the secondary and unintended proposition. In the second, the pronoun refers to the lover, obtained from the intended proposition. With either dialogue, the speaker would realize his error and would not find the addressee's response anomalous, as he would realize that he had unwittingly evoked two conflicting interpretations in the addressee's mind.

2. If the addressee does not know any more than the speaker, she would simply get the reference to the lover and would wrongly assume he was the husband. In this case, two propositions would not come to her mind as she would not detect the error. Of course, if she is unable to detect the

error, then she cannot also enter into either of the two dialogues above, which presuppose that she knows the full facts about the identity of the husband and lover.

The critical thing in both cases is that v_u is salient and this tells the speaker he can use HER HUSBAND referentially with respect to v_u. And it tells the addressee she can infer a referential use with respect to v_u (as opposed to an attributive, generic, or predicative use or a referential use with a different resource situation) as well. Equilibrium semantics provides a detailed account of how ambient facts translate into various interdependent games that enable the disambiguation of utterances, including the type of use, so little more needs to be said about the derivation of its content.

Going on to Kripke's other arguments, he refers to the different treatments of descriptions and names in cases such as ξ and ξ'' in the previous section 6.1.5. A detailed discussion of names is beyond the scope of this book, but suffice it to say that equilibrium semantics does not treat them differently as briefly discussed above. Since both accounts, Kripke's and mine, treat the data uniformly, it is not true that "the apparatus of speaker's reference and semantic reference, and of simple and complex uses of designators, is needed *anyway*, to explain the Smith-Jones case."

Next, Kripke says:

> We thus have two methodological considerations that can be used to test any alleged ambiguity. "Bank" is ambiguous; we would expect the ambiguity to be disambiguated by separate and unrelated words in some other languages. Why should the two separate senses be reproduced in languages unrelated to English? First, then, we can consult our linguistic intuitions, independently of any empirical investigation. Would we be surprised to find languages that used two separate words for the two alleged senses of a given word? If so, then, to that extent our linguistic intuitions are really intuitions of a unitary concept, rather than of a word that expresses two distinct and unrelated senses. Second, we can ask empirically whether languages are in fact found that contain distinct words expressing the allegedly distinct senses. If no such language is found, once again this is evidence that a unitary account of the word or phrase in question should be sought.

In section 4.2.3 and especially in section 6.1.4, it was made clear that lexical ambiguity may in general involve just the conventional map from **C**, or just the informational map from **I**, or both. When it involves the former, we get an ambiguity in conventional meaning or "sense" of the kind Kripke is referring to with BANK. On the other hand, when it involves the informational map, we have a lexical ambiguity but it is no longer one involving the conventional meaning or sense of the word.

Rather, it involves the way in which this conventional sense is ontologically transformed into an infon, into a possible content or referential meaning, as first discussed in section 4.2.3. This is exactly the situation with THE, which has the single conventional sense $\hat{P}(\dot{P} \mid Unique(\dot{P}, \dot{r}_{\dot{u}}, \dot{q}_{\dot{u}}))$ but four possible referential meanings corresponding to its four possible uses.

That is, since my notions of conventional and referential meaning are generalizations or refinements of the traditional distinctions between intension and extension, connotation and denotation, and sense and reference, and since my enlarged conception allows *multiple* possibilities to occur on either or both sides of these distinctions, Kripke's methodological tests should not lead us to expect either intuitively or empirically that THE would be explicitly disambiguated in other languages the way BANK is. The ambiguity in BANK is conventional, whereas the ambiguity in THE is informational or ontological, even though both ambiguities are lexical.

Kripke's tests would need to be revised to take this more complex notion of lexical ambiguity into account. Consequently, the absence of explicit disambiguations in other languages does not suggest that a unitary concept of THE is at issue. This would be so only if the lexical ambiguity were conventional.

In the initial part of section 6.1, I had said that the Gricean dictum to use a modified Occam's razor to block the multiplication of senses beyond necessity would be addressed. With regard to the case of THE and similar words, senses are not really being proliferated if what is meant by "sense" is conventional meaning. The term "semantic ambiguity" or "lexical ambiguity" is itself ambiguous, as we have just seen.

Finally, Kripke expresses some uncertainty about the correct linguistic intuitions regarding the truth or falsity of utterances such as "Her husband is kind to her" where some error is present.

> As I remarked above, if we had a direct intuition that "Her husband is kind to her" could be true even when her actual husband is cruel, then we would have decisive evidence for the D-language model.[18]

The reason why such uncertainty about a direct intuition would exist universally in such second-order situations involving misdescription should now be apparent. In cases like these, the situation is seldom spelled out fully and it is unclear how much the addressee knows about

18. By "D-language model" Kripke means to refer to Donnellan's semantic ambiguity model.

the error. As a result, there is some uncertainty about whether just one interpretation is triggered in the recipient's mind or two, even though the theorist is plainly aware that there are two. It is this lack of sharp demarcation between what the addressee knows and what the theorist knows that causes us to waver.

If we were to set aside what the theorist knows and assume the second case above where the addressee does *not* know the identity of the husband, then it is very clear that only one true proposition about the lover's kindness is generated in the addressee's mind "even when her actual husband is cruel."

When there are two propositions in the addressee's mind, each has a different truth value with the intended interpretation being true. However, it is possible that the addressee is not quite so clear that the resource situation v_u is really that salient and so she may opt for a reading in which the husband is the (determinate or indeterminate) referent (based on whether the reading is referential or attributive) and not the lover. This is why the situation needs to be spelled out more fully.

This matter ultimately touches upon the issue of indeterminacy in section 5.3. Just for convenience, I reproduce the last paragraph from that section:

> This raises the question of what the model for meaning ought to be. It is possible to identify one subjective (or, more correctly, intersubjective) content for each participant in a conversation. Moreover, there is no content that is the interlocutor-independent "objective" content of the utterance in question, even for the simplest utterance. This is because each game model and its solution depends integrally on the information and preferences of the relevant participant; there is no "objective" game that can provide an "objective" content. Thus, this fact introduces yet another aspect of indeterminacy into meaning.

A careful setup of the relevant doxastic facts for each game is required in order to determine the intersubjective content for the speaker, the addressee, and the theorist. Only then can we hope to get hold of a "direct intuition" or at least a direct solution to this problem. This I have shown how to do.

6.1.7 Definite Descriptions and Discourse Anaphora

It is worth remarking briefly that anaphorically used pronouns take on the uses of their antecedents. Adding to the sentences from section 6.1.3 in the same discourse situation d, we have:

1. The waiter is rude. He ought to be fired.
2. The waiter will take the order. He will be more polite.

3. The waiter is meant to serve customers in a restaurant. He takes the order and brings the food.
4. This is the waiter.

Here, each use of the pronoun is different. In the first discourse, it is referential, in the second, attributive, and in the third, generic. There is no predicative use.

Many things remain to be discussed in connection with definite descriptions, especially more complex descriptions as well as their interactions with anaphora, but I leave these for another occasion. In closing this section, I emphasize that variants of the theory offered here are certainly possible within equilibrium semantics.

6.2 Indefinite Descriptions

Indefinite descriptions are descriptions with the indefinite article A (or AN). Like the definite article, A has several uses. It has the same single conventional meaning $P^a = \hat{P}(\dot{P} \mid Unique(\dot{P}, \dot{r}_{\dot{u}}, \dot{q}_{\dot{u}}))$ and the same informational maps but with certain key differences.

In this section, I look at just these informational maps very briefly. A fuller examination is beyond the scope of this book.

For each of the examples below, assume an appropriate utterance situation u and corresponding resource situations r_u, q_u with $q_u = r_u$.

1. A waiter was rude (ω')
2. A waiter will take the order (λ')
3. A waiter is meant to serve customers in a restaurant (θ')
4. This is a waiter (κ')

It is possible to imagine each sentence above being used in the corresponding use below.

A/AN

- Referential use: a $\rightarrow P^a \overset{u}{\rightarrow} \langle\!\langle \hat{P}(e(\dot{P}, r_u) \mid Unique(\dot{P}, r_u, q_u)) \rangle\!\rangle$

Here, an utterance of ω' may be used to refer to a particular waiter in a particular resource situation, but it would have to be a situation to which the addressee does not have access. This means the addressee is not in a position to evaluate $e(\dot{P}, r_u)$ once $\dot{P}$ is replaced by P_1^{waiter} and figure out the identity of the waiter. Refer back to section 6.1.1 where it was pointed out that the step from Equation 6.2 to Equation 6.3 is not automatic. Of course, THE may also be used when the addressee does not have direct access, but in this case either the entity or resource situation containing it have to be mentioned in prior discourse. For example, one may say, "I got into a cab; the radio was blaring." Here, presumably, the addressee does not have direct access to the resource situation relevant for the first sentence and the cab has not been mentioned previously, so the speaker is forced to use the indefinite article. However, the new resource situation for the second sentence has been established by the situation described by the first utterance, so it is possible for the speaker to use the definite article with RADIO. This does not allow the addressee to evaluate Equation 6.2 in an absolute sense since she still does not know which cab, and therefore which radio, is pinpointed, but in a relative sense, that is, relative to the prior discourse: it is the radio in the cab mentioned earlier though the addressee does not know which cab it is. Thus, access to a resource situation not only means direct perceptual access but also discursively established access.

- Attributive use: a $\rightarrow P^a \overset{u}{\rightarrow} \langle\langle \hat{P}(e(\dot{P}, \dot{r}_u) \mid Unique(\dot{P}, \dot{r}_u, \dot{q}_u)) \rangle\rangle$

An utterance of λ' may be used to pick out a waiter whoever he is or whatever the resource situation, that is, pick him out *indeterminately*.

- Generic use: a $\rightarrow P^a \overset{u}{\rightarrow} \langle\langle \hat{P}[\dot{x} \mid r''_u \models \langle\langle \dot{P}; \dot{x} \rangle\rangle] \rangle\rangle$

An utterance of θ' may pick out the corresponding *type* as before.

- Predicative use: a $\rightarrow P^a \overset{u}{\rightarrow} \langle\langle \hat{P}(\dot{P} \mid Unique(\dot{P}, r_u, q_u)) \rangle\rangle$

Finally, the indefinite description in κ' may be used predicatively.

It appears that the key difference between A and THE is not in the contents expressed, but in their (epistemic) presuppositions. In any case, I do not explore these matters further here.

6.3 Names

I will be even briefer with names. Kripke's (1972, 1980) dramatic work has raised many difficult challenges for the Frege-inspired (1980) account I chose to give in section 3.2 with respect to the name HARVEY. It is not possible to meet these criticisms here. A summary of my account is presented below without argument.

A key element in my theory is the special property P^N associated with every name N, that of being *named* N (or put less directly, but more in line with the account of descriptions, of being *an* N). That every name is associated with such a property is obvious. However, historically, it appears that few theorists (for example, Kneale, 1962, and Burge, 1973) have given this important property its due.

Names are not in principle different from descriptions and an adequate theory of names must recognize that names can also be used in a number of ways. In section 3.2, just the referential use of HARVEY was considered to keep things simple.

1. Harvey is playing
2. Grothendieck is a great mathematician
3. January has thirty-one days
4. This is Harvey

It is possible to imagine each sentence above being used in the corresponding way outlined below. I use N to stand for each of the names above.

N

- Referential use: $N \rightarrow P^N \xrightarrow{u} \langle\langle e(P^N, r_u) \mid Unique(P^N, r_u, q_u) \rangle\rangle$

We have already seen the first referential use of HARVEY in section 3.2. It is perhaps important to mention that resource situations *are* required with referential uses of names, although they are more likely to differ for speaker and addressee. This need not prevent the same referent getting across.

- Attributive use: $N \rightarrow P^N \xrightarrow{u} \langle\langle e(P^N, \dot{r}_u) \mid Unique(P^N, \dot{r}_u, \dot{q}_u)) \rangle\rangle$

To those who have never heard of the reclusive Grothendieck (but not only to those), the second sentence above could be used to refer to him attributively, that is, whatever the resource situation may be. An addressee of such an utterance would learn that someone named Grothendieck—whoever he is or whatever resource situation may be used to identify him—is a great mathematician. A sentence using HARVEY or any other name could also involve an attributive use as long as the resource situation may be left parametrized.

- Generic use: $N \rightarrow P^N \xrightarrow{u} \langle\langle [x \mid r''_u \models \langle\langle P^N; x \rangle\rangle] \rangle\rangle$

This use of JANUARY is a relatively rare type of use.

- Predicative use: $N \rightarrow P^N \xrightarrow{u} \langle\langle P^N \rangle\rangle$

Finally, HARVEY may clearly be used predicatively as well.

I believe the special property P^N and this analysis can be made immune to Kripke's arguments, but I cannot pursue a defense here. Much of the theory of descriptions in section 6.1 may be extended to names and a counterargument mounted as I did there.

6.4 Generalized Quantifiers

The foregoing accounts for definite and indefinite descriptions and for names can be generalized to all the quantifiers. This yields a uniform theory of noun phrases in a way that makes it unnecessary to distinguish between referring expressions and quantifiers, as Frege had done. A key difference between the Montagovian approach and mine is that in the former quantifiers are treated as relations whereas in the latter they are treated as properties. Moreover, in sentences such as "Many waiters left" and "Some waiters served two customers," the verbs LEFT and SERVED are the main relations of the infon expressed, not the quantifiers MANY and SOME. This makes the treatment uniform across a much wider class of sentences and enables all noun phrases to be treated as *terms*. Two key texts in the literature on generalized quantifiers are Barwise and Cooper (1981) and Peters and Westerståhl (2006). My treatment here is quite sparse.

Once again, I will forgo a detailed analysis via equilibrium semantics and present just the conventional and informational maps. This is because the *Flow Constraint* works in identical ways across *all* words so there is no point in repeating the game-theoretic derivations.

Recall that there were two components of the contents of descriptions and names: one was $e(P,r)$ and the second was the conditioning infon $Unique(P,r_u,q_u)$. For quantifiers generally, we need $e(P,r)$ as before and analogous conditioning infons. Instead of developing each of these one by one, I present them all together. It is convenient to give these conditioning infons a name as there are many of them: I call them the *Q conditions*. As the set $\{y \mid r \models \langle\langle P; y\rangle\rangle\}$ occurs in the definition of all the Q conditions, I use $e(P,r)$ in the rest of this section with the understanding that when it yields just one entity, either this single entity or the corresponding singleton set is intended, whichever makes sense in the context. This greatly simplifies the notation.

To make things concrete, assume Alan and Barbara are at the restaurant as before. Imagine they are observing various waiters leaving or serving various customers with Alan reporting the results to Barbara in utterance situations, all of which will be denoted by u. Let r_u stand for the corresponding resource situation where the relevant waiters *serve* the relevant customers and let q_u stand for the wider more inclusive resource situation in the restaurant as such. That is, in all cases, we have $r_u \subset q_u$.

The Q conditions

- $Unique(P, r_u, q_u) = \langle\langle = | r_u \subseteq q_u; card(e(P, r_u)); 1 \rangle\rangle$
- $Two(P, r_u, q_u) = \langle\langle = | r_u \subseteq q_u; card(e(P, r_u)); 2 \rangle\rangle$
- $n(P, r_u, q_u) = \langle\langle = | r_u \subseteq q_u; card(e(P, r_u)); n \rangle\rangle$
- $Some(P, r_u, q_u) = \langle\langle \geq | r_u \subseteq q_u; card(e(P, r_u)); 1 \rangle\rangle$
- $Many(P, r_u, q_u) = \langle\langle \approx | r_u \subseteq q_u; card(e(P, r_u)); k_{Many} \times card(e(P, q_u)) \rangle\rangle$ where k_{Many} is a fuzzy number around 0.5 but greater than 0.5 and less than 1
- $Most(P, r_u, q_u) = \langle\langle \approx | r_u \subseteq q_u; card(e(P, r_u)); k_{Most} \times card(e(P, q_u)) \rangle\rangle$ where k_{Most} is a fuzzy number around 0.9 but less than 1
- $Every(P, r_u, q_u) = \langle\langle = | r_u \subseteq q_u; card(e(P, r_u)); card(e(P, q_u)) \rangle\rangle$

It is not important exactly how the approximate nature of many quantifiers such as MANY and MOST is rendered. It seemed easiest to use fuzzy numbers from fuzzy number theory,[19] but if other ways are preferred, they could be used instead. The key point is that there is an approximate relation between, say, waiters or customers in r_u and those in the larger, more inclusive situation q_u. It is reasonable to use MANY with WAITERS, for example, if the number of waiters in r_u is roughly more than half but less than all of the waiters in q_u with the actual fraction being closer to 1/2. Likewise, with MOST, 0.9 has been taken to be the approximate cutoff. The same sort of thing may be done with FEW and other such fuzzy quantifiers. Essentially, there is some indeterminacy here about exactly what proportion is meant by a speaker and what picked up by an addressee.

Incidentally, now the role of the second resource situation q_u should be clear. It is not required for several quantifiers like THE, but it is required when some fraction or proportion of a larger set of entities is involved, as with MANY and MOST and EVERY. I chose to retain q_u in all the Q conditions for uniformity, as it can always be set equal to r_u where it is otiose.

The Q conditions enable us to spell out the conventional and informational maps for the corresponding quantifiers. In section 6.1, we saw that with sentences like the following:

Some boys are playing.
Many boys are playing.
Most boys are playing.
Every boy is playing.

19. See Klir, St. Clair, and Yuan (1997).

it is possible to refer to sets of boys given suitable resource situations. Likewise, it is possible to use these quantified noun phrases attributively and predicatively as well. Generic uses seem to be absent. In what follows, just the referential and attributive uses are considered.

The quantifiers

Referential uses

- $N \rightarrow P^{N} \xrightarrow{u} \langle\!\langle e(P^{N}, r_u) \mid \mathit{Unique}(P^{N}, r_u, q_u)\rangle\!\rangle$
- $\mathit{The} \rightarrow P^{\mathit{The}} \xrightarrow{u} \langle\!\langle \hat{P}(e(\dot{P}, r_u) \mid \mathit{Unique}(\dot{P}, r_u, q_u))\rangle\!\rangle$
- $\mathit{Two} \rightarrow P^{\mathit{Two}} \xrightarrow{u} \langle\!\langle \hat{P}(e(\dot{P}, r_u) \mid \mathit{Two}(\dot{P}, r_u, q_u))\rangle\!\rangle$
- $\mathit{Some} \rightarrow P_1^{\mathit{Some}} \xrightarrow{u} \langle\!\langle \hat{P}(e(\dot{P}, r_u) \mid \mathit{Some}(\dot{P}, r_u, q_u))\rangle\!\rangle$
- $\mathit{Some} \rightarrow P_2^{\mathit{Some}} \xrightarrow{u} \langle\!\langle \hat{P}(e(\dot{P}, r_u) \mid \mathit{Unique}(\dot{P}, r_u, q_u))\rangle\!\rangle$
- $\mathit{Many} \rightarrow P^{\mathit{Many}} \xrightarrow{u} \langle\!\langle \hat{P}(e(\dot{P}, r_u) \mid \mathit{Many}(\dot{P}, r_u, q_u))\rangle\!\rangle$
- $\mathit{Most} \rightarrow P^{\mathit{Most}} \xrightarrow{u} \langle\!\langle \hat{P}(e(\dot{P}, r_u) \mid \mathit{Most}(\dot{P}, r_u, q_u))\rangle\!\rangle$
- $\mathit{Every} \rightarrow P^{\mathit{Every}} \xrightarrow{u} \langle\!\langle \hat{P}(e(\dot{P}, r_u) \mid \mathit{Every}(\dot{P}, r_u, q_u))\rangle\!\rangle$

There are two distinct conventional senses of SOME, one involving *more than one* and the other *one*. The only difference in the attributive uses below is that the resource situations are parametrized.

Attributive uses

- $N \rightarrow P^{N} \xrightarrow{u} \langle\!\langle e(P^{N}, \dot{r}_u) \mid \mathit{Unique}(P^{N}, \dot{r}_u, \dot{q}_u)\rangle\!\rangle$
- $\mathit{The} \rightarrow P^{\mathit{The}} \xrightarrow{u} \langle\!\langle \hat{P}(e(\dot{P}, \dot{r}_u) \mid \mathit{Unique}(\dot{P}, \dot{r}_u, \dot{q}_u))\rangle\!\rangle$
- $\mathit{Two} \rightarrow P^{\mathit{Two}} \xrightarrow{u} \langle\!\langle \hat{P}(e(\dot{P}, \dot{r}_u) \mid \mathit{Two}(\dot{P}, \dot{r}_u, \dot{q}_u))\rangle\!\rangle$
- $\mathit{Some} \rightarrow P_1^{\mathit{Some}} \xrightarrow{u} \langle\!\langle \hat{P}(e(\dot{P}, \dot{r}_u) \mid \mathit{Some}(\dot{P}, \dot{r}_u, \dot{q}_u))\rangle\!\rangle$
- $\mathit{Some} \rightarrow P_2^{\mathit{Some}} \xrightarrow{u} \langle\!\langle \hat{P}(e(\dot{P}, \dot{r}_u) \mid \mathit{Unique}(\dot{P}, \dot{r}_u, \dot{q}_u))\rangle\!\rangle$
- $\mathit{Many} \rightarrow P^{\mathit{Many}} \xrightarrow{u} \langle\!\langle \hat{P}(e(\dot{P}, \dot{r}_u) \mid \mathit{Many}(\dot{P}, \dot{r}_u, \dot{q}_u))\rangle\!\rangle$
- $\mathit{Most} \rightarrow P^{\mathit{Most}} \xrightarrow{u} \langle\!\langle \hat{P}(e(\dot{P}, \dot{r}_u) \mid \mathit{Most}(\dot{P}, \dot{r}_u, \dot{q}_u))\rangle\!\rangle$
- $\mathit{Every} \rightarrow P^{\mathit{Every}} \xrightarrow{u} \langle\!\langle \hat{P}(e(\dot{P}, \dot{r}_u) \mid \mathit{Every}(\dot{P}, \dot{r}_u, \dot{q}_u))\rangle\!\rangle$

It is easy to specify what the various properties P^{Two}, P_1^{Some}, P_2^{Some}, P^{Many}, P^{Most}, and P^{Every} are by analogy with P^{The}. Here they are:

- $P^{\mathit{The}} = \hat{P}(\dot{P} \mid \mathit{Unique}(\dot{P}, \dot{r}_{\dot{u}}, \dot{q}_{\dot{u}}))$
- $P^{\mathit{Two}} = \hat{P}(\dot{P} \mid \mathit{Two}(\dot{P}, \dot{r}_{\dot{u}}, \dot{q}_{\dot{u}}))$
- $P_1^{\mathit{Some}} = \hat{P}(\dot{P} \mid \mathit{Some}(\dot{P}, \dot{r}_{\dot{u}}, \dot{q}_{\dot{u}}))$
- $P_2^{\mathit{Some}} = \hat{P}(\dot{P} \mid \mathit{Unique}(\dot{P}, \dot{r}_{\dot{u}}, \dot{q}_{\dot{u}}))$
- $P^{\mathit{Many}} = \hat{P}(\dot{P} \mid \mathit{Many}(\dot{P}, \dot{r}_{\dot{u}}, \dot{q}_{\dot{u}}))$
- $P^{\mathit{Most}} = \hat{P}(\dot{P} \mid \mathit{Most}(\dot{P}, \dot{r}_{\dot{u}}, \dot{q}_{\dot{u}}))$
- $P^{\mathit{Every}} = \hat{P}(\dot{P} \mid \mathit{Every}(\dot{P}, \dot{r}_{\dot{u}}, \dot{q}_{\dot{u}}))$

The reader should check that the **C** and **I** constraints do, in fact, work as they should.

For the rest of this section, only referential uses are entertained as the corresponding attributive uses may be obtained by a simple parametrization of the relevant resource situations. It is time to look at some examples. Consider:

- Two waiters left
- Some waiters left
- Some waiter left
- Many waiters left
- Most waiters left
- Every waiter left

Instead of taking each example through the *Flow Constraint* **F**, the equilibrium infon is directly displayed for the last utterance given the circumstances described above. To simplify the notation, assume WAITER and LEFT are conventionally unambiguous.

$$C_u^{\ell}(\text{Every waiter}) = \langle\!\langle e(P^{waiter}, r_u) \mid Every(P^{waiter}, r_u, q_u)\rangle\!\rangle \tag{6.6}$$

$$C_u^{\ell}(\text{Every waiter left}) = \langle\!\langle P^{leave}; e(P^{waiter}, r_u) \mid Every(P^{waiter}, r_u, q_u)\rangle\!\rangle$$

It is possible to add the temporal constituent $(t \mid t \prec t_u)$ if desired. It should be checked that this is indeed the expected result. The form of the equilibrium infons for the other quantifiers is the same, so there is no need to spell them out.

Scope The phenomenon of scope requires a little more machinery. I look briefly at just one example.

Many waiters served two customers. $(\vartheta = \vartheta_1\vartheta_2\vartheta_3\vartheta_4\vartheta_5)$

There appear to be three readings of ϑ:

1. The wide reading: Each of many waiters served the same two customers.
2. The narrow reading: Each of many waiters who served two customers served different pairs of customers.
3. The "polyadic" reading: A set of waiters characterized by "many" served a set of two customers, each of these waiters serving one or two of these.

Since scope is a relation between two or more quantifiers, conditions connecting the two or more Q conditions are required. I call these the F *conditions* since the connections are of a functional or relational kind.

The F conditions

Let f be a (partial) correspondence and use the variable x for a member of $dom(f)$ and the variable y for a member of $ran(f)$.

- $F_{wide}(Many, Two, P, Q, r_u, q_u) = \exists f(dom(f) = e(P, r_u) \mid Many(P, r_u, q_u) \wedge ran(f) = e(Q, r_u) \mid Two(Q, r_u, q_u) \wedge \forall x \forall y(f(x) = y))$
- $F_{narrow}(Many, Two, P, Q, r_u, q_u) = \exists f(dom(f) = e(P, r_u) \mid Many(P, r_u, q_u) \wedge ran(f) = e(Q, r_u) \wedge \forall x \forall y(f(x) = y \wedge card[f(x)] = 2))$
- $F_{polyadic}(Many, Two, P, Q, r_u, q_u) = \exists f(dom(f) = e(P, r_u) \mid Many(P, r_u, q_u) \wedge ran(f) = e(Q, r_u) \mid Two(Q, r_u, q_u) \wedge \forall x \exists y(f(x) = y))$

The domain and range of f are picked up from the Q conditions directly, so this works well with the parse tree as one moves up the tree as shown below. Parsing right to left and using analogues to Equation 6.6 results in the following:

$$\langle\!\langle e(P^{\vartheta_2}, r_u) \mid Many(P^{\vartheta_2}, r_u, q_u)\rangle\!\rangle$$

$$\odot_u (\langle\!\langle P^{\vartheta_3}\rangle\!\rangle \odot_u \langle\!\langle e(P^{\vartheta_5}, r_u) \mid Two(P^{\vartheta_5}, r_u, q_u)\rangle\!\rangle)$$

$$= \langle\!\langle e(P^{\vartheta_2}, r_u) \mid Many(P^{\vartheta_2}, r_u, q_u)\rangle\!\rangle$$

$$\odot_u \langle\!\langle P^{\vartheta_3}; e(P^{\vartheta_5}, r_u) \mid Two(P^{\vartheta_5}, r_u, q_u)\rangle\!\rangle$$

$$= \langle\!\langle P^{\vartheta_3} \mid F_{wide}; e(P^{\vartheta_2}, r_u) \mid Many(P^{\vartheta_2}, r_u, q_u);$$

$$e(P^{\vartheta_5}, r_u) \mid Two(P^{\vartheta_5}, r_u, q_u)\rangle\!\rangle$$

Note how the relevant F_{wide} condition is built up from the respective Q conditions. This requires extending the $\odot_u$ operation a little.

The same thing happens with F_{narrow}:

$$\langle\!\langle e(P^{\vartheta_2}, r_u) \mid Many(P^{\vartheta_2}, r_u, q_u)\rangle\!\rangle$$

$$\odot_u (\langle\!\langle P^{\vartheta_3}\rangle\!\rangle \odot_u \langle\!\langle e(P^{\vartheta_5}, r_u) \mid Two(P^{\vartheta_5}, r_u, q_u)\rangle\!\rangle)$$

$$= \langle\!\langle e(P^{\vartheta_2}, r_u) \mid Many(P^{\vartheta_2}, r_u, q_u)\rangle\!\rangle$$

$$\odot_u \langle\!\langle P^{\vartheta_3}; e(P^{\vartheta_5}, r_u) \mid Two(P^{\vartheta_5}, r_u, q_u)\rangle\!\rangle$$

$$= \langle\!\langle P^{\vartheta_3} \mid F_{narrow}; e(P^{\vartheta_2}, r_u) \mid Many(P^{\vartheta_2}, r_u, q_u);$$

$$e(P^{\vartheta_5}, r_u) \mid Two(P^{\vartheta_5}, r_u, q_u)\rangle\!\rangle$$

and with $F_{polyadic}$:

$$\langle\langle e(P^{\vartheta_2}, r_u) \mid Many(P^{\vartheta_2}, r_u, q_u)\rangle\rangle$$

$$\odot_u (\langle\langle P^{\vartheta_3}\rangle\rangle \odot_u \langle\langle e(P^{\vartheta_5}, r_u) \mid Two(P^{\vartheta_5}, r_u, q_u)\rangle\rangle)$$

$$= \langle\langle e(P^{\vartheta_2}, r_u) \mid Many(P^{\vartheta_2}, r_u, q_u)\rangle\rangle$$

$$\odot_u \langle\langle P^{\vartheta_3}; e(P^{\vartheta_5}, r_u) \mid Two(P^{\vartheta_5}, r_u, q_u)\rangle\rangle$$

$$= \langle\langle P^{\vartheta_3} \mid F_{polyadic}; e(P^{\vartheta_2}, r_u) \mid Many(P^{\vartheta_2}, r_u, q_u);$$

$$e(P^{\vartheta_5}, r_u) \mid Two(P^{\vartheta_5}, r_u, q_u)\rangle\rangle$$

This concludes the brief discussion of my theory of generalized quantifiers.

The F conditions can be constructed from the relevant Q conditions. It means that one specifies the set corresponding to each noun phrase separately, and then from these sets one gets the correspondence between them as one moves up the parse tree. However, there may be no general way to construct the functional condition itself—it may just be a matter of looking at the full range of permutations possible.

It should be possible to consider more complex sentences like "Many waiters served two customers three desserts." The entire scheme appears to be fairly general and could encompass many quantifiers via suitably expressed cardinality relations and via suitably restricted functions or correspondences. It does not seem to require ad hoc determinations. Most importantly, each quantifier is a unary property rather than a relation and the central verb rather than a quantifier becomes the governing relation and syntactic and semantic uniformity can be maintained across all sentences. Inference also appears to work as it should.

The particular theory of noun phrases presented in this chapter gives a uniform account of definite and indefinite descriptions, names, and generalized quantifiers. All noun phrases work like terms and no very useful purpose is served by the Fregean distinction between referring expressions and quantifiers. In the same way, the notion of logical form also appears superfluous.

In section 2.3.2, the noun phrase THE TALL BLOND MAN WITH ONE BLACK SHOE was briefly considered in the context of conditioned infons. At that time, it had been incompletely rendered as $\langle\langle a_1 \mid \langle\langle P^{tall}\rangle\rangle \wedge \langle\langle P^{blond}\rangle\rangle \wedge \langle\langle R^{with}; a_1' \mid \langle\langle P^{one}\rangle\rangle \wedge \langle\langle P^{black}\rangle\rangle\rangle\rangle\rangle\rangle$ where a_1 and a_1' stand for the man and shoe respectively. Assuming a *referential* use of the phrase, its equilibrium meaning can now be expressed fully as:

$$\langle\!\langle e(P^{man}, r_u) \mid Unique(P^{man}, r_u, q_u) \wedge \langle\!\langle P^{tall} \rangle\!\rangle \wedge \langle\!\langle P^{blond} \rangle\!\rangle$$

$$\wedge \langle\!\langle R^{with}; e(P^{shoe}, r'_u) \mid Unique(P^{shoe}, r'_u, q'_u) \wedge \langle\!\langle P^{black} \rangle\!\rangle \rangle\!\rangle \rangle\!\rangle$$

Here, it is left implicit that the relation R^{with} has as its first argument the man himself—that is, it is the man who is with the shoe. Thus, the infon has been only partially expressed.[20] If desired, it may be made fully explicit as follows:

$$\langle\!\langle e(P^{man}, r_u) \mid Unique(P^{man}, r_u, q_u) \wedge \langle\!\langle P^{tall} \rangle\!\rangle \wedge \langle\!\langle P^{blond} \rangle\!\rangle$$

$$\wedge \langle\!\langle R^{with}; e(P^{man}, r_u); e(P^{shoe}, r'_u) \mid Unique(P^{shoe}, r'_u, q'_u) \wedge \langle\!\langle P^{black} \rangle\!\rangle \rangle\!\rangle \rangle\!\rangle$$

This makes evident the two arguments of WITH. The primed and unprimed resource situations may be taken to be the same or distinct depending on the utterance situation. When access to these resource situations is available, the speaker and addressee can set $e(P^{man}, r_u) = a_1$ and $e(P^{shoe}, r'_u) = a'_1$. The determiner ONE has simply been represented as the infon *Unique*. Notice again that there are two levels of nested conditioning: $e(P^{man}, r_u)$ has four conditions corresponding to THE, TALL, BLOND, and WITH ONE BLACK SHOE; the last condition itself has two conditions on $e(P^{shoe}, r'_u)$, namely, those corresponding to ONE and BLACK. Incidentally, if the noun phrase had been THE TALL SHORT MAN ..., the conjoining of the infons corresponding to TALL and SHORT would have resulted in the condition becoming contradictory and the entire infon becoming **0**.

This title of a 1972 French comedy points to the fact that many books, films, and other artworks have noun phrases as their titles. A theory that is able to express the contents of noun phrases in isolation is therefore required.

6.5 Resource Situations

Much use has been made of resource situations, especially in chapter 6. A little needs to be said about how they are identified and how the objects referred to in them are discovered.

20. It has also been assumed that there are no conventional ambiguities in the various properties that require subscripting.

In general, a resource situation is either perceptually given or is available through the prior discourse. When it is perceptually given, it is usually labeled "v_u" as visual scenes are among the most common perceptually given situations. Otherwise, we use "r_u." In section 2.6, I defined the discourse state $\mathcal{D}$, which I said contains all the resource and described situations accessed via the sequence of utterances in d, the discourse situation, as well as other information. Thus, r_u may come from $\mathcal{D}$.

But how exactly is the resource situation identified from among these possibilities in a way that makes it a more or less shared situation between speaker and addressee? There are two aspects to the solution of this problem.

The first insight here is that there is some kind of *salience* at work. Human beings are usually quite adept at homing in on the right part of a shared scene or on what situation has been or is being described. This probably has something to do with our brains' ability to attend to things in their environments (e.g., we are able to detect motion more easily than a state of rest and we are able to detect certain colors like red more readily than others like gray) or to identify some situation from memory or simply by construction. Indeed, this is just one instance of a larger and more pervasive fact.

In the preceding chapters, it was said that Barbara was able to infer from various facts in her environment—Alan and Barbara discussing their plans for the evening or the waiter's being rude at the restaurant—what the setting game was and what the appropriate payoffs and probabilities were or at least what the relevant inequalities were. But how did $\mathcal{B}$ know these were the right facts to focus on from the myriad things going on in their apartment or in the restaurant? This larger problem of selecting the few relevant features from an infinity of goings-on in the environment has again to do with salience. As I said in section 5.7, identifying the correct utterance situation is as much of a problem as identifying the correct resource situation.

In one respect, it may be argued that this *secondary* problem lies outside the immediate sphere of semantics proper and that it is more or less *separable* from this sphere. That is, the main problem of semantics is to derive the meaning of an utterance from first principles *given* certain ambient facts including those related to the resource situation. A related but distinct and subsidiary problem is how these ambient inputs are themselves identified. This is analogous to the problem of determining the so-called *initial conditions* in several areas in physics. If an athlete throws a javelin, where it lands depends on two things, the laws of motion and the initial conditions. These two things may be separated. I have attempted to solve the analogous problem of figuring out *the laws of meaning*; what remains is the subsidiary issue of determining the analogue to the initial conditions, the ambient facts. In other words, what has been done is to say that if the utterance and resource situations are such and such and, therefore, if the corresponding games of partial information have such and such probabilities and payoffs, then this is the meaning. A functional relation between such inputs and the resulting outputs has been established. Identifying various situations and the corresponding input inequalities requires solving a different problem, one that involves deriving such inputs from the ambient facts.

On the whole, it is much more likely that interlocutors in communication fix on a particular situation or other types of things like individuals, types, sets, and infons by recourse to a range of general cognitive strategies rather than the deployment of conventional linguistic rules. And if such cognitive strategies are involved, then it is likely that they can be modeled by some kind of optimization and equilibrium processes as well. Indeed, we may even be able to use the apparatus of game and decision theory itself to address this problem of salience.

Having said this, I will simply assume that some such game-theoretic model undergirds the conspicuousness of various entities in a flow of information between two agents. That is, the pivotal entity—whether the utterance situation u or a resource situation like v_u or r_u or a described situation like c or an individual like a in r_u—will emerge as the equilibrium of a suitable game, especially as a discourse progresses. The finite agents[21] will not consider infinite choice sets in such a game, but just a small range of possibilities from an otherwise large space selected by the constrained architecture of their brains and bodies.

Now we come to the second aspect of the solution to the problem of how these situations are identified, one that does not allow such a convenient separation between semantics proper and the ambient circumstances. That is, it is not possible to assume that the external inputs are *given*: indeed, they are themselves part of the equilibrium process involved in communication.

In speaking of utterance, resource, or described situations, it must be borne in mind that they may never be identified with full precision, just enough to enable the inputs to do their work. In other words, as we have already seen, this process is usually indeterminate. If an utterance

21. See section 2.5.

involves the definite article and if there are two candidates for a resource situation, one containing one waiter who is perhaps independently prominent and another containing two waiters, then the resource situation that enables the utterance to be true will be selected rather than the one that makes it false. Likewise with utterance and described situations. Consequently, there is an important interdependence—and *circularity*, which should be no stranger to us now—between resource situations and the referents they contain, and therefore among resource situations and interpretations and their truth! The same observation applies to utterance situations and described situations. This further circularity was deliberately left out as it would have needlessly complicated the central ideas of the equilibrium semantics framework.

Imagine that there are two tables in the restaurant in roughly the same direction from Alan and Barbara. Each table has a man drinking something that looks the same from a distance. Now suppose Alan says to their waiter:

The man drinking a martini looks happy tonight.

Let the two men be denoted by *a* and *b*. Assume that *a* is drinking water and that *b* is drinking a martini (both in martini glasses) and that Alan is attempting to refer to *a*. If the waiter has just served the two men and knows what they are in fact drinking, his interpretation of Alan's utterance will be affected by *a preference to make the content true*. He will be pushed toward selecting the resource situation that enables a true content. If, in addition, the waiter knows whether the two men are happy or unhappy, this will also influence his interpretation by pressuring him to identify the described situation in a way that makes the proposition expressed true. That is, *meaning and truth are interdependent*, like much else in communication. Of course, truth is just *one* more factor that colors content, along with various other determinants we have already seen, and pushes or pulls for or against different possible contents in exactly the same probabilistic way. It is not an absolute requirement for an interpretation. The waiter would also have to consider what Alan is trying to convey and what Alan is likely to know about the situation he is describing. In this example, there are many cases to consider and there may be several indeterminacies about which resource situation and described situation are selected and therefore which referent, and, consequently, whether an interpretation that is true gets selected or not. These would depend on how the utterance situation itself is identified, something that is equally a part of the equilibrium.

I will not spell out formally how a preference for truth governs how the various situations—utterance, resource, and described—get incorporated into this circular process, but it should be evident now how these important *external* factors may be added to the mix. The key point is that the formal structure of equilibrium semantics that I have elucidated makes it relatively easy to consider additional inputs that affect communication without requiring any fundamental change in its essential nature. All the factors involved in communication, whether internal or external, play a *partial* and *circular* role, each contributing some weight toward one or other possible contents, and together simultaneously determine the equilibrium contents (one for each interlocutor) of the utterance. It is in this sense that communication is a *balancing act* involving a variety of internal and external inputs, each vying to influence its outcome.

Thus, the identification of the various situations depends partly on their salience which is externally given and is more or less separable from semantics proper and partly on a preference for truth which makes their determination internal to semantics proper.

Finally, the ineluctable indeterminacy in all this helps in fact to partially explain the *productivity* of dialogue. If the u or r_u or c an addressee optimally selects is larger than it needs to be—say a larger than required visual scene is identified—then this larger situation may have other features the addressee can comment upon in an ongoing conversation.

7 Conclusion

It is the harmony of the diverse parts, their symmetry, their happy balance; in a word it is all that introduces order, all that gives unity, that permits us to see clearly and to comprehend at once both the ensemble and the details.
—Henri Poincaré

Equilibrium semantics has now been articulated as a theory that enables the computation of meaning, as an overarching framework that permits the construction of variant theories, and as a paradigm embodying the central idea and image of balance or equilibrium. The origins of the account in the four phenomena and corresponding ideas of reference, use, indeterminacy, and equilibrium has been demonstrated and the concomitant unification of semantics and pragmatics, or the *aufhebung* of these traditional disciplines, has been achieved. A philosophically sound, mathematically solid, and computationally tractable alternative to the prevailing mainstream view relying primarily on Grice and his followers to unify the two halves of meaning has been presented. Not only this, a kind of transmutation of words into numbers or language into arithmetic has been realized, enabling a single fixed point vector equation to capture the full meaning of an utterance. The notions of ambiguity and indeterminacy have been generalized in a way that enables one to incorporate some of the insights of Continental theorists such as Derrida. Many particular aspects and levels of meaning have been studied, including locutionary and illocutionary meaning, literal and implicated meaning, and, perhaps most unexpectedly, their circularity and interdependence. The role of truth in helping to identify the various situations involved in communication, and with this, the interdependence of meaning and truth, has been clarified. Even the psycholinguistics of garden path sentences has been analyzed. The framework has then been applied to the highly contested case of noun phrases and, again, an alternative to the dominant Russellian viewpoint has been identified together with a possible rebuttal of the latter viewpoint. Here, too, a uniform theory of noun phrases has been constructed, making otiose several assumptions about quantifiers that are often uncritically accepted. All of this has been done with innovative additions to both situation theory and situated game theory. Moreover, the universality of games of partial information in semantics has been proved. In Appendix A, a new construction of games from situation theory together with some speculations about solutions to games via an analogy with the meanings of utterances has been offered. Finally, some insights into the concept of strategic inference have been advanced.

A few things remain to round out this perspective and these I proceed to consider in this last chapter.

7.1 Equilibrium Semantics

Only as much of the framework as necessary for our purposes has been spelled out in the book. Many very important aspects of the **(P)SCIF** constraints have yet to be clarified.

7.1.1 The Syntactic Constraint S

S has played a critical but external role in my description of equilibrium semantics. It has influenced the shape of the trees on which the maps g_u and f_u act as well as affected the particular ontological transforms that come into play in **I** via a specification of the grammatical categories involved. The only marginal push in the other direction from the other three constraints to **S** has been the weeding out of suboptimal parses via **F** in cases of structural ambiguity, as we saw in section 4.10. But this still remains *external* rather than internal to syntax: **S** first generates all possible parses in isolation and then the unwanted ones are evicted.

This is both theoretically and practically unappealing. Practically, most sentences will have multiple parses and we do not seem to first generate and then discard most of them when we interpret utterances. That would be too costly. What is required is that the other three constraints act on the internal processes of parse generation and include them in the equilibrium process. This would enable the idea of equilibrium to apply to all four constraints and make the framework theoretically more attractive as well.

All that can be offered here is a conjecture. Just as the maps g_u and f_u are homomorphisms and therefore enable three alternative routes in principle to computing meaning, either via the left or middle or right sides of the equation $f_u[g_u(\alpha \circ \alpha')] = f_u[g_u(\alpha) \otimes g_u(\alpha')] = f_u[g_u(\alpha)] \odot_u f_u[g_u(\alpha')]$, likewise, there ought to be similar homomorphic maps that take one inside the parse generation process that suggest alternative routes to incorporating this process *both* internally and externally. And just as the maps g_u and f_u result in a single fixed point vector equation

$$\mathcal{C}_u(\alpha, P(x \mid u)) = f_u[g_u(\alpha, P(x \mid u))] = x$$

because of the interdependence of the various games of partial information requiring a *double* fixed point or *global* equilibrium, so these hypothetical syntax-related homomorphisms might be incorporable into this equation as well. If this were possible, then the problem of generating all possible parses may well be averted. For such a plan to be carried out, it would be necessary to figure out a way to introduce the notion of *value* or payoff and probabilities for syntactic elements as well. That is, here generativity and equilibrium might become even more closely entwined than has been shown so far and the rule-governed proof-theoretic processes of syntax may be replaceable with model-theoretic processes of game-theoretic optimization and equilibrium instead. Perhaps this idea of a *game-theoretic and equilibrium syntax* is in line with the ideas of model-theoretic syntax, perhaps it is not.

The natural way in which such a game-theoretic or equilibrium syntax may be realized is as follows: just as we had games of partial information g_u that involved a choice of utterance by the speaker and a choice of meaning by the addressee in semantics, so there would be similar games that involved a choice of utterance by the speaker and a choice of syntactic category and parse tree by the addressee. And there would again be lexical, phrasal, and sentential games here as well. Moreover, these games would interact and influence one another exactly as do the semantic games. Finally, the double fixed point solution to these interdependent games would yield the optimal parse tree rather than the optimal meaning. In other words, we could conjecture that the form of the solution to the optimal parse is exactly as before:

$$\mathcal{S}_u(\alpha, P(y \mid u)) = f'_u[g'_u(\alpha, P(y \mid u))] = y \tag{7.1}$$

where $\mathcal{S}$ stands for the syntactic category function providing full fine-grained syntactic information, y stands for the detailed category and parse of the phrase α, f'_u and g'_u are the analogous maps for syntax, and the rest of the symbols are the same as before.[1]

1. The alternative sentences uttered in g'_u would specify the relevant grammatical category explicitly.

Of course, this much merely asserts an obvious Fregean parallelism between semantics and syntax; what is missing is the *interactions* between syntactic and semantic elements at and across *every* level of the possible parse trees in a larger, truly global equilibrium. In the structurally ambiguous sentence from section 4.10:

Harvey saw her duck. ($\mu = \mu_1\mu_2\mu_3\mu_4$)

the lexical item DUCK can be either a verb or a noun; the optimal choice of syntactic category depends on the meaning of DUCK and vice versa. Not only this, each syntactic category (and parse tree) depends on each semantic meaning and vice versa in a completely circular and codetermining way. That is, the meaning of DUCK depends on the category of DUCK and the meanings and categories of all the other words, phrases, and entire sentence; likewise, the category of DUCK depends on the meaning of DUCK and the meanings and categories of all the other words, phrases, and the entire sentence.

In the *syntactic* lexical game in Figure 7.1, it is the category of DUCK, verb V or noun N, as well as the corresponding parse tree (not explicitly shown in the figure), that is being communicated and that the addressee has to figure out. And, as in the other semantic lexical games, the initial probabilities here are also strategic variables and are conditioned by all the other categories of the expressions in μ and all the meanings of the expressions in μ. Phrasal and sentential syntactic games are handled similarly.

The entire set of interdependent semantic and syntactic games for an utterance leads to a grander fixed point equation with the same form as before:

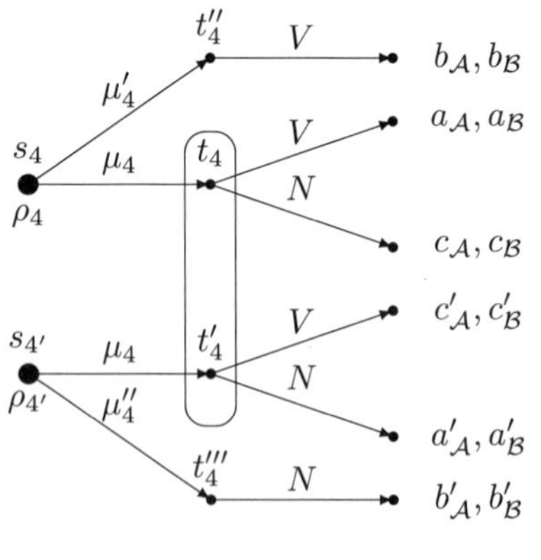

Figure 7.1
The algebraic lexical game for the category of DUCK

$$\mathcal{C}_u(\alpha, P(x \mid u)) = f_u[g_u(\alpha, P(x \mid u))] = x \tag{7.2}$$

except that now $\mathcal{C}$ doubles for both the category (i.e., parse) and the meaning function and x can be the equilibrium category/parse or content. The conditioned and conditioning variables in the vector $P(x \mid u) = (P_i(x \mid u)) = (P_i(x_i \mid x_{-i}, u))$ would now be not just the *meanings* of the other items but also their *parses*. This then is the fundamental equation that has to be solved when agents communicate. It represents a further generalization of Frege's *principle of semantic compositionality* involving the *parallelism* between syntax and semantics to what I will call the *generalized fixed point principle* that captures their *mutual determination* as well. Semantics not only mirrors syntax, as Frege suggested, the two interact and reciprocally determine each other's optimal selection as well. The universality result of section 4.11 can then be extended to include *both* syntax and semantics, and games of partial information are universal with respect to both syntax and semantics. To spell out its essential meaning with respect to syntax, if a method is found to map any utterance to its optimal parse tree,[2] then it will be equivalent to the alternative route via a game-theoretic or equilibrium syntax.

Earlier, the framework of equilibrium semantics was expressed in terms of two homomorphic maps between three isomorphic trees—the parse tree, the games tree, and the contents tree. Now the optimal parse tree is no longer available as it is itself selected as part of the equilibrium output computed by situated agents. A close look at the framework would reveal, however, that all that is required is the *monoidal* properties of $\mathcal{L}$, $\mathcal{G}$, and $\mathcal{I}$ together with *all* the possible lexical categories of each word in the utterance (e.g., verb or noun, as we have just seen). The *tree structure* was never used. Once the possible lexical categories are obtained from **S**, they would imply all the possible informational maps from conventional to possible referential meanings for each word in the utterance. These sets of possibilities together—the possible lexical categories (and ways of constructing parse trees with them) and the possible referential meanings—would provide all the required choice sets to form the interdependent syntactic and semantic games in the constraint **F** resulting in Equation 7.2 above.

It is instructive to reread section 4.9 on the garden path sentence from this new perspective. In particular, the unavailability of one of the possible parses as the addressee progresses to the end of the sentence is no

2. A set $\mathcal{P}$ of parse trees (or their equivalent) and an operation $\star$ to combine them would play a role analogous to the set $\mathcal{I}$ of infons and the operation $\odot_u$.

longer just part of the information in the utterance situation u, but becomes an explicit element of the expanded set of conditioning variables in the vector $P(x \mid u) = (P_i(x \mid u)) = (P_i(x_i \mid x_{-i}, u))$.

For the first time, therefore, communication and the flow of information appear not only as the communication and flow of optimal meanings but also as the communication and flow of optimal grammatical categories and parses. When a speaker utters a sentence like μ, he expects the addressee to figure out *both* its syntax and its semantics in a mutually determining way. The key insight of this view is to see syntax game-theoretically with the speaker uttering words, phrases, and sentences and the addressee figuring out both their grammar and their meaning simultaneously. Of course, since equilibrium syntax involves games, the speaker and addressee solve them as before by considering each other's best responses to their actions (and beliefs) and choosing equilibrium strategies accordingly. Notice that mixed strategies are always possible so that two or more parses may be obtained probabilistically when a unique optimal parse is not warranted.

A deeper way of stating this game-theoretic and equilibrium-based insight is that the content of an utterance is not just its meaning but also its syntax. Words when uttered not only have meanings but also have structure. Language is *about* the world, but it is also *about* grammar, and both types of content are required to mutually determine each other. The constraints **S** and **C** and **I** together provide the set of possible *contents* in this deeper sense for the words and phrases in an utterance and the constraint **F** provides the jointly optimal content from among these choices for both speaker and addressee. The homomorphic maps g_u and f_u and g'_u and f'_u (the latter from Equation 7.1) provide a compact way of expressing how to get from an utterance to its equilibrium content in this generalized sense. This way of looking at syntax makes it completely analogous to semantics at an abstract level. Just as semantics is a map from language to world, so syntax is a map from language to structure. These two maps interact to provide the equilibrium *content* of all utterances. Just as meaning is situated, so is grammar. Both concern the flow of information from speaker to addressee and are fully interdependent and circular: neither is prior to the other. The linear pipeline view involving syntax, semantics, and then pragmatics is now fully transcended.

The intricate connection between generativity and equilibrium can also now be seen more transparently. The rules of a grammar may generate various syntactic structures but the cutting power derived from equilibrium may also reduce the number of rules required in the constraint **S** as certain possibilities may get eliminated simply in virtue of their being suboptimal. Section 3.3.1 examined this very situation albeit from a more restricted standpoint that we can now view in a more general setting involving a sublated syntax and semantics.

Indeed, other constraints like **P** would be added on just like **S**, each constraint contributing its particular variety of *content*, whether meaning, structure, or sound, to the overall content of an utterance.

Needless to say, this view is speculative at this stage and based on rich analogies between the processes of semantics and syntax and their interaction. Integrating syntax and semantics the way I have integrated semantics and pragmatics would of course have to be worked out in detail.[3] But if this intuition turns out to be bear fruit, there would be not only an equilibrium semantics and not only an equilibrium syntax but a true equilibrium linguistics tying all the major parts of language into a single unified account, into a genuine science of language that is philosophically sound, mathematically rigorous, and computationally tractable.

I now summarize this insight visually. Recall that we have the following monoids, each with its own zero:

- $(\mathcal{L}, \circ)$
- $(\mathcal{G}, \otimes)$
- $(\mathcal{I}, \odot_u)$

with the following maps between them:

- $C_u : (\mathcal{L}, \circ) \rightarrow (\mathcal{I}, \odot_u)$
- $g_u : (\mathcal{L}, \circ) \rightarrow (\mathcal{G}, \otimes)$
- $f_u : (\mathcal{G}, \otimes) \rightarrow (\mathcal{I}, \odot_u)$

The commutative diagram of Figure 4.12 displayed again as Figure 7.2 captured the universality result for so-called *semantic* games of partial information.

Based on the foregoing discussion, I now add two more monoids with zeros, one for so-called *syntactic* games of partial information and the other, somewhat speculatively, for the set of parse trees $\mathcal{P}$ and an appropriate adjunction operation $\star$ on them:

- $(\mathcal{G}', \otimes)$
- $(\mathcal{P}, \star)$

3. While pragmatics gets assimilated to semantics, syntax and semantics would remain related but distinct counterparts.

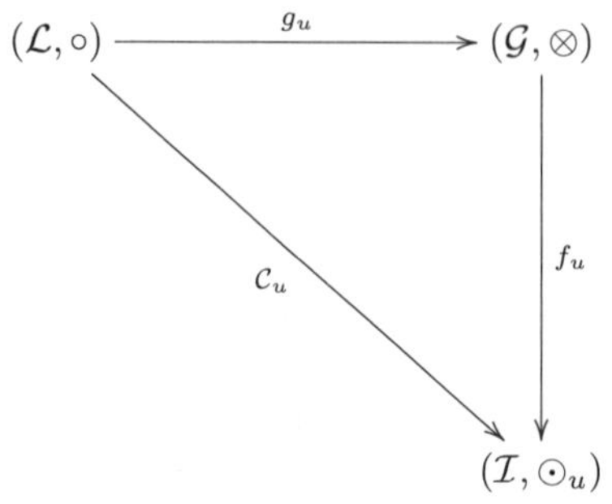

Figure 7.2
The commutative diagram: $\mathcal{C}_u = f_u \circ g_u$

The tree adjunction operations of tree adjoining grammar developed by Joshi (1985) are likely to be relevant here. In any case, I simply assume the monoid $(\mathcal{P}, \star)$ is available. I now define the following maps:

- $\mathcal{C}'_u : (\mathcal{L}, \circ) \to (\mathcal{P}, \star)$ A corresponding syntactic interpretation function
- $g'_u : (\mathcal{L}, \circ) \to (\mathcal{G}', \otimes)$ A corresponding syntactic game function
- $f'_u : (\mathcal{G}', \otimes) \to (\mathcal{P}, \star)$ A corresponding solution function to a syntactic game

If these additional monoids and maps are assumed as given, then the conjecture is that a corresponding universality result should hold for syntactic games of partial information as well and we can put the diagrams for the two results together in the following composite commutative diagram in Figure 7.3.

The diagram in Figure 7.3 captures more or less the full framework of equilibrium semantics and syntax. If we add—equally speculatively—

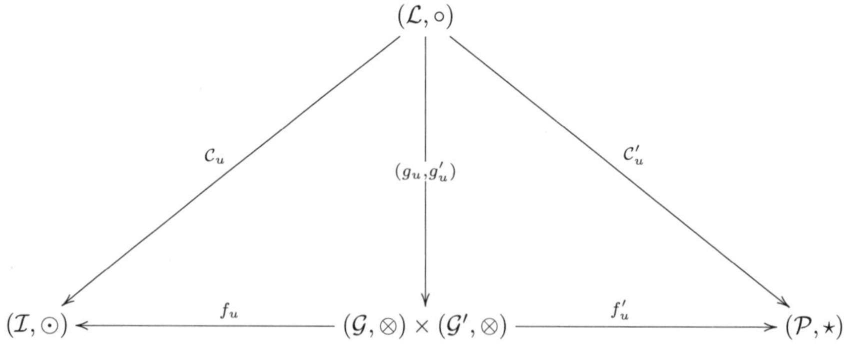

Figure 7.3
The composite commutative diagram: $\mathcal{C}_u = f_u \circ g_u$ and $\mathcal{C}'_u = f'_u \circ g'_u$

corresponding entities for the phonological constraint **P**, then we could presumably add a third triangle to the two above. For the moment, however, this must remain conjectural.

7.1.2 The Conventional Constraint C

There are three large issues connected with **C**.

The first has to do with the criticisms Putnam (1975) has leveled against the notion of meaning and the traditional notions of sense and reference, intension and extension, and connotation and denotation. In my generalization and refinement of these distinctions, I have blithely assumed that all words have a more or less fixed set of conventional meanings and that these meanings are properties or relations in $\mathcal{O}$. Not much has been said about these properties and relations; they have simply been taken as given.

Putnam's (1975) persuasive arguments compel us to accept that these properties and relations often have an indexical component rooted in the experience of each agent. Moreover, we are forced to accept that, as a result, these conventional meanings or associated properties are different for different persons. The property P^{water}, for example, associated with the natural kind word WATER may be something like *the same liquid as x* where "*x*" refers to some sample of water in the relevant agent's experience. I am *not* saying that the property P^{water} *is* a description; the property is an abstract but indexical entity that I am merely referring to with a piece of language. Also, it is this indexical component that allows both *intensions* and *extensions* to differ for the same word for different agents. If we allow such indexical components in our properties, then it appears that the force of Putnam's Twin Earth arguments against the traditional distinctions can be deflected because the view incorporates Putnam's main arguments; however, it is not possible to do justice to such a defense here. Beyond this, something would need to be said about the nature of such indexical properties and relations. It may still be the case that the concepts agents use to represent these indexicalized properties *are* in the head, which is what enables the computation of referential meanings on their basis. Finally, one consequence of this indexicalization is that agents share these conventional meanings only partially and this makes communication an even more subjective and indeterminate affair.

The second issue involves the assumption, made in section 4.2.2, that conventional meanings are conventional and independent of the utterance situation. This was a deliberate simplification. Many words are associated with contextually fixed properties based on the circumstances of utterance. WAITER and RUDE and a whole lot of other words we have considered can all embody subtle shifts of meaning based, perhaps, on certain pre-given properties. Whether an attendant in a self-service restaurant should be called a waiter or not depends on the situation; in many contexts, one can refer to such an attendant with a noun phrase like THE WAITER. What has happened is a small shift in the relevant property. Likewise, the precise degree of rudeness picked out from a possibly infinite and indeterminate range of gradations would depend on the resource situation and the utterance. Since it is the property itself that enters into the referential meaning of the word or phrase, it is this property that is being altered via the utterance. It may be necessary to introduce an intermediate step between the conventional and informational maps that allows the contextually identified property to be accessed. But things are not so straightforward. The attendant in the self-service restaurant or the intended degree of rudeness may require the addressee to take note of the resource situation and the described situation and then, via a principle of charity and further *circularity*, adjust the conventional meaning to fit with the described facts. That is, the very content being conveyed influences the property that enters into the content. This kind of interdependence may make the equilibrium processes more complex. I chose to ignore it as a first approximation, but just like the circularity with utterance and resource and described situations in section 6.5, it would need to be addressed in any complete account. Truth enters the determination of meaning yet again.

Incidentally, the cases of misdescription considered in section 6.1.5 may also be viewed in this light. A use of "The murderer is insane" may pick out the man on trial for the murder even if the death was a suicide. This involves a slight contextual shift in the relevant conventionally associated property. That is why flagrantly different and unrelated properties will not work: one cannot refer to the same man by uttering "the waiter is insane" in similar circumstances.

In section 4.2.2, it was said that conventional meanings are the sorts of meanings that can largely be found in a dictionary. Such a statement would have to be modified to take account of the two issues broached above. On the one hand, these meanings would have to be indexicalized and relativized to agents; on the other, they would have to provide for subtle alterations based on the content being conveyed.

The third large issue is: how do conventional meanings of words arise? This is a complex matter, one that Grice (1968) attempted to tackle informally. As I said in section 4.2.2, he saw speaker meaning as primary and saw the conventional meanings (of words and sentences) emerging as uniformities across utterances. Barwise and Perry (1983) largely endorsed this view of word meaning, but did not get any further in analyzing the phenomenon. My view is that this picture is correct, but is only half the story. The other half is that speaker meaning depends on conventional meaning. In other words, like much else in equilibrium semantics, the process is *circular* and is governed by an equilibrium or fixed point. This kind of society-wide game belongs to what was called *macrosemantics* in section 1.5. A sketch of a model exists in the unpublished note Parikh (1987a), but is beyond our scope here.

A partial derivation can nevertheless be provided to indicate some of what is involved. Consider the case where two lexical forms α and α' are candidates for some conventional meanings P and P' (e.g., α could be the lexical item TABLE, α' could be the lexical item CHAIR, P could be a conventional meaning of TABLE, say, the property of being *something conventionally used to write on*, and P' could be the property of being *something conventionally used for sitting*). That is, both α and α' can take on either of the conventional meanings P and P' and we are analyzing a situation prior to their having acquired either of these meanings. I ignore the fact that both words in fact have multiple conventional meanings and focus on just one of their conventional meanings in each case.

Incidentally, this formulation of the problem should already evoke the discussion of the special nature of a symbol in section 5.10. As I said there, a symbol is identified by its arbitrary and systemic link with reality. The place where language first connects with the world is via **C**, by words acquiring conventional meanings. The link thus forged will be arbitrary—each word TABLE and CHAIR could acquire either P or P'—and systemic in Deacon's (1997) sense—each word's connection to a property will be mediated by the other word's connection to the other property.

This quartet of two lexical forms and two meanings would lead to the game in Figure 7.4. If desired, the payoffs can be expressed algebraically as in Figure 7.5.

In this situation, since the words TABLE and CHAIR may be assumed to be equally costly and their possible uses may be assumed to be equally frequent in everyday life, we must assume symmetric payoffs and symmetric probabilities ($\rho = \rho' = 0.5$). The result here is that TABLE could have meant *something to sit on* and CHAIR *something to write on*—it is pure chance that in English they mean the opposite. If the words had been different, say TABLE and SESQUIPEDALIAN, the prediction would also have been different. In that case, there would be asymmetric payoffs and probabilities and so TABLE would turn out to have its regular meaning.

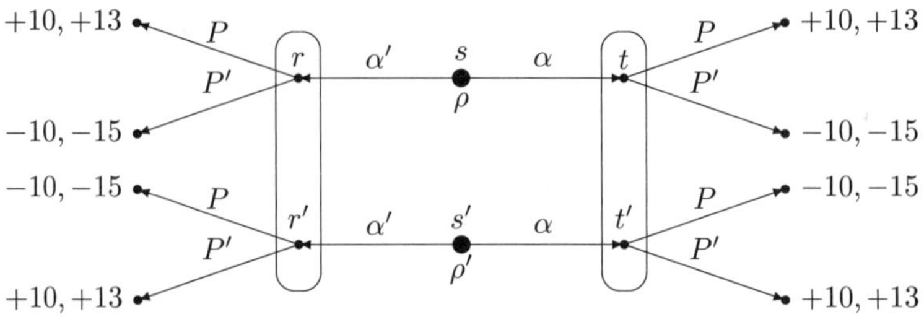

Figure 7.4
A partial derivation of conventional meaning

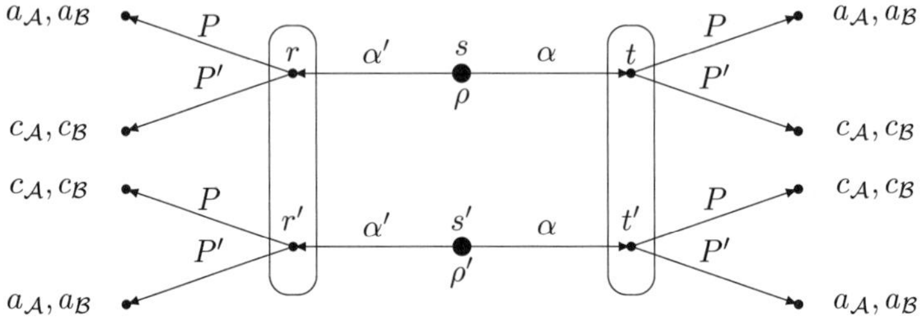

Figure 7.5
A partial algebraic derivation of conventional meaning

This is an incomplete view that ignores many other possibly more important determinants of conventional word meaning—determinants issuing from morphological and historical factors. This type of argument is a ceteris paribus argument—it assumes that if "other things are kept equal" then the conclusions follow. In practice, other things are generally not equal and one would have to delve into the etymological roots of forms to learn how they acquired the meanings they did. However, the import of the game-theoretic argument is that such trade-offs of cost and frequency of use may also be important determinants of conventional meaning in their own right and thus should be incorporated in any complete theory. Indeed, it is not difficult to see how such an account might be carried out—for example, morphology and existing meanings might constrain the possible new meanings a word might acquire, but the actual new meaning that emerges would also be tied to its strategic efficiency in use. Here the approach of evolutionary game theory as a way of solving and interpreting games might also be more apt, though a static approach could also yield some insights.

In any case, both key attributes of *symbolic* reference and communication should be evident from this simple model. Words take on conventional meanings more or less arbitrarily because both words could have acquired either meaning. Symbolization is also systemic because the solution to the game above is *simultaneous*: if TABLE acquires P, CHAIR simultaneously and systemically acquires P'. As Deacon (1997) has said in the first part of his book, the link between word and referent is mediated by a link between word and word, and these games show this cross-reference in an especially clear way. Nonsymbolic reference and communication (e.g., a dog responding to a command or a vervet monkey signaling the presence of a type of predator) are not mediatory and systemic in this way. The links are just from sign to referent without the presence of links between one sign and another.

The other way to derive conventional meaning extends the partial way just described to a macrosemantic society-wide game described in Parikh (1987a). The entire range of lexical forms in a language is considered over an entire population of users—it also ignores other historical and nonstrategic factors and involves a ceteris paribus argument. This society-wide model involves an analogy with the economic theory of general equilibrium first formulated by Arrow and Debreu (1954) in which conventional meanings are analogous to the prices of goods and referential meanings are analogous to the quantities supplied and demanded. The social equilibrium in this model results in the equilibrium conventional meanings and the equilibrium referential meanings in a linguistic community just as the general equilibrium model in economics yields the equilibrium price and quantity at which the markets in a competitive economy clear. It is also possible to formulate such a model in the setting of evolutionary game theory. The arbitrary and systemic nature of symbolic reference and communication comes across in an even more dramatic way in such social models. In a certain sense, both Peirce (1867–1913/1991) and Saussure (1916/1972, 1960) are combined in it, not to mention the later Wittgenstein's (1953/1968) slogan *meaning is use*.

I remind the reader that only words have conventional meanings; phrases and sentences are conventionally meaningless unless we simply collect the properties associated with their constituent words and call the collection the conventional meaning. This observation is reinforced by our analysis of the three issues above. Besides, as I have shown, conventional meanings of phrases and sentences, whatever they may be, are not required to derive the meanings of utterances.

7.1.3 The Informational Constraint I

The essential question for **I** is why the different grammatical categories are linked to different ontological and informational maps. Why, for example, does *Det* lead to four maps[4] and why do *N* and *V* lead to just one? In other words, are there underlying principles that enable a *derivation* of **I** just as there are for **S** and **C** and **F**?

If all the categories are enumerated, it may turn out that just the determiners (and anaphoric pronouns and possibly conjunctions as well) require multiple maps, in which case this question becomes much simpler to answer. But such an exhaustive enumeration is not possible here, so I leave the matter open.

7.1.4 The Flow Constraint F

A fair bit has been said about situated games of partial information, especially in chapters 3 and 4 and also in Appendix A.

It would have been too technical a digression to incorporate the fascinating insights of Halpern and Rego's (2006, 2007) recent work on unaware players in the exploration of common knowledge and subjective games in section 3.3.4. This is exactly the kind of extension required to look at what were called *strategic interactions*, that is, game-like interactions where common knowledge fails to obtain.

It has also not been possible to relax the constraints imposed by the assumption of rationality and include the contributions of behavioral economics. This is an area that ought to yield several new ideas for solving games as the situated agents that communicate in equilibrium semantics are definitely finite and limited in their capacities to perceive, remember, and reason. Some indication of alternative ways of approaching the solution of games was given in section 3.3.5 on perfect Bayesian equilibria as well as in the introduction to Appendix A. Only the latter of these involved something like behavioral considerations via the situatedness of agents and games.

Looking outward, it would seem a priori that the kind of two-level equilibrium structure of interdependent games uncovered here in analyzing an utterance might have wider applicability to other systems, especially social, ecological, and distributed computer systems. Imagine a system that has relatively weakly linked distinct subsystems, such as an utterance containing several words where the utterance is seen as a whole system containing several distinct subsystems involving the utterance of distinct words. That is, an utterance situation u, viewed as a system and involving the sentence $\varphi = \varphi_1 \circ \varphi_2 \circ \cdots \circ \varphi_n$, may be broken down into subsituations $u = u_1 \cup u_2 \cup \cdots \cup u_n$, each of which may then be viewed as

4. Actually, it leads to the fifth map *extensionalization* as well when plural descriptions are considered.

an interconnected subsystem. Each lexical game $g_{u_i}(\varphi_i)$ corresponds to u_i and the phrasal and sentential games correspond to appropriate collections of utterance subsituations. Then, just as these lexical, phrasal, and sentential subsystems interact with one another via the probabilities (and possibly the payoffs) of the various lexical, phrasal, and sentential games, so games corresponding to different social or other subsystems would be linked and interact with one another and with larger games involving subsets of subsystems. This is not unlike the kind of thing that happens in the film *Syriana* where relatively remote and unconnected events in weakly linked spheres result in a disastrous global equilibrium. Essentially, the idea of interdependent games and the concomitant double fixed point equilibrium may be extendable to whole-part relations in a variety of fields because it allows the whole to be dependent on its parts and the parts to be dependent on the whole in a natural and rigorous way.

7.1.5 The Isomorphic Trees and the Homomorphic Maps g_u and f_u

Not much more remains to be said here except to echo the comments made in the section on **S** above that this apparatus may be expandable if a game-theoretic syntax can be worked out.

I also remind the reader of the universality result of section 4.11, which may itself be widened to include syntax as well as semantics.

7.1.6 Language and Equilibrium

As I said in section 1.4.4, the general idea of equilibrium in equilibrium semantics is that all the sets of constraints corresponding to the different subsystems of language are in equilibrium—within each constraint and across constraints. In this book, I have explored the semantical part of this ideal conception with a few words about syntax.

7.2 Discourse

Something should be said about how equilibrium semantics would handle discourse. As we have seen, each utterance results in three isomorphic trees and two homomorphic maps that provide a complete solution to the problem of deriving the meaning of the utterance. The natural extension of this picture to a sequence of utterances is to have a sequence of such isomorphic trees and maps. The only task that would remain is to figure out a way to connect each element of the sequence with the other elements. It is well known that the meaning of a text is more than the conjunction of the meaning of its component utterances. It is less well known what the constraints are that define well-formed discourse. A new set of discourse constraints **D** would be required to handle text. These would presumably result in adding more cases to the concatenation operation $\circ$ to handle situations where two sentences are concatenated. This operation (as well as $\otimes$) may well require subscripting with the utterance (or discourse) situation just as $\odot_u$ does.

A single utterance itself is a complex event and has complex effects on the various situations it is related to including the utterance situation itself. Some of these effects are conveniently located in the discourse state $\mathcal{D}$. Others are best viewed as forming new situations that affect subsequent elements of the sequence of utterances. In principle, this is not difficult to do: much of it involves a kind of bookkeeping. But many indeterminacies lurk here and they need to be taken note of. Does an utterance change an addressee's belief or not? That may be probabilistically inferred only through the addressee's future actions, and so on.

Once this is carried out, analyses like the one in Clark and Parikh (2007) involving discourse anaphora may be readily incorporated.

7.3 The Semantics of Formal Languages

In section 1.4.1 on reference, how the semantics of formal languages has been applied to the semantics of natural languages was described. Several shortcomings of this approach were mentioned there. It was maintained, however, that the method worked for formal languages themselves. In particular, direct reference as opposed to the two-tier Frege-inspired viewpoint involving conventional meaning and referential meaning was felt to be adequate. Now it is possible to see why this may be so. In the case of formal languages, there is no ambiguity at the level of conventional meaning or informational meaning; that is, there is a single conventional map and a single informational map for each (lexical) item. This appears to permit a simpler direct referential approach.

There is, however, a potential problem that may require some relaxation of the strictures against ambiguity even for formal languages. This is the Fregean problem of informative identities: how is it that a mathematical statement like "$2+2=4$" conveys new information, if the left side of the equation represents the same entity as the right side? This is no different from the problem of the morning star and the evening star being the same object.

If we view mathematics as an activity, and in particular, the linguistic expression of mathematical propositions and proofs as a type of communicative activity (the speaker and addressee do not need to be distinct), then we should be looking at utterances, and not sentences, as with all communication. And we can then interpret "$2 + 2 = 4$" as containing not a referential but an attributive use of the first noun phrase "$2 + 2$." (The sum of two and two is equal to four.) This would explain how mathematical identities can be informative. Of course, they still remain necessary truths, unlike "Hesperus is Phophorus" when used attributively, and the question of how necessary truths can be informative is a different one. But the first step to answering it is to make clear that the content of mathematical utterances is at least not trivial.

7.4 How We Compute Meaning and Structure

A persistent question ought to have arisen throughout the reading of this book: if the framework of equilibrium semantics is to be believed, how do people ever manage to communicate in real time given the complexity resulting from all the interacting games? And, as we pretended in section 3.3.4, are agents really supposed to be representing and solving all these games in their heads? A further related question: can the account be used to enable an artificial agent to compute equilibrium meanings (and parses) in a tractable way? Now that the framework is in place, there are several ways of answering these very reasonable questions.

In section 4.12, the *forms* of games based on the number of initial nodes were identified. As strategic inference has a formal nature despite its situatedness, agents do not need to keep solving these games every time they encounter them. It is quite possible that solutions to each form are simply stored in the agent's brain after the first few times of working them out. Of course, equilibrium semantics and the strategic inferences that occur in communication involve not just the use of isolated forms but interdependent forms. This adds a layer of complexity to the process but does not change it in a significant way.

The neuroscientific evidence for decision-theoretic and equilibrium processes that take place at unconscious levels in the brain during decision making is also mounting. See Glimcher (2004) for just one fascinating account of this argument. Whether such views extend to the case of language and communication remains to be seen.

A third and related possibility is that agents use a number of heuristics and approximate strategies based on the Pareto-Nash Inequalities and Mixed Strategy Equilibria. One way is just to simplify the notion of form by making the blanket approximation that the case of mixed strategy equilibria applies only when the entire game is completely symmetric in payoffs and probabilities. This implies that most often just pure strategy equilibria obtain with mixed ones appearing only for completely symmetric games. This dramatically reduces the number of forms associated with each type of game involving n initial nodes and thereby reduces the complexity of the inferences involved significantly as well. This may suffice to make the whole process quite amenable for resource-limited, finite, situated agents.

This heuristic also has an unexpected consequence. It can be shown that if the approximation is assumed, the fixed point equation:

$$\mathcal{C}_u(\alpha, P(x \mid u)) = f_u[g_u(\alpha, P(x \mid u))] = x$$

simplifies to:

$$\arg\max_x P(x \mid u) = x$$

This is also a vector equation and one has to take the arg max of each component separately for x_i ranging over the set of all possible infons resulting from the conventional and informational maps applied to α_i. It is a special case of the fundamental equation. Needless to say, the equation can be generalized to include syntax as well.

All an agent has to do is to run through the alternatives, enumerating them one by one, until a vector x is found to solve it. If a further assumption is made that most people know and recall far fewer conventional meanings for a word than are available in a dictionary, then there will usually not be too many alternatives to try out, so that such an equation will often be solvable in real time.

If we take note of sections 3.3.3 and 4.9 on the psycholinguistics of garden path sentences, then it is possible to simplify even this simpler equation because we may allow the interpretations of earlier words to affect those of later words but not vice versa—until a garden path effect occurs. This reduces the number of interdependencies greatly and makes the computation much easier.

Remarkably, the simpler equation above is a generalized version of the standard Bayesian equation for word sense disambiguation:

$$\begin{aligned} s' &= \arg\max_{s_k} P(s_k \mid c) \\ &= \arg\max_{s_k} \left[\log P(s_k) + \sum_{v_j \in c} \log P(v_j \mid s_k) \right] \end{aligned}$$

where the s_k are the word senses, the v_j are the words in the context c, and the P represents probability.[5] The key generalization is that the condi-

5. See Manning and Schütze (1999) for more details.

tioning (and conditioned) variables in my equation are the "senses" themselves, as opposed to words, because of the circular and fixed point nature of my conception. This shows an unexpected connection between equilibrium semantics and the work in computational semantics, a connection that warrants a closer look. And if we throw syntax (and phonology) into the mix as in section 7.1.1, then the generalization is at an altogether different level.

7.5 Symbol Systems and Equilibrium

The painting by Piet Mondrian on the cover of the book was chosen because it is integrally about pictorial harmony and balance and equilibrium. But equilibrium semantics may also be used to understand the meaning of this and other visual utterances, because the parts of such visual systems also interact in ways that are similar to the interactions among words and phrases in a linguistic utterance.

The basic idea of equilibrium semantics (and syntax) is that each part of a symbol system has a certain semantic (and syntactic) value that interacts with the semantic (and syntactic) values of all the other parts so that they are all jointly in balance. This interaction is mediated essentially by situated human agency. Each map from a part of the system to its value is given by a game and its solution. Since the parts and their values interact via their use by agents, so do the games. Thus, the meaning (and structure) of the whole is given by the solution to interdependent games.

In the case of verbal languages, the parts are clearly identifiable as words (and phrases and sentences if we assume a syntax). In the case of visual and other continuous symbol systems, individuating the parts poses an additional problem. While the parts in the Mondrian painting may be especially clear and obvious, this basic idea is also true of other image systems that may lack a clear set of interacting parts or the elegant balance of the Mondrian artwork. The main challenge here is how to either handle a continuous space directly or to convert the continuous space into a discrete one. Of course, the counterparts of *illocutionary* meanings also need to be considered.

Thus, another avenue for exploration is the application of equilibrium semantics (and syntax) to other symbol systems in ways that may make possible the realization of a unified approach to communication and meaning (and structure) in the world.

7.6 Metaphysics and Equilibrium

In the entire book, the ontology $\mathcal{O}$ has been taken as given. It was also said in sections 1.2, 1.3, and 2.1 that agents of different kinds *individuate* the entities in $\mathcal{O}$. That is, there is an interaction between agents and the world that produces the world of entities as we know it via a process of simultaneous *codetermination*. I referred to Quine (1960) in section 2.1 who has argued convincingly that ontologies may not be unique even for the same species. However, it is not necessary to accept Quine's conclusions about *radical* indeterminacy because the jointly optimal processes of *equilibration* eliminate all the suboptimal ontologies and thereby make the indeterminacies *moderate* rather than radical, as has also been argued in chapter 5.

Equilibrium semantics (and syntax) could, in theory, be generalized to an *equilibrium metaphysics*. It would in that case not be just the parts of symbol systems that interact with one another to be about *preexisting* semantic values. Instead, all the parts (e.g., "gavagai," to use Quine's example) and all the possible semantic values (e.g., rabbits and rabbit parts and rabbit stages) would interact to result in one grand and evolving metaphysical equilibrium that is responsible for both meaning (and structure) in the world and the world itself. The phenomena of semantics (and syntax) and the world of objects are then just the solution to a system of simultaneous equations and inequalities arising from the interaction among agents with one another and with the world, equations that may be compactly represented by the fundamental fixed point vector equation:

$$\mathcal{C}_u(\alpha, P(x \mid u)) = f_u[g_u(\alpha, P(x \mid u))] = x$$

reinterpreted yet again, generalized from semantics which links language and world to include syntax on the side of language and ontology on the side of the world.

Our world is certainly far from being the best of all possible worlds but, ontologically speaking, if we take the limitations and finitude of human beings into account, we do inhabit one of the best.[6]

6. I hope I have not committed the error in Abraham Maslow's pithy statement: *if you only have a hammer, you tend to see every problem as a nail.* I have certainly applied what I have called the fundamental equation in ever-widening ways, from locutionary meaning to illocutionary meaning to meaning generally and from there on to syntax and phonology and other symbol systems and even the world. The idea of a system of simultaneous equations (or inequalities) and *equilibrium* to explain language and world has been with me for a long time, over twenty years. This book has enabled me to work it out.

Appendix A: The Mathematical Model

Though this be madness, yet there is method in 't.
—William Shakespeare, *Hamlet*

The basic task of this Appendix is to derive the map $g_u : \mathcal{L} \rightarrow \mathcal{G}$ from first principles. This will provide the necessary mathematical foundation for our informal discussion of situated games of partial information and related concepts in the book.

Recall that the elements of situation theory have already been spelled out as fully as required for the purposes of this book in chapter 2. Certain basic facts relating to agents and language were also identified in sections 2.5–2.8. I will take this material as given here.

The key innovation in my presentation, based on Parikh (1987b, 1990, 2001), is that games are constructed from situation-theoretic objects just as numbers can be constructed from sets. There are many reasons for preferring such an embedding of game theory in situation theory to defining games *directly* as is usually done.

First, situation theory is a foundational theory of information—philosophically as we have already seen, but also mathematically and computationally—and if games, which provide a framework for choice and action, are constructed from situations, then these more complex objects are explicitly related to their simpler, more basic building blocks, thereby making their ontological status clear. This is useful not just for semantics but for any application of game theory.

In pure mathematics, when one type of entity (e.g., numbers or games) is constructed from a simpler type of entity (e.g., sets or situations), then this construction has a *logical* character. However, when the same piece of mathematics is applied to some part of the real world, then such a construction additionally takes on the character of an *explanation*. Since situations and games are very much part of the world, my construction serves as an explanation of how games arise in communicative situations. The alternative is simply to assume that there is a game that models some flow of information and then show that its solution matches our intuitions. My construction goes a step further: instead of assuming a game to start with as an article of faith, I assume a more basic ontology, one whose objects are prima facie easier to accept, and show how a game naturally emerges in communication. This is a common feature in science where relatively complex objects whose existence is assumed in a theory that is more at the surface of things get accounted for by more fundamental objects in a deeper theory (e.g., explaining certain objects of particle physics—like hadrons—by using string theory or explaining diseases via genetics and epigenetics). In this sense, I take games to be real objects out there in the world just like individuals, properties, relations, infons, situations, and all the rest of the objects in the ontology $\mathcal{O}$. Indeed, situation theory provides a finer-grained universe of objects that even facilitates a natural derivation of more general choice-theoretic structures called strategic interactions in sections 3.3.4, 5.3, and 5.10 that permit weaker conditions than common knowledge. This is precisely the kind of consequence that one should expect from using a more general framework.

A third and related reason is that the elements of situation theory actually make certain aspects of the game theory clearer. For example, the information that agents possess at each stage of a game can be made explicit in a natural way since the progression marked by a path in a game tree is nothing but a progression of evolving situations that support different infons based on the action chosen by an agent. Likewise, the basis for the particular payoffs and probabilities in a game can be represented in the initial situations of a game. The definition of a product of two games also becomes easier to address because the information at each node of the product is readily expressible via set-theoretic operations on the situations at the nodes in the multiplicands. The circular and non-well-founded[1] aspects of strategic inference also become transparent, a matter I do not discuss here.

A fourth reason is that, in my view and as chapter 3 makes clear, I believe *all* choice is fundamentally *situated*. For example, an agent in a certain situation may prefer a scoop of ice cream to a glass of water. After he chooses the ice cream and eats it, he may face exactly the same choice in the ensuing new situation. Though his options are the same the second time around, his preferences in this new situation may be different: he

1. See, for example, Barwise and Etchemendy (1986).

may now prefer a glass of water to the ice cream and may act accordingly. This is something economists and others using game theory have seldom tried to capture explicitly. Games and decision problems become *actual* only with respect to a *setting* or situation. And real situations, being what they are, can seldom be enumerated exhaustively. This means real games themselves are *partial* objects, which can be more or less fully captured by the game-theoretic models we build. Sometimes, as we have seen, the agents in a situation may model the choices available to them differently, either because of their different epistemic constraints or because of their different preferences. As exemplified in section 3.1, the solutions to a game also sometimes depend on the ambient situation, as not all the information required for a solution may be located in the model of the game itself but may remain "outside," as it were, in the setting for the game. It is worth amplifying on this situatedness of choice and action despite the slight digression it entails.

In this book, I have relied largely on the Pareto-Nash equilibrium as a solution concept. This is not because I believe it is the one and only correct solution concept, but because it made it possible for me to be concrete in considering the solutions to games of partial information. Additionally, as discussed in section 3.3.5, it does seem that most other solution concepts are likely to yield results that are the same as the Nash or Pareto-Nash equilibria although, as we also saw, Pareto dominance (or payoff dominance) can diverge from risk dominance. Suffice it to say here that the universality result of section 4.11 does guarantee that a unique solution exists for all games of partial information.

In any case, often too much attention is given to solution concepts. Important as they are for completing the analysis, it is the games themselves and their various representations that are more fundamental, and I have tried to show throughout that they can model a very wide range of phenomena. In general, there are many different approaches to solving essentially the same game, some giving similar predictions and others that are not equivalent. Once one has the basic setup, one can explore multiple approaches to analyzing it without committing oneself to one or another approach. This is an ongoing task. Thus, a clear distinction needs to be made between the choice situation being modeled, the game one uses to model that situation, and finally, the analysis of the model with some solution concept.

Indeed, once this kind of separation is made, a very different view of game theory emerges, a view that does not seem to have been explored in the game-theoretic literature, at least as far as I know. This view was discussed in Parikh (2006a) and I revisit it here in greater detail. To introduce this perspective of what I have called *situated game theory*, let us consider an analogy.

As mentioned in chapter 1, it has taken a while to give full recognition to the context of utterance as an integral factor in the determination of content and even today the dominant position gives it a second-class status in semantics. But there should no longer be any doubt that it is only the sentence together with a context that can have a content. The proliferation of analysis strategies for games suggests that games may well be like sentences in this regard. Indeed, the fact that we could prove in section 4.11 that $\mathcal{L} \cong \mathcal{G}$, that is, that $\mathcal{L}$ and $\mathcal{G}$ are isomorphic, puts this analogy on a formal footing. Just as the same sentence can be used in a variety of ways in different situations to make different statements, so the same game can be solved in a variety of ways in different situations to yield different solutions. The same game in an economic context may be best analyzed in one way but in a political or communicative context in other ways. It is only the game together with a context that can have a solution.

Now games already incorporate a number of contextual factors internally—through the payoffs and probabilities and game tree—so what remains of relevance in the context after this has been done? Indeed, games are themselves models of situations, so why leave anything relevant out in the situation being modeled? This is a moot point because if something does remain, we could always try to enrich the model and incorporate it. This would be similar to the familiar move in the case of language of enriching the sentence itself or the sentence's logical form. While this is an ad hoc and therefore bad strategy for the analysis of utterances, it may be partially acceptable in the case of games: we can sometimes enrich the game model and sometimes leave things in an external context. Perhaps there are higher level things about the concerns of the players that are best left out of the game model and used externally to determine how the game should be analyzed, whether statically or behaviorally or evolutionarily, or given one of these choices, what solution concept should be employed, and further, which of multiple possible equilibria should be selected. Perhaps there are external things about the behavioral or architectural configurations of the agents involved, as mentioned in chapter 3: they may have all kinds of computational limitations, for example, that may vary from situation to situation and agent to agent.

In section 3.1, the protagonists faced multiple equilibria in G regarding their choices for how to spend the evening, and it was suggested there that the setting of the game that made it actual could contain further information about its solution. Different assumptions and different corresponding analyses would be germane for other settings and the behavior of the players would then be different. That is, just as the variation of context leads to different contents for utterances, so this variation can also lead to different solutions for games.

So the ambient situation is responsible not just for giving rise to the game model itself, but also partially for its solution. There is a kind of trade-off and indeterminacy between how much information is absorbed explicitly into the game and how much is left in the ambient situation, just as in section 5.6 there was an indeterminacy between how much of the content of an utterance should be inscribed on the side of the described situation and how much on the side of the infons. In one, we have the form $u \models G$ and, in the other, we have the similar form $c \models \sigma$, and the indeterminacy concerns which side of the turnstile the information in question is placed.

Since there are often additional facts in u that have been left out of the game (e.g., a preference for separating equilibria or a certain kind of mixed strategy equilibrium in a game of partial information), why not use a second higher-order game to model these additional facts? This would be an adaptation of the strategy of leaving certain facts external to the initial game model in the context u, and then using a second game to model these external facts. This move can be made clearer by recognizing what has been done for content:

phrase $\oplus$ utterance situation = content of utterance (i.e., $\mathcal{C}_u(\alpha) = \sigma$)

Here, games of partial information were introduced to model the utterance situation. A similar equation can be expressed for games:

game $\oplus$ game situation or setting = solution of game

(i.e., $\mathcal{C}_u(G) =$ solution)

If games of some kind were relevant for utterance situations, then it is plausible that games can be deployed to model "game situations" or settings. This is precisely the second higher-order game mentioned above. In the special case of communication, the game situation is nothing but the utterance situation. But for other settings, say in economics or political science or biology, there is no prior phrase or utterance.

This idea suggests that given a general situation u containing one or more agents, it is possible to model it as a sequence of games (or decision problems) $\langle G_0, G_1, G_2, \ldots \rangle$, G_0 being the initial model G, and each subsequent game being at a higher level than the one before it in a way that each successive game in the sequence captures some of the residual information in the initial (game) situation u. So G_1 might encode information about a preference the players may have for a certain type of solution concept in G_0, G_2 in G_1, and so on. Even though the information in a real situation is seldom fully exhausted, one can imagine situations where such a sequence "converges" so that in some G_n for finite n or possibly in the limit as $n \to \infty$, the solution is obvious. Then this would presumably cascade all the way back to G_0, yielding the solution to the original game.

And when an utterance of α is being considered, not an arbitrary game or decision problem G, then the relevant sequence $\langle g^0, g^1, g^2, \ldots \rangle$ would start with the phrase or sentence α itself and go on to a game of partial information $g_u(\alpha)$ followed by other games. That is, $g^0 = \alpha$ is the phrase or sentence uttered in u and $g^1 = g_u(\alpha)$ is the partial information game of equilibrium semantics. Each game helps to solve the one preceding it: g^1 enables the solution to g^0, g^2 to g^1, and so on, ad infinitum if necessary.

In the case of general games as well as the case of utterances, the setting u is the source of the entire sequence: u supports G and α, u supports G_1 and $g_u(\alpha)$, and so on.

Admittedly, this suggestion is a bit speculative, but there seems to be no immediate problem in carrying it out. Certainly, there may often be additional information in u that has not been exhausted by G_0 and this leftover information may be relevant for the solution of G_0. If this suggestion turns out to be valid, it would have interesting consequences for the use of game theory in wider contexts too, whether they are economic, political, or biological. And, of course, it would apply to games of partial information. We may also be forced to accept that if contextual information relevant for solving a game is not always fully exhaustible through the sequence of games above, then there may well remain a nonformal residue in our attempts to solve games satisfactorily. This may happen also because the initial situation u is simply not given clearly or differs for the agents involved, as mentioned in connection with the ambiguity of texts in section 5.7. Just as there is an element of creativity involved in coming up with a suitable context for the interpretation of a text, so there is an element of creativity involved in identifying the context for a game, as can be seen when two sides are involved in a difficult negotiation. This observation pretty much dashes all hopes for a fully formal theory for the determination of unique equilibria for games just as new readings for existing texts will always be possible by changing their context.

Incidentally, all of the foregoing refers to the situatedness of *choice*, not of action. In this book, the primary actions of interest have been utterances and interpretations, although actions were considered more generally in the setting game G. It is easy to separate an utterance into a sentence and a situation in which it is uttered and, likewise, it is easy to separate an interpretation into an infon and a situation. A point I have not pursued here but mention in passing is that *all* actions are situated and require reference to a situation, just as utterances and interpretations do. This observation makes it possible to develop an entire theory of action based on situation theory, something clearly outside our scope.

To return from the brief detour, a fifth and final reason for constructing games from situations is that I have already done it informally starting with chapter 3. All that needs to be done is to spell it out more formally here.

Quite apart from the applications to semantics, it is likely that such an integration of situation and game theory will have many uses in the wider domain of action, especially as it is studied in philosophy and artificial intelligence. For example, it could well be of interest in robotics.

Generally, if there are results that are relatively hard to prove, they are called theorems, whereas simpler results of this sort are called propositions. Because the proofs here are all quite simple, I have used "theorem" and "proposition" differently, to mark the importance of the result for equilibrium semantics.

A.1 The Background

In section 2.3, I named the sets of infons, situations, and propositions $\mathcal{I}$, **SIT**, and **PROP** respectively. These sets are assumed to be finite and represent just the range of infons, situations, and propositions of interest to us relative to a small part of reality called the environment $\mathcal{E}$. There are various operations defined on these entities and these should be borne in mind as well.

Agents were introduced in section 2.5 and elaborated on in later chapters. Language and its related situations were introduced in section 2.6. While any action can be communicative in the right context, I restrict my focus to linguistic communication. The constraints **S**, **C**, and **I** are also taken as given. The latter two constraints **C** and **I** together provide the set of possible contents of an utterance. If syntax is also considered game-theoretically, then the content of communication is viewed more broadly as either syntactic or semantic, and **S** contributes the set of possible grammatical contents or parse trees. Another way of describing the task of this Appendix is to say that the constraint **F** will be developed mathematically.

Since $\mathcal{A}$'s actions are utterances of sentences, they can be modeled by ordered pairs $\langle \varphi, u \rangle$, where φ is a sentence in $\mathcal{L}$. As the utterance situation u is a parameter, it is convenient to simplify the notation by specifying utterances by their sentences alone.

$\mathcal{B}$'s actions are interpretations of $\mathcal{A}$'s utterances, and can be modeled as pairs $\langle \sigma, c \rangle$, where σ is an infon and c the situation described partially by the infon. Once again, this can be simplified to just σ, because c is held fixed for all the infons that serve as interpretations relative to the utterance situation u. I have taken infons rather than propositions as the relevant contents. Clearly, both are transmitted in an utterance.

Initially, lexical games $g_u(\varphi_i)$ will be constructed, where φ_i is a word in the sentence φ. The corresponding possible contents of φ_i obtained from **C** and **I** will be denoted by σ_i^y where y stands for zero or more primes as before (see section 4.2.4). To avoid the proliferation of generic indices, I choose to replace i with just the number 1 with the understanding that the same construction would apply mutatis mutandis to all the words in the sentence uttered. Thus, φ_i is replaced by φ_1 and σ_i^y by σ_1^y.

Instead of referring back to the constraints **C** and **I** every time the possible contents of an expression have to be accessed, it is easier to define a function m_u that maps elements of $\mathcal{L}$ into their possible contents σ_1^y relative to u. $m_u(\varphi_1) = \{\sigma_1^y \mid y = 0, 1, 2, \ldots \text{primes}\}$ is assumed to be finite and generated via **C** and **I**.[2] Indeed, m_u is just the composition of the conventional and informational maps suitably defined. An added advantage of using this composed function is that the construction of $g_u(\varphi_1)$ can be applied beyond language to other symbol systems and other domains like social systems if m_u is reinterpreted for those other contexts. In other words, **C** and **I** and their corresponding maps may be viewed as just the *theory* of m_u for the case of language. Further, different parts of language require different theories for each part of the Informational Constraint **I**. The Conventional Constraint **C** belongs more to what was called *macrosemantics* in sections 1.5 and 7.1.2. A similar function m'_u that maps elements of $\mathcal{L}$ into their possible parse trees may be assumed if we wish to consider syntax.

This way of accounting for the possible contents of an expression suffices for *locutionary* meanings because they are generated by the expressions themselves via **C** and **I**. As we saw in section 4.4, the possible contents that arise in connection with the illocutionary meanings of an utterance are based not on any expression in the sentence but on the resolu-

2. Incidentally, m_u plays the same role that m played in section 5.10.

tion of *issues* that are raised. Crucially, as was pointed out in section 4.4.2, these issues have what was called a *support* in the sentence, which may be a single word or phrase or the entire sentence. So it is possible to extend the function $m_u(\alpha)$ to illocutionary meanings as well by identifying its argument α as the support of the possible illocutionary meanings of the utterance. This makes the function $m_u(\alpha)$ not a function but a correspondence since it would yield the set of possible locutionary contents of α as well as the set of possible illocutionary contents whose support is α. We could easily separate this into two functions m_u^ℓ and $m_u^\imath$, one for locutionary meanings and the other for illocutionary meanings, just as was done with the actual equilibrium contents $C_u^\ell(\alpha)$ and $C_u^\imath(\alpha)$, but this merely adds clutter so I will avoid it.

In any event, it should be kept in mind that the function m_u is nothing but a notational stand-in for the constraints **C** and **I** and represents the composition of the conventional and informational maps. It is to them one has to turn in order to actually know what the *possible* locutionary and illocutionary meanings are when considering linguistic communication.

The way the game-theoretic model works is that given an utterance situation u, the speaker $\mathcal{A}$ forms an intention to convey a (partial) content σ_1 (like the film *Harvey*) as part of a full utterance and chooses a possibly ambiguous locution φ_1 (like "Harvey") such that $\sigma_1 \in m_u(\varphi_1)$. If σ_1 is the only member of $m_u(\varphi_1)$, a trivial game ensues. If φ_1 is ambiguous (in my extended sense), then a nontrivial game results. In either case, the number of initial situations in the game equals the number of possible contents of φ_1. In the construction below, it is assumed that these starting points are given.

A.2 Some Prior Basic Elements

Some basic relations, infons, situations, and functions pertaining to communication are now defined.

The first is the relation *itc* of intending to convey something. This is a three-place relation with a speaker who does the intending, an infon the speaker intends to convey, and an addressee to whom the content is addressed. As discussed in sections 5.1 and 5.9, such intentions are understood to be either explicit or implicit. The second relation *hu* is the relation of having uttered something. Its first argument is a speaker and its second argument is a parameter that is anchored to an expression. However, instead of writing $\langle\langle hu; \mathcal{A}; \dot{\varphi} \rangle\rangle$ with $f(\dot{\varphi}) = \alpha$, as I did in section 2.6, I will write simply $\langle\langle hu; \mathcal{A}; \alpha \rangle\rangle$ to keep the notation uncluttered. The third relation is the relation *hi* of an addressee's having interpreted an utterance as communicating something. This is a three-place relation with arguments an addressee, an utterance, and an infon. From these three relations, corresponding infons and situations can be constructed.

We start with a specification of the *possible*[3] initial situations in a game of partial information.

Definition 1 $s_{1^y} = u \cup \{\langle\langle itc, \mathcal{A}, \sigma_1^y, \mathcal{B} \rangle\rangle\}$, where $\sigma_1^y \in m_u(\varphi_1)$.

This says simply that the initial situations s_{1^y} are just the utterance situation u augmented with an infon representing the appropriate intention $\mathcal{A}$ would have to convey σ_1^y to $\mathcal{B}$. This definition and the basic relations above are then used to specify the alternatives to φ_1 that $\mathcal{A}$ might consider and the consequences of $\mathcal{A}$'s and $\mathcal{B}$'s possible actions.

Definition 2 $alt_u : \mathcal{L} \times \mathcal{I} \to \mathcal{L}$ with $alt_u(\varphi_1, \sigma_1^y) = \varphi_1^{y+1}$ where $\varphi_1^{y+1} \in \mathcal{L}$ is a minimal cost alternative to φ_1 such that its unique possible content in u is σ_1^y. That is, $m_u(\varphi_1^{y+1}) = \{\sigma_1^y\}$. Moreover, the cost of φ_1^{y+1} is always greater than the cost of φ_1 for all y. In the special case when $m_u(\varphi_1) = \{\sigma_1\}$ is a singleton, then $alt_u(\varphi_1, \sigma_1) = \varphi_1$.

For the purposes of the model, the cost of uttering an expression and perceiving and interpreting it are taken as given. To keep things simple, the definition above refers just to "cost" without specifying whether it is the cost for $\mathcal{A}$ or $\mathcal{B}$ and whether these costs are identical. A whole *theory* of cost would be required to do justice to this aspect of payoffs and is obviously beyond our scope here. If there is more than one minimal cost alternative, one can be picked arbitrarily.

As we have seen, defining alt_u to yield just one alternative is *not* required. It could quite easily be defined as a *set* of alternatives that moreover do not necessarily have unique contents in u. But this needlessly complicates the model and we would lose sight of the forest for the trees![4]

Definition 3 $act_{\mathcal{A}} : \mathcal{S} \times \mathcal{L} \to \mathcal{S}$

$$act_{\mathcal{A}}(s, \alpha) = s \cup \{\langle\langle hu, \mathcal{A}, \alpha \rangle\rangle\}.$$

$$act_{\mathcal{B}} : \mathrm{ran}(act_{\mathcal{A}}) \times \mathcal{I} \to \mathcal{S}$$

$$act_{\mathcal{B}}(t, \tau) = t \cup \{\langle\langle hi, \mathcal{B}, \alpha, \tau \rangle\rangle\} \quad \text{where } \alpha = 2^{nd}[act_{\mathcal{A}}^{-1}(t)].$$

3. See footnote 31 in chapter 1.

4. Pun intended.

Here ran($act_{\mathcal{A}}$) is just the range of the function $act_{\mathcal{A}}$. These two functions give general descriptions of the consequences of $\mathcal{A}$'s uttering something in a situation and of $\mathcal{B}$'s subsequently interpreting it. All that happens is that the initial situations s get augmented first with $\mathcal{A}$'s utterance and next with $\mathcal{B}$'s interpretation. It should be easy to see that if s were taken to be one of the initial situations s_{1y} above and if appropriate utterances and interpretations were specified, then we would have the basic mechanism for generating the game tree via the updates given by $act_{\mathcal{A}}$ and $act_{\mathcal{B}}$. Thus, having started with the elements of situation theory and with some basic relations pertaining to communication, games of partial information will naturally follow.

It should be clarified that this is partly where using situation theory enables us to make the information available to each agent at each stage explicit. Uttering α in s has the consequence that $\langle\langle hu, \mathcal{A}, \alpha \rangle\rangle$ gets added to s, a fact that is explicitly available to both agents. Without this kind of underlying construction, this fact would remain implicit. This kind of articulation is especially useful in contexts where artificial agents that communicate have to be designed because such information can then be used in making situated and strategic inferences.

We first remind ourselves of the form of games of incomplete information which will be the approximate target of our construction.

A.3 Games of Incomplete Information

As I have said, traditionally, games are approached directly. Although Harsanyi (1967) was the first person to define games of incomplete information, he did so in normal or strategic form. What we need is their extensive form definition because that is where various aspects of the choice structure are made transparent. This was made clear by Kuhn (1953) who was the first to define extensive form games for games of perfect and imperfect information. Kreps and Wilson (1982) extended Kuhn's definition to games of incomplete information and their definition remains quite standard. We use their formulation of a game of incomplete information as a tuple of sets and functions as the approximate goal of the situation-theoretic construction. This goal is approximate because games of partial information are different in certain respects from incomplete information games. Incidentally, Lewis (1969) who based his signaling games on Schelling's (1960) normal form games implicitly used imperfect information games, although the informational aspects of such games were never made explicit. Later, they were generalized by game theorists to incomplete information games.

Kreps and Wilson (1982) define a game of incomplete information directly as an extended tuple $\langle T, \prec; ACT, act; N, \eta; P; H; v\rangle$. T is a set of nodes and $\prec$ is a partial ordering on T that makes the pair $\langle T, \prec\rangle$ a tree (more precisely, a forest). ACT is a set of actions and act is a function that maps every noninitial node of $\langle T, \prec\rangle$ into some action in ACT. This is intended to be the action that leads to this node. N is a set of agents (or players) and η is a mapping from the set of nonterminal nodes onto N. η establishes whose turn it is to act. P is a vector of probabilities on the set of initial nodes. This much of the tuple gives a tree with decision nodes connected by actions with an agent identified for each decision node. H is a partition on T that consists of subpartitions, one for each player. It is meant to capture the information sets of each agent, the sets of decision nodes of an agent that cannot be distinguished by the agent. Accordingly, each agent's subpartition is a collection of those sets of nodes that are his or her information sets. Finally, v is the payoff function, a mapping from the terminal nodes into the set $\mathbb{R}$ of real numbers. This is an informal description of the tuple constructed below and the reader is referred to Kreps and Wilson's (1982) paper for the formal definitions.

A.4 Games of Partial Information

I now construct what were called *local* games of partial information in section 3.3.5. This is a straightforward matter of defining the elements of the tuple characterizing a game of incomplete information one by one.

Situations and Choices

As was said above in section A.1, given an utterance situation u, the speaker $\mathcal{A}$ forms an intention to convey a (partial) content σ_1 (like the film *Harvey*) as part of a full utterance and chooses a possibly ambiguous locution φ_1 (like "Harvey") such that $\sigma_1 \in m_u(\varphi_1)$. The first element of the tuple that has to be constructed is the tree of *possible*[5] situations and to do this we start with the initial situations identified in Definition 1 in section A.2. Then we define $\mathcal{A}$'s choice sets in each of these initial situations based on the function alt_u from Definition 2. Next, we generate the situations that result from these possible actions based on $act_{\mathcal{A}}$ from Definition 3 and then identify $\mathcal{B}$'s choices in these resulting situations. Finally, we define the terminal situations that follow from $\mathcal{B}$'s interpretive actions

5. See footnote 31 in chapter 1.

based on $act_{\mathcal{B}}$. This collection of situations forms a tree under the subset ordering.

Definition 4 $T_0 = \{s_{1^y} \mid \sigma_1^y \in m_u(\varphi_1)\}$

$$C_{\mathcal{A}} : T_0 \to \mathcal{P}(\mathcal{L})$$

$$C_{\mathcal{A}}(s_{1^y}) = \{\varphi_1, alt_u(\varphi_1, \sigma_1^y)\} = \{\varphi_1, \varphi_1^{y+1}\}$$

$$T_1 = \{act_{\mathcal{A}}(s_{1^y}, \alpha) \mid s_{1^y} \in T_0, \alpha \in C_{\mathcal{A}}(s_{1^y})\}$$

$$C_{\mathcal{B}} : T_1 \to \mathcal{P}(\mathcal{I})$$

$$C_{\mathcal{B}}(t) = m_u(\alpha) \text{ where } \alpha = 2^{nd}[act_{\mathcal{A}}^{-1}(t)]$$

$$T_2 = \{act_{\mathcal{B}}(t, \tau) \mid t \in T_1, \tau \in C_{\mathcal{B}}(t)\}$$

$$T = \bigcup_i T_i$$

Each $C_{\mathcal{A}}(s)$ and $C_{\mathcal{B}}(t)$ are $\mathcal{A}$'s and $\mathcal{B}$'s choice sets in the relevant situations.

This is one place where games of partial information differ from games of incomplete information because the usual definition of the latter requires that all the choice sets $C_{\mathcal{A}}(s)$ be equal and correspondingly that all the choice sets $C_{\mathcal{B}}(t)$ also be equal. This goes back to Harsanyi's (1967) original definition of incomplete information games. Games of partial information relax this requirement.

Proposition 1 $\langle T, \subset \rangle$ is a "tree" (more accurately, forest).

Since the more basic building blocks of situations and actions have been strung together piece by piece, the fact that $\langle T, \subset \rangle$ is a tree is something that can now be *proved* rather than simply assumed as is conventionally done. The nodes of the tree can in general represent situations or *types* of situations.

Definition 5 $\forall t, t' \in T_0, t \equiv_{\mathcal{A}} t'$ iff $t = t'$.

$\forall t, t' \in T_1, t \equiv_{\mathcal{B}} t'$ iff $t = t'$

or for some α in both $C_{\mathcal{A}}(s)$ and $C_{\mathcal{A}}(s')$

there exist $s, s' \in T_0$

such that $t = act_{\mathcal{A}}(s, \alpha)$ and $t' = act_{\mathcal{A}}(s', \alpha)$.

Proposition 2 $\equiv_{\mathcal{A}}$, $\equiv_{\mathcal{B}}$ are equivalence relations.

These equivalence relations capture the relevant epistemic properties of the two agents because they have the following consequences.

Proposition 3

- For all $t, t' \in T_1$, $t \equiv_{\mathcal{B}} t'$ implies $C_{\mathcal{B}}(t) = C_{\mathcal{B}}(t')$.
- For all $t, t' \in T_1$, $t \equiv_{\mathcal{B}} t'$ implies $t \not\subset t'$.
- For all $t, t' \in T_1$, $t \equiv_{\mathcal{B}} t'$ implies $\eta(t) = \eta(t')$.

The first statement says that $\mathcal{B}$ has the same choices at each of various equivalent situations. This is important because if the choices were not the same, the agent could use that information to distinguish between epistemically equivalent situations, a contradiction. The second statement says that of two equivalent situations one cannot precede the other. This again makes intuitive sense because if such precedence were possible, the agent would know it, and it would make the situations epistemically distinguishable. The last statement requires Definition 9 made below and says simply that the same agent has to act in all equivalent situations. The corresponding properties for $\mathcal{A}$ are trivially true. The key thing to note is that all these properties can now be *proved* from more basic assumptions.

Actions

The third element of the game tuple above, the set of actions in the game, is nothing but the union of all the choice sets in Definition 4. This gathering of all the actions into a single set is just to maintain conformity with Kreps and Wilson's (1982) tuple, so that the game is rendered in a familiar form.

Definition 6 $ACT = [\bigcup_{s \in T_0} C_{\mathcal{A}}(s)] \cup [\bigcup_{t \in T_1} C_{\mathcal{B}}(t)]$

The map *act* assigns an appropriate set of actions in ACT to each noninitial situation in T.

Definition 7 $act : T_1 \cup T_2 \rightarrow ACT$

$$act(t) = 2^{nd}[act_{\mathcal{A}}^{-1}(t)] \quad \text{if } t \in T_1$$

$$= 2^{nd}[act_{\mathcal{B}}^{-1}(t)] \quad \text{if } t \in T_2$$

act maps a situation into the action that brings it about. The reason for labeling situations or nodes in the game tree with actions in this manner is because $\langle T, \subset \rangle$ is a tree and this means that each noninitial situation has a single action that generates it.

Agents

Definition 8 $N = \{\mathcal{A}, \mathcal{B}\}$ is the set of agents.

The function η below determines whose turn it is to act.

Definition 9 $\eta : T_0 \cup T_1 \rightarrow N$

$$\eta(t) = \mathcal{A} \quad \text{if } t \in T_0$$
$$= \mathcal{B} \quad \text{if } t \in T_1$$

This just offers a formal way of saying that $\mathcal{A}$ is the speaker and $\mathcal{B}$ the addressee.

Initial Probabilities

The next item in the tuple is the initial probabilities. As we have seen, they are, in a sense, the most complicated part of the game-theoretic structure because it is through them that each local game is connected with all the other local games, both locutionary and illocutionary, that materialize when a sentence is uttered. To enable the definition below, assume that the whole sentence uttered is $\varphi = \varphi_1\varphi_2 \ldots \varphi_n$ for some n, as was done in section 2.6. In addition, remember that x_{-1} is a variable that stands for any of the vectors formed by taking all the combinations of the possible contents of locutions other than φ_1.

Definition 10 $P : m_u(\varphi_1) \times m_u(\varphi_2) \times \cdots \times m_u(\varphi_n) \rightarrow [0, 1]$ such that $\sum_y P(\sigma_1^y \mid x_{-1}, u) = 1$ with $\sigma_1^y \in m_u(\varphi_1)$ and $x_{-1} \in m_u(\varphi_2) \times \cdots \times m_u(\varphi_n)$.

There are two things to note in the above definition. The first is that each m_u is intended to cover both locutionary and illocutionary possibilities as was clarified in section A.1. The second is that only lexical contents have been mentioned in the domain of P. To be complete, it would be necessary to include *all* the constituents α of the sentence, words and phrases, but this would require looking at the Syntactic Constraint **S** and would involve more encumbrances, so I avoid spelling out this more fully. The basic idea is clear enough and this is all I am after here.

This is another area where games of partial information differ from games of incomplete information. Incomplete information games have a single pre-given probability distribution; as was first explained in chapter 4, partial information games have multiple probability distributions for each local game. These form a *third* set of *strategic* choice variables along with the choice of utterance and interpretation from each $C_{\mathcal{A}}(s)$ and $C_{\mathcal{B}}(t)$. This strategic characteristic is made possible by the presence of the conditioning variables x_{-1} because each different instantiation of these variables creates a different probability distribution $P(\sigma_1^y \mid x_{-1}, u)$ and the agents have to *choose* one distribution from among many based on whether all such choices are in *global* equilibrium or not.

Information Sets

Definition 5 and the corresponding Propositions 2 and 3 allow us to specify the information sets of each agent. They are *information* sets precisely because they have been shown to have the appropriate epistemic properties.

Definition 11 $h_A : T_0 \to \mathcal{P}(T)$

$$h_A(t) = \{t' \in T_0 \mid t' \equiv_A t\} = \{t\}$$

$$H_A = \{h_A(t) \mid t \in T_0\}$$

$$h_B : T_1 \to \mathcal{P}(T)$$

$$h_B(t) = \{t' \in T_1 \mid t' \equiv_B t\}$$

$$H_B = \{h_B(t) \mid t \in T_1\}$$

$$H = H_A \cup H_B$$

Again, I observe that the situation-theoretic construction makes it possible to build information sets from the simpler objects $\equiv_A$ and $\equiv_B$ rather than just defining and imposing them outright. It provides an explanation of why they arise from the more basic epistemic properties of the game.

Payoffs

At one level, the payoffs are the easiest elements to define as all that is needed is two real-valued functions defined on the terminal situations in T_2, with the understanding that each function encodes the same underlying preferences up to positive affine transformations. This would be the most general case. However, it is desirable to constrain these functions to respect the inequalities introduced in chapter 3.

$$a_A > b_A > c_A$$

$$a'_A > b'_A > c'_A$$

$$a_B > b_B > c_B$$

$$a'_B > b'_B > c'_B$$

These inequalities pertain to games where there are only two initial situations. To consider games with more (or fewer) initial situations, all that needs to be noted is that the additional terminal situations that result all belong with instances where $\mathcal{B}$ has erred in interpreting the utterance. All such situations need to be mapped into the lowest level of payoffs $c_{\mathcal{A}}$ or its cognates.

Keep in mind that these inequalities were derived from the underlying preferences agents have for successful communication on the one hand and for minimizing effort or cost on the other. This is why it makes sense to constrain the payoff functions we define to obey these inequalities.

A little manipulation of prior constructs is required to express the condition that a terminal situation represents a correct interpretation or an incorrect one or the intermediate case where the interpretation is correct but the path to it involves a greater cost. This is not difficult to do but I rehearse it a bit to make it more readable.

To identify terminal situations where the interpretation is correct and is realized with the lowest cost, we require that the situation $t \in T_2$ satisfies:

$$1^{st}[act_{\mathcal{A}}^{-1}([1^{st}[act_{\mathcal{B}}^{-1}(t)]])] = s_{1^y} \in T_0$$

$$2^{nd}[act_{\mathcal{A}}^{-1}([1^{st}[act_{\mathcal{B}}^{-1}(t)]])] = \varphi_1$$

$$2^{nd}[act_{\mathcal{B}}^{-1}(t)] = \sigma_1^y$$

All of these conditions flow from Definitions 1, 2, and 3. The first condition simply traces the path back from the terminal situation t to the initial situation s_{1^y} in T_0 by Definition 3; the second condition states that the utterance that led to the terminal situation be φ_1, which implies that it is the lowest cost action by Definition 2; and the last condition requires that the interpretation leading to the terminal situation be σ_1^y, which is the content intended in s_{1^y} by Definition 1, thereby ensuring that the interpretation is the right one. These three conditions jointly capture the requirements for the highest payoffs, such as $a_{\mathcal{A}}$ and its cognates.

Similar conditions with suitable modifications are required to identify payoffs such as $b_{\mathcal{A}}$ and its cognates and $c_{\mathcal{A}}$ and its cognates.

Definition 12 $v_{\mathcal{A}} : T_2 \longrightarrow \mathbb{R}$

$$v_{\mathcal{B}} : T_2 \longrightarrow \mathbb{R}$$

such that $\forall t,\ t', t'' \in T_2$

if

$$1^{st}[act_A^{-1}([1^{st}[act_B^{-1}(t)])] = s_{1^y} \in T_0,$$

$$2^{nd}[act_A^{-1}([1^{st}[act_B^{-1}(t)])] = \varphi_1,$$

$$2^{nd}[act_B^{-1}(t)] = \sigma_1^y,$$

and

$$1^{st}[act_A^{-1}([1^{st}[act_B^{-1}(t')])] = s_{1^y} \in T_0,$$

$$2^{nd}[act_A^{-1}([1^{st}[act_B^{-1}(t')])] = \varphi_1^{y+1},$$

$$2^{nd}[act_B^{-1}(t')] = \sigma_1^y,$$

and

$$1^{st}[act_A^{-1}([1^{st}[act_B^{-1}(t'')])] = s_{1^y} \in T_0,$$

$$2^{nd}[act_A^{-1}([1^{st}[act_B^{-1}(t'')])] = \varphi_1,$$

$$2^{nd}[act_B^{-1}(t'')] \neq \sigma_1^y$$

then

$$v_A(t) > v_A(t') > v_A(t'')$$

and

$$v_B(t) > v_B(t') > v_B(t'')$$

$$v = (v_A, v_B)$$

The terminal situations t' are those where the interpretation is correct but the utterance is not the cheapest, and so lead to the intermediate payoffs $v_A(t')$ and $v_B(t')$ akin to b_A and b_B. Likewise, the terminal situations t'' are those where the interpretation is incorrect but the utterance is the lowest cost one and so lead to the lowest payoffs $v_A(t'')$ and $v_B(t'')$ akin to c_A and c_B. In general, there will be many terminal situations t'' when the number of initial situations in the game is greater than two.

Both v_A and v_B obey the same constraints, although the actual payoff numbers may be different for the two agents. v collects both these functions in an ordered pair.

I have deliberately not imposed any further conditions such as the Pareto-Nash Inequalities or the Mixed Strategy Equilibria conditions first introduced in section 3.2, or the risk dominance condition of Equation 3.3 in section 3.3.5.

If a theory of costs and benefits were available, it would have been possible to break down the payoff functions above into cost and benefit functions. Such costs and benefits depend on u and $\mathcal{L}$. Making this dependence explicit would reinforce the situatedness of choice and game theory.

The Game Tuple

All the elements required for a local game are now at hand.

Definition 13 $g_u(\varphi_1) = \langle T, \subset; ACT, act; N, \eta; P; H; v \rangle$

The full local game is of course $\langle g_u(\varphi_1), \mathcal{I}_g \rangle$, where $\mathcal{I}_g$ represents common knowledge between $\mathcal{A}$ and $\mathcal{B}$ of $g_u(\varphi_1)$. In general, as was said in section 3.3.4, $\mathcal{I}_g$ represents the *information structure* of the *strategic interaction* and it may range from no shared information to full common knowledge. This is part of the advantage gained by the situation-theoretic construction because it permits a natural extension of games where common knowledge obtains to more general strategic interactions where common knowledge may not obtain.

Earlier, in section A.1, I chose to avoid undue generality by fixing the utterance to be φ_1. It is now time to relax this constraint by letting the utterance vary freely over $\mathcal{L}$.[6]

Definition 14 $g_u(\alpha)$ where $\alpha \in \mathcal{L}$ is defined analogously by replacing φ_1 with α and making all other corresponding changes in each component of the game tuple above. $g_u(e) = g_e$ where g_e is the trivial game with a single initial node, a single branch labeled e, and a further single branch labeled **1** issuing from the node ending the first branch with any payoff at the terminal node, and $g_u(0) = g_0$ where g_0 is the the trivial game with a single initial node, a single branch labeled 0, and a further single branch labeled **0** issuing from the node ending the first branch with any payoff at the terminal node. $\mathcal{G}$ is defined to be just the collection of all the tuples so obtained. This gives us the map $g_u : \mathcal{L} \to \mathcal{G}$.[7]

6. Remember that $\mathcal{L}$ is the free monoid generated from the vocabulary $\mathcal{V}$ by the special concatenation operation $\circ$ together with the empty string e and the zero element 0 as mentioned in section 2.6. Needless to say, $m_u(0) = \{\mathbf{0}\}$ and $m_u(\alpha) = \{\mathbf{0}\}$ when $\alpha \in \mathcal{L}$ is a grammatical but meaningless expression.

7. I have already specified in section A.2 that we have an anchor f such that $f(\dot{\varphi}) = \alpha$ in order to secure that α is uttered in u. Just as we did in footnote 38 in

This completes the construction of the local game map g_u, the primary goal of the Appendix. The theorem below then follows.

Theorem 4 $g_u(\alpha)$ where $\alpha \in \mathcal{L}$ is a local game of partial information.

As observed above, instead of simply *defining* or legislating that the tuple above is a game, the situation-theoretic construction makes this fact a *consequence* derived from more basic assumptions. It is possible to *prove* that the tuple is a local game of partial information.

Games of partial information are in many ways similar to but slightly more general than games of incomplete information, the latter having been first systematically approached by Harsanyi (1967). The particular subclass of partial information games we are concerned with—those that apply to communication—are in fact similar to but again slightly more general than the subclass of incomplete information games known in economics as signaling games. The two types of game models of partial and incomplete information are predictively identical.

A signaling game starts with a move of Nature that reveals some private information to one player. This private information is called the type of the player and is known only to that player and not to the other player. The other player knows only the range of possible values of this type, that is, the other possible moves of Nature, but does not know which particular value was instantiated. Then the same extensive form, consisting of some actions (signals) by the first player followed by some actions (responses) by the second player, is appended to each of these types. Since the same extensive forms are attached, there are often many nodes between which the second player cannot distinguish and these are collected into appropriate information sets. The first signaling games were invented by David Lewis (1969) who represented them in normal or strategic form, as mentioned in sections 1.4.4 and 3.2. They were later studied by Michael Spence (1973), Crawford and Sobel (1982), and David

---

section 2.8 with the content map, it is necessary to make the game map a total function. We can do this as follows:

$$g_{u[f]}(\alpha) = \begin{cases} g & \text{if } f(\dot{\varphi}) = \alpha \\ g_\alpha & \text{otherwise} \end{cases} \tag{A.1}$$

where g is the game defined above when α is uttered in u and where g_α is the game below:

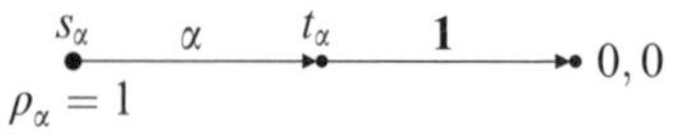

Kreps (1986) who represented them in extensive form which is now the standard form in economics for signaling games.[8]

This form, defined for incomplete information games by Kreps and Wilson (1982) and introduced in section A.3, is what we have used as the approximate target of our construction.

What are the precise differences between signaling games and the relevant subclass of partial information games we have constructed?

1. In incomplete information signaling games, the same extensive form is always attached to each type (see for example Myerson, 1995; Osborne and Rubinstein, 1994; Watson, 2002; see Kreps and Sobel, 1994, for a parenthetically expressed relaxation of this requirement). In partial information games, this is not necessarily true: in general, $C_{\mathcal{A}}(s) \neq C_{\mathcal{A}}(s')$ where both s and s' belong to T_0. Similar considerations apply, mutatis mutandis, to the sets of interpretive actions $C_{\mathcal{B}}(t)$ by $\mathcal{B}$.[9]
2. Another difference is that, in partial information games involving communication, the interpretive act—what Austin (1975) called an act of understanding—is always made explicit. In signaling games, there is usually an action the "Receiver" takes, and the interpretive act remains implicit and part of the solution process. Of course, since the action the Receiver can take is completely general, it can always be defined to be an interpretive action in purely formal terms. But it is in natural language communicative situations (e.g., with ambiguity) that the need for an explicit representation of this interpretive act becomes fully visible. Of course, if a further action is required after the interpretive act—such as the acceptance or rejection of a statement, or the carrying out of a request or command, or an answer in response to a question—then that act is appended to the interpretive act.[10] The interested reader is referred to Parikh (2009) for a generalization of this idea to *all* games, even those that do not involve communication.
3. A third difference, mentioned in section 3.3.5, is that $\mathcal{B}$ constructs the game $g_u(\alpha)$ only after $\mathcal{A}$ has uttered α, and similarly the game becomes common knowledge—when common knowledge is warranted—only after $\mathcal{A}$'s action. In signaling games, the entire game is common knowledge to both players before the start of the game.

8. Games of partial information were first invented by the author in 1985.
9. See Parikh (2006a) for more details.
10. See Parikh (2001), chapter 8.

4. A related difference is that $g_u(\alpha)$ need not be common knowledge for both players in games of partial information. As was made clear in section 3.3.4, it is generally enough to simply have each agent *believe* that a certain extensive form and payoff structure is common knowledge. When these beliefs are false, more general strategic interactions result.
5. Fifth, the initial probabilities are *strategic* choice variables, just like the utterance and interpretation, as a result of the interconnectedness of the various local games associated with an utterance. No game of partial information—in the context of communication—is an isolated and independent entity but is interdependent with other related games. They always exist as a family.
6. Lastly, this so-called *local* game is embedded in a larger *glocal* game described in section 3.3.5. Incidentally, it is now easy to construct glocal games situation-theoretically and I leave this to the reader.

To summarize the above, games of partial information generalize games of incomplete information (and their corresponding subclass of signaling games) but are predictively identical to them when they are analyzed in the same way. In some sense, the underlying game model is more important than the subsequent analysis through solution concepts, as there are usually several solution concepts that can be applied to a game model, most of which turn out to be equivalent for the simpler classes of games involved here.[11]

11. I quote from Parikh (2006a):

In his paper, van Rooij (2004) has the unfortunate title "Signaling games select Horn strategies"—the game model, whether it is a game of partial information or a signaling game (of incomplete information), can never select anything as such; it is only the analysis of a game model based on a solution concept that results in some strategy being selected. He contrasts games of partial information with signaling games implying that, in a certain context, the latter give the expected result whereas the former don't, but this is impossible because the two models are predictively identical when analyzed identically. In addition, because both types of models have relatively simple structures, it will turn out that most solution concepts will yield identical predictions. This means that even if the two types of games are analyzed differently, they are still likely to yield the same outcomes, though of course this would be an incorrect comparative procedure.

The particular difference in prediction in van Rooij's paper cited above arose from two faulty sources. One is whether one uses mixed strategies or behavioral strategies to do the analysis; however, it is a well known result—I believe going back to Kuhn (1953)—that the two modes of analysis are predictively identical. So this cannot be a source of difference, even though van Rooij wrongly believed that he was using a different solution concept. As regards the real source, van Rooij has clarified in an email that he inadvertently used certain incorrect numbers which resulted in the different predictions. My thanks to him for pointing this out.

A.5 The Product of Two Games

Now that games of partial information have been built and their collection $\mathcal{G}$ identified, it is possible to define their product $\otimes$ that plays a central role in equilibrium semantics. It is straightforward but time-consuming to carry this out. What has to be done is to start with two tuples, one for each multiplicand, and then construct the tuple for their product, building each component one by one from the components of the multiplicands. Along the way, it is necessary to prove, of course, that each component does in fact have all the properties required of it. For example, I asserted in section 4.2.4 when introducing the product $\otimes$ of two games that the payoff inequalities were preserved in the product when the payoffs in the product were defined to be the sum of the corresponding payoffs in the multiplicands. Such a fact would now be rigorously provable and would have to be proved to establish that the product game really is a game of partial information.

Once this is done, it becomes easy to show that $(\mathcal{G}, \otimes)$ is a monoid and that $g_u(\alpha_1 \circ \alpha_2) = g_u(\alpha_1) \otimes g_u(\alpha_2)$, facts that were required in section 4.11 to prove that $g_u : \mathcal{L} \to \mathcal{G}$ is an isomorphism in order to establish the universality of games of partial information in semantics.

I leave this construction and the proofs of the corresponding facts as an exercise for the reader. Instead of defining $\mathcal{G}$ directly as was done in Definition 14, it could be freely generated from just the lexical games via the product. Both approaches yield the same set.

A.6 Solution Concepts

The next step would be to define and examine various solution concepts. I did define a Nash equilibrium in section 3.1 and a perfect Bayesian equilibrium and risk dominant equilibrium in section 3.3.5 so I do not repeat this here. Beyond examining alternative solution concepts, it is necessary also to expand their scope in *two* related ways. One is to provide for the strategic nature of the initial probability distributions. The other is to build a definition of *global* equilibrium based on the solution concept one starts with.

Whatever solution concepts we employ, they make possible the construction of the second basic map of equilibrium semantics $f_u : \mathcal{G} \to \mathcal{I}$, whose existence and uniqueness were established by the universality result. Once we have both maps g_u and f_u, we are in a position to derive our fundamental global fixed point equation:

$$\mathcal{C}_u(\alpha, P(x \mid u)) = f_u[g_u(\alpha, P(x \mid u))] = x$$

This completes a mathematical rendering of the core framework of equilibrium semantics from first principles. It can be extended to account for syntax in a natural way.

Appendix B: An Exercise

Nothing is more abstract than reality.
—Giorgio Morandi

Situation

1. Alan and Barbara share the following background situation *B*:

a. John Smith is their local banker.

b. Fred Smith has a sailboat and sails frequently with them.

c. When they are at the bank and John Smith is not available, they go to the teller.

d. When they want to go sailing and Fred Smith is not available, they rent a sailboat.

2. u_1 and u_2 are two utterance situations as follows:

a. In u_1: Alan and Barbara are walking to their local bank to deposit a check.

b. In u_2: Alan and Barbara are walking to the river bank to go sailing.

c. $B \subset u_1$ and $B \subset u_2$.

3. Alan utters the same sentence in both u_1 and u_2:

SMITH HAS LEFT THE BANK (ψ)

4. The following assumptions may be made:

a. HAS has just the conventional meaning of the relevant auxiliary verb.

b. LEFT has just the conventional meaning of *gone from temporarily*, not permanently (as in *resigned*) or any other conventional meaning.

c. THE is being used referentially.

Questions

1. Derive and represent the (locutionary) content of the utterance in u_1 for $\mathcal{A}$ and $\mathcal{B}$ from first principles using the methods of equilibrium semantics.

2. Derive and represent the (locutionary) content of the utterance in u_2 for $\mathcal{A}$ and $\mathcal{B}$ from first principles using the methods of equilibrium semantics.
3. Relax the assumptions in #4(b) and #4(c) above by adding the possible conventional meaning *resigned* for LEFT (but no other conventional meaning) and adding the attributive use for THE (but no other use) and then do the same again for both utterances.
4. Derive and represent the illocutionary contents of both utterances for $\mathcal{A}$ and $\mathcal{B}$ from first principles using equilibrium semantics.
5. Suppose:
- A passerby $\mathcal{C}$ overhears $\mathcal{A}$ uttering ψ to $\mathcal{B}$.
- $\mathcal{C}$ does not have the information in #2(a) or #2(b).
- $\mathcal{C}$ knows the facts in B and #2(c).
- $\mathcal{C}$ is told that the content conveyed was that John Smith has left the (financial) bank.

Describe the utterance situation for $\mathcal{C}$ and use equilibrium semantics to argue what $\mathcal{C}$ can infer about the utterance situation for $\mathcal{A}$ and $\mathcal{B}$.
6. Suppose:
- $\mathcal{C}$ overhears $\mathcal{A}$ uttering ψ to $\mathcal{B}$.
- $\mathcal{C}$ does not have the information in #1 or #2 above, that is, he does not have access to either the background B or to the rest of the utterance situation.

Describe the utterance situation for $\mathcal{C}$ and derive and represent the (locutionary) content of the utterance for $\mathcal{C}$ from first principles using equilibrium semantics. What can $\mathcal{C}$ now infer about the utterance situation for $\mathcal{A}$ and $\mathcal{B}$?
7. Compare and contrast other ways of deriving and representing the locutionary and illocutionary contents of both utterances. Discuss the universality result of equilibrium semantics in this context.

References

Varol Akman. Context and the indexical "I". Powerpoint presentation at http://www.cs.bilkent.edu.tr/~akman/papers.html, presented at NASSLLI, Stanford University, 2002.

Kenneth J. Arrow and Gerard Debreu. Existence of a competitive equilibrium for a competitive economy. *Econometrica*, 22(3):265–290, 1954.

Robert J. Aumann. Lectures on Game Theory. Based on lectures delivered at Stanford University, 1976.

Robert J. Aumann. Correlated equilibrium as an expression of Bayesian rationality. *Econometrica*, 55:1–18, 1987.

J. L. Austin. *How To Do Things With Words*. Harvard University Press, Cambridge, second edition, 1975. ed. J. O. Urmson and Marina Sbisa.

J. L. Austin. How to talk—Some simple ways. In J. O. Urmson and G. J. Warnock, editors, *Philosophical Papers*, pages 134–153. Oxford University Press, Oxford, third edition, 1979a.

J. L. Austin. Performative utterances. In J. O. Urmson and G. J. Warnock, editors, *Philosophical Papers*. Oxford University Press, Oxford, third edition, 1979b.

J. L. Austin. Truth. In J. O. Urmson and G. J. Warnock, editors, *Philosophical Papers*, pages 117–133. Oxford University Press, Oxford, third edition, 1979c.

Kent Bach. Descriptions: Points of reference. In Marga Reimer and Anne Bezuidenhout, editors, *Descriptions and Beyond*, pages 189–229. Oxford University Press, Oxford, 2004.

J. Barwise and R. Cooper. Generalized quantifiers and natural language. *Linguistics and Philosophy*, 4:159–219, 1981.

Jon Barwise. Information and circumstance. In *The Situation in Logic*. CSLI Publications, Stanford, 1989a.

Jon Barwise. *The Situation in Logic*. CSLI Publications, Stanford, 1989b.

Jon Barwise. Situations and small worlds. In *The Situation in Logic*. CSLI Publications, Stanford, 1989c.

Jon Barwise. Situations, facts, and true propositions. In *The Situation in Logic*. CSLI Publications, Stanford, 1989d.

Jon Barwise. Situations, sets, and the axiom of foundation. In *The Situation in Logic*. CSLI Publications, Stanford, 1989e.

Jon Barwise and John Etchemendy. *The Liar*. Oxford University Press, Oxford, 1986.

Jon Barwise and John Perry. Semantic innocence and uncompromising situations. In Peter French, Theodore Uehling Jr., and Howard Wettstein, editors, *Midwest Studies in Philosophy: The Foundations of Analytic Philosophy*, volume 6, pages 387–403. University of Minnesota Press, Minneapolis, 1975.

Jon Barwise and John Perry. *Situations and Attitudes*. MIT Press, Cambridge, 1983.

Jon Barwise and Jerry Seligman. *Information Flow*. Oxford University Press, Oxford, 1997.

Anton Benz, Gerhard Jäger, and Robert van Rooij, editors. *Game Theory and Pragmatics*. Palgrave Studies in Pragmatics, Language and Cognition, Palgrave Macmillan, New York, 2006.

B. D. Bernheim. Rationalizeable strategic behaviour. *Econometrica*, 52:1007–1028, 1984.

Reinhard Blutner and Henk Zeevat, editors. *Optimality Theory and Pragmatics*. Palgrave Studies in Pragmatics, Language and Cognition, Palgrave Macmillan, New York, 2004.

T. Burge. Reference and proper names. *Journal of Philosophy*, 73, 1973.

Colin F. Camerer. *Behavioral Game Theory*. Princeton University Press, Princeton, 2003.

Herman Cappelen and Ernie Lepore. Radical and moderate pragmatics: Does meaning determine truth conditions? http://ruccs.rutgers.edu/tech-rpt/TR70-Lepore-Cappelen.pdf, 2004.

Robyn Carston. Relevance theory and the saying/implicating distinction. In Laurence R. Horn and Gregory Ward, editors, *The Handbook of Pragmatics*, pages 633–656. Blackwell Publishing, Oxford, 2004.

Vijay Chandru and John Hooker. *Optimization Methods for Logical Inference*. John Wiley, New York, 1999.

Gennaro Chierchia. Scalar implicatures, polarity phenomena, and the syntax/pragmatics interface. In Adriana Belletti, editor, *Structures and Beyond*, pages 39–103. Oxford University Press, Oxford, 2004.

In-Koo Cho and David Kreps. Signaling games and stable equilibria. *The Quarterly Journal of Economics*, 102(2):179–222, 1987.

Herbert Clark. *Using Language*. Cambridge University Press, Cambridge, 1996.

Robin Clark and Prashant Parikh. Game theory and discourse anaphora. *Journal of Logic, Language, and Information*, 16:265–282, 2007.

Ariel Cohen. Probabilistic approaches to semantics. In Rens Bod, Jennifer Hay, and Stefanie Jannedy, editors, *Probabilistic Linguistics*, pages 343–379. The MIT Press, Cambridge, 2003.

Vincent M. Colapietro. *Glossary of Semiotics*. Paragon House, New York, 1993.

V. P. Crawford and J. Sobel. Strategic information transmission. *Econometrica*, 50:1431–1451, 1982.

Steven Davis, editor. *Pragmatics: A Reader*. Oxford University Press, Oxford, 1991.

Terrence Deacon. *The Symbolic Species: The Co-evolution of Language and the Brain*. W. W. Norton, New York, 1997.

Jacques Derrida. *Limited Inc*. Northwestern University Press, Evanston, 1988.

Eliot Deutsch and Ron Bontekoe, editors. *A Companion to World Philosophies*. Blackwell Publishing, Oxford, 1997.

Keith Devlin. *Logic and Information*. Cambridge University Press, Cambridge, 1991.

Keith Donnellan. Reference and definite descriptions. *Philosophical Review*, 75:281–304, 1966.

Fred I. Dretske. *Knowledge and the Flow of Information*. The MIT Press, Cambridge, 1981.

Michael Fehling and Prashant Parikh. Bounded rationality in social interaction. In *Knowledge and Action at Social and Organizational Levels, AAAI Fall Symposium*, 1991.

Gottlob Frege. On sense and meaning. In Peter Geach and Max Black, editors, *Translations from the Philosophical Writings of Gottlob Frege*, pages 56–78. Basil Blackwell Ltd., 1980.

L. T. F. Gamut. *Logic, Language and Meaning: Intensional Logic and Logical Grammar*, volume 2. The University of Chicago Press, Chicago, 1991a.

L. T. F. Gamut. *Logic, Language and Meaning: Introduction to Logic*, volume 1. The University of Chicago Press, Chicago, 1991b.

Jean Mark Gawron and Stanley Peters. *Anaphora and Quantification in Situation Semantics*. CSLI Publications, Stanford, 1990.

Herbert Gintis. *Game Theory Evolving*. Princeton University Press, Princeton, 2000.

Paul Glimcher. *Decisions, Uncertainty, and the Brain: The Science of Neuroeconomics*. The MIT Press, Cambridge, 2004.

H. P. Grice. Meaning. *Philosophical Review*, 66:377–388, 1957.

H. P. Grice. Utterer's meaning, sentence-meaning and word-meaning. *Foundations of Language*, 4:1–18, 1968.

H. P. Grice. Utterer's meaning and intentions. *Philosophical Review*, 78:147–177, 1969.

H. P. Grice. Logic and conversation. In Peter Cole and Jerry L. Morgan, editors, *Syntax and Semantics*, volume 3, pages 41–58. Academic Press, New York, 1975.

H. P. Grice. *Studies in the Way of Words*. Harvard University Press, Cambridge, 1989.

J. Gronendijk and M. Stokhof. Dynamic predicate logic. *Linguistics and Philosophy*, 14:39–100, 1991.

Joseph Y. Halpern and Leandro Rego. Extensive games with possibly unaware players. *Proceedings of the Fifth International Joint Conference on Autonomous Agents and Multiagent Systems*, pages 744–751, 2006.

Joseph Y. Halpern and Leandro Rego. Generalized solution concepts in games with possibly unaware players. *Proceedings of the Eleventh Conference on Theoretical Aspects of Rationality and Knowledge*, 2007.

J. C. Harsanyi. Games with incomplete information played by Bayesian players. *Management Science*, 14:159–182, 320–334, 486–502, 1967.

J. C. Harsanyi and R. Selten. *A General Theory of Equilibrium Selection in Games*. The MIT Press, Cambridge, 1988.

Irene Heim. *The Semantics of Definite and Indefinite Noun Phrases*. PhD thesis, University of Massachusetts, Amherst, 1982.

E. D. Hirsch. *Cultural Literacy*. Random House, New York, 1988.

Laurence R. Horn and Gregory Ward, editors. *The Handbook of Pragmatics*. Blackwell Publishing, Oxford, 2004.

A. K. Joshi. Tree-adjoining grammars: How much context sensitivity is required to provide reasonable structural descriptions? In D. Dowty, L. Karttunen, and A. Zwicky, editors, *Natural Language Parsing*, pages 206–250. Cambridge University Press, Cambridge, 1985.

Daniel Kahneman, Paul Slovic, and Amos Tversky, editors. *Judgement under uncertainty: Heuristics and biases*. Cambridge University Press, Cambridge, 1982.

Hans Kamp. A theory of truth and semantic representation. In J. A. G. Gronendijk, T. M. V. Janssen, and M. B. J. Stokhof, editors, *Formal Methods in the Study of Language*, pages 277–322. Mathematical Centre Tracts 135, Amsterdam, 1981.

Hans Kamp and U. Reyle. *From Discourse to Logic*. Kluwer, Dordrecht, 1993.

David Kaplan. Quanitfying in. In Donald Davidson and Jaakko Hintikka, editors, *Words and Objections: Essays on the Work of W. V. Quine*, pages 178–214. Reidel, Dordrecht, 1969.

Stefan Kaufmann. Conditional predictions: A probabilistic account. *Linguistics and Philosophy*, 28:181–231, 2005.

George J. Klir, Ute St. Clair, and Bo Yuan. *Fuzzy Set Theory: Foundations and Applications*. Prentice Hall, Upper Saddle River, 1997.

W. C. Kneale. Universality and necessity. *British Journal for the Philosophy of Science*, 12, 1962.

Elon Kohlberg and Jean-Francois Mertens. On the strategic stability of equilibria. *Econometrica*, 54(5):1003–1037, 1986.

David Kreps. Out of equilibrium beliefs and out of equilibrium behavior. Working Paper, Graduate School of Business, Stanford University, 1986.

David Kreps and Garey Ramey. Structural consistency, consistency and sequential rationality. *Econometrica*, 55:1331–1348, 1987.

David Kreps and Joel Sobel. Signalling. In Robert Aumann and Sergiu Hart, editors, *Handbook of Game Theory with Economic Applications*, volume 2. Elsevier, Amsterdam, 1994.

David Kreps and Robert Wilson. Sequential equilibrium. *Econometrica*, 50:863–894, 1982.

Saul Kripke. *Naming and Necessity*. Harvard University Press, Cambridge, 1972, 1980.

Saul Kripke. Speaker's reference and semantic reference. In Peter A. French, Theodore E. Uehling Jr., and Howard K. Wettstein, editors, *Contemporary Perspectives in the Philosophy of Language*, pages 6–27. University of Minnesota Press, Minneapolis, 1977.

H. W. Kuhn. Extensive games and the problem of information. In H. W. Kuhn and A. W. Tucker, editors, *Contributions to the Theory of Games*, volume 2, pages 193–216. Princeton University Press, Princeton, 1953.

F. William Lawvere and Stephen H. Schanuel. *Conceptual Mathematics: A First Introduction to Categories*. Cambridge University Press, Cambridge, 1997.

David Lewis. *Convention*. Harvard University Press, Cambridge, 1969.

David Lewis. General semantics. In Donald Davidson and Gilbert Harman, editors, *Semantics of Natural Language*, pages 169–218. Reidel, Dordrecht, 1972.

Christopher Lyons. *Definiteness*. Cambridge University Press, Cambridge, 1999.

Saunders Mac Lane. *Categories for the Working Mathematician*. Springer-Verlag, New York, 1971.

Christopher Manning and Hinrich Schütze. *Foundations of Statistical Natural Language Processing*. The MIT Press, Cambridge, 1999.

A. P. Martinich, editor. *The Philosophy of Language*. Oxford University Press, Oxford and New York, 1985.

Arthur Merin. Information, relevance, and social decision making: Some principles and results of decision-theoretic semantics. In L. Moss, J. Ginzburg, and M. de Rijke, editors, *Logic, Language, and Information*, volume 2, pages 179–221. CSLI Publications, Stanford, 1999.

Richard Montague. English as a formal language. In Richmond H. Thomason, editor, *Formal Philosophy*, pages 108–221. Yale University Press, New Haven, 1974a.

Richard Montague. The proper treatment of quantification in ordinary English. In Richmond H. Thomason, editor, *Formal Philosophy*, pages 246–270. Yale University Press, New Haven, 1974b.

G. E. Moore. Russell's theory of descriptions. In P. A. Schilpp, editor, *The Philosophy of Bertrand Russell*, pages 177–225. Tudor, New York, 1944.

Charles Morris. Foundations of the theory of signs. In *International Encyclopedia of Unified Science*, volume 1. University of Chicago Press, Chicago, 1938.

R. B. Myerson. Refinement of the Nash equilibrium concept. *International Journal of Game Theory*, 7:73–80, 1978.

Roger Myerson. *Game Theory: Analysis of Conflict*. Harvard University Press, Cambridge, 1995.

Stephen Neale. *Descriptions*. The MIT Press, Cambridge, 1990.

Stephen Neale. Paul Grice and the philosophy of language. *Linguistics and Philosophy*, 15:509–559, 1992.

Martin J. Osborne and Ariel Rubinstein. *A Course in Game Theory*. The MIT Press, Cambridge, 1994.

Gary Ostertag, editor. *Definite Descriptions: A Reader*. The MIT Press, Cambridge, 1998.

Prashant Parikh. Conventional meaning and equilibrium. Unpublished, 1987a.

Prashant Parikh. *Language and Strategic Inference*. PhD thesis, Stanford University, Stanford, 1987b.

Prashant Parikh. Situations, games, and ambiguity. In Robin Cooper, Kuniaki Mukai, and John Perry, editors, *Situation Theory and Its Applications*, volume 1, pages 449–470. CSLI Publications, Stanford, 1990.

Prashant Parikh. Communication and strategic inference. *Linguistics and Philosophy*, 14:473–514, 1991.

Prashant Parikh. A game-theoretic account of implicature. In Yoram Moses, editor, *Theoretical Aspects of Reasoning about Knowledge*, pages 85–94. Morgan Kaufmann, San Mateo, 1992.

Prashant Parikh. Communication, meaning, and interpretation. *Linguistics and Philosophy*, 23:185–212, 2000.

Prashant Parikh. *The Use of Language*. CSLI Publications, Stanford University, 2001.

Prashant Parikh. Pragmatics and games of partial information. In Anton Benz, Gerhard Jäger, and Robert van Rooij, editors, *Game Theory and Pragmatics*, pages 101–122. Palgrave Macmillan, New York, 2006a.

Prashant Parikh. Radical semantics: A new theory of meaning. *Journal of Philosophical Logic*, 35:349–391, 2006b.

Prashant Parikh. Situations, rules, and conventional meaning: Some uses of games of partial information. *Journal of Pragmatics*, 39:917–933, 2007.

Prashant Parikh. Game theory and meaning. To be published, 2009.

Prashant Parikh and Robin Clark. An introduction to equilibrium semantics for natural language. In *LOFT 06: The Seventh Conference on Logic and the Foundations of Game and Decision Theory*, pages 151–160, 2006.

Prashant Parikh and Robin Clark. An introduction to equilibrium semantics for natural language. In Ahti-Veikko Pietarinen, editor, *Game Theory and Linguistic Meaning*, pages 149–158. Elsevier, Amsterdam, 2007.

Barbara H. Partee. Reflections of a formal semanticist as of Feb 2005. http://people.umass.edu/partee/docs/BHP-Essay-Feb05.pdf, 2005.

Judea Pearl. *Probabilistic Reasoning in Intelligent Systems: Networks of Plausible Inference*. Morgan Kaufmann, San Mateo, 1988.

Charles Sanders Peirce. *Writings on Semiotic*. University of North Carolina Press, Chapel Hill, 1867–1913/1991. Edited by James Hoopes.

John Perry. Thought without representation. *Aristotelean Society Supplementary Volume*, 60:137–151, 1986.

Stanley Peters and Dag Westerståhl. *Quantifiers in Language and Logic*. Oxford University Press, Oxford, 2006.

Ahti-Veikko Pietarinen, editor. *Game Theory and Linguistic Meaning*. Elsevier, Amsterdam, 2007.

Alan Prince and Paul Smolensky. *Optimality Theory: Constraint Interaction in Generative Grammar*. Blackwell Publishing, Oxford, 2004.

Hilary Putnam. The meaning of 'meaning'. In *Mind, Language, and Reality: Philosophical Papers*, volume 2. Cambridge University Press, Cambridge, 1975.

Willard Van Orman Quine. *Word and Object*. The MIT Press, Cambridge, 1960.

K. Kunjunni Raja. *Indian Theories of Meaning*. The Adyar Library and Research Center, Chennai, second edition, 1977.

François Recanati. Descriptions and situations. In Marga Reimer and Anne Bezuidenhout, editors, *Descriptions and Beyond*, pages 15–40. Oxford University Press, Oxford, 2004a.

François Recanati. *Literal Meaning*. Cambridge University Press, Cambridge, 2004b.

François Recanati. Pragmatics and semantics. In Laurence R. Horn and Gregory Ward, editors, *The Handbook of Pragmatics*, pages 442–462. Blackwell Publishing, Oxford, 2004c.

Marga Reimer and Anne Bezuidenhout, editors. *Descriptions and Beyond*. Oxford University Press, Oxford, 2004.

Richard M. Rorty. *The Linguistic Turn: Recent Essays in Philosophical Method*. University of Chicago Press, Chicago, Midway Reprint edition, 1988.

Ian Ross. *Games Interlocutors Play: The Unification of Implicature*. PhD thesis, University of Pennsylvania, Philadelphia, 2006.

Bertrand Russell. On denoting. *Mind*, 14:479–493, 1905.

Bertrand Russell. Descriptions. In *Introducton to Mathematical Philosophy*, pages 167–180. George Allen and Unwin Publishers Ltd., Sydney, 1919.

Uli Sauerland. Scalar implicatures in complex sentences. *Linguistics and Philosophy*, 27:367–391, 2004.

Ferdinand de Saussure. *Cours de Linguistique Générale*. Éditions Payot, Paris, 1916/1972.

Ferdinand de Saussure. *Course of General Linguistics*. Peter Owen, London, 1960.

T. C. Schelling. *The Strategy of Conflict*. Harvard University Press, Cambridge, 1960.

Stephen Schiffer. *Meaning*. Oxford University Press, Oxford, 1972.

John R. Searle. Proper names. *Mind*, 67:166–173, 1958.

John R. Searle. Referential and attributive. In Steven Davis, editor, *Pragmatics: A Reader*, pages 121–133. Oxford University Press, Oxford, 1991.

J. Seligman and L. S. Moss. Situation theory. In J. van Benthem and A. ter Meulen, editors, *Handbook of Logic and Language*, pages 239–309. The MIT Press, Cambridge, 1997.

R. Selten. Reexamination of the perfectness concept for equilibrium points in extensive games. *International Journal of Game Theory*, 4:25–55, 1975.

Claude E. Shannon and Warren Weaver. *The Mathematical Theory of Communication*. University of Illinois Press, Urbana, 1949.

Michael Spence. Job market signaling. *Quarterly Journal of Economics*, 87:355–374, 1973.

Michael Spence. Signaling in retrospect and the informational structure of markets. Nobel Prize lecture at http://nobelprize.org/nobel-prizes/economics/laureates/2001/spence-lecture.pdf, 2001.

Dan Sperber and Deirdre Wilson. *Relevance: Communication and Cognition*. Blackwell Publishing, Oxford, 1986a.

Robert C. Stalnaker. Pragmatics. *Synthese*, 22, 1970. Reprinted in Stalnaker, 1999.

Robert C. Stalnaker. Assertion. In *Syntax and Semantics*, volume 9. Academic Press, New York, 1978. Reprinted in Stalnaker, 1999.

Robert C. Stalnaker. On the evaluation of solution concepts. *Theory and Decision*, 37:49–73, 1996.

Robert C. Stalnaker. On the representation of context. *Journal of Logic, Language, and Information*, 7, 1998. Reprinted in Stalnaker, 1999.

Robert C. Stalnaker. *Context and Content*. Oxford University Press, Oxford, 1999a.

Robert C. Stalnaker. Introduction. In *Context and Content*. Oxford University Press, Oxford, 1999b.

Robert C. Stalnaker. Saying and meaning, cheap talk and credibility. In Anton Benz, Gerhard Jäger, and Robert van Rooij, editors, *Game Theory and Pragmatics*, pages 83–100. Palgrave Macmillan, New York, 2006.

P. F. Strawson. On referring. In Antony Flew, editor, *Essays in Conceptual Analysis*, pages 21–52. MacMillan and Co. Ltd., London, 1956.

P. F. Strawson. Intention and convention in speech acts. *Philosophical Review*, 73:439–460, 1964.

Deborah Tannen. *You Just Don't Understand*. Random House, New York, 1990.

Ian Tattersall. *The Monkey in the Mirror: Essays on the Science of What Makes Us Human*. Harcourt, New York, 2002.

Charles Travis. Meaning's role in truth. *Mind*, 105:451–466, 1996.

Robert van Rooij. Questioning to resolve decision problems. *Linguistics and Philosophy*, 26:727–763, 2003.

Robert van Rooij. Signaling games select Horn strategies. *Linguistics and Philosophy*, 27:493–527, 2004.

Kai von Fintel. Would you believe it? The king of France is back! (Presuppositions and truth value intuitions). In Marga Reimer and Anne Bezuidenhout, editors, *Descriptions and Beyond*, pages 315–341. Oxford University Press, Oxford, 2004.

Joel Watson. *Strategy: An Introduction to Game Theory*. W. W. Norton and Company, New York, 2002.

Deirdre Wilson and Dan Sperber. On defining relevance. In Richard Grandy and Richard Warner, editors, *Philosophical Grounds of Rationality*, pages 243–258. Clarendon Press, Oxford, 1986b.

Deirdre Wilson and Dan Sperber. Relevance theory. In Laurence R. Horn and Gregory Ward, editors, *The Handbook of Pragmatics*. Blackwell Publishing, Oxford, 2004.

Ludwig Wittgenstein. *Philosophical Investigations*. Macmillan Publishing Company, New York, third edition, 1953/1968.

Ernst Zermelo. Uber eine anwendung der mengenlehre auf die theorie des schachspiels. *Proceedings of the Fifth Congress of Mathematicians*, Cambridge University Press, Cambridge, pages 501–504, 1913.

Index